Art of Investing

5th Edition

Tony Pow

Why you need this book

This book encompasses all my proven investing techniques and the mistakes I've learned to avoid. Since my children are not interested in investing, I have no reason to withhold any insights.

- As of 2024, I achieved a return exceeding **five** times my initial investment by employing the sector rotation strategy detailed in this book. This involved investing an amount greater than my annual salary at that time.
- The average return of my last six books of the series "Best stocks" beat S&P 500 index by 184%. Most research is based on this book. http://tonyp4idea.blogspot.com/2024/01/incredible-stock-performances.html
- Among the 8 stocks recommended in my book "Best Stocks for 2023", SMCI has an annual return of 272% from 12/15/22 to 12/15/23.
- I recommended 20 stocks in an article Amazing Return in Seeking Alpha. If you bought them on the published date, you would have beaten the S&P 500 index by over 100% in a year without considering dividends.
- I achieved huge returns during the early recovery of the last two market crashes.
- On 5/26/2020, I searched for "Investing" under Amazon's Book for book price over $5 and the topic is related. All info is obtained from Amazon.com.

Book	Date	Size	Kindle $	Paper $	Stars
Art of investing 5th Edition	01/2025[1]	**770**[2]	**$9.95**	$24.95	4.5[3]
Perpetual Wealth	07/2019	235	**$9.95**	$24.59	4.5
Intelligent Investor	02/2006	640	$17.99	$14.29	4.5
Common Sense Investing	10/2017	304	$14.49	$16.49	4.5
Investing 101	01/2016	264	$10.98	**$9.78**	4.5
Investing All-in-One	05/2017	552	$15.99	$21.49	4.5

[1] Word indicates this book has about 580 pages (6*9).
[2] All data were obtained from Amazon.
[3] Based on "Complete the art of investing", the original book.

Contents

Why you need this book 2
Why you invest 13
Introduction 15
    Disclaimer 19
    How the rate of return is calculated 19
    How to start reading this book 20
Highlights 25
  Reviews 25
  The power of market timing 27
  How I beat the S&P 500 index by 100% 30
  Bubbles 30
Book 1: Simple Techniques 32
  1   Money Market, CDs & Bonds 33
  2   Sample portfolio 35
  3   Anatomy of a trade 37
  4   Investing for 'lazy' folks 38
  5   Simplest analysis of ETFs 40
    An example 43
  6   Simplest ways to evaluate stocks 44
  7   Simplest market timing 46
  8   Rotate four ETFs 49
  9   Simplest technical analysis 51
  10   The best strategy 51
  11   Don'ts for beginners 52
  12   Summary 53
Book 2: Finding Stocks 54
  1   Where the websites are 54
  2   *Finviz.com screener* 56
    A screener example 57
    Other sources 58

	Common parameters	59
3	Sectors to be cautious with	64
4	GuruFocus	67
5	Piotroski's F-Score	68
6	NASDAQ	71
7	Fidelity	72
8	ChatGPT	74
9	Performance of my screens	75
10	A scoring system	78

Book 3: Evaluating Stocks ... 83

1	Performances	84
2	Amazing returns	85

Section I: Fundamental metrics ... 90

3	Mysteries of P/E	90
4	*Fundamental metrics*	97
5	Finviz's parameters	107
	Your broker's website	114
	Other sources	114
	Gurus	115
	Quick and dirty	115
	5-minute stock evaluation	116
	More info from Fidelity	118

Section II: Beyond fundamentals ... 119

6	Intangibles	119
7	Qualitative analysis	123
8	Manipulators and bankruptcy	127
	Mergers	128
9	Avoid bankrupting companies	129
	An example from a guru on Micron	131

Section III: Selling stocks ... 132

  10 *When to sell a stock* 132

    Selling a winner 136

  11 Examples of overpriced stocks 139

  12 Should you hold stocks forever? 140

  13 Monitor your traded stocks 142

Section IV: Other sources 143

  14 Good pointers from a popular book? 143

  15 Seeking Alpha 144

  16 Making sense 145

  17 Fidelity 146

Book 4: Scoring Stocks 148

Section I: ASSS, Adaptive Stock Scoring System 149

  1 Adaptive Stock Scoring System 149

    An illustration by implanting a score system in a spreadsheet 153

  2 Get metric data from Finviz.com 154

  3 How to use the grand score 159

  4 Get metric data from Fidelity 162

  5 Compare the two sources 167

  6 An extension to the scoring system 169

  7 A scoring system for growth stocks 171

  8 A scoring system for momentum stocks 171

Section II: Monitor parameters 172

  9 *Monitor my big gainers* 172

  10 Monitor my big losses 178

  11 My performance monitor 182

  12 Metric performances & market cycle 185

  13 Investing: Long Term vs. Short Term 186

Book 5: Trading Stocks 188

  1 Chronology of a trade 188

  2 Order prices 190

  3 Stop loss 195

4	Short selling	198
My experience in selling short		201
Common parameters for short candidates		204
5	Covered calls	206
6	Diversification	209
7	High frequency trading (HFT)	212
8	Tax avoidance	213
9	Trading plan	217
10	My A.B.C. on bonds	221
11	Muni bonds	225
12	Annuities	227
13	Buyback, Diluting and Spinoffs	228
14	Brokers	229
15	Fidelity	232
Summary		234
Book 6: Market Timing		235
1	Market timing example	236
Management summary		236
Mid-year update		240
Canary warning?		242
A correction or a crash?		243
2	Another example of early 2022	244
Section I: Spotting big market plunges		245
1	*Spotting big market plunges*	*245*
2	More tools	253
Using VIX as a timing model		253
Other technical indicators		253
Sound Advice Risk Indicator		253
Buffett's Equity to GDP		254
3	Related topics	254

Other related hints on value 254
Fear and Greed 255
Lazy man's market timing 256
Fidelity 256
My experiences 256
False alarm 256
4   Why the market fluctuates 257
5   Double tops & a faster indicator 259
     A faster, confirming indicator 261
6   Retail investors and market timing 262

Section II: Market cycle 265

1   Market cycle 265
2   Bull / Bear market 271
3   Profitable Early Recovery 275
4   A non-correlation of the market and business 276
5   A tale of two market plunges 280
6   Secular bull market is coming! 287
7   Market prediction for a new year 293
8   What to do in mid-year 294
9   The worst scenario 295
10   Market timing from 2008 to 2015 296
11   Market timing of 2022 297
12   2023 Market Outlook 298

Section III: Correction 300

1   Correction 300
2   Six signs of a correction 302
3   Anticipating a correction 304
4   Market correction example 308

Section IV: Market timing by Calendar 309

1   Market timing by calendar 309

2	Summary	313

Section V: Peaks and bottoms ... 315

1	Market peaks / bottoms	315
2	Peaking and Overbought	321
3	Design a test for market peaks/bottoms	322
4	Market peak example	324

Section VI: Miscellaneous ... 325

1	A sideways market	325
2	Market timing by asset class	327
3	My predictions	329
	Fidelity	331
4	Reasons for the coming market crash	332
5	A simple but risky strategy on market timing	334
6	Navigate in a stormy market	335

Book 7: Investing Strategies ... 336

1	Introduction	339
	A Sample Strategy	340
	Testing strategies	341
	Monitor performances of strategies	343
	Execution of a strategy	344
	More on strategies	344

Section I: Common strategy ideas ... 347

2	Screening stocks	347
	A simple tutorial	349
3	Experiences in strategies	350
4	*The best strategy*	355
	The second-best strategy	357
	The third best strategy	358
	Buy and Monitor	359
	My long-term grade	360
5	Different investment styles	361

6	Summary on value investing	363
7	AAII, a source for strategies	365
8	Profit from a proven strategy	366
9	An illustration of testing strategies	369

Section II: Safer strategies 371

Super safe strategies 371

10	Tom's conservative strategy	373

An alternative to Tom's strategy 374

John's Strategy 374

Jill's Strategy 375

11	Define Swing trading	376
12	Top-down investing	382

Section III: Riskier strategies 385

13	The contrarian	385
14	Refined "Dogs of the Dow"	387
15	Multi baggers	390
16	Trading by headlines	396
17	Earnings season overreactions	402
18	Strategies on earnings	405
19	Strategies that worked before	406
20	Short Squeeze	409

CALM, a candidate 409

21	Year-end strategies	413
22	Rocket stocks	419

FAANG stocks 419

23	Small caps vs. big caps	421
24	An aggressive strategy	422
25	A turnaround strategy for value stocks	427

Book 8: Sector Rotation: The Basics 430

1	Sector rotation in a nutshell	430
2	Outline on how to start sector rotation	437

3	The 5G revolution	439
4	Computer chips	441
5	Artificial Intelligence (AI)	442
	Summary of AI investing performance	443

Book 9: Insider Trading 444

1	Define Insider Trading	444
2	How to profit	446
3	Screen the Insiders' purchase.	448
4	Other Considerations	451
5	My trades based on insider purchase trading	453

Book 10: Penny stocks and micro caps 454

1	My micro-cap performance	457
2	Penny stocks	458
3	Micro caps	462
4	Hints	463
	Summary	463

Book 11: Momentum investing 466

	Introduction	466
1	My momentum performance	473
2	Five strategies for momentum	476
3	Herd theory	480
4	Characteristics of momentum trading	481
5	Good News/Bad News	482
6	Business news	483
7	Missing opportunities	484
8	Ukraine impact	485
9	Momentum stock basic	487

Book 12: Dividend investing 488

1	The basics	489
2	More on dividend stocks	492
3	Potential problems	494

4	Dividend growth	496
5	Are dividend stocks better?	497
6	Passive income	501

Book 13: Technical Analysis (TA) ... 502

1	Technical analysis (TA)	503
2	Examples of using TA	508
3	Easy TA without charts	511
4	Bollinger Bands	512
5	MACD	513

A TA strategy ... 513

6	Other TA indicators/patterns	514
7	More on technical analysis	515
8	Using Fidelity	517
9	Determine the exit point	518

Book 14: Investment advice ... 519

1	Newsletters and subscriptions	519
2	Advantages of a retail investor	524
3	Future trends	527

Book 15: Buffettology ... 529

1	Debunk the myths	529
2	Preaching that works	536
3	Search value stocks like Buffett	541
4	Buffett	543
5	Efficient charities donation	545

Book 16: The economy ... 547

1	My economic theories	547
2	My Coconut Theory	549
3	American first: Challenges and risks	551
4	Politics and the stock market	552
5	The evils of printing money	553
6	Shenzhen	553

7	Why market rises or falls	555
8	Investors' psychology 101	556

Review what we've discussed 557

Epilogue 563

    Afterthoughts 565

    Recommend the next books. 566

Appendix 1 - Our window to the investing world 566

Appendix 2 - ETFs / Mutual Funds 568

Appendix 3 - Links 573

Filler: Real joke

My six-year-old grandson called the library about the availability of the book Mine Craft. The lady told him that only "Mine Craft for Dummies" was available. He told her it was not for him as he was not a dummy.

#Filler: My choice

My doctor asked me to try an experimental drug to cure my psoriasis. The drug is so strong that it would kill me. However, in either case, my psoriasis will be cured.

Why you invest

Learning to invest is an essential life skill, crucial for financial growth and long-term security. Calculated risks, when approached with discipline, can lead to significant rewards. Compare the returns of various asset classes, such as cash, certificates of deposit (CDs), treasury bills, bonds, real estate, and stocks.

We begin with the safest assets and move toward riskier ones. Interestingly, the average returns follow the opposite order. For instance, while cash and CDs may seem risk-free, inflation erodes their value. A CD offering a 2% return with a 3% inflation rate results in a negative real return. Additionally, taxes further reduce these modest returns. In essence, our capitalist system penalizes inaction.

To protect your portfolio:

- Use stop-loss orders to limit potential losses.
- Avoid leverage, including options, if you're a beginner.
- Start as a "turtle investor," focusing on value stocks and long-term gains rather than speculative trading.

Understanding Risks

There are two types of risks:
1. Blind Risk: Investing based on tips or unverified recommendations, similar to buying a house without inspecting it.
2. Calculated Risk: Buying stocks backed by proven strategies, thorough research, and proper evaluation.

In the long run, calculated risks tend to yield profitable results. For instance, "Buy and Monitor" strategies outperform "Buy and Hold" because they adapt to market changes, such as avoiding losses from corporate failures like Enron.

For Beginners

If you're just starting, prioritize steady strategies:
- Invest in diversified market ETFs.
- Use simple market timing techniques to minimize losses during downturns.

- Gradually transition to advanced techniques like short-selling or covered calls after gaining experience.

Cautionary Notes

- Avoid heavily marketed financial products, such as annuities and high-fee insurance plans.
- Don't entrust your portfolio to poorly managed hedge funds.
- If you're inclined to real estate, focus on properties in growing areas and take advantage of tax benefits like 401(k) contributions and Roth IRAs.

The Long-Term Case for Stocks

Historical data supports investing in stocks. For example:
"The historical average yearly return of the S&P 500 is 9.775% over the last 20 years as of January 2023, assuming dividends are reinvested. Adjusted for inflation, the 20-year average return (including dividends) is 7.077%."

#Filler: Why?

Why do the majority of my friends find more beautiful ladies when they grow old? Most likely they use their spouses as the yardstick. I am the minority. Do not tell my wife please.

Introduction

Overview
Art of Investing: 5th Edition is a comprehensive guide to investing, offering practical advice and strategies for retail investors of all levels. Drawing on decades of experience and rigorous analysis, the book emphasizes disciplined approaches to investing, avoiding common pitfalls, and maximizing returns through calculated risks and informed decisions. It has over 570 pages (6*9), equivalent to the size of two average books on investing.

Notable Achievements Highlighted:
The author shares instances of beating the S&P 500 index by substantial margins using the strategies described:
- As of 2024, I made more than **5 times profit** using sector rotation.
- As of 2024, the average return of my last six books of the series "Best stocks" beat S&P 500 index by about 184%.
- Among the 8 stocks recommended in my book "Best Stocks for 2023", SMCI has an annual return of 272% from 12/15/22 to 12/15/23.

Who Should Read This Book? This book is ideal for:
- Beginner investors seeking to understand the basics of stock and ETF investing.
- Intermediate and advanced investors looking for proven techniques and strategies to enhance their portfolio.
- Anyone interested in improving financial literacy and taking control of their investments.

Key Themes
1. **Investment Philosophy**:
    - Focuses on blending proven techniques with innovative strategies to outperform the market.
    - Encourages readers to adopt a "turtle" approach—slow, steady, and consistent growth rather than speculative leaps.
2. **Practical Strategies**:
    - Market timing techniques to avoid downturns and capitalize on recovery phases.
    - Step-by-step methods to evaluate and select stocks using fundamental, technical, and qualitative analyses.
3. **Diversification and Risk Management**:

- Advocates for a balanced portfolio tailored to individual risk tolerance and market conditions.
- Recommends simple diversification strategies like sector rotation and ETF-based investing.
4. **Advanced Techniques for Experienced Investors**:
   - Covers short selling, momentum investing, and strategies for exploiting insider trading.
   - Provides detailed advice on using tools like Finviz and Fidelity for stock screening.
5. **Market Insights**:
   - Discusses bubbles, economic cycles, and the influence of government policies on markets.
   - Offers perspectives on navigating volatile markets and capitalizing on unique opportunities, such as during early recovery phases.
6. **Accessible Guidance**:
   - Designed for readers of all experience levels, with clear organization by skill level (beginner, intermediate, and advanced).
   - Provides actionable advice on creating trading plans, managing losses, and evaluating long-term versus short-term strategies.

Book Structure The book is divided into 16 interconnected "books," each focusing on specific investing topics such as:
- Simple techniques for beginners.
- Sector rotation and scoring systems.
- Dividend and momentum investing.
- Insider trading and technical analysis.
- Advanced market timing and strategy implementation.

Each section offers detailed examples, metrics, and tools, making it both a reference guide and a practical manual for hands-on application.

Unique Features:
- **Personal Insights**: The author shares personal successes, mistakes, and lessons learned, making the content relatable and actionable.
- **Extensive Use of Tools**: Highlights free and low-cost tools like ETFdb, Finviz, and Fidelity to enhance research and decision-making.
- **Focus on Education**: Contains practical exercises and encourages paper trading for risk-free practice before using real money.

Final Takeaway *Art of Investing: 5th Edition* serves as a valuable resource for anyone aiming to improve their investing acumen. With a blend of simplicity and depth, Tony Pow provides readers with the tools, techniques, and insights needed to navigate and profit in a complex financial world.

How to use this book

Do **not** trade the stocks discussed in this book, as they may be outdated. Learn the reasons they are recommended.

This book is not a novel that you should read sequentially. The novel could be more entertaining and are connected with each chapter. However, most have one or a few tips on investing, and this book on the average has at least one useful tip on every page. This book is organized as a reference book. You can start any chapter or find the related topic as needed. I recommend starting to glance at the table of contents that is usually available. I have read a few novels on investing. They are entertaining, but I learn nothing. One best seller describes using ROI in the entire book.

Most graphs and tables are in landscape orientation (recommended for small screens) for both paperback and e-readers. Some graphs may not be displayed adequately on a small screen of an e-reader. Use a PC to read the graphs on the larger screen. For better orientation, just flip your e-reader device 90 degrees if it is available. Most e-readers let you select a table or a graph to display it to fit the screen.

The **font size** (Ctrl Minus for browser implementation of e-readers) should be adjustable for e-books.

There are clickable links to web articles and/or YouTube videos, which are usually more entertaining than reading. Most of them are from public websites such as Wikipedia. Some public links may not be available in the future as they are not under my control and my book may change. For security, get the information such as "RSI(14)" directly from the source; the primary ones are Wikipedia, Investopedia, YouTube and Fidelity.

These links extend the usefulness of this book by making available specific topics that may not be interesting to every reader. It also provides articles (most are not written by me) for more in-depth analysis. Instead of typing the links to your browser, you can access the following website to access most of the links easier. One reader commented, "(the links have) lots of useful information. The author also has a sense of humor."

http://tonyp4idea.blogspot.com/2021/05/web-links-for-printed-copy-of-my-book.html

Fidelity provides video clips to explain some of the basic terms. Fidelity does not require a balance to open an account; I have no affiliation with them except I retired from Fidelity. Take advantage of their extensive research and info. YouTube offers similar video lessons. This book provides many of the links for the paperback readers. In any case, get the same information or extra information by entering a search in Wikipedia and/or Investopedia (http://www.investopedia.com/) such as "Dogs of the Dow".

'Afterthoughts' includes my additional comments and ideas of minor importance. There are fillers with tips, refreshing pictures (most were taken by me) and jokes (most original) to fill up some empty space of the printed book. Fillers, links and afterthoughts should not disrupt the flow of reading this book. One user commented on my fillers: "Thanks for the jabs (Fillers) to make the reading fun while getting an education".

For convenience, this book uses SPY, an Exchange Traded Fund (ETF) simulating the S&P 500, as the benchmark for the market.

Since most of the stock recommendations are probably obsolete by the time you read about them, use them as examples and do not trade the mentioned stocks without consulting your financial advisor first. For simplicity, I treat ETN the same as ETF. This book hopefully can make you a better investor.

About the author

I graduated from Cal. State University at San Jose in Industrial Engineering and the University of Massachusetts in Amherst with a MS in Industrial Engineering. I have retired from a job in IT. I have been an investor for over 30 years and have written over 30 books on investing. Here is the link to some of the articles I have written.

Dedication
To all retail investors and future retail investors including my grandchildren.

Acknowledgement
Thanks to Seeking Alpha, Wikipedia, Fidelity, Yahoo!Finance and Investopedia for the many helpful links to enrich this book. Special thanks to Douglas Brindle II for helping me with AI to enhance this book.

Important notices

© 2025 Tony Pow. This is the 5nd Edition and is based on the first edition ("Complete the art of investing"), which was published in 2016.

Version	
Initial	01/25

No part of this book can be reproduced in any form without the written approval of the author. My email address is pow_tony@yahoo.com and my blog is https://tonyp4idea.blogspot.com.

Book store managers can order the printed books from Creatspace.com. Publishers please consider publish my books.
https://tonyp4idea.blogspot.com/2024/12/dealers-and-publishers.html

Disclaimer

Do not gamble with money that you cannot afford to lose. Past performance is a guideline and is not necessarily indicative of future results. All information is believed to be accurate, but there is not a guarantee. All the strategies including charts to detect market plunges described have no guarantee that they will make money and they may lose money. Do not trade without doing due diligence and be warned that most data may be obsolete. All my articles and the associated data are for informational and illustration purposes only. I'm not a professional investment counselor, a tax professional or any other field. Seek one before you make any investment decisions. Remember to consult with a registered financial adviser before making any investment decisions. The above mentioned also applies for all other advice such as on accounting, taxes, health and any topic mentioned in this book. Tax laws change all the time, so talk to your tax advisors before taking any action. Some articles may offend some one or some organization unintentionally. If I did, I'm sorry about that. I am politically and religiously neutral. I have provided my best efforts to ensure the accuracy of my articles. Data also from different sources was believed to be accurate. However, there is no guarantee that they are accurate and suitable for the current market conditions and /or your individual situations. The values of some parameters such as RSI(14) are arbitrarily set by me. I have made a lot of predictions that may not materialize. My publisher and I are not liable for any damages in using this book or its contents.

How the rate of return is calculated

They are for education purposes only, and do not make your investing decisions based on them. I usually use annualized for better comparisons; 4% in a month is more than 5% in a year for example. For short-term strategies including momentum, shorting and year-end strategy, I use the returns for a month, and sometimes including returns for 2 months for comparison. Annualized returns are usually used for long-term strategies. The holding periods may have a few days off due to holidays and weekends. For simplicity, most of my returns do not include commissions, exchange fees, order spread and dividends. Most numbers have been rounded up for better readability. The return = profit / investment. I and my publisher are not liable for any error. I use SPY and sometimes RSP as a yardstick; RSP and SPY have the same S&P 500 stocks, but the stocks are weighted evenly in RSP. However, many readers do not know RSP.

How to start reading this book

Many investment books are easy to read with continuation from one chapter to the next. They usually deal with one or two investing tips such as using ROE. Even if it worked for the author, it may not always work as the market is always changing. After one strategy was publicized in a popular book, it did not work, as there were too many followers.

This book covers most topics in investing and many strategies. Investing is multi-disciplined and there is no evergreen strategy. We have to match the best strategy to the current market conditions. For example, during the year end, you want to use the year-end strategy described in this book. Even if it does not always work, it is better to use a strategy that has worked before.

You should glance through this book and use this lengthy book as a reference. Glancing through the whole book is time-consuming. First ask yourself what level of investing you are: beginner, intermediate or advanced. I have two choices for selecting chapters appropriate to you, one is by books and the other is by chapters.

By books:

Beginner investors: Book 1, 14, 15 and 16.
Intermediate investors: Book 1 (may find some simple techniques useful) and 2 to 5.
Advanced investors: Book 6 -- 13.

By chapters:

In addition, I select more useful articles to make use of your limited time. Here are the three tables of selected chapters for beginners, the intermediate and the advanced.

Beginners:

Article	Book	Chapter
Simple techniques	1	1-5
Advanced beginners:		
Finviz.com screener	2	2
Amazing returns	3	2
Finviz's parameters	3	5
Intangibles	3	6
Qualitative analysis	3	7
When to sell a stock	3	10
Adaptive Stock Scoring System	4	1
Get metric data from Finviz.com	4	2
Chronology of a trade	5	1
Order prices	5	2
Diversification	5	6
Market timing example	6	
Market timing by calendar	6	
Tom's conservative strategy	7	10
Basics in dividend investing	12	1
Read articles that are interesting to you	14	
Select value stocks like Buffett	16	3

Intermediate investors:

Article	Book	Chapter
Simple market timing	1	1
Simplest way to evaluate stocks	1	4
Finviz.com screener	2	2
Amazing returns	3	1
Finviz's parameters	3	5
Intangibles	3	6
Qualitative analysis	3	7
When to sell a stock	3	10
Fidelity's stock research	3	27
Adaptive Stock Scoring System	4	1
Get metric data from Finviz.com	4	2
Order prices	5	2
Short selling	5	4
Tax avoidance	5	8
Diversification	5	6
Trading plan	5	9
Market timing example	6	

Article	Book	Chapter
Spotting big market plunges	6	1
Market cycle	6	
Actions for different stages of a m. cycle	6	6
Market timing by calendar	6	19
Tom's conservative strategy	7	10
Trading by headlines	7	18
Year-end strategies	7	23
Rocket stocks	7	24
A turnaround strategy for value investors	7	25
Sector rotation: Section I	8	
Screen the insider's purchase	9	3
Four strategies for momentum	11	2
Technical Analysis	13	1

Advanced investors:

Article	Book	Chapter
(All of the above for intermediate investors if they are appropriate and helpful to you.)		
Simple market timing	1	1
Simplest way to evaluate stocks	1	4
Finviz.com screener	2	2
Amazing returns	3	1
Finviz's parameters	3	5
Intangibles	3	6
Qualitative analysis	3	7
When to sell a stock	3	10
Fidelity's stock research	3	26
Adaptive Stock Scoring System	4	1
Get metric data from Finviz.com	4	2
Short selling	5	4
Tax avoidance	5	8
Diversification	5	6
Trading plan	5	9
Market timing example	6	
Spotting big market plunges	6	
Market cycle	6	
Actions for different stages of a m. cycle	6	
Market timing by calendar	6	
Tom's conservative strategy	7	10
Trading by headlines	7	18
Year-end strategies	7	23
Rocket stocks	7	24
A turnaround strategy for value investors	7	25
Sector rotation (Section I and III)	8	
Screen the insider's purchase	9	3

Four strategies for momentum	11	2
Technical Analysis	13	1

The chapters that have not been selected are useful for reference. For example, if you are into momentum investing, read all chapters in Book 11.

#AFiller: Caution in investing

As with everything in life, there is no guarantee that this book will make you a lot of money. However, the chance of success will be substantially improved especially when you practice with most of the ideas presented in this book. Most beginners should start with paper trading first.

1. First determine your objectives. Retirees select safer strategies. Millionaires can afford to select riskier strategies for larger returns.
2. Determine your risk tolerance, how much time you have for investing, your knowledge on investing, the desire to learn and your portfolio size.

   To illustrate, when the market is risky, do not buy any stock. However, for investors who can tolerate higher risk, buy contra ETFs to bet against the market for larger return. Retirees may be less risk tolerant unless they're rich.

   If your job is very demanding, you should spend less time investing even if you're knowledgeable and have a desire to learn about investing.

   Check your net worth (= what you own – what you owe) and cash flow (incomes – debt payments). Reserve your emergency cash equal to expenses for at least 3 months.

   Prioritize your investments: Roth IRA (if qualified), the matched part of 401K if offered to you, down payment for a house for starters, and then the unmatched part of the 401K. Everyone's priorities and situations are different.
3. When the market is peaking, invest cautiously. Use trailing stops described in this book. The same for stocks that have appreciated a lot.
4. When you have lost two trades in a row, take a break and return to paper trading until you're comfortable.
5. Find stocks with one of the many strategies described in this book using Finviz.com, your broker or any free screen sites.

   Start with one of the safer strategies including the long-term swing trading strategy for starters and/or trading ETFs.
6. Except for bottom fishing used in the Early Recovery phase of the market cycle, ensure the stock is trending upwards (for example, SMA-200% in Finviz.com should be positive).

7. Ensure the screened stocks are fundamentally sound except for momentum strategies.
8. Sell the stock when it fulfills your objective, there is better buy, or the market is plunging as detected by my simple technique.
9. Test your strategy on paper. This book requires you to try out the various strategies, and select the one you are comfortable with. All theories may not work for real trading.
10. When a strategy has been thoroughly tested out recently and the result is good, use real money slowly and gradually. Monitor your performance including the screens and the fundamental metrics.

This book is full of useful information and some chapters require you to test the described techniques out such as "Detecting market plunges" and "Finding stocks". Not all of my predictions are materialized, so always use stops to protect your portfolio. Learn from the arguments for the predictions, not merely the accuracy of the predictions. Predictions are based on educated guesses, and hence hopefully more of them will materialize in the long run.

#Filler: The world is round, honey

My spouse complained I made the wrong turn. I replied eventually we would be right as the world is round. Time wise I was wrong but logic wise I was right.

Highlights

My motivation to write this book
I would like to share my experiences, both good and bad. I use simple-to-follow techniques using the free (or low-cost) resources available to us. I have been successful in investing for decades. I am enjoying a comfortable financial life. I do not hold back my 'secrets' as my children are not interested in investing.

If you are looking at how to make a 100% return overnight, this book is not for you. This book describes how to be a 'turtle' investor making a fortune gradually and surely. Before you begin, first define your objectives.

My steps to trade stocks (ETFs are far simpler)
1. Search for valued stocks (there are many strategies to choose from).
2. Evaluate the screened stocks by
    a. Fundamental Analysis.
    b. Intangible Analysis.
    c. Qualitative Analysis.
    d. Technical Analysis.
3. Sell stocks.
   Every 6 months (shorter duration for some strategies), perform the same as in Step #2 to determine whether you need to sell the stocks you own, or just keep them for another 6 months.

Reviews

Some readers' comments are on "Debunk the Myths in Investing", which this book is originally based on.

"I skipped ahead to his chapter book 14 (of "Complete the art of Investing"), Investment Advice just to get a feel of his writing style. His research is phenomenal and doesn't overwhelm with big words or catchy "sales-like" tactics.

I truly believe this ordinary man, Mr. Tony Pow, has a gift of explaining his experience as an investor without the bullshit of trying to make you buy his stuff. He seemingly just wants to share his knowledge, tips, and clarity of definitions for the kind of folks like me who want to understand something FIRST before jumping in with emotions of trying to make a boat load of money. I like the technical analysis side he brings.

Mr. Tony Pow talks about hidden gems in his book; ....quite frankly, he is a hidden gem. Thank you and I will also post my comments about this author to my Facebook page!" – JB.

"Tony, I just finished reading your 2nd edition. It's my pleasure to report that I found it most interesting. You're welcome to use this blurb if you like:

Debunk the Myths in Investing is an all-encompassing look at not only the most salient factors influencing markets and investors, but also a from-the-trenches look at many of the misconceptions and mistakes too many investors make. Reading this book may save not only time and aggravation but money as well!" - Joseph Shaefer, CEO, Stanford Wealth Management LLC.

"Tony, Great work!" from James and Chris, who are portfolio managers.

"'Debunk the Myths in Investing' is a comprehensive book on investing that deals with many aspects of this tense profession in which with a lot of knowledge and a bit of luck (or vice versa) one can greatly benefit...

Therefore 'Debunk the Myths in Investing' is an interesting book that on its 500 pages offers a lot of knowledge related to investing world and a lot of practical advice, so I can recommend its reading if you're interested in this topic."
- Denis Vukosav, Top 500 Reviewers at Amazon.com.

"490 pages (Debunk) of a genius's ranting and hypothesis with various theories throughout, written light-heartedly with ample doses of humor...Yes, the myth of not being able to profitably time the market is BUSTED...

One might ask... Why is he giving away the results of his hard-earned research for only $20? He states that his children are not interested in investing and wants to share his efforts with the world." - Abe Agoda.

"Excellent book, recommend to all investors... great knowledge. It has fine-tuned my investing strategies... Your book is hard to set aside, as I read it all the time learning good techniques and analysis of stocks, ETF... Since I purchased your book in March, I have underlined, highlighted and placed tabs on top of pages for quick reference." – Aileron.

"Great stuff, Tony. It's great to meet experienced traders such as yourself. I had a browse through the book and think your method is a little more refined than mine."

"Your strategy is very rules based and solid. I sometimes envy people who have developed something like this."

"I have read so many investing books that have only maybe 1 or 2 ideas in a 400-page book. I really wish I had got proper advice sooner." J. Shaw.

The power of market timing

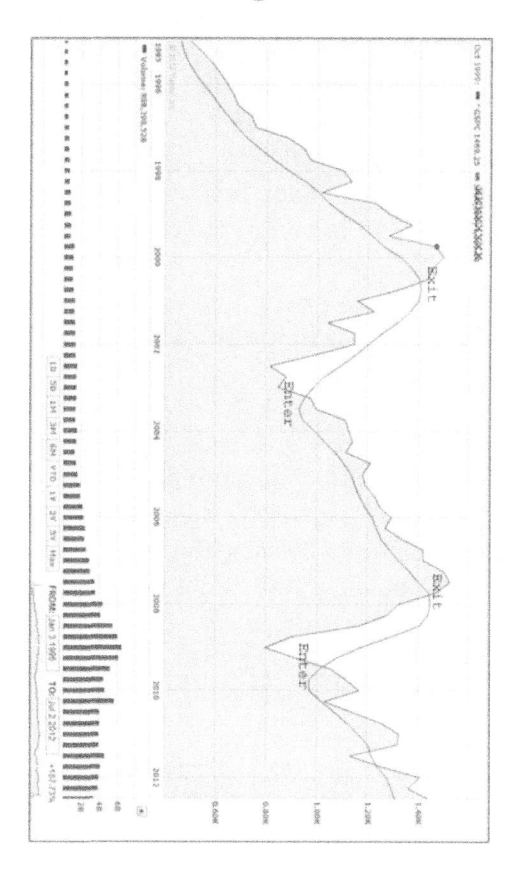

Many e-readers allow you to zoom in on graphs for better visibility. Throughout this book, I use SPY, an ETF that tracks the S&P 500, as a benchmark for market trends. Detecting market plunges as seen in this graph indicates the exit points and reentry points also from 2000 to 9-2009 as follows.

Market Plunge	Peak	Bottom	Indicator Exit	Indicator Reenter
2000	08/28/00	09/20/02	10/01/00	06/01/03
2007	10/12/07	03/06/09	02/01/08	09/01/09
			08/01/11	11/01/11

Table: Vital Dates

For simplicity I skipped a few brief exits and reentries since 2011. You can run the simple chart once a month. When it indicates a potential market plunge is close, run the chart once a week. The last row represents a false signal.

This is based on stock prices so it may not identify the peaks and bottoms precisely, but so far it has not failed to avoid big losses and ensure big gains by reentering the market. I hope the next market plunge will most likely give us enough time to act as these two did.

Unbelievable return with market timing
Calculate how much you made if you followed the above exit points and reenter points from 2000 to today. I bet you would have made a good fortune.

I compared the above returns with the SPY without market timing from 1-2000 to 9-2013.

There are many assumptions. Dividends and compounding are not considered. My return should be substantially better if I include buying contra ETFs during the exits and selling them during the reentries. I was shocked by the incredible return by using this simple market timing. Again, past performance does not guarantee future performances.

Summary info:

S&P 500 1-2000 to 9-2013	With Market Timing	Without Market Timing
Better	500%	
Gain	1,000	167
Gain %	68%	11%
Annualized gained	5%	1%
Days	4,959	4,959

Calculations:

S & P 500	With Market Timing	Without Market Timing
1-2000	1,469[1]	1,469[1]
Exit 10/01/00	1,041[2]	1,041
Enter 06/01/03	1,041	964[4]
Exit 02/01/08	1,489[3]	1,379[4]
Enter 09/01/09	1489	1,020[5]
Exit 08/01/11	1,888	1,293
Enter 11/01/11	1,888	1,251
09/03/13	2,469	1.638
Gained	2,469 – 1,469=1,000	1,638-1,469=167
Gain %	1000/1469 = 68%	167/1469 = 11%
Annualized gained	68% * 365/4959=5%	11%*365/4959=1%
Better	(1,000-167)/167 = 500%	

Portfolio with Market Timing:
[1] Both start with S&P 500 of 1,469 on 1-3-2000.
[2] 10/01/00
The market timing portfolio exits the market and remains the same value of 1,041 until 6/1/00.
[3] 02/01/08
The market timing portfolio exits the market and remains the same value of 1,489 until 9/1/09.

> '1,489' is calculated as follows:
> 1,041 * (1 + Rate) = 1,041 * (1 + 1,379-964)/964) = 1,489
> where the S&P 500 is 964 on 6/1/00 and 1,379 on 2/1/08.

The other calculations are based on the S&P 500 at 1,020 on 9/1/9, 1,293 on 8/1/11, 1,251 on 11/1/11 and 1,636 on 9/3/13.

Portfolio without Market Timing:
[1] Both starts with the S&P 500 of 1,469 on 1-3-2000. We could use the 9/3/13 the S&P 500 value, but it would not account for some compounded interest considerations.

[4] S&P 500 is 964 on 6/1/00 and 1,379 on 2/1/08.

[5] 02/01/08. The portfolio value is calculated to be 1,020 as follows:
> 1,379 * (1 + Rate) = 1,379 * (1 + (1020-1379)/1379) = 1,020
> where S&P 500 is 1,379 on 2/1/08 and 1,020 on 9/1/09.

The other calculations are based on the S&P 500 at 1,293 on 8/1/11, 1,251 on 11/1/11 and 1,636 on 9/3/13.

I cannot believe the shocking return with market timing. I checked my calculations and there was nothing wrong that I could find. If you find something wrong, send your findings to me (pow_tony@yahoo.com).

Even if I made a mistake somehow and got 100% instead of 500%, it still doubles the return without market timing! Ask any fund manager what it means to his or her fund performance and his / her career.

My simple technique that does not use chart told us to **exit the market** on around March 20, 2022.

How I beat the S&P 500 index by 100%

I recommended 20 stocks (pretty diversified) in an article Amazing Return in Seeking Alpha, a website for investors. If you bought them on the published date, you would have beaten the S&P 500 index by over 100% without considering dividends in one year. It is demonstrated in my other article A Tale of Two Portfolios in the same website.

Bubbles

Bubbles have existed throughout history. They occur due to excessive valuations, most often driven by big institutional investors (fund managers, pension managers, hedge fund managers, etc.). These asset valuations are then driven even higher by retail investors. For example, in March 2014, a market bubble was caused by government stimulus, which injected capital into an excessive money supply and subsidies. Early investors riding the wave made significant profits, while those buying at the peak suffered losses.

In recent history, we have seen the 2000 internet bubble and the 2007–2008 housing bubble. The chapter "Spotting Big Market Plunges" demonstrates effective methods to detect these market downturns. Employing these strategies could potentially save over 25% of your portfolio in the event of a future plunge.

Today, many bubbles are caused by governments pumping excessive money into the economy. However, this cannot continue indefinitely, nor can we expect future generations to shoulder the burden of our debts. When these injections cease, the market is likely to drop quickly and deeply.

USD

As of mid-2020, the USD is performing relatively well, though this may be because other countries (such as those in the EU and Japan) are worse off. As Einstein said, "everything is relative." A strong USD negatively impacts exports, and global corporations may see reduced profits when converting foreign earnings back to USD. However, excessive money printing and high government debt levels threaten the USD's status as a reserve currency. This risk is further heightened if China decides to sell its holdings of U.S. Treasury bonds.

Bonds

The bond bubble will likely burst when interest rates rise. Interest rates may have bottomed by mid-2020, though it's even possible they could turn negative.

Stocks
There are several bubble stocks, such as the FAANGs. The market was peaking in January 2020 before the virus outbreak. Employ defensive strategies, including stop-loss orders. The record-high margin debt is a significant concern. If credit tightens due to higher interest rates, this bubble may also burst.

When to Act
Without a time machine, no one can predict exactly when these bubbles will burst. Market timing depends on your risk tolerance, knowledge, and level of greed.

Recently, we face several bubbles, including the housing bubble (2007–2008), gold bubble, market bubble, second housing bubble, debt bubble, bond bubble, and second market bubble. It seems we are trapped in a never-ending bubble cycle. By 2020, the world faced a global recession, exacerbated by the ongoing trade war between the two largest economies. A military conflict would undoubtedly worsen the situation.

The world is more economically interconnected than ever before. When the U.S. economy falters, it affects trading partners such as European nations, China, and Japan, as well as their partners in resource-rich regions like South America, Australia, Russia, Canada, and Africa.
For me, it's safer not to chase the last dollar when the reward-to-risk ratio is too low. A good night's sleep, after all, is invaluable and worth more than all the gold in the world.

#Filler: Your Complaint Department

Depending on your level of investing knowledge, more complex concepts can be harder to grasp. Some strategies even require paper trading to practice. The book may seem even more challenging if read out of sequence, as it is designed to guide readers through beginner, intermediate, and expert-level chapters.

Do not complain about the fillers—they are simply used to occupy blank space in the printed book. Consider them an opportunity to take a breather while reading this lengthy text.

Book 1: Simple Techniques

The first step on investing is to protect your broker and bank accounts. For better security, use a two-factor login that should be available in most if not all brokers and most financial institutions such as banks. To illustrate, after you have logged in, your broker sends a code to your phone, and you use the code to have a second logon to verify you are the rightful owner. Personally, I use a Chromebook or a PC dedicated to financial transactions.

Avoid scams by showing your wealth. Do not click unknown web links. Do not give out your credit cards to vendors you do not know. Do not be greedy. For example, avoid financial products that give you 12% return while the best CDs are paying 5% interest.

This book has a chapter on CDs. When you are first ready to invest in stocks, trade ETFs such as SPY or VOO (an ETF simulating S&P 500 stocks), and you can skip the rest of the book for now. I prefer VOO which has an expense ratio of 0.03% vs. SPY's 0.09% as of 12/2022). It has been proven, the SPY or VOO has beaten most funds by a good margin. Do not waste time and money in hiring hedge funds as most of them do not beat the S&P 500 index. When you are ready in term of investing knowledge, time and money, study the several chapters on how to trade stocks.

It only takes a few minutes every month to time the market as described in Chapter 7. It is very simple and does not require any skill. When the market is down, sell the ETF(s) you own. When the market recovers, return to the stock market. Many investors miss the best profit opportunity, as they have bad experiences when the market is down.

More hints:

- If you have less than $50,000 to invest, just buy ETFs.
- Improve your investing skills by reading investment articles from this book and your broker's website. For example, Fidelity has a lot of information for investors.
- Subscription to AAII is recommended. When your portfolio grows more than $50,000, invest on a subscription such as Value Line, GuruFocus, Zacks or IBD (for momentum traders). Initially, use the information for paper trading on value stocks, which may be usually available from your broker.

- The following is from Portfolio Visual (https://www.portfoliovisualizer.com/backtest-portfolio#analysisResults).
  From 2000 to Nov., 2022 and including reinvested dividends, the portfolio consisting of 25% SPY, 25% RSP and 50% MDY returns (CAGR) 10% with a max drawdown of 51%.

- More useful websites and most are free.

Click here for Morningstar classroom.
http://morningstar.com/cover/classroom.html
Click here for Vanguard.
https://investor.vanguard.com/investing/investor-education
Click here for Investopedia's Tutorials.
http://www.investopedia.com/university/
Click here for Yahoo!
http://finance.yahoo.com/education/begin_investing
Click here for Fidelity basic in investing.
https://www.fidelity.com/investment-guidance/investing-basics

1   Money Market, CDs & Bonds

Overview

CDs are suitable for conservative investors or for temporarily parking money during market downturns. While they offer lower returns compared to stocks or ETFs, they provide stability in uncertain times.

Key Points about CDs

1. Rates and Returns:
   - One-year CD rates have varied from 1.5% in 2020 to 4% in 2024.
   - After accounting for inflation and taxes, returns may be negative. CDs serve better as a defensive investment rather than for growth.
2. Laddering Strategy:
   To ensure liquidity while maximizing returns:
   - Split your investment across CDs with staggered maturity dates (e.g., 3 months, 12 months).
   - Renew maturing CDs for shorter terms to adjust for changing interest rates.
3. FDIC Insurance:

- o FDIC insures up to $250,000 per bank, not per account.
- o Some foreign bank CDs are also FDIC-insured and may offer higher rates.
4. Tax Considerations:
    - o CDs from local banks may receive favorable tax treatment in some states.
    - o However, brokered CDs often offer better rates and convenience.
5. Avoid Callable CDs:
    - o Callable CDs allow banks to terminate the agreement early, typically when rates drop.
    - o Be careful on non-callable CDs unless the offered rates are significantly higher.

Alternatives to CDs

- Money Market Funds:
Brokers like Fidelity offer competitive money market funds (e.g., SPAXX). These provide liquidity and variable yields but are more sensitive to interest rate changes.
- Bond Funds and ETFs:
Bond funds like HYG or JNK provide higher yields but come with added risk. Remember, bond prices generally fall when interest rates rise. The following is my illustration.

Their annualized returns are compounded. SPY is the benchmark I use. Check out their past performances. In 2008, the market crashed. It was a bad year for both bond funds and ETFs, but the bond funds lose less than SPY.

	2007	2008	2009
HYG	3%	-18%	29%
JNK	Not avail.	-25%	38%
SPY	5%	-37%	26%

Link: Government bond default? https://www.youtube.com/watch?v=wMxj6iB92ZA
- Broker CDs (Recommended):
https://www.youtube.com/watch?v=zhEiyW2N7KE
- More on CD: https://www.youtube.com/watch?v=FRWMsGJ2-NE
- Money market fund: https://www.youtube.com/watch?v=N53wZ_80abU
- Its risk: https://www.youtube.com/watch?v=k3wGqD_9SzY
- Better than cash: https://www.youtube.com/watch?v=SrQTOhafE4A

2   Sample portfolio

It is a suggested sample. You need to tailor it to fit your personal requirements and your risk tolerance. In general, you should have an emergency fund for at least 3 months (6 months preferred). Many of my generation have one or even no layoff during my work life. However, I estimate the current generation will have at least 3 layoffs in their work life. It is due to automation, artificial intelligence, global economy, etc.

The rough estimate of stock holding in distribution between stock and bond is equal to 100 – Your Age. To illustrate in the following three portfolios, I use a 30-year-old, and hence he should have 70% in stocks and 30% in bonds (including gold, CDs and cash).

In addition, some sectors are better than others according to the market conditions. The following three portfolios are for regular, todays' market and one during a market crash. I use low-cost ETFs exclusively. ETF is exchange-traded funds. They are traded similar to stocks, but most are more diversified; their fees are usually lower than mutual funds.

ETF	Normal	As of 2/2021	Market Crashing[5]
SPY[1]	40%	30%	0%
QQQ[2]	10%	10%	0%
VTIAX[3]	20%	5%	0%
LQD[3]	15%	20%	5%
GLD	5%	15%	15%
CD	5%	0%	0%
Cash	5%	20%	60%[6]
SH[4]	0%	0%	5%
PSQ[4]	0%	0%	15%

[1] VOO is a low-fee alternative to SPY.

[2] QQQ has more tech stocks.

[4] SH and PSQ are contra ETF to SPY and QQQ. They are shorting the corresponding index. When the market is recovering, switch them back to SPY and QQQ.

[5] Need to balance the allocations about two times a year as ETFs can grow or shrink. When the market crashes, rebalance it right away. All markets

will crash, and the last two (2000 and 2008) have an average loss of about 45%. Refer to the chapter "Simplest marketing timing".

[6] Today's low interest rate does not benefit us for CDs. I would leave the cash not invested and wait for the recovery to move back to stocks.

Of course, everyone's situation is different. If you are conservative, do not buy SH and PSQ. If you are afraid of inflation (especially due to the excessive printing of money), allocate more on GLD, a gold ETF.

Do not listen to financial news. They are used by institutional investors / analysts to manipulate the market. Many times they act the opposite from what they preach. This is the primary reason retail investors do not do better. With the GameStop incident, do not invest in most hedge funds. Buffett has proved the **hedge funds** with their high fees cannot buy an indexed ETF such as SPY.

The above is my recommendation. In the long run, it should work fine. Consult your financial advisor before taking actions. If you have more time, time the market as described. If you are interested in investing, study the more sophisticated techniques described in my book "Art of Investing 5th Edition".

Link
Best Vanguard ETFs https://www.youtube.com/watch?v=mSEyghlZchQ

VTI or VOO: https://www.youtube.com/watch?v=v7staXdVE8c

#Filler "How to make a 50% return"

https://www.youtube.com/watch?v=eEto5nEkf1Y

#Filler Buffett, the person.
https://www.youtube.com/watch?v=w-eX4sZi-Zs

3 Anatomy of a trade

- Ensure the market is trending up before you trade (Chapter 7). You do not need charting knowledge. It is simpler than it looks.

- Beginners. If you are not ready to buy stocks, buy CDs with different maturing dates (Chapter 1). Buy ETF(s) such as VOO, a low-fee ETF for S&P 500 index.

- Non-beginners. Screen stocks with the screens that have the best performances recently. Evaluate stocks with metrics from Finviz.com such as avoiding stocks being dumped by the insiders, negative Q-Q earnings, etc.

- Metrics are generally divided into short term and long term. For me, long term means holding the acquired stocks for more than one year.

- Consider the lower taxes on capital gains on non-retirement accounts.

- Recommend buying less than 10 stocks with less than 3 stocks in the same sector. To illustrate, for a $10,000 portfolio, buy 10 stocks with a position of $1,000 each.

- Sell stocks when your objectives are met or the market is trending down (Chapter 7).

- The reason why investors making good profits when their success rates are only 50%: stop orders. Many recommend set stops so you can lose only 5% (or 10% for volatile stocks) of a trade. Use trailing stops for winners (i.e. periodically renew the stop based on the current price).

Everyone's situation is different, so tailor the above to your own requirements, knowledge and available time for investing. Usually, I hold more than 10 stocks and I use covered calls to maximize my profits.

Do not put new money on losers but on gainers if the trend is positive. The above are my opinions only. Read the Disclaimer in the Introduction section.

4 Investing for 'lazy' folks

You have better things to do than investing or you do not have the time, the desire to learn and/or the expertise in investing. Then you should be better off buying ETFs.

I recommend the following 4 ETFs. If you have $100,000 to invest, buy $25,000 for each recommended ETF. Consult your financial advisor before taking any action. The recommended ETFs should have large market caps and have a high volume.

Most returns started on July 1 and ended on July 1 the following year; this article is written on July 20, 2021. All are annualized returns for easy comparison. Fees, commissions and dividends have not been included.

Symbol	Name	YTD[1] Return	1 Year[2]	5 Years[3]	Bear[4]
IWF	Russel1000Grow	30%	34%	40%	-33%
QQQ	QQQ	30%	46%	42%	-31%
VTI	Vang. Viper Tot	34%	22%	42%	-35%
VUG	Vang. Growth	37%	33%	41%	-32%
Avg.		31%	34%	41%	-33%
SPY[5]		34%	21%	39%	-35%
Beat[6]		-9%	60%	6%	7%

[1] The start date is 1/4/2021 and the end date is 7/1/2021.
[2] The start date is 7/1/2020 and the end date is 7/1/2021.
[3] The start date is 7/1/2016 and the end date is 7/1/2021.
[4] The start date is 1/2/2008 and the end date is 4/1/2009. My estimates.
[5] SPY is the ETF for the S&P 500 index. It is used as a yardstick.
[6] = (Avg. – SPY) / SPY. Again, it does not include fees, commissions and dividends.

Comments:
- The YTD is the only period that this portfolio does not beat SPY (the market to many). However, 31% return is far above the average of the market.
- The one-year return beats the market by 60%.
- The 5-year return beats SPY only by 6%, but the return of 41% is nothing to sneeze at.
- All except Vanguard's Viper Total are ETFs for growth stocks. Hence, I expected it would not beat the market, but it still did it by 7%.
- You can time the market using the techniques described in this book as often as you can. When the indicator tells you to exit, you can sell these ETFs and reenter the market when it recovers. Riskier investors can buy

- contra ETFs such as PSQ and SH instead of holding cash when the market is down.
- At least once in a year review the selection. Use ETFdb.com for more information. If you do not have time, it is fine skipping the review. When you switch ETFs, taxes on any capital gains should be considered.
- Most ETFs replace some stocks periodically to ensure better appreciation potential.
- SCHD should be evaluated and considered if you have only one ETF to buy.
- I prefer VOO due to lower fees (about .03% as of this writing) fee over SPY (about .06%) for long-term investors and SPY for short-term investors due to lower spread (difference between ask price and sell price) as a larger fund. One proven and simple strategy: Periodically (say every month), buy more shares of VOO when the market is down, and less when the market is up.
https://www.youtube.com/watch?v=SGXiOzu0N7I
- Beginners. Do not think hedge funds are your answer. As Buffett pointed out, **most hedge funds after fees cannot beat most index ETFs**.

#Filler: Silence is golden

I am glad I did not give advice to a friend who had to decide whether to take a lump sum payment or an annuity. The correction in March, 2020 would wipe out a lot of his portfolio if he took the lump sum payment. No one would share his profits when the predictions are correct, but the blame if it does not materialize.

It is the same in investing that nothing is certain. With educated guesses, we should have more rights than wrongs especially in the long run.

#Filler: The Ten Commandments of Investing

http://www.investopedia.com/articles/basics/07/10commandments.asp

- Set goals. * Personal finances in order. * Ask questions. * Do not follow the herd. * Due diligence. * Be humble. * Be patient. * Be moderate. * No unnecessary churning. * Be safe. * Do not follow blindly.

- My additions: * Diversify. * Study market timing. * Protect your losses and profits. * Monitor your screens and your metrics. * Be emotionally detached from investments.* Learn from mistakes. * Stay away from bubbles. * Be socially responsible.

5 Simplest analysis of ETFs

Evaluate an ETF

ETFs are a basket of stocks according to the market, a specific sector, country or a specific theme.

Yahoo!Finance used to give the P/E of an ETF. Try to get it from ETFdb.com. Enter the symbol of the ETF such as XLU, and then select Valuation. If it is below 15 and above zero, it could be a value ETF. Also, if the current price is lower than its NAV, it is sold at a discount (or premium vice versa). Compare its YTD Return to SPY's.

Alternatively, get similar info from http://www.multpl.com/. In addition, this website provides the following metrics: Shiller P/E, Price/Sales, and Price/Book.

From Finviz.com, enter the ETF symbol. If SMA-20%, SMA-50% and SMA-200% are all positive, most likely the ETF is in an uptrend. To illustrate, SMA-200 is Simple Moving Average for the last 200 trading sessions (no trading on weekends and specific holidays). The percent is how much the stock price of the ETF is above the SMA. If the percent is negative, it means the stock price is below the SMA (i.e. downtrend).

If your average holding period of your stocks is about 50 days, SMA-50% is more appropriate to you. If RSI(14) > 65, it is probably oversold; if it is < 30, it is probably under-sold.

In addition, ensure the ETF's average volume is high (I suggest more than 10,000 shares), the market cap is more than 300 M, and it has low fees. Most popular ETFs have these characteristics. Beginners should avoid leveraged ETFs.

How to determine if the sector has been recovered

It is easier to profit by following the uptrend of an ETF using the above info. If SMA-20%, SMA-50% and SMA-200% are all positive, most likely the ETF is in an uptrend or it has recovered. It does not always happen as predicted, so use stops to protect your investment.

Link: Fidelity ETF https://www.youtube.com/watch?v=tUsFTN7iDcQ
Vanguard offers many low-cost ETFs.

An example

First, determine whether the market is risky. Most beginners should not invest in a risky market. Advanced investors can bet against the market or a specific sector by buying contra ETFs or puts.

Next, you want to limit the number of sector ETFs by selecting those that are either in an uptrend or hitting a bottom (bottom is hard to predict). Personally, I prefer sectors with long-term uptrends (indicated by articles found from many websites including cnnfn.com and Seeking Alpha.

To illustrate, I compare the following ETFs: SPY (simulating the market based on large companies) and XLP (consumer staples). XLP should perform better than XLY (consumer discretionary) during a recession as those products are the necessities.

Technical indicators such as SMA-50 (Simple Moving Average for the last 50 sessions), SMA-200 and RSI(14) are obtained from Finviz.com and the rest are obtained from Yahoo!Finance.com. After you buy the ETF, use a stop loss to protect your investment. Change the stop loss value every month to protect your gains in this case.

As of 2/5/2016	SPY	XLP (staples)	XLY (discreet.)
Price	190	50	71
NAV	192	50	73
• Technical			
SMA-50	-4%	0%	-7%
SMA-200	-6%	2%	-7%
RSI(14)	44	50	36
Other	Double bottom at $186		
• Fundamental			
P/E	17	20	19
Yield	2.1%	2.5%	1.5%
YTD return	-5%	0.5%	-5%
Net asset	174 B	9 B	10 B

Explanation
- The figures may not be identical among websites due to the dates they are using.
- XLY has the best discount among the 3 ETFs as most investors predict a recession is coming.
- XLP has less down trend among the 3 ETFs as expected.

- XLY is more undersold among the three as expected.
- Double bottom is a technical pattern that indicates the stock would surge upward (opposite to double top).
- SPY has a better value according to its P/E.
- XLY's dividend is the least among the three as they have more tech companies in the ETF; they have to plow back the profits to research and development.
- XLP has the best YTD return among the three.
- As long as the asset is above 500 M (200 M for specialized ETFs), it is fine and all three pass this mark.

There are many metrics such as Debt/Equity not readily available from most websites. Many sites list the top holdings of a specific ETF. Just average the metrics of the top ten or so of its stock holdings. You can simulate it by averaging the top 10 companies if the ETF is weighed by market cap.

Links
Fidelity ETF: https://www.youtube.com/watch?v=tUsFTN7iDcQ

#Filler: Illogical logic
If we do not test for the pandemic, we would have zero increase in this pandemic. Some silly folks buy this argument. What happens to the once-great country?

Filler: The problems of the U.S.
1. Our political system. We waste time arguing between the two parties. There is no long-term planning, as the other party could claim the credit. Same as corporations' CEOs who care about their yearly bonuses.
2. The politicians have to satisfy their voters. Today give them free cash by jacking up the printing press. And ignore the long-term consequences.
3. We have to protect our workers, our environment... Hence, we cannot compete with many countries.
4. We have spent too much on the military and ignore our crumbling infrastructure.
5. Historically no country can rule the world forever.
6. We blame China, but ignore how hard-working Chinese are.

An example

This example evaluates RING, a gold miner, using ETFdb and Finviz that are free from the web. The data is from July, 6, 2020.

Bring up ETFdb and enter RING for the search. The following are the basic info that are important to me: Sector (gold miners), Asset Size (Large-Cap), Issuer (iShares), Inception (Jan. 31, 2012), Expense Ratio (0.39%) and Tax Form (1099).

They fit all my requirements. The expense ratio is higher than most ETFs. I would like trading ETFs using Tax Form 1099 in my non-taxable accounts only as too much work to file for taxable accounts.

Select "Dividend and Valuation". P/E of 17.39 is fine for this sector. It is hard to evaluate miners. I buy this ETF primarily to fight the possibility of inflation and the potential depreciation of USD. The dividend rate of 0.52% (0.70% from Finviz) is in the low range of the scale; it is fine for me as dividend is not my primary concern for this ETF.

There is more info from this website. Alternatively, bring up Finviz for this ETF:
- The short-term trend is up (SMA-20% = 8% and SMA-50% = 7%).
- The long-term trend is up (SMA-200% = 26%).
- It is close to overbought (RSI(14) = 64%; 65% to me is overbought).
- It is -4% from 52-w High. It has performed well from the YTD, Last Year, Last Quarter, Last Month and Last Week.
- It almost doubled in price from mid-March this year.
- Avg. Vol. is fine.

From ETFdb, check the Holding. It has 39 stocks, so it is quite diversified for this industry. The two top holdings are NEM (19%) and ABX (18%). I also consider buying these two stocks in addition to RING. You can estimate the other metrics that are not available by averaging these two stocks. Here is my summary:

STOCK	NEM	ABX
Forward P/E	20	25
Debt / Share	0.31	0.24
ROE	17%	22%
Sales Q/Q	43%	30%
EPS Q/Q	389%	254%
SMA50	2%	4%
RSI(14)	59%	60%
Insider Trans	-13%	N/A
Fidelity's Equity Summary Score	6.1	6.8

6   Simplest ways to evaluate stocks

Who is this for?

This section is for intermediate investors ready to move beyond ETFs and into individual stock trading. Beginners are advised to focus on ETFs due to their diversification and lower risk.

Step-by-Step Stock Evaluation

1. Use free web sites
- Fidelity: Offers Equity Summary Scores for comprehensive ratings and many metrics.
- Finviz: Provides detailed financial metrics and screening tools.
- Yahoo! Finance: Useful for key financial ratios like EV/EBITDA.

2. Focus on Key Metrics

Metric	Preferred Range	Purpose
Forward P/E	5 to 20 (up to 25 for tech)	Measures expected profitability.
EV/EBITDA	Below industry averages	Evaluates valuation, including debt and cash.
Debt/Equity Ratio	Below 0.5 (higher for utilities)	Indicates financial stability.
ROE (Return on Equity)	Greater than 5%	Assesses efficiency in using shareholder capital.
Insider Transactions	Positive or minimal selling	Tracks confidence from company insiders.
Momentum Metrics	Positive SMA-50% and SMA-200%	Confirms the stock is trending upward.

3. Compare to Sector and Historical Averages
- **Sector Comparison**: Compare the stock's metrics (e.g., P/E) to others in the same industry.
- **Historical Comparison**: Look at the stock's 5-year averages for key metrics.

4. Assess the Market Environment
- **Risky Market**: Avoid buying when SMA-50% and SMA-200% of major indices (e.g., SPY) are negative.

- **Sector Trends**: Use Finviz to evaluate the ETF representing the stock's sector. Only buy when the sector is trending upward.

5. Additional Considerations
- **Volatility**: Prefer stocks with a beta under 1 if you are risk-averse.
- **Event News**: Check recent developments like lawsuits, earnings surprises, or management changes.
- **Cap and Volume**: Ensure the stock's market cap is above $800M and daily trading volume exceeds 10,000 shares for stability.

Example: Scoring a Stock
Use a scoring system to assess potential investments. Assign points to each metric and sum them to evaluate overall viability.

Metric	Good	Bad	Score
Forward P/E	5–20: +2 points	Over 50 or < 0: -1 point	
P/FCF (Price/Free Cash Flow)	<12: +1 point	Over 30 or < 0: -1 point	
Sales Q/Q Growth	>15%: +1 point	Negative: -1 point	
EPS Q/Q Growth	>20%: +1 point	Negative: -1 point	

Passing Grade: Total score of **3 or higher**. Stocks scoring 2 may warrant further analysis.

Very Basic Advice for Beginners
1. Stick to U.S. stocks with market caps over $800M.
2. Avoid highly leveraged companies (Debt/Equity > 0.25, except for utilities).
3. Diversify: No more than 20% in one stock and 30% in one sector.
4. Practice paper trading or use simulators like Investopedia Simulator.

Link: Buy stocks/ETFs: https://www.youtube.com/watch?v=4vjkeC_4EmU
https://www.youtube.com/watch?v=wMxj6iB92ZA

7 Simplest market timing

Why Market Timing Matters
Before the 2000s, market timing was often dismissed. However, with major market plunges (e.g., 2000 and 2008) averaging losses of 45%, timing has become a practical tool to minimize losses and improve overall returns.

The goal of market timing is not to predict exact peaks and bottoms but to reduce exposure during downturns and re-enter during recoveries. Using Finviz, no charting is used.

Most gurus do not believe in market timing. The following simple techniques have been proven profitable in 2000 and 2008 market plunges. Accumulate cash when the market plunges and re-enter the market when the indicator tells you so. My most profitable years are the early recovery stage of the market for both 2000 and 2008.

My key Indicators for Market Timing

1. **Death Cross:**
   - Occurs when the 50-day Simple Moving Average (SMA-50) crosses below the 200-day Simple Moving Average (SMA-200. Note: I use 200 as it is readily available from Finviz).
   - Signals a potential market plunge.
2. **Golden Cross:**
   - Occurs when SMA-50 crosses above SMA-200.
   - Indicates market recovery and signals it's time to re-enter.

How to Detect a Market Plunge

- **Use a site like Finviz:**
  1. Search for SPY or RSP (representing the S&P 500).
     Check the SMA metrics:
     - SMA-200%: Positive values suggest no immediate downturn.
     - SMA-50% vs. SMA-200%: If SMA-50 is more negative than SMA-200, it signals a market plunge.
  2. Look for a negative trend in the Buy/Sell ratio (B/S) week over week.

Action Steps During a Plunge:

- **Conservative Approach:**
    - Sell riskier stocks (e.g., those with negative earnings or high P/E ratios).
    - Hold cash or low-risk assets like CDs or money market funds.
- **Aggressive Approach:**
    - Sell all stocks.
    - Consider buying contra ETFs like PSQ (shorts the NASDAQ) or SH (shorts the S&P 500).

How to Detect Market Recovery

- **Reverse the process used for detecting a plunge:**
    1. SMA-200% turns positive.
    2. SMA-50% crosses above SMA-200% (Golden Cross).
    3. Look for a positive week-over-week trend in the Buy/Sell ratio.

Action Steps During Recovery:

- Sell contra ETFs and close short positions.
- Reinvest cash in broad-market ETFs like SPY or VOO.

Tips for Monitoring Indicators

- Frequency: Check indicators monthly. Increase to weekly if prices approach SMA thresholds.
- Advanced Method: For fewer false signals, use SMA-350 (or SMA-400) instead of SMA-200.

Limitations of Market Timing

- Does not capture exact market peaks or bottoms due to reliance on past data.
- False signals may lead to minor losses (e.g., selling early and re-entering).
- Requires discipline to follow the strategy despite market noise or volatility.

Example Application
As of February 12, 2022:

ETF	SMA-200%	SMA-50%	Death Cross?
SPY	-0.8%	-4.2%	Yes
RSP	-0.5%	-1.9%	Yes

This data indicated a confirmed market downturn, suggesting a shift to defensive assets.

Another Simple chart example.
Bring up StockCharts.com and enter SPY. It indicates Death Cross occurred on around March 20, 2022.

8 Rotate four ETFs

We can beat the market by rotating one ETF that represents the market such as SPY and cash via market timing. Aggressive investors can add SH or PSQ (contra ETFs) to the four to have better returns during market plunges.

During a market uptrend, rotating the following four ETFs could be more profitable than staying with SPY (or any ETF that simulates the market). Be warned that a short-term capital gain in taxable accounts is not treated as favorably as the long-term capital gain; check current tax laws.

The allocation percentages depend on your individual risk tolerance. You can use indexed mutual funds. Compare their expenses and restrictions. Some mutual funds charge you if you withdraw within a specific time period.

Select the best performer of last month (from Seeking Alpha, cnnFn, or one of many ETF/mutual fund sites). Add a contra ETF such as SH to take advantage of a falling market for more aggressive investors. Add sector ETFs to the described four ETFs such as XLY, XLP, XLE, XLF, XLU, IYW, XHB, IYM, OIL and XLU to expand your selection.

ETFs	Money Market	U.S.	International	Bond
Fidelity		Spartan Total Market	Spartan Global Market	Spartan US Bond
Vanguard		Total Stock Market	Total International Market	Total Bond Market
My choice	Fidelity	SPY	Vanguard	Fidelity
Suggest %				
During Market plunge	90%	0%	0%	10%
After plunge	10%	60%	20%	10%

Explanation

- The above are suggestions only. If your broker offers similar ETFs, consider using them.
- Check out any restrictions of the ETFs and commissions.

- 4 ETFs (one actually is a money market fund) are enough for most starters. They are diversified, low-cost and you do not need rebalancing except during a market plunge.
- The percentages are suggestions only. If you are less risk tolerant, allocate more to a money market fund, CD and/or bond ETF.
- Have at least 10% allocated to the money market fund for safety.
- When the market is risky, reduce stock equities (i.e., increase money market and bond allocations).
- The symbols for Fidelity ETFs are FSTMX, FSGDX and FBIDX.
- The symbols for Vanguard ETFs are VTSMX, VGTSX and VBMFX.
- If you are more advanced, use additional sector ETFs to rotate. Also buy long-term bond funds (such as 30-year Treasury) when the interest rate is 10% or more.

#Filler: Glad to be an investor

After watching the following YouTube video, I am glad my parents did not push me to play piano and also glad I do not have any musical gene. How can I compete with this kid?

https://www.youtube.com/watch?v=yf0B4rVoq44

Also, glad not into some life-threatening professions such as surgical doctors, soldiers, fire fighters, etc. I can make mistakes in investing from time to time without suffering from the consequences. With the uptrend market for most of the last 50 years, most investors should make good money. Thank God.

#Filler: Where common sense is not common sense

Excessive printing of money is not a long-term solution. Servicing the huge debt weakens our competitiveness. The politicians just want to buy votes today and finance their campaigns. Our next generations have to pay for these huge debts.

#Filler: Cayman Island
Most global corporations are making fun of our tax system. Moving the "headquarter" to low-tax countries such as Cayman Island with a mailbox, a bank account and/or an office that has never been used is a norm. The profitable Boeing has negative tax liability. What a shame!

9 Simplest technical analysis

When the stock, the sector that the stock is in and the market are all above its SMA-N averages (Single Moving Average for the last N sessions), most likely the stock is trending up. In simple words, technical analysis is a study of trends and the change of trends.

1. Bring up Finviz.com from your browser.
2. Enter SPY. Write down the SMA-200 (Single Moving Average for 200 sessions). Positive numbers indicate that the trend for the market is up long term (for simplicity).

    However, the market could be peaking or overbought. Be careful when SMA-200 is over 5% and / or RSI(14) is over 65%. RSI is a metric on overbought / underbought.
3. Enter the sector ETF the stock is in. Write down the SMA-50. Positive numbers indicate that trend for the sector is up short-term.

    However, the sector could be peaking or overbought. Be careful when the SMA-200 is over 10% and / or RSI(14) is over 65%.
4. Enter the stock symbol. If your average holding period of the stocks is 200, use SMA-200 and so on. I recommend SMA-200 for holding value stocks long term and SMA-50 for momentum stocks. Write down the SMA-N for your stock. Positive numbers indicate that the trend is up. However, the stock could be peaking or overbought. Be careful when the SMA-200 (or SMA-50) is over 25% and / or RSI(14) is over 65%.

If the above three criteria and the fundamental criteria are satisfied, most likely it is a good buy. If you buy sector ETFs or mutual funds only, you can skip step #4. In any case, use stop loss to protect your investment.

10 The best strategy

The best-kept secret in investing is to buy a weighted ETF. I use SPY as an example here. This ETF is well diversified as it keeps all 500 stocks in the S&P 500 index. The ETF has a higher position (in percentage) on stocks with higher market cap. The stocks with higher market caps usually grow the market cap by having good management and good products. The bad stocks are deleted from the index periodically.

The second best-kept secret is using simple market timing as described in this book to reduce the losses in market crashes.

It is very hard to beat this strategy. You do not need any knowledge in investing, and you only spend a few minutes every month to time the market. The market is risky when the metrics show you so such as the price is close to the simple moving average in using SMA-350 method; in this case you time the market more frequently.

11   Don'ts for beginners

- Do not use leverage: options, margin and leveraged ETFs.
- Do not short stocks.
- Buy low and sell high.
- Buy value stocks. Sell profitable stocks after a year and losers before holding 12 months for favorable tax treatments in non-retirement accounts. Be a turtle investor.
- Limit momentum trades. Prefer trade them in non-taxable accounts.
- Use stops to protect your portfolio, and trailing stops for gainers.
- Do not follow 'experts' blindly (most have their own agenda).
- Do not trade penny stocks (i.e., stocks less than 200M and/or price less than $1 to my definitions).
- Do not day trade. Most beginners lose most of their money.
- Do not take classes / seminars that promise you big money; if it works, they will give out their secrets.
- Avoid most hedge funds. After the hefty fees, most cannot beat SPY.
- Be selective on investing subscriptions. If they give you a handful of stocks to thousands of subscribers, most likely the actual performance will not be good. Check their past performances that use real money.
- Do not miss many opportunities by avoiding stocks with small caps (such as 300 to 1,000M).
- Do not buy stocks making new lows, as there could be another bottom.
- Do not add position to your losers.
- Buy stocks on their way up, especially when the market is in an uptrend.
- Favorable market conditions: low interest rate and low inflation.
- Do not buy products from financial planners and/or promoters, but pay them for advice. Avoid annuities and some insurance products unless you have good reasons.

Link
Common mistakes: https://www.youtube.com/watch?v=zkNueyFs8zQ

12   Summary

The following improves the odds of success but there is no guarantee.

Risky Market?
Bring up Finviz.com. Enter SPY. If both SMA-50% and SMA-200% are both negative, do not invest especially when SMA-50% is more negative than SMA-200%.

Evaluate value stocks from others' researches
Gather a list of stocks from screens and/or recommendations from magazines. Use researches that are free. Value stocks should be kept for at least 6 months. In six months or so, evaluate the bought stocks again to see whether you want to sell the stocks. Some other sites may provide free trial or one-time evaluation: IBD, GuruFocus, Zacks and Morningstar. Fidelity requires an account but there is no minimum position.

Name	Pass Grade
Fidelity's Equity Summary Score	>=8
Value Line[2]	Timeliness > Average
	Proj. 3-5 yr.% > 5%
VectorVest[1]	VST > 1 and RV > 1

1   Should be available from your local library.

2   Free for limited number of stocks and free trial.

Evaluate stocks
Bring up Finviz.com and enter the stock symbol.

Metric	Passing Grade
Forward P/E	Between 5 and 20 (25 for tech stocks)
P/FCF	< 15 and ratio is positive
Sales Q/Q	>10
EPS Q/Q	>15

Intangible Analysis

Bring up Finviz, Fidelity, Yahoo!Finance or Seeking Alpha (fewer articles now) and enter the stock symbol. There should be a few articles on the specific stock. To prevent manipulation, the stocks should have larger cap (> 300 M) and higher daily average volume (> 10,000 shares).

Book 2: Finding Stocks

There are about 4,000 of stocks (about 30,000 if you include smaller stocks and stocks on foreign exchanges). How can you find the winners? Screening stocks can give you a manageable list of candidates worth your further evaluation.

You can use one of the simple screens that are available to you free from many websites such as Finviz.com and the one from your broker to find a handful of stocks. The filter criteria could be "P/E < 10", "Sales Growth by 20%" or a combination. If the screens consistently find you winners, they are good.

It is more complicated than that. Otherwise, there will be no poor folks. However, most screened stocks should be evaluated. Among the 50 or so screens, there is only one evergreen screen that gives consistent stocks that perform. Some screens work better than others in different phases of the market cycle and/or different market conditions such as during the end of year. You need to use different screens for different purposes. For example, stress on value parameters such as "P/E" for value stocks that have to be held for a longer time than momentum stocks. Use long-term screens for long-term stocks, and vice versa.

Link: Five steps in investing
https://www.youtube.com/watch?v=-i-MS4nX5G4

1 Where the websites are

- **Free and simple screen sites**

    They are described in this article or type the following
    http://stocks.about.com/od/researchtools/a/071909screenlist.htm

    o Yahoo!Finance.
       Click here or type
       http://screener.finance.yahoo.com/stocks.html

    o Finviz.
       Click here or type
       http://Finviz.com/screener.ashx

How to scan using Finviz (YouTube).
https://www.YouTube.com/watch?v=aQ_0FTg9Cfw

Screening using technical indicators (particularly useful for momentum stocks).
https://www.YouTube.com/watch?v=RZRP2NeSX0s

- o Your broker.
  Fidelity's screens are more sophisticated than most.

- o More options: Google, CNBC.com and Moringstar.com.

Here is a list.
http://stocks.about.com/od/researchtools/a/071909screenlist.htm

- **Sophisticated screens (usually not free)**

Most of them are more complicated and need time to learn. Both VectorVest and Stock123 provide historical databases for back testing your screens. Zacks has an earnings revision database at extra cost. GuruFocus has an easy-to-use but powerful screen function.

AAII provides screened stocks from various screens in its low-priced subscription. Both AAII and Value Line take care of some specific industries, but they provide no historical database at least for regular subscriptions. AAII provides historical performance summaries of their screens included in its subscription.

Afterthoughts

Here are the links to screens provided by MarketWatch and NASDAQ.
http://www.marketwatch.com/tools/stockre...
http://www.nasdaq.com/reference/stock-sc...

How to find quality stocks.
http://seekingalpha.com/article/2381395-how-to-identify-quality-stocks-and-is-there-really-alpha-to-be-had
Swing trading: https://www.youtube.com/watch?v=cMmW12Smmt4

Filler
"Sell in May" could be a self-fulfilled prophecy. I prefer to sell on April 1 and come back on Oct. 15 to avoid the herd.

2   Finviz.com screener

You should use fundamental metrics for fundamental stocks, growth metrics for growth stocks, momentum metrics for momentum stocks, or a combination. Basically, you want to keep the fundamental stocks longer so the market would realize their values.

Finviz.com provides a screening function incorporating both fundamental and technical metrics and is one of the best free sites. Bring up Finviz.com in your browser and select screener. You have 4 tabs: Descriptive, Fundamental, Technical and All. It has the following features:

- The criteria specified can be saved but the number is limited.
- The searched stocks can be saved in a portfolio (for paper trading and performance monitoring).
- Technical indicators.
- For an extra fee, you can have a historical database. This would help you to test your strategies. The historical database is quite limited for some technical parameters only.
- Some advanced technical indicators work well, especially useful in momentum trading.
- Use technical patterns. My favorites are Head and Shoulder and Double Bottoms (Peaks).
- Combine fundamental metrics and technical metrics to narrow down your selection.
- Combine fundamental metrics and technical metrics to narrow down your selection.
- Add Insider Trans (> 5% for me), Short Squeeze (> 20%), etc. for specific purposes.
- Candlesticks is hard to master. You need to read a book dedicated to it.

http://www.investopedia.com/terms/c/candlestick.asp
https://www.youtube.com/watch?v=FsqoV1aVrUc

https://www.youtube.com/watch?v=vQHAOcKVmA0

Finviz's screener lacks the following features:

- Stocks with prices trending up in the last several weeks (such as increasing X% in the previous week).
- Using exponential moving averages that supposedly have better predictive power than simple moving averages for momentum investing.

- Selecting ranges such as selecting all three major exchanges and market cap ranges.
- P/E for an ETF. It can be obtained from other sources such as ETFdb.com.
- When the earnings (E) are negative, you may have the wrong values for P/E and the metrics using E. For example, if you want stocks with P/E less than 20, the screener returns you stocks with negative earnings.
- Combine fundamental metrics and technical metrics to narrow down your selection.

All of these missing features can be worked around. The paid version may provide better functions.

A screener example

The following is an example. Fine tune the selection criteria according to your personal criteria and risk tolerance.

- Bring up Finviz.com from your browser. Select Screener, the third tab. As of 3/24/2015, we have 7066 stocks.
- For illustration purposes, we would like to find stocks with double bottoms, a positive technical indicator. Select the Technical tab. Select Pattern and then Double Bottom. Now we have 257 stocks.
- Select the Fundamental tab that is next to the Technical tab. Select Forward P/E and then select "under 20". Now, we have 86 stocks.
- Select Debt/Equity less than .5. Now, we have 45 stocks. Some industries such as utilities are traditionally high in debt, so you can use 'less than 1'.
- Select EPS growth Q-to-Q over 10%. Now, we have 19 stocks.
- Select the Description tab. Select Country to USA. Now, we have 17 stocks.
- Select Price > 1. Select Avg. Volume "Over 100K". Select Float Short "Under 10%. Select Analyst Recs. "Buy or better". Now we have 9 stocks.

Now we can evaluate them one by one using Fundamental Analysis, Intangible Analysis, Qualitative Analysis and Technical Analysis. The purpose of screening is to filter the 7000 stocks to a small number (9 stocks in this case).

Skip the stocks that have the Earnings Date within 2 weeks. If you already have too many stocks in the same industry, skip that stock. You can save the screen when you have registered with Finviz.com. It is free. Check the performance of your selections after 3 months or so.

Other sources

Paper trade and check the actual performance before investing your money. Many popular screens provided by many sites worked before but may not work now. It could be too many folks using the same strategy. Hence it is important to check the current performances of the screen you are using. For yardstick, use SPY or similar ETF that simulates the market. Here are some sources beside Finviz.com.

Your broker
Most broker sites have screen functions. Some have screens to simulate what a specific guru such as what Warren Buffett would buy.

IBD (a subscription service)
From my check on the IBD 50, they're good in the last 10 years, but not that good in the last 5 years – the victim of their own success? They provide stocks from their screens. Most screens are for momentum stocks and large caps. Here are the updated days for specific lists as of this writing.

Stocks Group	Published
Sector Leaders	Daily
Stock spotlight	Daily
Top World	Daily
IBD 50	Mon. and Wed.
Weekly Review	Fri.
Big Cap 20	Tue.

You may want to check out individual stocks with Stock Checkup and then analyze them again. The following are good parameters: Composite Rating, Industry Ranking (finer and better than Sector Ranking) and Relative Price. Understand their parameters and apply accordingly - the same for most other vendors.

IBD prefers large and growing companies with institutional ownership. Some of their parameters may not make sense for small, value and/or turn around companies.

Common parameters

Different styles of investing use different parameters for screening stocks. Here is my suggested group of parameters for using Finviz.com. Vary them to your risk tolerance and market conditions. Finviz.com is not complete in all functions, but it could the best free screener that incorporates both the fundamental and the technical criteria. The first table is for Value and the next one for Growth. The last one is for finding stocks that the institutional investors are trading.

Screening value stocks

Value Screens	Common	Penny	Micro Cap	Dividend
General				
Market Cap (M)	>500 M	<50 M	50-200 M	+Mid(>2B)
Price	>5	<5	1-15	>5
In all 3 Exchanges	In	Not In	Most are In	In
Avg. Volume	>100K	>5K	>10K	>100K
Country	USA	USA	USA	USA
Dividend%				>3%
Float Short	<10%	<10%	<10%	<10%
Analyst Rec	Buy or +	Buy or + if avail.	Buy or +	Buy or +
Fundamental				
Forward P/E	<20	<20	<20	<25
ROE	>10	>10	>5	>15
QQ earning	>0			>0
QQ sales	>0			>0
PEG	<1	<1	<1	<1.2
Payout%				20-50%
P/S	<10	<10	<10	<10
Technical				
Price above 200 SMA	Yes	Yes	Yes	Yes
RSI(14)	<70	<70	<70	<70

There may be no analysts or very few following penny stocks and micro-cap stocks. QQ is quarter to quarter.

Screening Growth Stocks

Growth Screen	Common	Technical	Momentum
General			
Market Cap (M)	>50	> 1,000	>500
Price	>1	>10	>5
Exchanges (Major 3)	In	In	In
Avg. Volume	>50K	>200K	>100K
Fundamental			
Forward P/E	<30	<30	<30
Return of Equity	>5	>0	>0
QQ earning	>10%	>15%	>20%
QQ sales	>5%	> 5%	>10%
PEG	<1	<1	<1
Analyst recs.	Buy or +		
Technical			
Price above 200 SMA	Yes	Yes	
50 SMA	Yes	Yes	Yes
RSI	< 75	< 75	

Short-term trends are important for momentum stocks.

Explanation
The above are suggestions only. Adjust them to your personal preferences and risk tolerance.

- Finviz screener lacks ranges, such as market cap and multiple of exchanges. Most Finviz's parameters do not have a range option such as Exchanges, so you need to run the screen three times, one for each of the three major exchanges.
- Average Volume. When the price of the stock is less than $3, double the average volume requirement. In most cases, 10K is quite acceptable to me. When the volume is small, you may have to pay more (a.k.a. spread) to trade.
- There are many fundamental metrics such as Debt/Equity and Price/Free Cash Flow that are not included here, but they should be included in your further evaluation. Each industry sector has different thresholds. For example, the P/S is very different for a supermarket rather than a high-tech company. Compare the company to the average value of the companies in the same sector. Many sites including GuruFocus.com and Fidelity.com have the average values displayed.
- For momentum stock, you can ignore most of the fundamentals and concentrate on the price trend such as SMA-20% (Simple Moving Average for the last 20 trade sessions) and SMA-50%. The higher the

percent, the higher it is away from its own average. You do not want to hold momentum stocks too long (max. 3 months unless the momentum is still uptrend); personally my max. is 1 month.
- For growth stocks, ensure the PEG (P/E growth), quarter-to-quarter earnings and quarter-to-quarter sales are above the averages in its own sector and/or the market.
- Technical analysis favors large cap stocks with large volumes. I prefer stocks with positive earnings and they are fundamentally sound.
- When the SMA-20%, SMA-50% and SMA-200% are all positive, they should be in an uptrend.
- RSI(14) indicates whether the stock is oversold (>65) or under bought (<30). The range is my suggestion only.
- You may want to check out your strategies using a virtual account from your broker.
- Some websites do not have the most updated price info and that would affect many other metrics such as P/E. If they have an icon Current, check it out for the last updated date. It usually does not matter unless the stocks have big swings, such as TGT losing about 25% in one day.

A general guideline for Institutional investors

Criteria	Value
Description	
Relative Volume	Over 2 M
Country	USA usually
Institution Ownership	Over 50%
Technical	
SMA-200	>10%
Volatility	Week – Over 3%
RSI(14)	>40%
Fundamental	
Market Cap	>1B
ROE	>10%

- Again, these are my suggested metrics. I prefer USA companies and many are global companies. If you use foreign countries, ensure they are larger companies and/or in countries that have regulations similar to our SEC's.
- For value investors, select Forward P/E less than 20 (25 for high-tech companies) and their Earnings are positive.

- Check out how many analysts are following the stocks that you are interested in.

To illustrate, I find 12 stocks. I narrow them down to 3. First, I skip all stocks that already have had more than 10% rise recently. They may have risen too high already.

Select profitable stocks with forward P/E less than 25. "Debt/Equity" is less than .5 (50%). Then, ROI is higher than 25%. Stop when you have reached the optimal number of stocks (3 for me in this example). If you find too many stocks, tighten the criteria and vice versa. Save the criteria and the selected stocks in a portfolio for paper trading.

Screens for specific searches

The current free version lacks combination operations such as AND. Adjust it accordingly and you may need more than one screen to achieve the same requirements. The table includes the most important parameter(s) only.

Purpose	Criteria	Value
Long:		
Insider	Insider transactions	Very positive
Momentum	50-Day Simple Moving Avg.	Price > SMA-50
Double Bottom	Pattern	Double Bottom
Short:		
Short	20-Day Simple Moving Avg.	Price < SMA-20
Double Top	Pattern	Double Top
Information:		
Earnings Announcement	Earnings date	Next week

Links

Basic Finviz https://www.youtube.com/watch?v=cHNUMPgEYGY
https://www.youtube.com/watch?v=3la_e6D1-XA

Under YouTube, search "Finviz".
Recommended YouTube: https://www.youtube.com/watch?v=CJoN7wLfWNo

Short-term parameters:
https://www.youtube.com/watch?v=BvMzYyynaoI

Investopedia.
http://www.investopedia.com/university/features-of-Finviz-elite/other-chart-features.asp

How to scan using Finviz (YouTube).
https://www.YouTube.com/watch?v=aQ_0FTg9Cfw
Finviz's screener tutorial.
https://www.youtube.com/watch?v=glMtwB7OVf4
https://www.youtube.com/watch?v=tHtovnCY6uY
(Recommended)
Swing trading: https://www.youtube.com/watch?v=M8sNMhPJINU
Screening using technical indicators (YouTube).
https://www.YouTube.com/watch?v=RZRP2NeSX0s

Filler: Chicken feet, lobsters and trade war
Lobsters are literally flown to China for the rich. The trade war changes all these. Chicken feet, a delicacy for the Chinese, will be thrown into the ocean. I can finally enjoy a $12 plate of lobster in Boston.

Many farmers have gone bankrupt as the banks do not loan them money to buy seeds for the next year. Our storage is over-flowed. Soybeans and pork are rotting. Trump's subsidies will not help a lot for farms who have small farms and he is going to lose all the votes from these farm states.

3 Sectors to be cautious with

There are many reasons to be very cautious when investing in the following sectors. However, Technical Analysis (a.k.a. charting) would give you more hints than the fundamentals for stocks in these sectors.

Loan companies/banks
The financial statements do not show the quality of their loan portfolios. Banks should make easy money when you compare the CD rates to the mortgage rates. However, they could lose money in the following: 1. Default of loans / mortgages that happen frequently during recessions. 2. Banks are making risky investments that fail such as Bitcoins. 3. Investing in losing vehicles, such as the 'safe' Treasuries during rapid interest hikes (happened in 2023). 4. Poor management and/or frauds. Following this advice, you may be able to skip the banks that melted down in 2007. The peak of Citigroup was $550 and several banks including Lehman Brothers went bankrupt.

To protect ourselves, do not have one bank account with our assets over $250,000, which is protected by FDIC. Be careful on foreign banks, especially the small ones and those that are not protected by FDIC.
https://www.youtube.com/watch?v=qmpVABboOKQ

Failure of Silicon Valley Bank in 2023. If Biden did not mention about paying deposits back in full (many companies have deposits more than the insured amount), it would have shaken our financial system and the entire economic system. The failure is partly due to the rapid interest rates hikes and partly due to the loss of the loans from startup companies in a slowdown in the tech sector. Any unlawful insider trading? Be cautious on small banks; in 2008, about 1/3 of the small banks failed. I expect money from small banks would move to precious metals and larger banks.
https://www.youtube.com/watch?v=atIyLIP9sFs

Drug (generic is ok)
Understanding the complexities of the drug pipelines, its potential profits for new drugs and the expiration of its current drugs may not be worth the effort for most retail investors. In addition, a serious lawsuit and / or a serious problem with a drug could wipe out a good percentage of the stock price. When a drug shows unpromising sign(s) in any trial phase, the stock could plunge and vice versa.

Miners
It is extremely difficult to estimate how much ore (sometimes a miner owns several different types of ores and/or of different grades in the same or different mines) that the company has. It is further complicated by the complexities to extract and transport them. When the total of these costs is greater than its

production price, the company will not be profitable. Understanding the market for ore futures is another discipline.

Many mining companies are in foreign countries such as Canada, Australia and countries in South America. Their financial statements of Canada and Australia are more trustworthy than those from most other emerging countries.

One potential problem of mining companies from many emerging countries is nationalization.

Mining rare earth ore is extremely risky when the profit depends on how China, a major producer of these ores, will price its ores. After China announced the export restrictions on rare earth elements, several non-Chinese companies announced to reopen their mines for rare earths but few have made any profits as of 2013. Developed countries have stricter environmental regulations. Coal suffers from the rising use of cleaner oil and gas.

Insurance companies. Insurance companies profit by:
1. The difference between the total premiums received and the total claims minus expenses in running the company.
2. How well they invest your premiums; you pay your premiums earlier than you may collect from the claims.

They can protect the profits in #1 by restricting claims by natural disasters such as earthquakes and by re-insuring. However, a bad disaster could wipe out a lot of their profits.
Even if the insurance company shows you its investment portfolio, most of us, the retail investors, do not have the time and expertise to analyze it.

Emerging countries (not a sector)
Their financial statements especially from small companies cannot be trusted and many countries use different accounting standards. Emerging countries are where the economic growth is. I trade FXI, an ETF, rather than individual Chinese companies. I have lost a lot in small Chinese companies due to fraud. To check out whether the stock is an ADR, try ADR.COM.
https://www.adr.com/

Stocks with low volumes (not a sector)
Most likely you pay a high spread to trade these stocks. They can be manipulated easier. I remember when I had a hard time trying to sell a stock of this kind. The majority of this company is owned by one person.

For simplicity, I trade stocks with the average daily trade volume over 6,000 shares (double it if the price is $2 or less). A better way could be in calculating the percent of your trade quantity / average daily trade volume to reduce the effect of penny stocks that have larger volumes due to the low prices. You need special skills to trade these stocks but it could be very profitable.

Good business and bad business
Banking is a good business. My deposit in them makes virtually zero interest, and they loan the same money making 3%. If they are more selective in loaning my money, they should make a good profit.

Restaurant is an easy business to open/run, but it is very hard to make good money. With the rising of minimal wages, it will get even tougher. That could be the reason for so many coupons today. The high-end restaurants are doing better due to the rising stock market. As of 8/2014, the newcomers Noodles & Company (NDLS) and Potbelly (PBPB) are not doing very well.

Retailing is a tough business. Looking at the top 10 retailers 15 years ago, I can only find two including Macy's that are still surviving. Most are either bankrupt or being acquired. Even Macy's was at one time in financial trouble.

Airlines are a tough business. You can tell by the average increase in fares in the last 10 years. It cannot even beat inflation. They have to charge you for everything. The next frontier charge is the restroom (especially for long-distance flights). Now I understand why they call themselves "Frontier Airline". As of 2014, it is quite profitable due to mergers and lower fuel cost.

There are several software companies that produce software such as virus detecting programs and tax preparation software. The customers faithfully buy new versions every year. That's great business.

Afterthoughts
As of 8/2013, is the emerging market oversold?
http://seekingalpha.com/article/1658252-have-emerging-markets-gotten-oversold
When an index of an emerging market is up by 10% and the currency exchange rate to USD is down by 20%, then it is not profitable.

Links
Nationalization:
http://en.wikipedia.org/wiki/Nationalization
Spread:
http://en.wikipedia.org/wiki/Bid-offer_spread
Insurance:http://seekingalpha.com/article/1239671-property-casualty-insurance-and-reinsurance-what-you-need-to-know
Bank failure: https://www.youtube.com/watch?v=FRWMsGJ2-NE

Filler: Irresponsible is my best defense
I told my date that I would not be responsible after the second drink due to the lack of an enzyme.

4 GuruFocus

There are many interesting features in Gurufocus.com. It provides the recent stock picks from gurus. Gurus have evaluated the stocks and you just follow them. Gurus' picks and insiders' purchases are one of the best picks without doing a lot of work yourself. It will not replace my production system in evaluating stocks, but it should supplement and improve my system.

They provide a very comprehensive screener and several screens to simulate what gurus would pick. If you do not have any paid subscription, this one is recommended. Take the free offer to see whether it is useful to you. I have not been paid by any one of them except those free subscriptions and /or services that are for my evaluation.

They do not have a historical database for me to test how effective my screens are. For the price they're charging, I do not complain.

They have a choice on the S&P 500 index, but not a choice of exchanges. They do not have Average Volume. It is effective to find the stocks, but you need further evaluation. Gurufocus.com provides a lot of information on a specific stock and some are quite unique such as the F-Score and the warning messages of a stock.

Filler: Incredible coincidence

My best man met the maid of honor in my wedding and they got married later. My best man was my elementary classmate in Hong Kong. The amazing coincidence is that I met him unexpectedly in a Greyhound bus station in Albany at 3 am when I was coming to Mass. for grad school from Cal., and he was changing buses on his way to Toronto. The chance could be higher than hitting the lottery. I prefer to hit the lottery. LOL.

On our flight back from Hong Kong, the one who introduced my future wife to me was two seats away from us on the same row. I cannot believe there is no God arranging our lives.

#Filler: Nobel Prize
Deng did not get a Nobel prize for saving millions from starving to death while Obama got one for doing nothing. It explained the serious prejudice and the dumb discrimination of the committee members.

5 Piotroski's F-Score

Piotroski's system is an interesting strategy. I first noticed it from a screen from AAII, which is very selective. Hence, most of the time I do not find any stock using this screen. In addition, AAII recommends you to sell the purchased stocks if they fail to meet the criteria. Its F-Score is described in the following SA article:

"Here are the nine variables used to calculate the F-Score. Each variable gets scored a one (1) if the condition is met.

1. Positive (+) net income in the current year.
2. Positive (+) cash flow from operations in the current year.
3. Return on Assets [ROA] is higher in the current period compared to the previous year.
4. Cash flow from operations exceeds net income before extraordinary items.
5. Lower ratio of long-term debt to assets in the current period compared to the previous year.
6. Higher current ratio this year compared to the previous year.
7. Company did not issue new shares/equity in the preceding year.
8. Higher gross margin compared to the previous year.
9. Higher asset turnover ratio year on year.

Piotroski only selected stocks that had an F-Score higher than 6 (i.e., 7 to the maximum of 9)."

Gathering the above information is quite time-consuming. However, Gurufocus's "All-in-one-Screener" includes F=Score.

Gurufocus.com's (http://www.gurufocus.com/)

To illustrate, on 11/13/2013, I found the following 12 stocks: SGA, EXAC, ODC, FRS, ANEN, BGFV, LBMH, LDL, RUTH, LWAY, ITRN and GHIFF with the following criteria:

1. F-Score 8 or higher.
2. Market Cap between $100 M and $500 M.
3. Financial Strength between 7 and 10.

The market cap is selected as most institutional investors will not evaluate these stocks.

My modification using their concept

Most readers do not have GuruFocus. The modifications resemble the original criteria and you can incorporate them to your screener including Finviz.com. In general,

- Add negative numbers.
- Adaptive criteria as described in the book. We omit the criteria that do not work in the current market.
- Add ratios that are not available in Piotroski's era.

The first line is the original and it is followed by my changes (if any). Use Finviz.com. Most screeners use Null value for unavailable data, and some use Zero which is a mistake.

1. Positive (+) net income in the current year.
   P/E is positive and less than 25: Add 1.
   P/E is null (or zero) or negative: Minus 1.

1. Positive (+) cash flow from operations in the current year.
   P/FCP is positive: Add 1.
   P/FCP is null or negative: Minus 1.

2. Return on Assets [ROA] is higher in the current period compared to the previous year.
   ROA > 10: Add 1.
   ROA < 2: Minus 1.

3. Cash flow from operations exceeds net income before extraordinary items. (Not used).

4. Ratio of long-term debt to assets in the current period compared to the previous year.

   Debt/Eq < .25: Add 1.
   Debt/Eq > .75: Minus 1.

5. Current ratio this year compared to the previous year.

   Current Ratio > 1.5: Add 1.

Current Ration < .8: Minus 1.

6. Company did not issue new shares/equity in the preceding year. (Not used.)
7. Gross margin compared to the previous year.

    Profit Margin > 15%: Add 1.

    Profit Margin < 5%: Minus 1.

8. Prefer high asset turnover ratio year compared to the previous year.

#3, #6 and #8 are not applicable to me or hard to find equivalent ratios. They are replaced with the following criteria.

1. Short Float < 5: Add 1.
   Short Float > 15 and < 25: Minus 1.
2. Sales Q/Q > 10: Add 1.
   Sales Q/Q < 2: Minus 1.
3. EPS Q/Q > 5: Add 1.
   EPS Q/Q < 1: Minus 1.
4. SMA50 > 10%: Add 1.
   SMA50 < -10%: Minus 1.

I called it FM-Score (M for modification).

Another alternative is to use the color code (green, black and red) from Finviz.com. For example, P/FCF in green color is 'Add 1', P/FCF in red is 'Minus 1', and no score for black color.

Need to adjust to specific industries. Supermarket has high turnovers but low profit margins. Utilities have high debts.

Links
F-Score System:
http://www.investopedia.com/terms/p/piotroski-score.asp

SA article:
(http://seekingalpha.com/article/1806542-a-dividend-portfolio-built-using-the-piotroski-f-score

6   NASDAQ

It is quite similar to GuruFocus's screens in some aspects, but quite simplified. Currently it is free. Bring up Nasqaq.com from your browser. Select "Investing" and then "Guru Screeners".

The following is an illustration on 6/9/2016. Select "P/E Growth Investors" and change "Some" to "Strong". Click on "Go".

I had 5 stocks with "Strong": THO, MPX, GGAL (ADR), BRDCY (ADR) and BMA (ADR). If you prefer U.S. companies only, you only have THO and MPX and both had a desirable "Proj. P/E" under 20.

Alternatively to reduce the number of screened stocks, include stocks with "Some Strong". Sort the "Proj. P/E" in ascending order. If it is blank, most likely it is losing money or there is no estimate for this stock. Use Finviz.com or Yahoo!Finance to confirm.

PEG (P/E growth) is a growth metric and it is available for sorting. You need to evaluate each screened stock. For example, a low P/E stock may not be good if it has excessive debt, or serious pending lawsuits.

Click on the stock THO. It explains how Peter and other gurus score this stock. If you use 70% as a passing grade, 7 gurus rate it a pass and 3 gurus rated it failed.

Click on "Detailed Analysis". Peter rates 4 "Pass" and 2 "Neutral" together with the description.

Try other gurus and select the guru(s) who fit your requirements. For example, if you are a value investor, find a guru or gurus using value metrics.

7 Fidelity

Fidelity offers a strong screen function. The most unique feature is incorporating its Equity Summary Score (used to be Analyst's Opinion) and some outside researches such as Zacks and Ford.

From the main menu, select "News and Research", "Stocks" and then "Lauch stock screen" (under "Find stocks" sub-window).

The following example selects stocks with the following criteria: Security Price (2 to 250), Market Cap. (300 and above), Equity Summary Score (8 and above), Zacks (Strongest) and Ford (Strongest).

It displays the 10 stocks. Research each stock. Read the News about each stock. You may want to use Finviz.com, Yahoo!Finance and other sources to double check.

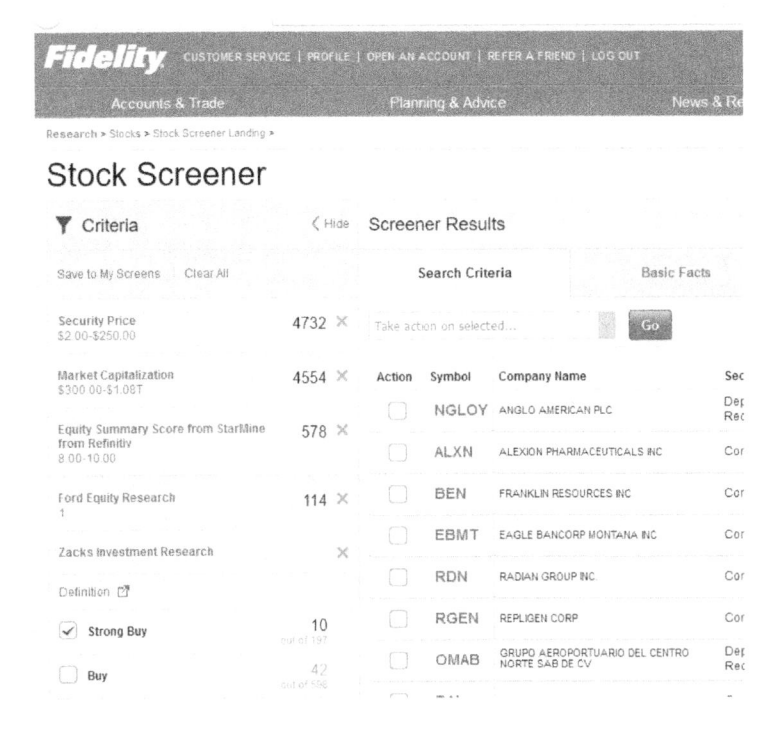

The following describes some of the features.

- Equity Summary Score. It is one of the major metrics I use in my proprietary scoring systems. They are not available to many small stocks. From my limited database in 7/2015 and for short durations, the results are:

Short Term: (7% return for the average)

Metric	Parm. 1	No. of Stocks	%	Parm. 2	No.	%	Predictability
Equity Summary Score	Buy	150	10%	Sell	279	3%	Good

Long Term: (8% return for the average)

Metric	Parm. 1	No. of Stocks	%	Parm. 2	No.	%	Predictability
Equity Summary Score	Buy	90	17%	Sell	208	4%	Good

It has its own limits, but they are very minor to me. First, it does not have a historical database for verifying the screen performance such as the return after a year. However, I do not know any site that provides this function free. To work around this, I save the results in a spread sheet and update the performance.

Secondly, it does not provide many other filter criteria that can be found in other systems such as technical indicators or insider transactions found in Finviz.com. I use other sites for further evaluation.

Most investors should find that this screening is a very good tool and very easy to use.

More info:
Under YouTube, search "Fidelity".
Recommended YouTube:
https://www.youtube.com/watch?v=fxE5577LaxE
Filler
Starbucks is being sued for too many ice cubes in the ice coffee. If he wins, he would sue MacDonald's, Burger King... and be a billionaire. Why did I not think of this? The lady won for the spilling of hot coffee. The jury did not know that eventually we had to pay for all of these and made the lawyers rich. Too many unproductive lawyers make it tough to operate a business including small businesses. In many countries besides the U.S., the one who sues and loses has to pay for court expenses.

8   ChatGPT

Besides Finviz and Fidelity as the major sources for gathering information, today we have ChatGPT, which is AI based.

Screening stocks. You can create a free account. I asked "best stocks for now", and it gave me 10 stocks. It gave me FB instead of the new name META and made me suspicious of the accuracy of the rest of its database. Currently, the database is updated to 2021, and hence it is not good to use it to evaluate stocks. Most are high-tech and all are large companies. It could lead to many asking the same questions and it would result in these stocks rising consequently.

Analyzing stocks with MSFT as an example.
Enter "Microsoft MSFT stock". It would give you general information about the stock.
Enter "Fundamental analysis". It would give you the most fundamental data on MSFT, which are appropriate for long-term holding.
Enter "Technical analysis". It would give you the most common technical data on MSFT, which are appropriate for short-term holding.

Most sites provide duplicate data. The following lists some unique data or data that can be easily accessible from the following sites.

Use Fidelity's equity summary score and at least one report for further evaluation. Comparing its P/E to the industry's P/E is helpful. As of 2/2023, comparing to the average 5-year P/E is not available.

Finviz provides most data. Insider Transaction, SMAs, Shorting % ... are quite easily accessible.

Yahoo!Finance provides EV/EBITDA under Statistics.

#Filler: Globalization

We used to dump chicken feet into sea. The Chinese treat them as a delicacy. Hence, we ship them to China and make a good profit. With the profit, we ask Chinese to assemble iPhones at about one fifth of our cost at home. The Chinese enjoy our chicken feet at less than their market prices and have many of the factory workers employed. A win-win situation!

9 Performance of my screens

I monitor the performance of my top screens every 6 months or so. Here is my September, 2013 summary. The purpose is identifying the screens that have performed well recently. It is for illustration purposes only. All returns are annualized. They are sorted by Grand Avg. in descending order.

Screen	Last Monitor 2/13	Current Test Avg.	Long-term Avg.	Short-term Avg.	Grand Avg.	Avail.
EP	39%	66%			59%	75%
BB3	35%	70%			53%	25%
LPSER	-21%	72%			49%	75%
MN	19%	53%			45%	75%
CW	64%	49%	39%	20%	38%	100%
LR	30%	37%			35%	100%
TT	30%	26%	71%	8%	35%	100%
TV2	50%	76%	14%	19%	35%	100%
BFSCB	5%	38%			31%	100%
DO	29%	24%	30%		28%	100%
AR	56%	53%	23%	6%	28%	100%
BE	81%	44%	10%	13%	25%	100%
FA	16%	27%			25%	100%
BS5BV	21%	25%			24%	100%
SE		53%	20%	-3%	23%	100%
CAO	-3%	17%	37%	12%	21%	100%
...	...	...	---	...	...	
Avg.	34%	19%	23%	5%	19%	

Screen.
They are the abbreviations. To illustrate, CAO is the screen looking for candidates for acquisition with low market caps. I have about 25 production screens. They have been selected among over 100 screens.

Last Monitor 2/2013.
Copied from the "Current Test Avg." from my last monitor in 2/2013.

Current Test Avg.

It is the average of the four tests on recent months. The four test dates are: 03/11/13 to 7/9/13, 4/9/13 to 8/7/13, 5/9/13 to 8/17/13 and 6/8/13 to 9/6/13. They are about 4 months apart. It is the most important average to reflect what worked recently.

Long-term Avg.
It is the long-term performance (about 12 months) of the actual, screened stocks. These are stocks that have been actually screened and some may have been purchased.

Short-term Avg.
It is the short-term performance (about 6 months) of the actual, screened stocks.

Grand Avg.
It is a weighted average of the above 4 return categories (Last Monitor, Current Test Avg., Long-Term Avg. and Short-Term Avg.) and they're sorted in descending order.

Run the top screens first as they have given me better returns in the past. It does not guarantee that they will perform as well as before, but they have a better chance to perform well than the screens scored below the average.

Availability.
To illustrate, if the screen found stocks in 1 out of the 4 tests, it is 25% available. These screens may not have enough data for prediction on the future results and there is a higher chance that I will not find any stocks using these screens.

Observations
The following are the personal findings on my own screens. You can do something similar to separate your top screens from the rest of your screens. Test and monitor the performances of your own screens.

- Usually, the top half of the screens from the last monitor show up in this monitor though their ranks may vary.

- CAO in the last monitor should be better than it indicates. At least two companies had been acquired and they had very good returns. These two companies did not show up in the test as they're taken out from the historical database; it is termed as survivorship bias.

- CW is quite consistent to the last monitor.

- EP and BB3 have not found any stocks in actual usage. MN proves to be a good screen in these two performance monitors. I missed the opportunities to make good money from this screen – my mistake.

- LPSER is a risky screen demonstrated here and from the previous monitors. I prefer not to take unnecessary risk. Include a column of maximum drawdown as it is a good indicator to avoid risky screens.

- LR was below the average and that's why it had not been used. It is above the average in this monitor, so it will be used to some small extent.

- TT is above the average in these two monitors. The returns of screened stocks during this monitor are better in both long term and short term and hence it will be used.

- The original table (not shown here) has comparisons to SPY (an ETF simulating the market). Beating the market is my yardstick. If most of your screens beat the market, most likely they will beat the market again. However, there are exceptions such as when the market is plunging. In this case, value stocks are better than growth stocks, and cash is the king.

    The market during my last monitor is better than this period. If the return of SPY is negative in the last three months, there is a good chance that the market is trending down.

- There are some screens that just do not perform for a long while. They will not even be monitored next time. However, when the phase of the market cycle changes, the performance of these screens may respond differently.

- The test results are not always consistent. It could be due to my limited data, or the market does not behave normally.

10   A scoring system

This scoring system helps you to select whether you should buy a stock or not. In this system, when a stock scores higher than 2, it is a buy. As a group, the highly-scored stocks usually perform better than the lowly-scored stocks in a year. The basic concepts are described here.

An Example

For illustration purposes, we use two metrics: Forward P/E and ROI.

First, we convert Forward P/E into Forward E/P by flipping the two values. Assuming Forward E/P should have a higher weight than ROI, multiply E/P by 5. The average ROI is 10% (simplified for illustration), so minus it by .1.

Score = Forward E/P * 5 + (ROI -.1)

For example, a stock has a P/E of 10 (E/P = 1/10= .1) and ROI is expressed as 25%.

Score = .1 * 5 + (.25 - .1) = .5 + .15= .65

Some parameters by some sites are expressed in grade such as A, B, C and D. For simplicity, if it is A, then the value is 2 otherwise it is zero.

Score = if (Grade = "A", 2, 0) + ...

Test your system on paper with at least 3 months of data. Check whether your scoring system works. It works when the higher the score corresponds to the better the return. Adjust the weight on each metric and see whether your scoring system improves its predictability.

Again, it is simplified for educational and illustration purposes. Try even more different metrics and check whether the metrics still work in the current market. The next metrics to include could be Equity Summary Score from Fidelity, Debt/Equity and Quarter-to-Quarter Earnings / Sales.

Monitor your scoring system

I am sure that many have tried to use most of the metrics and they still cannot find the Holy Grail. I believe the predictability power of each metric is influenced by the current market conditions. For example, the fundamental metrics such as P/E predict better than the growth metrics such as PEG during the market bottom. You should test the performance of each metric every 6 months or so.

You may have two scores: one for short term and one for long term. The stocks you want to keep in the short term may not be the same kind of stocks you want to keep in the longer term. Short term is 3 months (one month for me) and the long term is 12 months for me. My definitions could be different than yours. Value metrics are more important for the long term while growth metrics are more important for the short term.

However, 12 months is too long a period of time and during this period the market may change, so it is better to change it from 12 to 6. To illustrate, energy stocks were great in 2007, but they plunged in 2008. If your scoring system for long-term holding was constructed based on 12 months' data in 2007, the system would have been misleading in 2008 for energy stocks in this example.

I find the short-term scores have a better prediction power than the long-term scores. However, I keep profitable stocks more than 12 months to qualify for the better tax treatments in taxable accounts, and sell the losers less than 12 months. Evaluate the purchased stocks every 6 months to decide whether you want to keep them for another 6 months. Use stops and trailing stops (for winners) to protect your portfolio.

Besides monitoring the metrics in your scoring system, monitor the scores.

The market is not always rational

Sometimes the scoring system fails: When the poorly-scored stocks perform better than the highly-scored stocks. The market is not always rational. Most scoring systems depend on fundamental metrics. When the market switches its favor from value to growth, adjust the score system accordingly. I have found that more than one time that the stocks scored in the top 5% did not perform, so be careful or skip the top 5% (sometimes 10%). The events such as a pending lawsuit or an expiring drug do not show up in metrics, and that is why we need to do other analysis such as Intangible Analysis.

Some metrics almost always work such as the positive predictions of excessive insider's purchases. The insiders know the company typically better than others. When they buy their own company's stock at market prices, they must know it has good appreciation potential. They have many reasons to sell their company's stocks. However, when they sell a large percent of their holdings, be cautious.

When the stock loses more than 30% in a month and you cannot find valid reasons, it may be a good indicator for potential appreciation ahead. Some suggestions are:

- Do not modify your scoring system during market plunges.
- The best strategy is to use the screens (same as searches) that have worked well for the last 90 days.
- Find out why your fundamental metrics that used to work do not work now. You may want to add more weight on growth metrics, and vice versa on value metrics.

An example of monitoring the metrics

This is what I found in monitoring the performances of the metrics as of 3/2013. It is based on a limited database of about 300 stocks with holding periods varying from 1 to 15 months. It has an average of 8% (16% for shorter term). The following is for educational purposes only.

1. The foreign stocks are not doing well: South America (average return is -21% for 7 stocks), Israel (-18% for 2), China (-10% for 7). Europe (0% for 17) and Canada (5% for 16, and most are in natural resources). If I ignore the foreign companies, the return of the portfolio would increase substantially.

2. The following metrics work fine for the long term only: Forward (same as Expected) Earnings Yield (E/P) and Fidelity's Equity Summary Score.

3. P/B. The stocks with P/B less than 1 perform better than the stocks with P/B greater than 2 (10% vs. 4%).

4. There are no definitive conclusions on Cash / Market Cap, PEG and Return of Equity (a surprise to me) in this monitor.

5. The stocks that were cheaper by 50% to their average 5-year P/E (available from Fidelity) have performed better than those stocks that were cheaper by less than 2%.

6. The ratio of Short / Market Cap between 25% and 30% has better performance than other percentages. It is a contradictory ratio and it

could be a short squeeze (a condition that the stock is running out of shares to sell short).

7. There are many composite scores from different vendors that I subscribe to and they are not disclosed here.

8. Based on the above, I will modify my scoring system. I will still have two scores, one for short term and one for longer term.

Short-term scoring system

The scoring system should work better in the shorter term. For testing this system, I used the above database, but deleted stocks that have been over 8 months old. It is still a small database of about 190 stocks.

The result is different from the above as the time frame has been reduced. Here is the summary.

1. The predictability of screens (same as searches) performs about the same as the last monitor. A few screens are better than others. I will not use the under-performing screens with real money.

2. The stock grades from several vendors are not a good indicator this time.

3. Expected (same as Forward) Earnings Yield (E/P) has been a good indicator.

4. Cash Flow is a good indicator (different from the last monitor).

5. Fidelity's Equity Summary Score is a good indicator. Finviz has a similar score, but I prefer to use Fidelity's. Fidelity places higher weight on opinions from analysts that have a better prediction on this stock than others. It eliminates some of the conflict of interest between the analysts and the investing banks s/he works for.

6. The Short Percentage between 25 and 30 is a good contrary indicator (could be a good chance for a short squeeze).

   Its value of less than 10 % is a good indicator. The rest of the range is not conclusive.

7. Cash / Market Cap, Insider Purchase, P/B, ROE and Dividend stocks (>3%) are not conclusive in this monitor.

8. P/S with values less than 0.8 are a good indicator.

9. For some reason I do not know why and how to explain: the top 10% of the top-scored stocks did not perform better than the other stocks that pass.

    It happens in both my two scoring systems. Be suspicious of them and it has happened for more than once. However, the stocks that scored in the bottom 10% are consistently poor performers and that's a good indicator.

There are many other parameters that may be of interest to you. Include them in the performance monitor.

Book 3: Evaluating Stocks

The simple formula to make money is to find value stocks and wait for the market to realize their values; it could be a year away. Momentum investors buy stocks that are trending up, and evaluate the purchased stocks again within 3 months. Personally, I sell within a month as usually there are better momentum stocks to buy. Only buy when the market is not risky. Aggressive investors find the worst stocks to short. Most successful investors are doing this.

The book value of a stock is simply the net worth of a company (= Assets − Liabilities). When the stock price is higher than the book value per share (i.e., 'Stock Price / Book Price' > 1), it is overvalued. When this ratio is more than 2 or less than 0.5, conservative investors have to be cautious. When it is way underpriced, there may be a critical reason.

Intrinsic Value includes the intangibles such as patents. However, both the Book Value and Intrinsic Value have not been convincing predictors from my tests. I briefly describe some basic but important metrics here.

- Expected (same as Forward) Earnings Yield (E/P). The future appreciation depends on future earnings and the current price of the stock (you do not want to overpay). I prefer a range from 5% to 30%.
- Growth of Earnings and growth of sales. Compare them to their numbers in the same quarter of last year. I prefer 10% or higher.
- How good is the management? It is measured by ROE. I prefer 10% or higher.
- How safe is the company? 'Debt/Equity' is one important metric and Cash Flow is another. The warning sign is that the company does not have enough cash to pay back the debt obligations. I prefer it to be less than .5 (same as 50%). However, some industries are debt-intensive.

Most ratios are readily available from many sites including Finviz.com. In most cases there is no need to dig into the complicated financial statements initially. If you do, ensure they are up-to-date. For example, when a stock has a one-to-two split, the price is updated but may not be the Earnings per share, Book per share, etc.

The predictability of most metrics changes according to the current market conditions. Monitor their performance and act accordingly.

Why you need further stock analysis after screening

First, you may have too many screened stocks. Second, it is for better performance. I listed the rejected stocks (12) in my recent book "Best stocks for 2024". From 12/20/23 (the publish date) to 3/29/2024 (today). The average return of the rejected stocks is about 2%, while the RSP (an ETF for unweighted S&P 500 stocks) has a return of about 10%. The average return of the recommended 8 stocks is about 14%. There are many other examples.

How to start

First, we filter stocks from about 7,000 selected stocks available from Finviz.com for example; the number is variable from different websites and/or services. To start with, skip stocks that are not in the three major exchanges, market caps less than 50 M, or daily average volumes less than 10,000 shares.

Check out the "Simplest Way to Evaluate Stocks" in the Common Tools section to evaluate stocks for beginners and couch potatoes. Furthermore, refer to Scoring Stocks to evaluate stocks via a scoring system.

1   Performances

They are the recommended stocks in the primary lists (for long-term stocks) of my last five books in this "Best Stocks" series:

Book	Stocks	Return	Ann.	Beat RSP by
Best stocks to buy for 2022	10	4%	4%	153%
Best Stocks to buy as of July, 2021	8	5%	13%	487%
Best Stocks for 2021 2nd Edition	10	42%	52%	220%
Best Stocks for 2021	4	29%	44%	118%
Best Stocks to Buy from Aug, 2020	14	45%	45%	3%
Avg.	9	25%	32%	196%

The details can be found in the following link.
http://tonyp4idea.blogspot.com/2022/12/best-stocks-series.html

2 Amazing returns

To achieve a consistent 10% return above S&P 500 over many years is every fund manager's dream. To double one's investment above the S&P 500 return is amazing while tripling it is unheard of. I beat the S&P 500 by 700% and I can detail the history of my transactions.

Many analysts show their average yearly returns and/or their returns of their top 10 stocks this time of year. The market has closed early today on Christmas Eve, so I have the time to check my recent performance. As a trader with many trades, it would be far too complicated for me to do the same for the entire year. I selected all the stocks I purchased in the last 90 days. Most of them are deeply-valued stocks. Let's check how I performed so far on these stocks.

Whenever you have achieved a high return such as this one, take the profit as it may have reached its peaks. To me, most profits are made in swing trades with an average holding period of just 90 days.

Stocks bought and their returns as of 12/25/12

Stocks	Date Bought	Return	SPY Return
BANR	12/07/12	3%	-.13%
KTCC	12/06/12	0%	.7%
QCOR	12/07/12	15%	-.1%
KTCC	12/06/12	-1%	.7%
ACTV	12/05/12	-5%	.7%
IAG	12/05/12	-1%	.7%
ADES	12/04/12	6%	.6%
NC	12/03/12	15%	-.3%
VELT	12/03/12	64%	-.3%
ANR	11/28/12	33%	4.8%
AAPL	11/16/12	1%	4.8%
C	11/14/12	13%	3.0%
DECK	11/13/12	16%	2.7%
MSFT	11/13/12	0%	2.7%
ALU	11/13/12	38%	2.7%
DLTR	11/09/12	7%	3.4%
CAT	11/08/12	4%	1.9%
MSFT	11/07/12	-8%	.5%
BSX	10/24/12	14%	.3%
BSX	10/19/12	7%	.3%
20			
AVG:		11%	1.35%

Beat SPY (in %) = (11%-1.35%)/1.35% = 716% or 7 times

Average Return = averaging each return of 20 stocks = 11%
Average Annualized Return = 148% or 122% (= 11% *365 / avg. holding period)
Average Return = Profit / Capitalization = 10%[1]

How the returns are calculated
Using BANR to illustrate how the return and the SPY return are calculated.

| BANR | 12/07/12 | 3% | -.13% |

BANR was bought on 12/07/12 (17 days from 12/24/12) at 27.93 and it was at 30.43 on 12/24/12.
Rate of Return = (30.43 – 27.93) / 27.93 = 3%

SPY was at 142.53 on 12/07/12 and at 142.35 on 12/24/12.
  Rate of Return = (142.35-142.53) / 142.53 = -.13%

Commissions and dividends are not included for simplicity. Commissions are negligible and dividends could add about another 2% for the annual returns.

Interpreting the performance results
The quantity of each stock bought is not important as I am comparing the return of the stock. However, a few stocks have been listed twice as I bought two times usually on separate dates. If I chose them as one purchase instead of two, my return would appear even better. The purchases are real, so the amount of each stock is not identical to each other.

I'm not too excited yet. This phenomenal return could be just this one time only. 90 days is a short period. Consistency could be achieved with an improved stock picking technique, plain luck or a combination. By any measure, it is an extremely decent return. However, I do not expect to beat S&P 500 by 7 times again.

My best return is from 2009 in my largest taxable account. It was over 80% beating the SPY by about 3 times. 2003 was another good year for profit.

These two years are defined by me as the Early Recovery stage in a market cycle and the market provides the best profit opportunity.

The four losers are MSFT (-8%), ACTV (-5%), KTCC (-1%) and IAG (-1%). The best winners are: VELT (64%), ALU (38%), ANR (33%) and QCOR (19%). The following are in a 14% to 16% range: DECK, NC and BSX (2 purchases). Click here for the entire list.

Cheating the results

I could 'cheat' for better results by doing the following, but I did not:

1. Exclude stocks only purchased in the last 20 days (instead of 15).

2. If my purchases of CSCO were included, the result would be even better. CSCO has been bought three times on 7/24/12 and it has gained 31% as of 12/25/12. I still have CSCO, but it is not included as it just hit the 90-days requirement.

3. I could include those buy orders that had not been executed due to their fast appreciation.

Hence, there are many ways to cheat, so you should read others' results carefully.

What stocks were included
There were 20 purchases. I bought some stocks twice and that counted as two purchases. None of the stocks have been sold as of 12/25/12. I have excluded the stocks that I am testing a strategy by trading them every month and most are in a separate account.

How the stocks were picked
The majority of the stocks were screened by my selected screens that had been proven profitable in the last 3 to 6 months, or are historically profitable at this stage of the market cycle. I also analyzed most of the screened stocks and assigned a score (15 and higher is a buy) based on the metrics that had a reliable prediction recently. I do not stick with the scoring system 100% of the time, but most of the stocks that I purchased twice have high scores.

The poor performers were scored as: MSFT with a score of 13, ACTV 16, KTCC 27 and IAG 23. The scoring system is OK. MSFT should not be bought judging from its low score. However, I believe MSFT has long-term appreciation potential. The other three are the latest purchases in this portfolio and they may perform better in a longer period of time.

The winners were scored as: VELT 34, ALU was not scored, ANR was not scored and QCOR 30. The scoring system is great for this group. ALU and ANR were selected from two Seeking Alpha articles and their selections were not based on these scores. I read several Wall Street Journal articles on ALU and CSCO to convince myself to buy both of them.

The average winners were scored as follows: DECK 9, NC 26 and BSX was not scored. DECK was selected based on an article from Seeking Alpha and it seemed DECK was experiencing the same short squeeze as CROX once did. BSX was selected from a Sunday paper article.

Observations
1. I notice that most big winners (ALU is $1) have a stock price less than $10. The myth of holding quality stocks with prices higher than $15 is not true here as most of my big winners were below $10 including ALU.
2. I did not double my normal purchases on VELT and ALU, which both turned out to be my best performers. VELT scored high in my analysis. ALU was very convincing but it seemed to be risky. 'Nothing risk and nothing gained' applies here. I did triple my purchase on CSCO, which is a large company with good fundamentals that were not yet 'discovered' by the market.

   Both AAPL and DECK gained more than 25% and then lost most of their gains during my short holding period. I should have sold AAPL as many of my fellow investors sold the winners expecting higher capital gains taxes next year. The myth of 'buy and hold' does not work here.
3. During this period, I had several buy orders that were not executed due to their rising stock prices. Market orders could be the solution. It is another example of pennies smart and a pound foolish.
4. It will be interesting to check the results again in 6 and 12 months. Except ALU, all are in my taxable accounts and I usually keep them for a year to qualify for the lower tax rates due to capital gains.
5. I have not described any specific method, but these concepts help you to build better strategies to customize to your individual situations and/or market conditions. Invest the money you can afford to lose. Past performance does not guarantee future results.
6. Reading articles such as Seeking Alpha can be beneficial providing they are not 'bump-and-switch' scheme. However, you should do your own analysis. It is your money after all.

7. The market has been up by .8% in the last 90 days and this portfolio increased by 11%. If my portfolio amplifies the market, I wonder whether it will be down by the same rate in a down market.
8. This portfolio is quite diversified even that I have not planned that way except weighing more with high tech companies. There are no big winners and no big losers that could change the average returns.
9. I tried not to include emerging countries such as China as I do not trust their balance sheets.
10. I have never achieved such an amazing return. I'm emotionally detached to big wins and big losses. It could be plain luck. Even the best strategy will have its "black swan" moment eventually.

11. To achieve over 100% annualized return is not sustainable by checking the top performers of the S&P 500 index and their returns. However, it is possible but not likely if you churn your portfolio more than once and you time the market correctly.

12. Time to take profits as most stocks here have achieved my objectives. Use the cash to buy stocks with a similar appreciation potential. You will never go broke taking profits.

Conclusion
My three steps of making a stock purchase are: 1. Market timing, 2. Screening stocks, 3. Stock Analysis and 4. When and what to sell. They have all been discussed throughout the book. Market timing and strategy (#2 and #3) does not always work, but it will go better with using them.

I am the living proof *against* the Efficiency Theory and the claims that stock picking does not work. It may not work from time to time, but in the long run it works.

Footnote
[1] Profit / Capitalization should be a little less than 20%. The original 10% is correct when you invest all the 20 stocks at the start of the beginning of the investment period. I bought these stocks on different dates. If I assume the average time of all the stock purchases is at a mid-point, then my average capitalization is only half and hence giving a 20% return.

It is slightly less than 20% as I did not include the stocks that I bought in the last 15 days. Use the number for a comparison and that's why we have to be concerned with the performance from most investment subscriptions.

Link: Intrinsic value: https://www.youtube.com/watch?v=nX2DcXOrtuo

Section I: Fundamental metrics

3   Mysteries of P/E

If you believe you can make good money by selecting stocks with low P/Es solely, dream on. If it were that easy, there would be no poor folks. However, buying fundamentally sound companies would reduce the risk and improve the chance of its appreciation.

P/E is the most misunderstood indicator. To me, it is the most useful one among all metrics if it is properly used. Earnings is the key to stock appreciation and P/E measures its value. To illustrate on P/E, you pay a million for a hot-dog cart in NYC. Even if its earnings increase year after year, you will never recoup your investment as you have paid too much even for a good business.

"Buy stocks with P/E below 15 and earnings positive" is not true in many cases. P/E growth (PEG) should be considered at least as a prospect of the company. Many retailers were destroyed by Amazon and many newspapers were destroyed by Facebook and Google. Which sector do you want to buy: the sector in up trending or the dying sector even with a better P/E?

Most old books on value are based on old industries that are no longer applicable in today's market. Read these books but ask the above question.

Better definition
P/E should be inverted as E/P, which is termed as Earnings Yield. Earnings Yield is easy to be compared and understood. It takes care of negative earnings for screening stocks and ranking (comparing stocks with the better P/E first). If you sort P/E in ascending order, your order will be wrong with the negative earnings but right with E/P.

It is usually compared to a 10-year Treasury bill yield (or 30 years) or a CD rate. If the stock has 5% earnings yield and your one-year CD is 1%, then it beats the CD by 4% in absolute numbers and four times better. However, the CD is virtually risk free (with deposit amount limits in most banks). Earning yield is an estimated guess and it may not materialize.

Many ways to predict E/P
- Based on the last 12 months. Project it to the Forward E/P. It is also called the last twelve-month E/P.

- Based on analysts' educated guesses. Guesses may not materialize. Based on my experience, the expected usually predicts better than the one based on the last 12 months. This is the one I use most and many investing subscriptions provide this Forward P/E (same as the Expected P/E) or expected E/P.

Usually, I do not trust the analyst's opinions due to their conflict of interest. However, the earnings estimate is my exception.

- Based on the last month or the last quarter. Latest information could be better for predictions. However, they are not good for seasonal businesses such as the retail where most sales are done during the Christmas season.
- Besides the Pow PE described later; I take the average of the earnings yield EY as:

The Avg. EY = (EY from the last twelve month + Expected EY + EY from the current month of prior year) / 3

It averages out using figures from the past, the present and the future. If no one has used it, I claim shamelessly it is my original idea.

Best E/P could not be the best

Very high E/P could be signs of troubles ahead such as a lawsuit pending, fraud, etc. If you find companies E/P over 50%, it means two years' profits could be equal to the entire cost of the company! I can tell you right away that they probably smell fishy unless you believe that there is a free lunch in life.

However, from time to time, some bargains do exist due to certain conditions, or the Wall Street is just wrong about the company. I found one in my year-end screen and that gave me huge return. You need to find out whether they are bargains or traps. When the E/P is low (sometimes even negative) but is improving fast, it could mean big profits for you. Fundamentalists may miss this opportunity in the early stages due to the unfavorable E/P, but it could be the most profitable time to buy. Sometimes, it could be a turnaround.

During a recession, most good companies have a hard time in promoting new products as the consumers are thrifty. At the same time, it usually is the best time to develop products if they have enough cash to finance them. In this case, there will be no alarm even with negative earnings. The only alarm is when a company cannot meet the debt obligations.

Some companies can manipulate earnings via dirty tricks in accounting. It could make this year look really good, but it is harder or even impossible to continue the same trick for many years. Check out the footnotes in the financial statement.

E/P and PEG

For value investing, E/P is usually used and the higher the better. Watch out when it is extraordinarily high.

PEG (P/E growth) measures the rate of improving P/E. '1' is supposed to be neutral to most investors. When it is below 1, it is undervalued, and vice versa.

PEG = (P/E) / Earnings Growth Rate

They have a similar problem with P/E with negative earnings.

Which of the following two stocks do you want to buy based on their historical earning yields and earnings growth?

1. A stock that has a 10% earnings yield with no earnings growth.
2. A stock that has an 8% earnings yield with 50% earnings growth.

If the earnings growth continues, in next year the second stock should pay 12%, substantially better than the first stock. This is another reason we should use forward earnings rather than historical earnings.

PEG may give a low value for companies that pay high dividends. To correct it,

PEG = (P/E)/ (Earning Growth Rate + Dividend Yield)

When the general market favors growth stocks, weigh more on growth metrics including PEG. I claim no credit on the adjusted PEG.

Fundamental metrics

E/P is one of the metrics you should use but not exclusively. If the earning yield is high but the % of debt is high too, then a good bargain may not be as good as it appears to be.

Some other metrics may not be easily found in the financial statements such as the intangibles, insider buying, pension obligations, trade secrets, losing market share, brand name, customers' loyalty, etc. It is interesting that most metrics change its ability to predict from time to time.

P/E variations

There are other P/E variations like Shiller P/E (same as CAPE and PE10). Shiller P/E can also be used to track the current market valuation. It is controversial and its value is easily misinterpreted. Hence, use it as a reference only unless you understand all its issues. I prefer to use a two-year average of the P/E instead of 10 as I believe the market changes too much over a ten-year span. Currently Shill P/E does not work that well as before. It is due to the excessive printing of money.

Compare a company's current P/E to its average P/E in the last 5 years. Also compare it to the average value of the companies in the same industry. The average P/E for high-tech companies is different from supermarkets for example. They are available from Fidelity.

P/E is more reliable for a group of stocks (SPY for example) instead of individual stocks which have too many other metrics and intangibles to deal with. When you compare the total return of an ETF to a corresponding index, you need to add the respective dividends to the index to ensure a fair comparison of total returns. As of this writing, the S&P 500 is paying about a 2% dividend.

EV/EBITDA is another way to measure the value of a company. This metric has its advantages and disadvantages over P/E. It includes other important data such as cash and debt. EBITDA/EV is equivalent to E/P including other mentioned metrics. I prefer to use it over E/P. Some sites do not provide it if the earnings is negative. The disadvantage to me is it does not use expected earnings. This ratio can be found under Yahoo!Finance.

Garbage in, garbage out
I do not trust most financial statements from emerging countries, especially the smaller companies. Watch out for fraudulent data. Most metrics can be manipulated. Recently I have a US stock that lost 18% in one day due to the SEC's investigation of its financial data.

The announced earnings may not be reflected in the financial statements that you use from the web. Ensure your data is up-to-date by checking the date of the financial statements. Seeking Alpha has transcripts for the earnings announcements that would save you a trip to attend the companies' quarterly meetings.

Sector and entire market
You can find the value of a sector using the P/E of an ETF for that sector. It is similar for the market. For example, use SPY (an ETF simulating the S&P 500 index). If it is lower than the average (15 to me), then most likely the market is good value and a buy signal. It is one of the many hints for market timing.

Where to use P/E
Each highlight of the following corresponds to one of my books. Click it for the description of the strategy.

My book on top-down approach starts with a safe market, then sector analysis, fundamental analysis, intangible analysis and optionally technical analysis. P/E is one of the many metrics in fundamental analysis.

There are many styles of investing. In general, fundamental analysis is important when you hold the stock longer.

- P/E is important in Long-Term Swing, Dividend Investing, Retirees and Conservative Strategies.
- My max value is 20 and 25 for tech companies. I ignore it if they have high potential for appreciation that could be indicated by insider purchases. However, many unknown companies then had a P/E over 50. Tesla had a P/E over 1,000 at one time.
- P/E is moderately important in Short-Term Swing and Sector Rotation.
- P/E is the least important in Momentum Strategy and Day Trading.
- Be careful of the falling companies when the P is low due to stockers are leaving due to events such as a major lawsuit.

Summary

Again, one metric should not dictate the reason to trade a stock. Compare the company P/E to its industry average and its own five-year average. In addition, many industries have cycles. If you buy it at the peak of the industry, the P/E may mislead you. Besides fundamental analysis, you need to consider intangible analysis and time the entry / exit point by using technical analysis. Intangible analysis evaluates information that cannot be summarized into numeric metrics such as a lawsuit pending.

True P/E

"EV/EBITDA" is available from Yahoo!Finance and other sources. The true EY is "1/Ture PE". I call it "True" for the lack of a better term as it represents the financial situation of the company better. This could be the most important metric for many.
EBITDA: https://www.youtube.com/watch?v=C2eoh3X4efM

Earnings can be manipulated. For example, the company management can lower the P/E ratio by buying back its stocks. In this case the earnings per share is boosted but in reality, there is no change in the company's financial fundamentals. The true P/E takes into consideration the reduced cash. EBITBA stands for "Earnings Before Interest, Taxes, Depreciation, and Amortization".

Be careful when EV or "EBITDA" is negative. Most likely you should avoid the stocks with a negative EV.

Yahoo!Finance usually leaves EV/EVITDA blank for financial institutions such banks, loan companies and REITS. In this case, use forward earnings yield (= 1 / Forward P/E or Pow Earnings Yield described next.

I prefer True Yield based on Forward P/E instead of P/E as it has better predictable power to me. To illustrate, Apple has a P/E of 21.61, Forward P/E of 19.46 (both from Finviz), and Enterprise Value / EBIT of 16.72 (from Yahoo!Finance). The True Yield is 6% (1/16.72). The True Yield based on Forward P/E is 7% (6% * 21.61/19.48).

Pow P/E

You should use the described "EV/EBITDA" and hence "Pow P/E" can be ignored. There are some cases that Pow P/E is better: 1. "EV/EBITDA" may not be available for reasons such as negative asset and 2. Use of Forward Earnings instead of Earnings based on the last twelve months. The following is an exercise on how I simulate it from Finviz.com with metrics that are readily available.

I modified P/E to take care of cash and debts. I use my last name due to being easier to distinguish from P/E and it has nothing to do with my ego.

Pow P/E = (P - Cash per Share + Debt per Share) / (Earning - Interest gained per share - Interest paid per share)

Pow Earnings Yield = 1 / Pow P/E

Here is a comparison of E/P (Earnings Yield), Expected Earnings Yield (Forward E /P), True Yield (EBITD/EV) and Pow Earning Yields, which is based one Forward (Expected) Earnings as of 10/14/2021.

	CARS	MPAA
Earnings Yield	1%	7%
Expected Earnings Yield	12%	12%
True Yield	13%	11%
Pow Earnings Yield	5%	9%

P/E is not always important

The following is my test from 1/2/2020 to 10/14/2020. RSP is similar to SPY except that the stocks in the S&P 500 index are equally weighted. EY (= E/P) is Expected Earnings Yield and there are no stocks with EY less than 0. DY is Dividend Yield. GPE is the growth of P/E. As in my book, I use annualized returns and dividends are not included. This test does not mean a lot, but it tells us what these metrics behave during this period, or it indicates **Value is not a good metric in this period**, and it may indicate momentum is better in this period. Most big winners start as small companies with **high P/E** (from 30 to 100). Many of them have important technologies or special systems that would change the world such as Microsoft, Facebook, Amazon and Walmart to name a few. Their sales have increased substantially year after year. In early 2023, P/E for many AI chips such as Nvidia is not important when the industry looks rosy and the Forward P/E is far better than the P/E (based on the last 12 months).

Examples of not depending on low P/Es. Before the financial crisis in 2008, P/Es of most bank stocks had 10-year low. After they announced the earnings, P/Es of many of them surged to over 100 and the stock prices suffered losses of more than 80% within 12 months. The stock price of Bethlehem Steel with P/E of 2 at one time went to zero. Need to find out why the stock is so cheap via intangible analysis and qualitative analysis.

The following is very rough testing and there are many limitations in the database. However, the conclusion is quite convincing to me and some are opposite to the contrary beliefs. For example, I expected the higher EY the better, but not in this test.

	Ann. Return	Indicator	Comment
RSP 500 All	-2%		
EY (top 10)	-54%	Bad	Contrary
GPE (top 10)	-20%	Bad	Contrary

Select All or top 100.			
DY = 0	16%	Good	
DY (top 100)	-19%	Bad	
DY / 1 and 2	2%		
EY 3 to 4	15%	Good	Second best
EY 2 to 3	6%	Good	Third best
EY 1 to 2	31%	Good	Best
EY 0 to 1	-39%	Bad`	

I use some metrics from a service I subscribe to that are not included here. Two major metrics of this subscription have a return of around 20%. Most subscriptions including the free Fidelity (to some extent) give you three composite scores: Total, Fundamental and Timing. I wish to check out the recent predictability of Fidelity's Equity Summary Score if they have a historical database. Most of them take out the delisted and /or bankrupt companies in their databases.

Link: P/E: https://www.youtube.com/watch?v=4KkTGx2bK_4

4   Fundamental metrics

ROE
Return of equity (ROE = Net Income / Equity) could be the most important financial indicator to determine how well the management is doing their job. However, in recent years, this metric has been overused and loses its prediction reliability.

The company's return on equity for at least the last five years would indicate how the stock price endures major financial downturns as well as upturns.

Comparing the ROE to the average ROE for the sector is a good indicator on how well the company is managed compared to its peers. Some sectors including utilities have low average ROEs.

Market Cap (Capitalization)
Market Cap = Total no. of outstanding shares * share price

I recommend the beginners buy U.S. stocks with a market cap greater than 800 M (million). Here are the current conventions (everyone's convention is different) and they should be adjusted to inflation.

Class	Market Cap (million)
Nano Cap	< $50M
Micro Cap	$50M to $250M
Small Cap	$250M to $1B (billion)
Mid Cap	$1B to $10B
Large Cap (Blue Chip)	$10B to $50B
Mega Cap	>50B

The higher the cap is, usually the less risky the stock would be. Nano Cap and Micro Cap are reserved for speculators or owners of the companies. Small Cap and Mid Cap are for knowledgeable investors as most institutional investors would skip these stocks in these caps especially Small Cap. Large Cap, Mega Cap and some Mid Cap are the stocks traded by institutional investors. They are thoroughly researched continuously.

My metrics

My current favorites are Forward P/E, PEG, Fidelity's Equity Summary Score, Short % of outstanding shares, Free Cash Flow, ROE and Debt Load / Equity.

In addition, I use many summarized metrics from different sources. For example, one of my subscription services gives me a composite rank for fundamentals and another one for momentum. To illustrate, click here for Blue Chip Growth which is no longer free for stock analysis. Enter IBM as the stock symbol. As of 2/2013, it gives C for a Total Grade, D for Quantity Grade and B for Fundamental Grade. The Total Grade is usually a composite grade of other grades.

Use the metrics to screen through the stocks to reduce the number of stocks for further consideration.

Mid, high and low values of common metrics

Metric	Mid Range	Low Range	High Range
P/E (last 12 months)	< 10	>40	< 4
Price / Cash Flow	< 12	>30	< 4
Price / Sales	< 2.5	>3	< .2
Price / Book	< 2.0	>4	< .2
PEG	< 1.5	>2	< .2

High Range means good values (although in this table it means low numbers), but sometimes it is too good to be true. Low Range means bad values. To illustrate, many internet stocks in 2000 had P/E over 40 (bad) while a neglected bargain stock has a P/E of 3 (supposed to be good). A bargain could also mean they could have some hidden problems. In reality, I prefer the Mid Range. Using P/E to illustrate, it should be between 4 and 10. Adjust the range according to your personal tolerance and the current market conditions. If the market trend is up, you may want to relax the range to 5 to 12 for example otherwise you cannot find too many stocks for further evaluation.

These values are my selections based on data for about 10 years. They are used for predicting the performance of a stock in a year; review the ranges every 6 months in the current market.

The metrics with the high-range and mid-range values offer better predictions for the stock price appreciation. From the above table, the stocks with the low-range values have a better chance than other stocks to lose money in a year or so. Some favorable numbers could be high values instead of low values such as ROE.

However, the range values could change. When the market favors momentum or you do not keep stocks for less than a month or so, the momentum metrics including PEG and price growth could be better predictors. We need to check to see whether the current market favors which metrics: Value or Growth – some websites and subscription services identify the current favorite. In addition, the performance of each metric should be evaluated every 3 to 6 months. In addition, new range values need to be adjusted with the above table.

Fundamental metrics take a longer time (about 6-12 months vs. 1 month for momentum metrics) for the performance to materialize. The metrics in the above table besides PEG are all fundamental metrics. Except for financial stocks, P/B is always worthless.

Examples of searching with high range values

Stocks with low-range values for most metrics (such as 40 in P/E in the above table) could be risky. Hence, select the stocks with the mid-range value (e.g., 10 for P/E). Avoid the low-range values indicated by the metrics.

Here is one example of selecting stocks with high range values of P/E and P/B. Most likely, you will not find too many stocks with these criteria.

> E > 0   and
> P/E < 4 and
> P/B < .2

E is earning per share and we need the company to be profitable.

High range values could indicate something is wrong with the company, e.g., a lawsuit pending. I would consider a P/E of less than 4 is suspicious. However, very small companies are often neglected by the market, so they could be solid companies. Don't forget to do your due diligence and spend more time in thoroughly evaluating the stock and its industry.

The stocks with the low-range values have a greater chance of losing money in the next year or so. That is proven statistically as a group despite some exceptions. AMZN[2] is not a valued stock by its high P/E or its high P/B. However, if the company is investing for the future by building infrastructure and capturing the market share, you may ignore these unfavorable metrics. Personally, I prefer fundamentally sound companies today.

Note. P/B is not a good metric for established companies and / or companies with a lot of research such as IBM. Many metric formulae are outdated due to ignoring intellectual properties, patents and market appeals such as brand names.

Example of a search for mid-range values
E > 0 and
P/E < 10 and
P/E > 4

In this case, you only include companies with positive earnings and P/Es within the range from 4 to 10 exclusively. You should find many companies with the mid-range values of P/Es.

Add other filters such as minimum price, market cap and average volume. If you do not find too many stocks, relax your criteria (start with mid-range values in the table), and vice versa to limit the number of stocks. If you usually find stocks with a screen but not today, it usually means that the market is overvalued and that you cannot find many bargain stocks.

Again, it is the first step to narrow down the number of stocks to be analyzed. Your metrics will not cover stocks with special situations. For example, IBM always has had a high Price/Book value for as long as I can remember and therefore it does not mean it should be excluded.

The searches based on fundamental metrics help us to narrow stocks for further evaluation. Occasionally I abandon the scoring system for some stocks under special conditions.

Compare a company's metrics to its sector's averages
This could be the most powerful comparison: Compare Apples to Apples.

You may want to compare the metrics of a company to the averages of that sector. The average of supermarket's P/S is extremely low and hence it has no meaning to compare a supermarket's P/S to most other sectors. Some sectors like utilities need high debt to run a utility company.

However, when the average P/E or other metric of a sector is suddenly lower than its historical average, it could mean that sector is out-of-favor and/or the sector is having a better value.

This following table compares Apple to its sector and a retail sector on a specific date for illustration. All the metrics will change.

Metric	Apple	Computer	Retail
P/E	11	19	24
(5-year average)	16	17	15
PEG	.6	N/A	1.4
Price /Cash Flow	9.4	8.1	9.2
Price /Book	3.3	3.0	3.6
EPS Growth	-6%	-42%	2.6%
(last 5 years)	62%	45%	11%
Operating Margin	20%	15%	8%
ROE	30%	14%	19%
Debt / Equity	2%	7%	88%
Inventory Turnover	76%	53%	4.55x

From the above table, some metrics only make sense for an industrial sector (Computer for Apple). In this case, you may want to compare AAPL to Computer, and not to Retail. "Debt / Equity" indicates that the retail sector needs to borrow more than the computer sector for example. Of course, retail stores have high Inventory Turnover.

Top-down approach
First, compare whether the market is risky. Second, select the best sector; there are many sites including Finviz.com to select the best sector. Then compare the fundamental metrics of the major stocks within that sector.

Some metrics do not apply

Using financial institutions as an example, usually P/B is more useful than P/CF. However, the quality of a loan (not a metric here) is more important than all metrics as we found out in 2007. P/S is more important for retails. However, the expected P/E is most important for most other sectors.

When you believe a sector is the currently best (a criterion available in many screeners), select the best stocks in this sector.

Compare metrics to its five-year average

If the company's five-year average of P/E (available from Fidelity and many other sites) is 20 and today it is 10. It is 100% under-valued by this standard. Also, you may want to try other metrics such as debt/equity and compare it to the five-year average.

Growth Metrics
The growth metrics are growth rates of the stock price, sales, earnings, etc. They are useful for growth investors.

Even for value investors, the earnings growth rate is very important, as most stocks with substantial gains have increased their earnings growth first. If the earnings have grown but the price remains the same (i.e., PEG), then the potential for price appreciation will be higher and most likely it will return to the historical average P/E.

Momentum Metrics
Momentum metrics is part of growth. The rates of increase of the stock price, the volume... are the major metrics. Earnings revision is another one especially in earnings announcement seasons (usually 4 times a year).

Fidelity and many subscription services provide a composite rank with name Timely or similar name. The following could be part of this Timely score: SMA-50, Q-Q sales increase and recent price appreciation. In my momentum portfolio, I use these metrics and ignore all the other metrics as my average holding period is less than 30 days for momentum strategies.

Insiders' buying
Insiders sell their stocks for many reasons. When insiders buy a lot of their companies' stocks at market prices, take notice. Insiders know better than anyone about the health of their companies and their industries.

Select Insiders' purchases from one of the available sites such as Finviz.com. Ignore the option exercises. I prefer the high ratios of Net Total Purchase Value / Market Cap and the purchases by more than one insider. Be careful that the insiders purchase the stocks after selling a similar amount of stock in a brief time span.

OpenInsider is a good site for this info.
InsiderSights is a good one too with more capable tools that would take more time to learn.

Where to get the metrics
You can get this information from the website with no or low cost such as Finviz.com, your broker's site, AAII (very low cost) and Fidelity.

The following subscriptions are at a little higher cost but they are still less than $1,000 per year: Value Line, IBD, Zacks, VectorVest and Stock Screen 123. Many data from different vendors are duplicated such as P/E. You will save time by concentrating on one or two sources.

Many vendors provide a composite metric such as a value metric to cover P/E, debt… and a timing metric to cover Technical Analysis indicators, PEG, price appreciation rate…

Short % is a useful metric available in Finviz.com. For Fidelity customers, you can click on Research and then Stock. Enter the stock name, and then click on Detailed. I find Fidelity's Analysts' Opinions quite useful.

Finviz.com provides a lot of useful information free of charge. It also provides a screen function. The 'Help' button describes Finviz's functions and all the metrics monitored.

Other sources are: Insider Cow, NASDAQ Guru Analysis …

Monitor the recent performance of the metrics
The predictability of most metrics has proven not to perform consistently as many investors and fund managers found out. My theory is that the specific metric works better in some market conditions than others. To test

which ones work better currently, check their performance in the last three months and use those that perform well. This is what my scoring system in the book Scoring Stocks is based on.

Why some metrics fail sometimes

Most investors are using metrics to screen stocks, but few are successful consistently. Some investment companies have top analysts dedicated to projects looking for the right strategy. My guesses why they fail are:

1. Metrics need to be monitored to see its effectiveness on current market conditions.

2. Besides fundamental metrics, there are many intangibles.

3. When they have too many followers on the same metrics, they will not work such as ROE in the last several years.

4. Fundamentals need time (at least 6 months) to reflect the value of the stock. You're swimming against the tide as a fundamentalist. Trading momentum stocks using basic fundamentals will not work.

5. Watch out 'Garbage in and garbage out'. Some emerging countries do not have an organization similar to SEC to ensure the integrity of the financial statements of a company and some audit firms are being paid to cover their eyes. Even though there are frauds in some U.S. companies and with their auditors.

6. The metrics may be derived from obsolete financial statements. Check out the date. The most updated one could be available from the company's website.

7. Some companies borrow a lot of money to dress up the metrics such as P/E and ROE. They will look good short-term but not long-term. Ensure the debt/equity has not been increased recently for this purpose. I recall one utility spin-off had incredible fundamentals except the debt load. It is so high that all these fundamentals will deteriorate in the future due to servicing its high debts.

Footnote

[1] The stocks are classified into sector and then sectors are divided into industries (same as sub sectors). For example, oil is a sector and oil exploration and oil services are industries under the oil sector. For

simplicity, I intermix the terms here as many sectors do not need further sub classifications for this discussion.

[2] AMZN is not a value stock by any standard. As of 1/1/2013, its P/E (from last 12 months) is 157 and P/B is 15. Both fall far into my low-range values. Its price rises from 256 from 1/1/13 to 270 today (1/22/13). Today its P/E is ridiculously over 3,000. The investors are betting AMZN's internet sales will take over the concrete stores and its investors do not care about profit but rather for market share. Does it sound familiar in the internet era? Its price momentum is indicated positively by any chart. It may be a good stock for traders, but it is too risky for a swing trader and a long-term investor like me (yes, I wear two hats). I do not short stocks in a rising market, but this could be an exception.

Afterthoughts

- The only recommendation from a very popular investment book I read is to select stocks by the return of equity (ROE). I will save you the time and money to read that book. I read the entire book in an hour at Barnes and Noble's and it saved me some money / time, not to mention cutting down trees for that book. Basically, it does not work today.
- DAL has an interesting Debt / Equity of over -1000% due to the negative equity. For a comparison, you may want to use Debt / ABS(Equity).
- Once in a while, I found the financial data was not consistent from different sources. Try to check out any discrepancy in the dates of the financial data of your sources. The financial statements from the company websites usually have the most updated data.
- Current Ratio = Current Asset / Current Liability. If it is below 1, then the company is having a tough time in meeting its current cash obligations.
- Dividend Yield is a valid metric for matured companies. I do not use it to evaluate growth companies or companies that need to plow back cash for research and development.
- If you use Finviz.com, you find three margins: profit, gross and operating. I prefer to use profit margin that is more useful for most companies. The other two may be relevant in some sectors.

http://www.investopedia.com/terms/p/profitmargin.asp

http://www.investopedia.com/terms/g/grossmargin.asp
http://www.investopedia.com/terms/o/operatingmargin.asp

Use Wikipedia for more description.

- Enron had millions in profits but negative cash flows. Earnings can be manipulated but not the cash flows.

    Insiders' selling usually does not cause any alarm unless excessively. Most insiders sell most of the stocks they have before these companies go bankrupt. Just common sense!

- Why fundamentals are important.
(http://seekingalpha.com/article/1612442-its-shorting-season)

    On the same day when this article was published, RVLT was up 10% due to increasing sales in the earnings conference. However, the company is still not profitable. It shows how tough shorting is even with good arguments. That's why do not expect every purchase is profitable. However, with the educated guesses, you should beat the market in the long run.

- Due to my ignorance, limited time or my short period of holding stocks, I have not used intrinsic value that often.

    Book value is different from intrinsic value. Book value is calculated by summing up the values of all pieces of a company such as a building and all equipment. Intrinsic value is the real value of a company. When two companies have the same book value and market cap, the company that generates more profit than the other one usually has a higher intrinsic value. When the intrinsic value is higher than the stock price, it is underpriced in theory.

Links:
Income statement: https://www.youtube.com/watch?v=ht-tzwyLPU
The following link provides more info on intrinsic value.
http://en.wikipedia.org/wiki/Intrinsic_value_%28finance%29
https://www.youtube.com/watch?v=l-T-Vyk2txc&authuser=0

5   Finviz's parameters

Most metrics are described in Finviz (via Help), Investopedia and/or Wikipedia and my articles on P/E and fundamental metrics if available. We use the metrics for screening stocks and then evaluating the screened stocks.

The following are my personal comments and why I feel some metrics are more important than the others. Personally, I divide the metrics into fundamentals and technical, which are more important for long-term investors and short-term investors respectively.

Compare the ratios to the companies in the same sector (industry) and also its averages from the last few years (5 preferable) from many other websites such as Fidelity.

From your browser, enter Finviz.com. Enter a symbol (I used ABEO for discussion). A chart is displayed with the prices and volumes for the last eleven months. SMAs (Single Moving Average) are displayed sometimes with other technical indicators. Intraday, Daily and Weekly options are available for day traders, short-term traders and long-term traders respectively. I prefer Candle – Advanced for drawing charts.

Besides the chart and the metrics described next, it describes what the company does, analysts' recommendations (I prefer Fidelity's Equity Summary Score), insiders' trading and articles that are good for intangible and qualitative analysis. Many free websites such as Yahoo!Finance provide a list of articles about the company.

"Financial Highlights and Statements" are materials for more in-depth analysis and they were more important decades ago when most financial ratios had not been calculated for you. It is important for investors with good knowledge in financial accounting. The current version also includes the basic balance sheet, income statement and cash flow for the current (TTM) and the last two years. Click on the following YouTube links for more detail.

Balance: https://www.youtube.com/watch?v=DMv9JC_K37Y
Income: https://www.youtube.com/watch?v=0--AvwZablQ
Cash flow: https://www.youtube.com/watch?v=hMBN6yTIDb0

A section on Insider Trading is also included. Do not be alarmed when insiders dump small quantities of the stocks. Buying large quantities (e.g., insider transaction more than 5%) at prices close to the market price could be favorable news.

The following metrics are roughly based on the flow of Finviz from top to bottom and left to right. I skip those metrics that I believe are not too important. You can also place your cursor on the metric to retrieve the description from Finviz or via Finviz's Help. Some metrics are left blank to indicate they are not applicable (for example, zero, negative or not available). For example, the Debt/Equity of YRCW in 1/2019 is blank (same as null) due to its negative Equity. From Yahoo!Finance at the time of writing, it has a total debt of 888M.

- **Index**. Most of us trade stocks in the three major exchanges in the USA. Stocks listed over-the-counter are too risky for most of us. Skip the stocks in local exchanges and foreign exchanges unless you are an expert on these stocks and/or have insightful (not illegal info from insiders) information. I screen the stocks and then ignore the stocks that are not in the Dow, NASDAQ and Amex. Other screeners may let you select a group of exchanges.
- **Market Cap** (MC). To me, stocks below 50M are risky even though they could be very profitable. Ensure the Avg. Volume is at least 10,000 shares and / or your order is less than 1% of the average volume. Some small stocks are controlled by the owners and have small volumes. You cannot trade these stocks easily.

    Float = Outstanding shares – Insider shares

    Usually, Float does not matter as they are typically the same. However, it does for small companies with large insider shares. Most of these owners do not want to sell their family businesses and hence they reduce the chance of being acquired entirely or partially for good prices. In this case, you may have to hold this kind of stock for a long time or you may have to sell it at a very unfavorable price.
- If **Forward P/E** (a.k.a. Expected P/E) is not provided, use the P/E which is based on the trailing last 12 months (TTM). Alternatively, calculate the E by using the E from P/E and multiplying it by its growth rate. It may not be seasonally adjusted. I prefer using Forward P/E as it provides a better predictability power to me. Successful investing is usually a result of correct guessing the future earnings.

Finviz.com leaves the P/E blank (same as null) if the earnings are negative. In this case, I would check out Yahoo!Finance's EV / EBITDA, which also considers taxes, cash and interests. The blank condition also happens in some other metrics such as negative assets (very seldom).

Earnings Yield is equal to E/P. I call it 'True Earnings Yield' for EBITDA / EV. It is easier to understand. Compare Earnings Yield or True Yield to the annual dividend yield of a 10-year Treasury – with the low interest rate in 2021, skip this comparison for this year.

E/P is easier in screening and sorting the screened stocks. If you use P/E instead of E/P, you need to screen or sort stocks with a clause "P/E > 0".

When the P/E is less than 5, be careful and there may be a reason why it is so low. Many bankrupting companies have low P/Es at one time before their stock prices go to zero.

Compare the P/E or Forward P/E with the average P/E for the sector (such as high tech) and its average P/E for the last 5 years that are currently available from Fidelity.com. Some sectors such as technology have high P/Es (such as 25 for me). If the sector is cyclical, the earnings could be affected.

Do not solely use P/E to determine the value of a stock. The other metrics are P/E Growth (PEG), P/B, Debt/Equity to name a few.

When the prospect of the company is good such as Tesla in 2020, ignore P/E. Investors are betting on the future. Do not short these rocket stocks.

- **Cash / share**. It is used to calculate Pow P/E and Pow EY when EV/EBITDA for the stock is not available. To illustrate, if the stock is $10 and it has $10 cash / share without debt (i.e., Debt/Equity = 0), most likely it is underpriced as you can get the whole company for nothing. You should find out why the price is so low. It could be the market ignoring the stock, or there is a serious event happening such as a major lawsuit. P/C is a better choice than Cash/Share; the lower the better.
- **Dividend %** is useful for income investors. The payout ratio should not be more than 30% except for matured companies. Most developing companies and tech companies plough back the profits into research and development, and hence they do not pay dividends.

- **Recs**. Select stocks with 1 or 2. Do not base your stock selection on this recommendation alone. There have been many bad recommendations that could cost you a fortune in losses. Use Fidelity's Equity Summary Score instead.
- **PEG** is a measure of the growth of P/E and hence a growth metric (the other ones are Sales Growth Q-Q and Earnings Growth Q-Q). It is similar to P/E, but it takes the expected earnings growth rate into account. The lower value is better as long as earnings is positive. If earnings is negative, then the reverse is true. It is a defect in using P/E and PEG and that's why I recommend EY (Earnings Yield) and EYG, Earnings Yield Growth. The chance of appreciation of the stock is high when the PEG is less than 1.

  If there are two companies with the same P/E, the one with a better PEG ratio is better. For similar logic, if two companies have the same E/P, the company with higher Earnings Growth (EPS Q/Q) would be better.
- **P/B**. Book value or Asset (= Total Assets – Total Liabilities) may not include intangible assets such as patents. Do not trust it 100%, so is ROE and other metrics which are based on the book value. Negative equity is possible when Total Liabilities is more than Total Assets. This popular metric is outdated for most matured companies as it is now made up of more intangible assets including patents, management, the quality of their employees, brand names, market share, partners, free cash flow and customer base to name a few. Some assets such as gold mines and real estates can be easily calculated. To illustrate, when gold price is falling, the P/B of a company's stock could be less than 1. It could be a good buy, but it is not if the trend continues downward.
- **P/S**. If two companies are unprofitable, this ratio could be more useful. A retail company such as Walmart is very different from a research company in P/S. This metric is only meaningful for stocks within the same sector or related sectors.
- **P/FCF**. I prefer it to be greater than 0 and less than 50 for value investors. Most metrics can be manipulated easily, but not this one. This is a major metric to avoid bankrupting companies.
- **Sales Q/Q** reduces the seasonal deviation. To illustrate, retail sales for the Christmas season should be compared to the same season in the prior year.
- **EPS Q/Q**. Same as above. I prefer the growth of EPS over Sales. Both of these Q/Q ratios are growth metrics. When a company terminates its unprofitable product(s), its Sales Q/Q could be down but its EPS Q/Q

could be up. In 2000, many internet companies had great Sales Q/Qs but negative EPS Q/Qs.

Q/Q comparison (quarter to quarter) takes out the seasonal variations as Sales Q/Q. I prefer both Sales Q/Q and EPS Q/Q increase. When EPS Q/Q increases far higher than Sales Q/Q, it could mean the EPS Q/Q could be temporary such as the oil company when the oil price rockets. When the company buys its own shares, EPS could be misleading as E is fixed and the number of shares is reduced. In most cases, the fundamentals of the company have not changed.

In 2021, many companies such as many energy stocks have incredible EPS Q-Q and most of their Forward P/E are better than the P/E. They could be momentum play unless they are sustainable.

- Positive **Insider** Transactions are favorable. Sometimes, they are misleading. Need to scroll to the end of the screen and check out more info there. If the transactions are outdated such as 3 months or so ago, and or they are purchases in a similar amount than the sales a while ago, they are not important. Insiders know the company better than us.

  So is **Institutional Transactions** as institutional investors move the market. Most institutional investors do not trade small stocks, and hence this metric is not important for small cap stocks.
- Insider Own, Shares Outstanding and Shares **Float** determine the number of shares that are available for trading. The stock with a small Float and a high Insider Own limits trading and the stock, and hence it should be avoided in most cases. Also, compare your trade positions for this kind of stock to their Avg. Volumes.
- **Profit Margin**. I prefer it over Gross Margin and Oper. Margin which does not include interest expenses and taxes. When you sell software, the Gross Margin is high as it does not include development, support and marketing, etc. A retail store has low Gross Margin. It all depends on the industry, and hence it is better to compare companies in the same industry.
- **Short Float**. I prefer it to be less than 10%. If it is greater than 10%, the shorters could find something wrong with the company. If it is over 25%, I would check the fundamentals and any important events such as a major lawsuit. If they are good, I would buy it expecting a short squeeze potential. It is risky but it has been proven profitable in some of my trades.
- Technical metrics: SMA-20, SMA-50 and SMA-200. Finviz expresses them in convenient percentages. If they are all positive, it means the

trend is up. SMA-20 and SMA-50 are a short-term trend indicator and SMA-200 is a long-term trend indicator. If you are a short-term swing investor, stick with the short-term trend and vice versa. The first two are also used as momentum grades. Many long-term investors do not buy stocks when the SMA-200% is negative. Some buy stocks when both SMA-20 and SMA-50 are positive and SMA-20 crosses SMA-50,. Some sell the owned stocks when both SMA-20 and SMA-50 are negative and SMA-20 crosses SMA-50. Some use SMA-50 and SMA-200 instead. They are called the Golden Cross and the Death Cross.

- **RSI(14)**. If it is greater than 65%, it is overbought (could turn around) to me. If it is under 30%, it is under-bought for me to me. Some use 5% up or down than my percentages. Use it as a reference. Most stocks making new heights are always overbought, and many of these stocks keep on rising. I recommend using trailing stops to protect your profits on rising stocks.
- **Beta**. A volatile stock fluctuates a lot. Higher beta stocks are good for short-term traders. A beta of 1 means the stock would fluctuate with the market, and it is more volatile if it is higher than 1. For volatile stocks (higher than 1), the stops should be higher. For example, if your stops are normally 10%, you may want to use 15% or even higher for volatile stocks.
- **Perf**. If the stock lost more than 50%, there is a good chance it could be a candidate for bottom fishing, or it could be heading to bankruptcy. Need more research if you want to buy these risky stocks.
- Management performance is measured by <u>ROE</u>. It is also judged by **Analysts' Rec.** and Institutional Ownership (except for small companies). The confidence of their own ability, the company and its sector are measured by Insider Ownership and Insider Purchases.
ROE = Net Income / Average Shareholder's Equity

According to Investopedia, a normal ROE for utilities should be 10% while high tech companies should be 15%. Compare this ratio and many other ratios with its peers that are available from many sites including Fidelity.
- Avoid all companies that are going to bankrupt at all costs. Debt/Equity, P/FCF, Cash/Sh., P/B, Profit Margin, Forward P/E, Short Float, RSI(14), SMA20% and SMA50 would give us some hints. Need to summarize all the info and study many other factors such as obsoleting products (including drugs going to be generic). Study articles which are available from Finviz and many other sites.
- Unless you have concrete information, do not buy stocks a week or so before the Earnings Date (available in Finviz). It is seldom to make great

profits when the announcement is better than the expected as the stock price is usually priced in, and the reverse could hurt the stock price a lot.

More useful information:
- **Equity** = Total Asset − Total Liability. When the Equity (Book) is negative, many of the metrics based on Equity would not be displayed. In May 5, 2022, TUP has Equity of -207M (from Finviz's Balance Sheet reported on 12/25/21). The related metrics are blank or null such as P/B, Debt/Eq, LT Debt/Eq in Finviz, and so is EV/EVITDA (from Yahoo!Finace). However, the P/E is less than 4. It could be a buy.
- The price chart. It has a lot of features such as the resistance line. Some charts include technical indicators such as double top (a bearish warning) and double bottom (a bullish sign).
- Description under the symbol. It briefly describes what the company (sector and industry) does and its country of registration. You want to buy a stock within a sector that is trending up. For example, according to Finviz Apple is in the Consumer Goods sector and the Electronic Equipment industry.

    If you do not want to buy foreign stocks, skip it if it is not listed in the US exchange or headquartered in a foreign country. Buying a foreign stock could be profitable, but risky due to the currency fluctuation, lack of regulations, and politics (such as Russia in 2022 and China in 2021). Some foreign stocks ask you to pay additional taxes when you sell them. Some foreign companies listed in the U.S. exchanges take out a good portion of the dividends.
- Articles on the company for qualitative analysis.
- Insider trading. Pay more attention to the insider purchases at market prices. Use common sense.
- The last line lets you open Yahoo!Finance and other sites.
- There are many ways to calculate intrinsic value of a stock. Many web sites (most require subscriptions) include this information. Use it as reference only, and evaluate the stock your yourself. Buy it when the intrinsic value is below the stock price, and sell it otherwise. It is "Buy Low and Sell High" concept. They work in general and in the long run. Need to consider other intangibles. Many stocks such as Tesla and Amazon had low intrinsic values, but they kept on rising.

Other important sites

Yahoo!Finance.

From Statistics, you can find Enterprise Value / EBITDA. I call it True Yield when I flip them to EBITDA / Enterprise Value. In case it is not available, I use Earnings Yield. In my spreadsheet without considering the cell designations,
=IF (Earnings Yield = "", True Yield, Earnings Yield)

Fidelity

Compare the P/E of the average PE of the last 5 years by using spreadsheets.
Cheaper By Historically =IF(PE="","",(Avg. of 5-year PE -PE)/Avg. of 5-year PE)

Compare the P/E of companies in the same sector. In my spreadsheet for demonstration,
Cheaper By To the peers =IF(PE="","",(Industry PE - PE)/Industry PE)

Your broker's website

Your broker website should have plenty of tools to analyze stocks. As of Dec., 2018, Fidelity lets you use their extensive research free by opening an account with no position restriction. I describe some of their metrics that should be beneficial to your research.

- Equity Summary Score. Potentially good buy when it is 7 (8 for conservative investors) or higher. With some exceptions, you should avoid buy or short stocks if the score is 3 or below. The stocks ranking from 4 to 6 could be turnaround candidates if they are supported by good Q/Q Earnings and/or good news. The above are my suggestions.

- The 5-year averages are good yardsticks. For example, in Dec., 2018, C's P/E is about 9 and the average for the last 5 years is 14. Hence it is a value buy.

Other sources

If you have other sources (most require a subscription or being a customer), skip the stocks that have one of the failing grades. The exceptions are a new positive development and increased insider purchases.

Vendor	Grade	Fail
Fidelity	Equity Summary Score	< 7
IBD	Composite grade	< 50
Value Line	Proj. 3-5 yr. return. Also, its composite rating	< 3%
Zacks	Rank	5
VectorVest	VST	< 0.7

You may be able to find Value Line and IBD in your local library. Try out the free stock reports from your broker first. Finviz and Seeking Alpha should have articles (now fewer free articles from Seeking Alpha) on stocks and earnings conferences, which could have important information after separating from the "welcome" and garbage talks.

Yahoo!Finance has good info. "EV/EBITDA" is better than "P/E" as it considers debts and cash. Most use Earnings from the last 12 months, which has poorer predictability than Forward Earnings to me.

When negative values such as Equity in Finviz.com, we need to adjust many related metrics or do not use them at all.

MarketWatch.com has many articles on the market in general and personal investing.

If the stock is close to the Earnings Date (found in Finviz.com), you should avoid trading the stock; as earnings could have a big swing for the stock price. Consult Zacks' ranking which is currently free for individual stocks.

Gurus

It is nice to know how gurus would rate the interested stocks. GuruFocus is a good source but requires subscription. NASDAQ is a simplified version. Bring up Nasdaq.com from your browser. Select "Investing" and then "Guru Screeners". On the third selection, enter the stock symbol such as THO. Click "Go". You will find how 10 or so gurus would evaluate this stock in theory. Click "Detailed Analysis" for each guru.

Quick and dirty

Many times we need to evaluate a stock fast such as taking action due to some development. Or, when you have over 30 stocks from your screen, you may want to reduce the number by using the following two methods.

Refer to my other article "Simplest way to evaluate stocks". The following should take a few minutes. Bring up Finviz.com and enter the stock symbol.

Using SWKS on 6/10/16 to illustrate, Forward P/E is about 11 (fine between 3 and 25), Debt/Eq. is 0 (fine less than .5), ROE is 30% (fine greater than 5%) and P/PCF is 31 (fine if not negative).

Also, check out Market Cap, Avg. Volume, Dividend, Short Float (fine between 0% and 10%), Country and Industry. Judging from the above, it is a buy.

If you have more time, check out the following: Recom. (Ok if less than 2.5), P/B (fine between .5 and 4), Sales Q/Q (fine if not negative), EPS Q/Q (fine if not negative), Cash/Sh (compare it to Debt/Sh) and Profit Margin (fine >5%). Check some articles described for this stock.

5-minute stock evaluation

It takes even less time than the above "Quick and Dirty". However, I recommend you should spend more time researching stocks.

- From Finviz.com, enter the stock or ETF symbol. Look at the number of reds in metrics. If there are more than greens, most likely it is not a good stock.

- It should be fine if Fidelity's Equity Summary Score is greater than 8.

If you have more time, I recommend you to check the following:

- Check out Forward P/E (E>0 and P/E < 20), Debut / Equity (< 50%) and P/FCF (not in red color).

    If time is allowed, replace Forward P/E with True P/E (same as "EV/EBITDA"), which is available from Yahoo!Finance and other sources.
- SMA20 (or SMA50 for longer holding period). If SMA20 is > 10%, it is trending up.
- It is fine if the Insider Transaction is positive.
- Be cautious on foreign stocks and low-volume stocks.
- If most of the above are positive, it is likely a buy. As in life, nothing is 100% certain.

Links

PEG: http://en.wikipedia.org/wiki/PEG_ratio
Short %: http://www.investopedia.com/university/shortselling/shortselling1.asp#axzz2LNDvpemo

Openinsider:	http://www.openinsider.com/
Finviz:	http://Finviz.com/
terms:	http://www.Finviz.com/help/screener.ashx
Insider Cow:	http://www.insidercow.com/
Current Ratio:	http://en.wikipedia.org/wiki/Current_ratio
Cash Flow:	https://www.youtube.com/watch?v=1v8hRZ36--c

How to find quality stocks.
http://seekingalpha.com/article/2381395-how-to-identify-quality-stocks-and-is-there-really-alpha-to-be-had

Over-priced stock: https://www.youtube.com/watch?v=VeMrOn4pvtM:
Outperform the market
https://www.youtube.com/watch?v=3DdY0JdUilM

Reading financial sheet.
Balance sheet: https://www.youtube.com/watch?v=DZjU0CHKyV4
Earnings report: https://www.youtube.com/watch?v=Ite4I_y08Gg

https://www.youtube.com/watch?v=DMv9JC_K37Y&t=954s
https://www.youtube.com/watch?v=8NelYFn07jg
Intrinsic Value: https://www.youtube.com/watch?v=I-T-Vyk2txc

More info from Fidelity

Besides Finviz, I get the EV/EBITDA from Yahoo!Finance under the Statistics tab. This chapter describes more metrics from Fidelity. The described three sites have duplicated metrics.

It all starts from "News & Research" tab. "Markets & Sectors" and "Viewpoints: Market Sense" (https://www.youtube.com/watch?v=o1q34vguEv8) give you a glimpse, and includes many related articles and insights. Fidelity's Screener can also be accessed.

We can build our income stream and CD ladder based on the info from "Fixed Income, Bonds and CDs". "ETFs" is recommended for beginners and investors who have limited time for investing.

"Stocks" will be described here in more detail. The Home page gives you a lot of general information. Try it out feature by feature.

It also gives you virtually everything about the stock. To illustrate, I enter AAPL on "Enter a symbol". Equity Summary Score is useful to me. It used to give a 5-year average of P/E. "

"Analysis and Sentiment" determine whether the stock is undervalued (good for long-term holding" or short-term sentiment (good for short-term holding).

"Analyst Opinions & Reports" typically has two reports and even more. Read them before taking any investment decision – start with high StarMine Relative Accuracy first. Some reports have more than 5-year values for specific metrics. Balance Sheet and Income Statement are also available.

For more info on Fidelity, search it in YouTube.

Section II: Beyond fundamentals

Buy stocks based on appreciation potential, not based on when and what you traded the stock for.

6   Intangibles

I give a score for each stock I evaluate. Occasionally some stocks with poor scores have great returns and vice versa. In general, the scoring system works. It has been proven statistically and repeatedly from my limited data. I stick with high-score stocks with some exceptions.

Once in a while I change my scoring system to adapt to the current market conditions. To illustrate, the market bottom phase and early recovery phase of the market cycle favor value more than momentum/growth. Here are some of my recent experiences and strategies:

- I double or even triple my stake on stocks with high scores. In the longer term, they are consistently better winners than the average with some minor exceptions. Besides the score, look at the intangibles described in this article.

- Watch out for the stocks with outrageous metrics such as P/E of 4 or less. It could be a big lawsuit pending, an expiration of some important drugs, etc. Also, be careful with scores in the top 5%. From my statistics they do worse than the average. Their problems may not show up in the current financial statements.

- The technology of a tech company cannot be ignored even though the company's P/E is high, that I set a limit of 25 instead of 20 for other stocks. The value of the company's technology and patents will not be shown in the fundamental metrics except from the insiders' purchases at market prices.

    For example, IDCC rose about 40% in 2 days. There was a rumor that Google was buying the company and/or Apple was bidding on it too for its mobile technology. Charts usually would flag this kind of event. For non-charters, use the SMA-20% from Finviz.com. They could be a little late as the charts depend on rising prices.

- There are more acquisitions during a market bottom (same as early recovery). The companies with good technologies are bargains and the larger companies especially those in the same sector understand their values better than most of us. These potentially profitable companies will not be shown by their scores explicitly. When corporations have a lot of cash or the credit is cheap, they are looking for smaller companies to acquire or invest in. The candidates are usually small, beaten up, low-priced and having valuable intangible assets such as technologies, customer base and/or market share of the industry segment. 2009-2012 was just the perfect environment and the before that was 2003. I had at least one stock in each of these periods and they appreciated a lot.

- The opposite is Netflix, Chipotle in 1/2012 and Amazon in 1/2013. They are overpriced by any measure. However, the mentioned companies are investing in the future. The shorters (not for beginners) are having a tough time making money on them. When their P/Es are higher than 40, watch out. Some could be OK in the mentioned companies, but usually they are not. Do not follow the herd and your due diligence will verify whether they will still go up.

    Use reward/risk ratio. It is based on experiences. To illustrate, if the company has the equal chance to go up 50% and go down 25%, then it is a buy and the reverse is a sell.

- The retail investor just cannot possibly know about some events until they actually happen. For example, ATSC dropped 15% due to losing its second primary customer. Fundamentals cannot predict this kind of event. Charts can signal this event, but usually they are too late unless you watch the chart all day long.

- After a quick run up, TZOO plunged due to missing some negligible earning expectations. It seems the original climbing prices already had the perfect earnings growth built-in.

    I do not understand why a company loses 10% of its market cap when it missed by 1% of the expected earnings. It could be driven up and down by the institutional investors. Evaluate the stock before you act. Acting opposite to the institutional investors could be very profitable for the right stocks. Avoid trading before the earnings announcement dates (about 4 times a year for most stocks).

- The following are not easily found in financial statements: industry outlook, patents, good will, market share, competition, product margins, management quality, lawsuits pending, potential acquisition, pension obligations, advertising icons, etc. That is why we need to read articles on the stocks in our buy list or our purchased stocks.

- The financial data could be fraudulent or manipulated. I do not trust small companies in emerging markets. I have been burned too many times. Check the company names such as foreign names, ADR and their headquarter addresses (from the company profile in most investing sites).

  Earnings can be manipulated with many accounting tricks. A jump in earnings from last year may not be as rosy as it looks. Check the footnotes in the accounting statements. I usually skip financial statements unless I have big purchases in mind as my time in investing is limited.

- Cash flow cannot be easily manipulated. It is good information whether the company will survive or not, but to me it does not prove to be a consistent predictor in my tests, but an important red flag for companies on their way to bankruptcy. Examples abound.

- Repeated one-time, non-recurring and extraordinary charges are red flags.
- Stay away from the companies where the CEOs are over-compensated. As of 7- 2013, Activision's CEO raised his salary by more than 600%, while the stock lost its value in double digits.
- Value stocks. Need to know why they become value stocks (i.e., fewer investors want to own them) even if they are fundamentally sound. For example, there are two primary reasons for the downfall of a supplier to Apple: 1. Apple is declining in sales and 2. Apple is switching suppliers to replace their product. Technology companies are continually building better mouse traps. They could turn around in a year or so with better products.
- Quitting of a CEO or CFO is not a good sign in addition to heavy insider selling.
  https://www.youtube.com/watch?v=ENNOx7y1pTU

Conclusion

Buying a stock is an educated guess that its stock price will rise. Fundamentals do not always work, but they work most of the time:

1. When we buy a value stock, we're swimming against the tide. Hence, we need to wait longer (usually more than 6 months) for the market to realize its value. The exception is the Early Recovery phase (see the Market Cycle chapter) and it has faster and larger returns than most other stocks from most other stages of the market cycle.

2. Some metrics are misleading. Book value could be misleading for an established company such as IBM. The image of the cowboy in a tobacco company could be a very important asset that is not included in its financial statement.

3. The market is not always rational.

Afterthoughts

- Brand names of big companies are one of the most important intangibles. Here is a strategy to buy big companies in a down market. It has been proven that it works. However, do not just buy these companies without analysis.
  http://seekingalpha.com/article/1324041-buying-brand-names-in-a-bear-market-can-make-you-rich

- The reputation of a company takes a long time to build but a bad incident to destroy in the case of GM such as the delay in recalling the killer switches.

#Filler: Carrie Fisher, another sad American story

Unless drug addiction is part of the culture now as evidenced from the legalization of certain drugs, we're in a permissive society! Brits pushed opium as a nation when they had nothing better to trade. Opium killed millions of Chinese and bankrupted China. When we do not learn from history, we will repeat history. It is another sad story of fame and money and then losing it all. I bet she would be happier in a normal life instead of being born in a privileged class. Same can be said for many celebrities such as Presley, Houston and her daughter. RIP.

7 Qualitative analysis

This is the last analysis to evaluate a stock fundamentally. Then the next is technical analysis which is used to find an entry point (also the exit point) for the stock. The market is not always rational. It also depends on the available of money such as easy credit to pump up the market.

Where quantitative analysis fails and why

I find that some stocks with high scores fail and some stocks with low scores succeed as indicated by my performance monitor. The scoring system still works statistically for the majority of my stocks.

- Reasons why stocks with low scores perform:

    - Oversold. The institutional investors (fund managers and pension managers) dump them first, and then followed by the retail investors. These big boys will buy these stocks back when they reach a certain price range. RSI(14), a technical indicator described in the Technical Analysis article and is available from many sites including Finviz, is useful to detect these oversold stocks.

    - The falling price (P) improves all fundamental metrics that have the stock price such as P/E and P/Sales. However, the trend of the price is down. Improving Forward P/E is usually a good hint.

    - The company has turned around after fixing its problems and/or the market has changed for the better. A new management team could improve profitability such as recalling Steve Jobs for Apple.

    - The current problems have been resolved but not known to the public that could be evidenced by the increase in Insiders' Purchases (from Finviz to start). It includes resolving a lawsuit, a new product, a new drug, or a new big order, etc.

    - Heavy purchases by insiders. The company's outlook is not shown in its financial statements. Sometimes the insiders hide them so they can buy more of their companies' stocks for themselves.

- Reasons why stocks with high scores plunge in addition to the described in the previous discussion:

- The company's fundamentals and its prices have reached or closed to the maximum heights. They have no way to go but down. It is particularly true when the stock's timing rating is at or close to the highest point. TTWO that I gifted to my grandchildren had been 5-baggers in the last few years before it plunged in 2018.

- It has reached its potential value (or a target price) and it is time for many investors to take profits.

- Sector (or finding another stock or sector with better appreciation potential)) rotation, particularly by institutional investors who drive the market.

    - The outlook of the company, its sector and/or the market is deteriorating. Most companies with P/E less than 5 have problems, and you need to find out the reasons why the stocks are so cheap. Via Finviz, check out debt / share (more than 0.5), negative Q-Q Sales, negative Q-Q Profits, and/or outdated products like typewriters.

- The stock price may be manipulated. There are many reasons to pump and dump the stock. Shorting is not recommended for most investors. However, some experienced shorters make money consistently when they find valid reasons to short stocks.

- It could be due to a new serious lawsuit, a new competing product or drug, canceling a major order, etc.

- Downgrade by analysts. They could spot some bad events such as product defects, violations of regulations or accounting errors / frauds. The downgrades are more important than the upgrades that could have conflict of interest.
- The financial statement had been manipulated. The SEC may ask for an investigation.
- Does not meet the consensus in earnings announcements, which have been over-acted by many investors.

Qualitative Analysis

We need to do further analysis after the quantitative analysis and the intangible analysis. Check out the company's prospects. Check out the date of the article and any potential hidden agenda items from the author. Older articles may not have much value.

Be careful on 'pump-and-dump' manipulation written by authors with a hidden agenda. It has happened especially on small companies before even SeekingAlpha.com has its share. Here was an article that tells you to sell NHTC. There was another article to tell you to buy ARTX. They fit into this category.

The sources are:

1. Seeking Alpha.
   Type the symbol of the company to read as many articles on the company as you have time for. Today this site and many other similar sites require you to be a paid member. If you cannot find too many good articles, check out the articles from Finviz.com.

   Recently, I read an article on AMD and it said it may have good profits in the next two years with the game consoles. The outlook of a company is not shown by any fundamental metric which are far from favorable.

   Following a well-known writer, I bought IBM without doing my due diligence (my fault). It went down more than 15% quickly. You can learn from my mistakes.
2. Research reports from your broker. If you do not find many, open an account with one that provides such reports. Some subscription services such as Value Line provide such reports.
3. Yahoo!Finance board. Most comments are garbage. However, once in a while you find some great insights. Usually, you cannot find any info from other sources on tiny companies.
4. The most recent company's financial statements. They are usually available from the company's website.
5. 10-Ks from Edgar database (www.sec.gov/edgar). Check out new products and its potential competition, key customers, order backlog, research and development and pending lawsuits.
6. Check out the outlook of the sector the company is in and the company itself.
7. Check out its competitors.
8. Some companies are run by stupid people. I received information via my email saying that my mutual fund account could be treated as an abandoned property. I have been cashing dividend checks every year

and why it would be considered as an abandoned property. I called them right away to close my account.

The tall and handsome guy presented articulately how he would turn around JC Penny on TV. I could tell you right away that all his tricks had been tried by other companies such as Sears, and most did not work. The intelligent investor does not care about how handsome, how articulate, how rich his family is and how many advanced degrees from prestigious colleges he possesses. If he does not make sense, do not buy his preaching and his company's stock. [Update. As of 5/2020, J.C. Penny filed for bankruptcy protection. If you had this stock and my book, you would have saved a lot of money minus $10 for my book!]

9. Check out its business model. Some business models do not make business sense and some do. Here are some samples.
- Giving razors makes sense, as the customers have to buy the blades eventually and keep on buying blades for life.
- Supermarket M lowers prices on common merchandise such as Coke and it works. They make money by providing inferior (but profitable to them) products that you cannot compare prices easily such as meat and seafood.

    Eventually there will be a supermarket in my area to satisfy me both in price and quality or at least make a good tradeoff.
- Last week it had been brutally hot. I went to a Barnes & Noble's bookstore to enjoy reading the updated books and enjoyed the air conditioning. When there are more free loaders like me than customers, this business model does not work.
- Market dumping works to capture the market. Microsoft used to do it with their new Office and Mail products that could not compete with the established products at the time. Google is following the same model to dump its equivalent products to compete with Office. Now, Microsoft is taking a dose of the same medicine. As of 2015, Google is not winning.

    Amazon.com gives writers (like myself) great deals if you only sell your digital books via them. This model will work so far, as it has captured the self-publishing market today.

8 Manipulators and bankruptcy

If we can avoid bankrupting companies and/or companies losing most of their stock values, our portfolio would be improved substantially. Some companies make bad bets and lose, such as Enron betting on energy futures. Here are some signs of bad situations.

- Foreign companies. I do not have too much luck in developing countries, especially their stocks of small companies. They include China, Ireland and Israel to name a few. However, as of 2019, many large Chinese companies are doing very well.
- When the P/E is too good, find out why. If the P/E is too bad, stay away.
- P/PFC should be greater than 0 and less than 50. Even a healthy cash flow may not be able to service the debt if it is huge. Hence, compare the cash flow to Debt/Equity.
- Altman Z-Score. I prefer a score above 3, a sign not to be bankrupt. However, Z-Score is not designed for financial sectors.
- Beneish M-Score. I prefer a score less than -2.22, a sign that the earnings is not manipulated. Both Z-Score and M-Score are available from GuruFocus.com for a fee.
- Z-Score metrics are: "Working Capital / Total Assets" (A), "Retained Earnings / Total Assets" (B), "Earnings Before Interest & Taxes / Total Assets" (C), "Market Cap / Total Liabilities" (D) and "Sales / Total Assets" (E).
  Z-Score = 1.2 A + 1.4 B + 3.3 C + .6 D + E
- Skip companies with bond ratings less than B.
- New government regulations such as taking out the credit for solar panels.
- Extraordinary profits such as Timber Liquidator and many banks in 2007-2008.
- Accounting manipulation: Excessive buying of stocks to boost Earnings per Share, excessive loans to officers, companies betting on futures such as Enron, too many one-time charges and reinstating the previous earnings.
- Skip thinly-traded stocks especially those stocks with the majority owned by a few owners.

The current financial statements could be the best source to look for them. If you read something you do not understand, be cautious.

We need to consistently monitor our stock holdings and sell them before they lose most of their value. I Recommend use stops.

This is why we need to have a focused investment portfolio of about 10 stocks; the number depends on your time available for investing. To illustrate, I have about 10 stocks with larger investments and about 100 stocks in smaller purchases. I would likely spend more time in monitoring the 10 stocks than the rest.

Mergers

Mergers are usually good for the merging companies to eliminate duplicate corporate functions such as payroll administration and researching on similar subjects.

The company being acquired usually has a high appreciation. I have a screen to search for the potential candidates. The Early Recovery (a phase of the market cycle defined by me) has more of these candidates. Big companies know their values and see good values when these stocks have been beaten in the market.

Then I do an intangible analysis on items that are not available from the financial statements and/or cannot be quantified. They are patents, technologies, research, customer base, the brand name, the barriers to entry, the distribution channels, the competition, the product cycle, the management and the pension obligations.

In 2003 I bought stock in a software company that was acquired by IBM profiting more than double. In the 2008 cycle, I bought ALU at $1 and sold it shortly at 40% profit. I expected Cisco would acquire it as Cisco did not build a network. Cisco and the U.S. did not acquire this valuable technology. In two years, it was acquired by another competitor for more than $3. I need patience.

The company going to be acquired tries to make the financial statements look very rosy. A Chinese company tricked Caterpillar in acquiring it and Caterpillar lost huge in this deal. Even big companies can be fooled. The record mergers in 2015 may not be good for the companies involved judging from the past history. When two losing companies merge, there will be one big loser.

#Filler: Why do poor countries remain poor?

One reason is suffering from repeated natural disasters such as earthquakes and hurricanes.

Even though the U.S. has been spending a lot of resources on Puerto Rico, some politicians want to be kings and queens as they do not care about their citizens.

#Filler: One way to evaluate a company

https://www.youtube.com/watch?v=fGVtypWv04Y

9 Avoid bankrupting companies

Avoid the bankrupting companies at all costs. Here are some hints that a company is going bankrupt:

- I had several companies that had lost most of their stock values. It turns out that most were Chinese companies. I did have some losers from Mexico, Israel and Ireland. I believe most were set up to cheat investors. Most if not all had 'rosy' financial statements. Avoid them, especially small companies in emerging countries.
- Many U.S. companies failed due to fraud, poor management, and/or the management betting wrongly. When the CEO is using the company as his own AMT, or having an extravagant lifestyle, watch out. If they promise you a return doubling the current rate of return of the market, listen to your wise mother: there is no free lunch. Despite so many real examples, still fools are born every day, because greed is a human nature.
- Do not follow the 'commentators' on TV. They have their own hidden agenda which usually is not in your interest.
- Many companies fail due to their lack of ability to pay back their loans. Except for specific industries and situations, avoid companies with high debt (Debt/Equity over 50%). Financial institutions and companies that have high debt in order to finance their products for their customers such as utilities are the exceptions.
- I have a screen named Big Losers beating the market by more than 600% in Early Recovery (a phase defined by me). However, some bankrupt companies are not included in the database which is termed as survivor bias. Hence, the actual result is far worse than the 600%. I still use this screen but skip these companies using the following yardsticks.
    - The companies are usually safe with high Free Cash Flow / Equity and high Expected Profit / Stock Price.
    - The following are red flags: low Free Cash Flow / Equity, high Inventory and high Receivable (esp. relative to its Payable), high P/B (over 30) and high net Debt/Equity (over 1 to 3 depending on the industry).
    - P/PFC should be greater than 0 and less than 50. A healthy cash flow may not be able to service the debt if it is too huge. Hence, compare it to Debt/Equity. Compare the cash flow per year to debt obligations per year.
- New government regulations could bankrupt an industry. What would happen when the U.S. takes out the rebates and subsidies of solar panels? When the U.S. banned solar panels from China, one of my

Chinese stocks went bankrupt. Also, the government bailed out bankrupt companies such as Chrysler (that I made a good profit from) and AIG Fannie Mae in 2008.

- Serious lawsuits- Most U.S. companies are required to file this information in their financial reports.
- Obsolete products. Newspapers, retail and similar products would be replaced by the internet. The opposite is new products such as virtual reality products.
- Many companies run out of money during the development phase of the major products. Many are too optimistic in their business plans.
- If you expect the market will recover in 2 years, ensure the company's cash and net income can support their burn rate for at least two more years.
- Many investing sites (most require subscriptions) have safety scores.
- If the Beneish M-Score is greater than -2.22, the company is likely an accounting manipulator.
- Choose companies with Z-Score higher than 3; it is not applicable to financial companies. Both M-Score and Z-Score are available from GuruFocus, a paid subscription. Z-Score does not work for financial institutions.
- Z-Score metrics are: "Working Capital / Total Assets" (A), "Retained Earnings / Total Assets" (B), "Earnings Before Interest & Taxes / Total Assets" (C), "Market Cap / Total Liabilities" (D) and "Sales / Total Assets" (E).
Z-Score = 1.2 A + 1.4 B + 3.3 C +.6 D + E
- Market timing- It does not always work, but it is far better to follow a proven technique than not. It is far safer to take money out of the market when the market is too risky or is plunging. The big losers are companies that provide non-essential products in a downturn.
- Small companies could be risky but very profitable. Typically, they have a low stock price (less than $5), small market cap (less than 50 M), low sales (less than $25 M) and low institutional ownership (less than 5%).
- Avoid companies when their own bond ratings are not equal to AAA or AA (www.moodys.com).
- The fall of a sector such as oil in 2015 could drive the related companies, or even a country to the brink of bankruptcy.

Investing is risky to start with. However, investing especially in stocks has been proven to be the best vehicle to beat inflation.

An example from a guru on Micron

On 5/22/2023, I have been looking for info on shorting MU (Micron). There was a YouTube article on MU with a good decent way to evaluate this stock and is quite appropriate for most other stocks too.

The web site: https://www.youtube.com/watch?v=X1W_qVal1ik

I agree you should read the Form 10-K for the potential stocks to trade. It is quite hard to get the data for the last 9 years, and data for the last five years are appropriate for me. His basic metrics are:

Metric	9-Yr Avg,	Current Yr[1]	Finviz
Revenue Growth	8%	-53%	Sales Q/Q
Earnings (EBITDA) Growth	15%	-206%	EPS Q/Q
Strong Free Cash	13%	N/A	P/FCF
Debt / EBITDA <3X	1.0X	0.26	Debt / EQ
Well Priced (EV/EBITDA)[2]	5.7X	7.11	
		49	P/E
		110	Forward P/E

[1] Most are from Finviz and EV/EBITDA is from Yahoo!Finance.
[2] It is similar to P/E except considering many metrics such as taxes.

The only consideration is MU's second (could be the first depending on how you link Hong Kong and other Asian countries) is China. China is developing their own memory chips. The politics between the US and China should also be considered, especially when China is the primary customer for most U.S. chip companies.

From the P/E, Forward P/E and Sales Q/Q and EPS Q/Q, I would consider more to short this short than buying it.

Links
After I wrote this article, China bans Micron due to "national security", which is the same argument for banning Huawei. Micron: https://www.youtube.com/watch?v=dy9vhwXN1SY

#Filler: G7
G7 in 2023 without China does not make any sense., so is 'de-risk'. These nations finally realized they could not decouple with China without hurting themselves. China is #1 in GDP (adjusted to purchase power) and #1 in global trade.

We are repeating history: bad mouthing China for not opening ports for trades, importing opium as a nation, using force to semi colonize China and stealing all the silver.

Section III: Selling stocks

We sell stocks when the reasons to own no longer apply by a good margin. In most cases, the sell decision should be based on data more than one quarter.

I sold ALU when it gained 40% in a few weeks' time. It gained more than 300% later when it was acquired. For rising stocks, we should adjust the stop orders. Do a mental stop order instead of just a stop order to avoid flash crashes. When the price of a stock purchased below a specified order, you place a market order to sell it. Use trailing stops for appreciated stocks.

10   When to sell a stock

There are many reasons to sell a stock as follows.

Personal

1. Has met my targets/objectives.
   It could be a 10% gain in a very short-term swing, x% return in 4 months for a short-term swing or y% gain after a year for long-term trades. Define x and y depending on your risk tolerance and how often you trade.

   I bought 4 stocks in one day during the August, 2015 correction and placed sell orders with 10% more than my purchase prices. I sold one in a day and another one within a month. This is my strategy for correction – sometimes it works and sometimes it does not.

   Never look back. Do not blame yourself when the prices are better than your trade prices. When the market is volatile, use a higher percent of the current prices. Be disciplined. Stay on the same strategy and detach yourself from emotions.
2. Realize that we have made a mistake. Do not let your ego block your eyes. It could be due to bad analysis, bad data, unexpected fraud, lawsuits, and/or unforeseeable events that you have no control of. It is better to get out with a small loss. I prefer a 25% loss as a threshold for long-term strategies and a 10% (or less for some strategies) loss for short-term strategies.

   We have to determine whether it is a mistake or not. If the 'mistake' is just bad luck or due to conditions we cannot possibly predict or control, then it is not a mistake. If it is a mistake, learn from it. When we diversify, one bad loss should not cause a big dent in our portfolios. The stop loss is a good tool most of the time except when there is a flash crash.

If the criteria have been faithfully followed and it does not work well, check out whether your criteria are wrong, or it does not work on the current market conditions.

3. When we have too many stocks in the same sector, we will want to replace some stocks to better diversify our portfolios.

When the sector is rising, we want to weigh more on that sector at the expense of diversification, and vice versa. Set a limit of how many sectors you should hold.

4. Need cash for living expenses.
5. To reduce a tax burden by selling some losers. Tax consideration should not be the primary reason for selling. Take advantage of the favorable tax treatment for long-term capital gains. In short, sell losers within the short-term limit (currently a year), and sell winners after 365 days; check the current tax laws.

Harvest tax losses. Sell losers and buy back similar stocks (or same stock after 31 days to avoid wash sale). It is not too clear in which you can buy back the same loser in your children's account under the current tax law.

6. To take advantage of a lower tax. In 2013, we can pay virtually zero (except the increase of tax on social security payment) Federal income taxes on long-term capital gains when our income is below a specific tax bracket (15% as of 2015). Check out the current tax laws. Evaluate the sold winners for a possible buy back.

Market Timing

7. When the market or the sector plunges, sell stocks or stocks within the sector.
For temporary peaks, evaluate which stocks in your portfolio to sell based on fundamentals. The objective is to raise cash for buying opportunities.

Deteriorating appreciation potential

8. There may be some stocks that have a better appreciation potential than the ones you currently own. Churning the portfolio by replacing

better stocks may cost some brokerage commissions (some are free today) and taxes for taxable accounts, but it improves the quality and the appreciation potential for the entire portfolio.
9. The company's fundamentals have changed for the worse. If you use a scoring system, compare the current score with the score you actually bought the stock for. Apple is a good example from 2013 to 2015. Buy when the fundamentals are good and sell when they are not.

The basic fundamentals are expected P/E, the quarter-to-quarter earnings growth rate / the sales growth rate, and Debt /Equity. They are available from Finviz.com.

When your stocks have passed the peak and started to decline, sell them. When they are heading to bankruptcy, sell them fast.

Hints that the fundamentals are degrading

Evaluate the stocks you own at least every 6 months and check their daily news at least once a week that can be easily done using Seeking Alpha's portfolio function.

- The cash flow is decreasing fast. Cash flow is not a particularly good predictive indicator for appreciation, but a good indicator on whether the company will survive. This metric is very hard to manipulate.
- A new or pending lawsuit. Check out how serious the lawsuit is and be aware that a minor lawsuit can be ignored. Companies always sue against each other.
- A big drop in sales. Do not be alarmed when a new product, or a new drug is going to replace a major product. Compare sales to the same quarter of prior year to avoid seasonal fluctuations (Q-to-Q info I available from Finviz.com).
- Management deteriorates- One hint is the deteriorating ROE from the last quarter.
- The extravagant lifestyle of the CEO and the many easy loans to officers.
- Poor operations. They include recalls of products such as the GM recall on ignition switches, product secrets being stolen and customers' credit card info being stolen. Boeing's 747-Max is a warning call.
- A successful product from the competitor, or the current product is losing its market share, or becoming a low-profit commodity.

- Insiders and/or institutional investors are dumping the companies' stocks far more than the averages (2% for me) especially in heavy volumes and by more than one insider. Info is available from Finviz.
    - Have more than one insider dumping a lot of the stock within a month and no insider purchase in that month.
    - Have more than one insider decrease their holdings by more than 10%.
- When the SEC or any government agency pays attention to a company, it usually means bad news.
- Deceptive accounting practices have been discovered.
- Increasing receivable and/or inventory at an alarming rate.
- Earnings have been restated too many times.
- Short percentage is increasing fast – someone found something wrong with the company.
- The invalidity of 'one-time charges'.
- Abnormal return rate of the company's pension fund comparing to the average of the companies in the same sector.
- Too many and too costly reconstructing charges.
- The entire stock market is plunging as indicated by our chart in detecting market crashes.
- The stock price does not move up with good news. It shows the price has peaked.
- The accumulation amount is far less than the sold amount. When the stock price is up, the accumulation is less than the sold stocks when the stock price was down the last time. It indicates that no more accumulation is ahead and hence the stock will be down most likely.
- Death Cross. Many times the stock price falls for unknown reasons. Technical tells us something is wrong. "A death cross **appears when the 50-day moving average crosses below the 200-day moving average**, an event that many chart watchers view as marking the spot a shorter-term correction morphs into a longer-term downtrend." The opposite is the Golden Cross.
  https://www.youtube.com/watch?v=BaZxE12cZP4

Afterthoughts

- Another article on this topic.
  http://buzz.money.cnn.com/2013/04/05/stocks-sell/
  An article from Investopedia. Nothing new but it is worth having the same second opinion.

http://www.investopedia.com/financial-edge/0412/5-tips-on-when-to-sell-your-stock.aspx

- It also depends on your strategies. I sell most of my stocks in my momentum portfolio within a month. At least one strategy I know of does not keep any stock during the peak stage of the market cycle – the easiest time to make money but also the riskiest time.

    If you use charts for trading, sell the stocks that are below your moving averages or other technical analysis indicators. Personally, I do not use charts for making sell decisions due to my limited time.
- Sell when the company is heading into bankruptcy as described before. The red flags are: 1. Negative cash flow. 2. Heavy insiders dumping the stocks. 3. Pending major lawsuit. 4. Fraud from the management.
- Risky periods for a stock.
    Earnings announcement (4 times a year), settling a major lawsuit and/or during an FDA event in approving a drug are risky periods for a stock. A fluctuation more than 5% in either direction is normal. Some use options to buy insurance. Most ignore it. For the majority of the time, heavy insider purchase is a good indicator. There are rumors (or educated guesses) on earnings before their announcements. Zacks is supposed to be a good subscription for earnings estimates.

Selling a winner

Let the profit rise and at the same time protect your profit. Tesla quadrupled its value in 6 months. Examples abound such as Amazon and Yelp.

If you do not know what to do, here are my suggestions:
- Sell half of the stocks.
- Sell the dollar amount equal to what you paid for.
- Use trailing stops. I did not do this when my GameStop stock appreciated by 300% and it turned out for far more appreciation. Guilty as charged.

You do not want to sell these rocket stocks even if their fundamentals do not make sense. Buffett does not touch these rocket stocks and he usually misses these big gains. However, many of these rocket stocks such as BRRY (Blackberry) will eventually fall losing most of their value. I bet the institutional investors move the market in either direction and usually they read the same analysts' reports. You profit as a contrarian if you have a good reason to act against the herd.

The following example uses a 10% trailing stop – mine is a little different from the official trailing stop described in the link section. Set the stop at 10% of the current price (i.e., 10% less than the current price), not the purchase price. You need to change the stop when the price rises but do not change it when the price falls. Review your stops every month or more frequently if time allows.

To illustrate, when the stock price rises to 100, set the stop at 90. When the stock price falls to 90, sell the stock at the market price. When the stock price rises to 200, change the stop price at 180.

The stop should also be set according to how volatile the stock is. Some stocks are more volatile than others. Most charts show the resistance line. This line assumes the stock price should not fall below this line in normal fluctuations. Set the stop at 2% below this line so your stock will not be stopped out in theory.

Do not stop orders on stocks with low volumes as they can be manipulated, especially after hours. In this case, you just place market orders to sell them.

To avoid flash crashes, do not place stop orders. Instead, do it mentally (mental stop is my term). When you see that the stock falls below your stop with no sign of a flash crash, sell the stock using a market order.

Of course, there is no bullet-proof scheme. This one should work in the long run. This is my suggestion only, so examine whether it works for you. Small cap and/or stocks with small average volumes fluctuate more.

Examples
I have too many bad examples of selling the stocks too early and sometimes holding them too long.

I made over 40% in a few weeks on ALU, but it went up more than 300% in the next two years. It was acquired in early 2016 by Nokia paying a good premium. I was right that ALU had a lot of valuable patents and I was wrong to dump it when I found out Cisco did not have any intention to acquire it – a big mistake by Cisco and the U.S.

FOSL is another example to teach us to use mental stop loss. FOSL was priced at $33.70 on 1/4/2010. Its fundamentals were just fine with an expected E/P (expected earnings yield) at 6% but decreasing earnings. It gained 115% later in 2010 - not expected.

On 1/3/2011, the expected E/P was still at around 6% and improving earnings. It gained 9% for the year – a little disappointing.

On 1/3/2012, the expected E/P was 7% and a huge earnings growth. Now, we expected a better performance for the year and it did by gaining 20%.

On 1/3/2013, the expected E/P was about 6% and the earnings gain was respectable. It gained 28% to $121. So far, so good.

On 1/2/2014, the E/P and the earnings growth were about the same as in 1/3/2013. However, it lost 7% for the year while SPY (an ETF simulating the market) gained 12%. There was no warning. Did the institutional investors lose the interest of this stock?

On 1/2/2015, the E/P was 7% and the earnings growth was about the same as the previous year. It lost 69% (vs. SPY's 0% return with dividends)!

From 1/4/2010 to 1/3/2016, the annualized return of FOSL is 0% (vs. SPY's 13%). Actually, after dividends, SPY should have an annualized return of about 15%. The lessons gained here are:

- Fundamentals (using EP and earnings growth in this example) may not always work. Otherwise, 2015 should have the same gain as 2014.
- The rosy outlook of the stock may be priced in already. When the outlook fails to materialize, the stock tanks.

Links: Fidelity Video: Trailing Stop Loss. 2 3
https://www.fidelity.com/learning-center/trading/trailing-stops-video
https://www.youtube.com/watch?v=I7EHWyOrfu4

https://www.investopedia.com/terms/t/trailingstop.asp

11   Examples of overpriced stocks

In 2011, there were discussions on the high valuation of Netflix in several articles in Seeking Alpha, an investment website. LinkedIn and Facebook shares were believed to be overvalued even before their IPOs.

Here are some of my thoughts on Netflix and the same concept can be applied to other stocks.
- Reward / Risk ratio.
  If the stock has the same probability to move up by 30% and move down by 50%, it is overvalued by 20% (50% - 30%). As of 2011, Netflix shares may rise, but it is too risky for me.
- Compare the P/E to its five-year average.
  The current P/E is 60 and the average for the last 5 years is 30. From this metric it is overvalued by 100%.

  The 'E' in P/E can be either expected (same as forward) earnings or based on the last 12 months (same as trailing or historical). It has been proven that the 'expected' is a better indicator than the 'historical'. AAII demonstrated this by comparing the performances of the expected PEG screen and the historical PEG screens over a long period of time.
- Fools who invested in the high P/E stocks and did not do their due diligence in 2000 had parted with their money fast. I could not convince my friends to take money off their internet stocks. It is similar to asking the lottery winners not to buy lottery tickets.
- Buying an expensive stock is like over paying for a hot dog cart in NYC for $100,000. The buyer will sell many hot dogs, but the rate of return of the investment will be minimal, and it will never recover the initial investment. "Buy high and sell higher" is a momentum play. It works if it is played with stops, but I prefer to "Buy low and sell high".
- Following a decent and proven investing strategy consistently should lead to success through persistence and adjustments. In the long term, a bad strategy always loses money.
- When the market favors growth / momentum (vs. value), it is OK to buy stocks with prices higher than the intrinsic values by a small percentage. The tide is on your side. However, be attentive to any indication that the market is changing direction.

NFLX has an average annual return rate of 177% vs. SPY's 14% from 1/3/2011 to 1/3/2020 without considering dividends. Hence, a trailing stop would do the job for the rocket stock.

12   Should you hold stocks forever?

There are many examples that you should hold onto some stocks forever such as Apple, Netflix, Amazon and Google. Interestingly there are more opposite examples such as AIG and Lehman Brothers. Hence, there is no right or wrong answer. Always continually monitor your stock holdings and the sectors they are in.

Even IBM could suffer its dips when it does not react to its market and / or make the wrong strategic decision. The Washington Post has to react to the free articles from the internet.

I have set up guidelines on when to sell. One selling indicator is when those shares lose over 25%. We have to admit that we have made a mistake, or the fundamentals of the stock have changed. Evaluate the fundamentals of the purchased stocks periodically.

Boston Chicken is one of my many big losers. I could use the money I lost to have chicken dinner every night for the rest of my life! This kind of thinking is not healthy. I decided not to buy any restaurant stock again and that is not rational either. It is an art to sell a loser, or wait for its potential recovery. From my experiences, it is better to sell the loser.

If you have a historical database, you can test out your strategy on when to sell and adjust the sell criteria accordingly. Do not try to fit data to your strategy.

Never fall in love with a stock and never be afraid to buy back a sold stock. Use fundamental metrics for making a buy/sell decision.

Taxes and diversification

Tax should not be a major consideration in selling a stock. However, you may postpone selling losers in December if your tax rate (so your tax loss value) will be better next year. If you need to offset short-term capital gains, sell some losers eligible for short-term capital losses. Postpone selling a winner to a month or so, if it can be eligible for long-term capital gain.

When your stock appreciates many, many times and you're close to your life expectancy age, hold it and the cost basis will step up to the day you pass away. Instruct your heirs to buy a newspaper to get the prices of your stocks you hold or instruct your heirs to inform your broker on the unavoidable day. Today's tax law provides a range of days around the date of death; check the current tax laws.

Instead of selling a stock with huge gain, consider options: 1. give it to your children who have lower tax brackets, 2. give it to charity, and 3. save it for your estate.

When the market is plunging as detected by market timing techniques, sell most of your holdings. Be warned that market timing does not always work.

No stock is sacred

That's why we need to churn the portfolio by replacing the bad stocks with better ones. More examples of failing companies that had been very promising at one time:

- The bankrupt companies due to competition: Circuit City (due to BestBuy) and BlockBuster (due to Netflix).
- The failing internet companies in 2000 and the financial institutions in 2008.
- HP when PCs, servers and printers are no longer kings.
- BestBuy killed Circuit City and then it is being eaten alive by Amazon, Walmart, Costco and BJ. However, it recovered in 2014.
- Many retailers went bankrupt. I lost count of so many of the retailers in the Boston area alone.

Filler: Dream high

I heard this. The girl wanted to be a president when she grew up. She went to a circus and she said she wanted to be a clown. Her wise father said, "You can be a president and a clown at the same time". Reality?

Should we modify the Constitution to ban our presidents from tweeting especially in private places?

It is a laughing stock for injecting disinfectants to cure the virus. At least we fix the racial discrimination when everyone has been bleached.

I am neutral in politics. I complained a lot about Obama.

13   Monitor your traded stocks

After you have bought (or shorted) a stock, you need to monitor the progress and any new information about the stock.

First, you need to place stop orders to protect your portfolio unless you want to hold it forever. When the stock is rising, you may want to place trailing stops and review them periodically. You can check out the performances from your broker's statement (on-line preferred).

Second, you need to read as many articles about the stock. If you have a handful of stocks, Finviz is all you need. If you have a lot of stocks, I recommend some websites such as SeekingAlpha and MarketWatch to store your portfolio. Most have basic features and some have some features that are important to you. The following is a list of features you may consider.

- Let you create and delete watch lists. You may want to delete watch lists that you no longer need. Let you add / delete stocks in the watch list.

- Let you create multiple watch lists. You may have one for long-term holding (usually value stocks) and one for short-term holding (usually momentum stocks).

- Let you select the stock and display a list of articles related to that stock.

- Categorize the stocks by sectors. Unless you have a reason, you may want to diversify your portfolio such as not putting 50% of your portfolio in one sector.

- The performances of the stocks (from the date the stock is entered) and the performance of the watch list. The number of days held is useful to figure out the long-term or short-term capital gain/loss for non-retirement accounts.

Section IV: Other sources

14 Good pointers from a popular book?

I read a popular book on how to make money. It works for the author, but most likely it will not work for you. I have provided all the reasons here. It is similar to many books. A good book should provide useful hints on investing and why the stocks fail.

- His book has been read by tens of thousands. When the strategy is overused, it will not be effective. Hence, I do not believe his simple strategy will be useful as there are many similar examples.

    When you follow the same strategy to find stocks, most likely you end up finding the same stocks as tens of thousands of his readers.

- Basically, it uses Buffett's philosophy to pick stocks. Some work, some do not work, and some are not available to the retail investor. Judging from Buffett's mediocre return in the last three years, it could be a waste of your time and money.

- Always diversify. The stock market is not always rational. Even a good stock could lose half of its value without warning. If you have $50,000 or less, stay with 3 stocks in 3 different sectors. Preferably, one stock is an ETF. No diversification is described in his book.

- If you do not consider market timing, you could lose half the value of your portfolio in a market crash. No market timing is described in his book.

- Today stocks are screened every day by many. I bet you do not find stocks selling at 50% discount in a bullish market. If you do, watch out. There could be reasons why they're selling at these steep discounts. We usually only find these discounts in the recovery state of a market cycle.

- When you find value stocks with a huge margin of safety, watch out again. From my limited tests. Margin of safety has not been a good predictor.
- Reading annual reports.
  https://www.youtube.com/watch?v=7OjsEF04V8o

15 Seeking Alpha

Seeking Alpha is a great site for investors. Here are my hints on using it.

- Use the portfolio function to enter all the stocks you own and/or the stocks you want to buy. When there are articles or news on the stock, you will be alerted in the Portfolio of the main menu. It is handy to keep track of all news about your stocks. Its function is similar to Finviz.com and your broker may provide a similar function. Small stocks may not be covered.
- There are many good articles from the main page.
- Read articles by authors you selected to follow. There are many experts in their respective fields.
- Follow the authors with strategies similar to yours such as dividend income.
- From the main page, Market Performance via ETFs gives us which sectors are trending. Wall Street Breakfast is a summary of the events of the day and last session. It is useful for sector rotation and seeking momentum stocks.
- I enjoy articles on market timing and summary of the current market.
- Here is a good article: 60 Value Resources. http://seekingalpha.com/article/3485446-60-best-value-investing-resources-youd-be-crazy-to-miss

However, you have to watch out for the following:

- Promotion. Seeking Alpha is not set up as a charity organization. They are selling the products for their clients. Some promotions are good if they are applicable to you.
- "Pump and dump". Be careful of reviews on small and/or low-volume stocks.
- One shorter made bad comments on EBIX that I owned. It turned out she did this all the time. EBIX has gained about 150% in a year.

16   Making sense

I read Dr. Campbell's The China Study book. He recommends a whole food, a plant-based diet. Avoid meat and processed food such as cakes, chips and soda to prevent heart diseases, cancers and most other diseases. If you still do not believe, read his book and it has been life-changing for many.

What in his book has anything to do with investing? There are a lot of similarities in both disciplines. This idea occurred to me before and Dr. Campbell confirmed it. Here are the primary similarities.

- Statistics.
  You have 1,000 in a plant-based diet and 1,000 in an animal-based diet. After 10 years, more folks in the animal-based diet have cancers and heart problems than the other group. The conclusion is clear.

  It is similar in our testing. If there are more winners in a screen or a strategy for a long period of time, in the long run they will perform better than the market. Statistics never lies.

- Market noises.
  A lot of health reports are controlled by the big conglomerates such as the meat industry, fast food chains and soda companies. Even their lobbyists control what they want to pass their messages to suit their agendas. If everyone followed Dr. Campbell's preaching by eating right, many drug companies would be out-of-business.

  It is the same as the junk mails promoting stocks. The TV business programs want to give you what you want to hear in order to capture larger audiences, which the advertisers want. Do your own research.

- Read and do.
  Many read the books, but do not do or practice what they have read. I recommend paper trading what you learn from this book.

  Dr. Campbell's book helps you be a healthier person and my book hopefully makes you a better investor.

17   Fidelity

Fidelity does not require any balance in an account. Take advantage of the extensive research for free. Access the research by selecting "News and Research" and then "Stocks". I only describe the unique features of Fidelity research.

Equity Summary Score. It has been proven. Personally, I prefer to buy stocks that are 8 or above for long-term hold. I short stocks that are 4 or below. Do not use it for momentum trades. I do not agree with this score all the time. In 6/2020, the score of around 9 for ZM and SHOP is quite misleading to long-term investors as the long-term metrics are bad.

P/E (5-year Avg.). Some stocks are bargains due to its low P/E compared to its 5-year average. Identify why they are bargains. The average does not tell you a lot, and hence I use the following to see how much of a bargain they are. As of 9/2023, this metric has been moved to 'More; under the 'Statistics' tab.
Cheaper by (%) = -(P/E – Avg) / Avg = -(17.8 – 14.95) / 14.95 in this example

Negative percent means "more expensive". Be careful if P/E is zero or negative. I prefer to use the Forward P/E (earnings being guessed).

P/E (Industry average). It is better to compare the company with the industry average. As of 9/2023, it is available from 'Statistics' tab.
Cheaper by (%) = -(P/E – Avg) / Avg

Environmental, Social & Governance (ESG). It is handy for social conscious investors.

Research Reports are available from the "Analyst Opinions and Reports". tab. Start the ones with high StarMine Relative Accuracy. Form 10-Q and balance sheet should be researched for experienced investors. "News" gives us many related articles and you can search articles on individual stocks without subscription that Finviz and Seeking Alpha usually require.

Select the **best stock(s)** from the same sector under the "Comparisons' tab. The top-down approach is: When the market is up, select the best stock(s) in the best sector(s) or best industries.

Momentum Analysis. It is available under Technical sentiment for short term, mid term and long term. Compare them to SMA-20, SMA-50 and SMA-200 and RSI(14) – available from Finviz.

Fundamental Analysis   MORE >

PROVIDED BY S&P CAPITAL IQ AS OF 07/31/2019

Analysis is driven by underlying factors specific to the Information Technology sector.

Metric	Score	Scale
Valuation	88	Overvalued — Undervalued
Quality	92	Low — High
Growth Stability	9	Low — High
Financial Health	77	Less Healthy — Healthy

How to interpret this data

Most stock research sites group the related metrics, weigh them and have a score. The following is my guess only and over-simplified. Basically, they should have 3 scores: Valuation (for long-term trades), Momentum (for short-term trades) and Combined (Valuation + Momentum). Safety or Financial Health is whether the stock is safe (i.e., the chance to go bankrupt).

Valuation. Forward P/E. Insider Transactions.
Quality. ROI, P/E and Debt/Equity.
Growth Stability. Q-Q Earnings.
Financial Health. Debt/Equity. Earnings.

Links

Platform tutorial: https://www.youtube.com/watch?v=fxE5577LaxE
Fidelity index funds: https://www.youtube.com/watch?v=xdEunmLrhb4
Investing tips: https://www.youtube.com/watch?v=twMNKMhL_KY

Book 4: Scoring Stocks

Enter the fundamental metric
information such as P/E for any 100 stocks into a scoring system. If the top 25% of the stocks perform a lot better than the rest in 6 months consistently, then it is a good scoring system.

I have been using my own scoring system for years. It sums up the individual scores for selected fundamental metrics. When the total score passes a set number, I evaluate the stocks further for potential purchase. This scoring system has been updated many times for refinements and adapting to the changing market conditions. All basic metric information can be obtained from free websites.

Many companies and academic projects must have worked on this kind of stock scoring system. However, few if any can prove their systems work consistently.

I may have found the reason why it does not work consistently. The fundamental metrics change when market conditions change. To illustrate, the current market conditions may favor value stocks while some other conditions favor growth stocks. I monitor the performances of all the fundamental metrics periodically and make changes accordingly. Hence, I call my scoring system Adaptive Stock Scoring System (do not use the acronym).

In writing this book, I switched the illustrative example from IBM to Apple IBM scored very low. Apple scored very high. This book was published in 06/2013. The performance of the two stocks from 06/03/2013 to 06/03/2014 are as follows:

Stock	Return
IBM	-12%
Apple	41%
SPY (for comparison)	17%

Section I: ASSS, Adaptive Stock Scoring System

1 Adaptive Stock Scoring System

It also applies to sector investing.

No.	Metric	Good	Bad	Score
1	P/E (use expected P/E if available)[6]	Between 2.5 and 12.5, Score = 2	> 50 or =< 0, Score = -1	
2	Price / Free Cash Flow	< 12, Score = 1	>30 or < 0, Score = -1	
3	Price / Sales[1]	< 0.8, Score = 1	< 0, Score = -1	
4	Price / Book[1]	< 1, Score = 1	< 0, Score = -1	
5	Analyst's Opinion[2]	> 7, Score = 1	< 4, Score = -1	
6	Short % (check reason for high %)	Between 30% & 40%, Score = 1[4]	Between 10% & 20%, Score = -1	
7	Insider Purchase[3]	Score = 1		
8	Profit Margin[3]	> 25%, Score = 1	< 5%, Score = -1	
	Compare Q to Q last year for #9 and # 10			
9	Revenue Growth[3]	> 15%, Score = 1	< 0, Score = -1	
10	Earning Growth[3]	> 20%, Score = 1	< 0, Score = -1	
11	Intangibles	Positive, Score = 1	Negative, Score = -1	
			Grand Score	
	Stock Symbol Date[5]	Current Price	SPY	

Footnote.

[1] Negative values for Sales (due to accounting adjustments), Equity and Book are possible but not likely.

[2] It is from the Fidelity website. If you have no access to it, use Finviz's Rec.: Score =1 if Rec=1 and Score = -1 if Rec = 5.

[3] This metric can be found from many sources. They may use different terms for the same data.

[4] A short squeeze could be coming when a stock is oversold. If the critical problem of the company cannot be recovered easily, change the Score from 1 to -1.

[5] The SPY in the last row is for your information only. SPY is used to measure whether it will beat the market by comparing the return of this stock to the return of the SPY.

[6] Earnings yield E/P (the reversal of P/E) should be between 8% and 40%.

Score

Score each metric and then sum up all the scores giving you a Grand Score. If the Grand Score is 3 (I use 2 for my passing grade), the stock passes this scoring system. Even if it is a 2, it still deserves further analysis if you have time.

For some reason I do not know why and how to explain this, the top 10% (15% for long term and 5% for short term) of the stocks we score and why they do not perform better than the passing grade. It happens in two of my scoring systems. Be cautious with this as it has happened more than once. The stocks scoring in the bottom 10% are consistently poor performers and that's good. To simplify the usage, ignore the stocks that have scores greater than 7.

The metrics from #1 to #6 are yearly metrics based on the last twelve months except the 'expected P/E'. These are popular value ratios.

Metric 9 and 10 are quarterly comparisons of the same quarter last year. They are readily available from Finviz.com.

Some metrics such as the Analyst's Opinion can be obtained directly from Fidelity. If you do not have access to it, use Rec. from Finviz.com.

Metric

For more information, search the metric in Wikipedia or any financial site.

- P/E.
  Price to Earning is a primary value ratio. The Expected Earning has better predictive power than the one from the last two months.

- Price / Cash Flow (same as Price / Free Cash Flow).
  Cash Flow is one of the few metrics that cannot be manipulated. **It is a red flag when it is increasing fast**. Statistically, it is not a good indicator for the long term but it does add safety.

- Price / Sales.
  Different industries have different averages for this metric. A supermarket business should have a very low ratio. Adjust it according to the industry the stock belongs to.

- Price / Book.
  Usually, it is not a good indicator for matured companies such as IBM.

- Equity Summary Score.
  Fidelity has a good handle on this metric. It is based on the past predictive accuracy of the analysts.
- Short Percent (= Shares being shorted / shares outstanding).
  The stock buyers who short the stocks frequently are right more times than they are wrong. The percent between 10% and 20% is high to me.

  However, when it is too high, a short squeeze may be coming. When there are too few shares to sell, the stock price could boost up due to supply and demand. You need to find out the reason why it is so high. If the reason is valid to short the stock, stay away from this stock no matter how high the stock scores. Any scoring system is not sacred and it can be ignored for many situations such as a pending serious lawsuit.

- Insider's Purchase
  When the insiders purchase their company's stock at the market price, most likely the company is doing well. No one knows the company and its sector better than the officials of the company. Ignore options. Ignore the purchases after the insiders sell. Insider Purchases explains why some lowly-scored stocks appreciate fast. Hence, ignore the low scores for stocks with heavy insider purchases and include them for further analysis.
- Profit Margin.
  Ignore or relax this metric during a recession. For those industries that do not have a gross margin, use operating margin instead.
- Revenue growth.
  Ignore or relax this metric during a recession.
- Earning growth.
  Ignore or relax this metric during a recession.
- Intangibles.
  The outlook of the company, its industry and the stock market.

  For simplicity, each outlook scores -1 for poor and 1 for good. Add up the three scores. There is more to it such as serious lawsuits pending, new products, sector rotation, changing market conditions....

  Analyze the high-scored stocks further. If a red flag surfaces, skip the stock. Red flags can be detected from or not from the financial statements. When you use financial statements, ensure they are the most updated ones that usually can be found in the company's website.

Holding Period

The performance monitor uses the holding period of 6 months. After six months, some metrics may change. Hence, evaluate the bought stocks again at that time using the same scoring system. In my last monitor, the metrics did not lose the predictive accuracy, but in the long run it should.

Check out your tax rates for long-term and short-term capital gains. For non-retirement (same as taxable) accounts, you need to make more adjustments such as selling the losers/winners before/after the required holding period for long-term capital loss/gain (as of 2016, it is 366 days to qualify for long-term capital gains).

Fundamentalists are swimming against the tide. It takes time for the market to realize their values. Hence, selling too early (3 months or less) without good reasons is not recommended. When a stock passes the profit target, consider selling it even if it has been bought just over several days ago.

Variations

Enter your changes to this scoring system to suit your investing style and/or different market conditions. The current system uses fundamental metrics. For growth investing, add the appropriate metrics such as PEG, price momentum, etc. This described scoring system **will not work on momentum strategies** (holding stocks less than a month) and day trading.

#Filler: lessons from a strategy named Turtle with my inputs
The experiment to train students who have no experience in two weeks worked. The technical analysis strategy would not work today for many reasons. However, the concepts are still good and explained here.

Do not time the market (not agree totally). Find a good strategy (easier said than done) and stick with it consistently. Cash management (agree with stops from 5% to 15% depending on your risk tolerance and the volatility of the stocks). Do not use leverage that could wipe out your entire portfolio. Follow the trend of the stock with higher positions.

An illustration by implanting a score system in a spreadsheet

The following is used for demonstration purposes only with only three metrics (EY, INSIDER and Debt/Equity all from Finviz.com). It is for long-term scoring. Short-term scoring should include SMA-20% and any timing ratings such as the one from Fidelity. The code in the spreadsheet for the score is:

=IF(A1="",0,(A1-1)*15)+
IF(B1="",0,IF(B1>0,MIN(B1*20,3),MAX(B1*20,-3)))+
IF(C1="",0,IF(C1>0,MIN(C1*15,3),MAX(C1*15,-3)))

Name	Spread sheet symbol	Spreadsheet code
EY = 1/ Forward P/E.	A	IF(A1="",0,(A1-1)*15)
INSIDER	B	IF(B1="",0,IF(B1>0,MIN(B1*20,3), MAX(B1*20,-3)))
Debt / Equity	C	IF(C1="",0,IF(C1>0,MIN(C1*15,3), MAX(C1*15,-3)))

Explanation.
- EY. If there is no input for EY, use 0, otherwise add 15 for any value higher than 1.
- INSIDER. We set a maximum value of 3 and a minimum value of -3.

Format
- If the symbol (D) is blank, the score is blank too.
=IF(D1="","", IF(A1="",0,(A1-1)*15)+
IF(B1="",0,IF(B1>0,MIN(B1*20,3),MAX(B1*20,-3)))+
IF(C1="",0,IF(C1>0,MIN(C1*15,3),MAX(C1*15,-3)))
)
- You may want to set up default values for some metrics on the sample line.

Link: Watchlist https://www.youtube.com/watch?v=cm5ZLtPFisc

2   Get metric data from Finviz.com

Get data from Finviz.com, a free website. Finviz provides everything on the same screen including the 'Forward (a.k.a. Expected) P/E' that I prefer over P/E.

An Illustration

Use AAPL as an example and note that today is 4/19/13. Enter the value in the last column of the table, and then add the individual scores to get a grand score, which is used to determine whether the stock is value or not.

No.	Metric	Good	Bad	Score	Value
1	P/E (use expected if possible)	Between 2.5 and 12.5, Score = 2	> 50 or < 0, Score = -1	2	7.92
2	Price / Cash Flow[1]	< 12, Score = 1	>30 or < 0, Score = -1	1	8.75
3	Price / Sales[1]	< 0.8, Score = 1	< 0, Score = -1	0	2.2
4	Price / Book	< 1, Score = 1	< 0, Score = -1	0	2.89
5	Equity Summary Score[2]	> 7, Score = 1	< 4, Score = -1	1	
6	Short % (check reason for high %)	Between 30% & 40%, Score = 1[4]	Between 10% & 20%, Score = -1	0	1.12%
7	Insider Purchase[3]	Score = 1		0	Few
8	Gross Margin[3]	> 25%, Score = 1	< 5%, Score = -1	1	42%
	Compare Q to Q last year for #9 to # 10				
9	Revenue Growth[3]	> 15%, Score = 1	< 0, Score = -1	1	18%
10	Earning Growth[3]	> 20%, Score = 1	< 0, Score = -1	-1	-.4%
11	Intangibles	Positive, Score =1	Negative, Score = -1	1	My view
			Grand Score	6	
	AAPL	$390.05	SPY = 155		4/19/2013[5]

Footnote
1. If negative values for Sales (due to accounting adjustments), Equity and Book are possible but not likely.
2. It is obtained from Fidelity's website. If you have no access to it or try to save time, use Finviz's "Recom".
3. This metric can be found from many sources.
4. A short squeeze could be coming when a stock is oversold. If the critical problem of the company cannot be recovered easily, change the Score from 1 to -1.
5. The last row is for your information. SPY is used to measure whether it will beat the market by comparing the return of this stock to the return of SPY.

Step-by-step instructions

1. Bring up Finviz.com from your browser.

2. Enter AAPL for 'Company or Symbol'.

3. The company's profile is described after the metric section. Try Yahoo!Finance if you feel they are not well summarized.

4. The sector is Computer, not one of the sectors (bank, insurer, mine, drug and biotech) we want to be cautious about.

5. It is not a foreign company judging by the address and names of the officers. You need more research on companies that are not well-known.

6. It passes the basic criteria (my recommendations only):

    a. Average Daily Volume higher than 6,000.
    b. Price greater than $2 per share.
    c. Listed in one of the three major exchanges.
    d. Capital Cap greater than 200M.

    Modify, define and / or add your own criteria here. If you want to be in micro-cap stocks or large-cap stocks only, change your criteria accordingly.

7. Enter 1 for Equity Summary Score (used to be Analysts' Opinion) from Fidelity.com. Fidelity uses StarMine which tracks the analysts'

past performance. There is a third choice after Finviz: TipRanks and also its consensus on sectors.

8. The Insider Trans (i.e., insider purchases) is positive when the color is green. Scroll down the screen to get the details of the insiders' info. Ignore this metric if the purchases are far below the current price. For more info on Insider Purchase, try out OpenInsider.com.

9. Most other metrics can be retrieved quite easily.

10. The forward (same as expected) P/E is 7.92. Enter 2 for its score (metric #1) as it is within the favorable range. It is also better than the P/E of the last twelve months. It predicts that the earnings would be better in the future.

11. Revenue (same as Sales) Growth compares to the quarter of the prior year to avoid seasonal fluctuations.

12. Earnings Growth has barely passed negative. You decide whether you want to put a 0 or -1 in Score. This metric is more important to Revenue Growth.

13. Add SMA50 (simple moving average for the last 50 sessions) for technical analysis which is not in the original score sheet. If it is over 10%, Score is 1. If it is -10% or less, Score is -1.

14. Determining Intangibles is very subjective. The outlook for Apple and its industry is good, but the current (as of 4/13) market is not.

AAPL scores 6 as of 4/18/13. It passes the passing grade of 3 by 3. It scores one point higher when using Fidelity's Equity Summary Score instead of Finviz's Recom.

Try it yourself. Your score may not be the same as my score as your date of performing this exercise is different from mine.

Some mature companies such as IBM may not score high, but they should be re-considered. Compare its score to its historical scores if it has been scored before. There are always exceptions to any scoring system. There may be current events or situations developing that will not be found in the financial statements such as a new lawsuit or a new, promising drug.

Check out the intangibles, its company's outlook, its industry's outlook and the market's outlook. When the market is plunging, do not buy any stocks with some exceptions such as contra ETFs. Even If the market is risky, you can use the scoring system to have a watch list of stocks ready for when the market returns.

If you trade in shorter terms (less than 3 months), select high-scored stocks and use technical analysis to enter and exit a trade such as SMA-50. It is better to trade stocks that are on their way up.

Again, this scoring system is based on fundamental stocks. The prediction is better on stocks to be held for more than 6 months. Use the scoring system as a guideline. Statistically the scoring system works but there are exceptions otherwise there would be no poor folks. It is better to use a good scoring system to trade stocks than to go without.

Fillers:

For folks who do not want to move to cash during market plunges

If holding cash is boring to you, just throw a gold coin into the ocean every 15 minutes. You will attract a crowd if not a diver or a police man to take you to the nearest mental hospital. In any case, you will make it to the 6 o'clock news.

#Do we need amendments for the Bible

I do not believe in "A tooth for a tooth" but forgiveness.

Screenshot on research screen from Finviz:

AAPL [NASD]
Apple Inc.
Technology | Personal Computers | USA

financial highlights

Index	S&P 500	P/E	10.74	EPS (ttm)	41.89	Insider Own	0.03%	Shs Outstand	938.65M	Perf Week	7.86%
Market Cap	422.37B	Forward P/E	10.16	EPS next Y	44.31	Insider Trans	3.68%	Shs Float	937.18M	Perf Month	5.20%
Income	39.67B	PEG	0.51	EPS next Q	7.40	Inst Own	64.10%	Short Float	2.14%	Perf Quarter	-0.22%
Sales	169.10B	P/S	2.50	EPS this Y	59.51%	Inst Trans	0.00%	Short Ratio	1.17	Perf Half Y	-23.63%
Book/sh	144.12	P/B	3.12	EPS next Y	10.86%	ROA	22.95%	Target Price	543.62	Perf Year	-21.56%
Cash/sh	41.69	P/C	10.79	EPS next 5Y	20.88%	ROE	33.34%	52W Range	385.10 - 697.80	Perf YTD	-14.95%
Dividend	10.60	P/FCF	10.82	EPS past 5Y	62.22%	ROI	28.53%	52W High	-35.51%	Beta	1.00
Dividend %	2.36%	Quick Ratio	1.75	Sales past 5Y	44.81%	Gross Margin	39.50%	52W Low	16.85%	ATR	11.37
Employees	72800	Current Ratio	1.78	Sales Q/Q	11.27%	Oper. Margin	30.92%	RSI (14)	64.29	Volatility	2.29% 2.51%
Optionable	Yes	Debt/Eq	0.00	EPS Q/Q	-17.95%	Profit Margin	23.46%	Rel Volume	0.75	Prev Close	445.52
Shortable	Yes	LT Debt/Eq	0.00	Earnings	Apr 23 AMC	Payout	18.91%	Avg Volume	17.20M	Price	449.98
Recom	2.00	SMA20	7.12%	SMA50	4.01%	SMA200	-16.73%	Volume	12,883,904	Change	1.00%

24-Apr-13   Reiterated   UBS   Buy $560 → $500

3 How to use the grand score

This scoring system is used to identify stocks with a higher appreciation potential. Statistically from my last performance monitor, this scoring system works. Sometimes a highly-scored stock may not perform. Check out the intangibles, the company's outlook, its industry's outlook and the market's outlook.

As in any strategy or scoring system, you should use paper trade first and then commit real money gradually and slowly. In any case, do not bet the entire farm on one strategy, and / or one scoring system.

The six steps of trading:

1. Is the market too risky to get in?
2. Screen stocks to reduce the number of stocks to be analyzed.
3. Evaluate stocks using the scoring system in this book.
4. Analyze each stock: Intangible Analysis, Qualitative Analysis and Technical Analysis (skip this one for long-term stocks).
5. Buy the stock.
6. Sell the stock. Analyze and score the purchased stocks to see if they have met your objectives.

All these steps will be described further here:

1. Market risk

If the market is too risky, do not buy any stocks.

2. Screen stocks

There are many good screens (same as searches) available. Try your broker's site first and then Finviz.

3. Score the screened stocks

Screens provide us with a limited number of stocks to evaluate; I prefer less than 10. Reduce the number further using the following criteria if they are not readily available in your screener.

- Take out any foreign companies including those that are listed in the US exchanges if the market does not favor foreign companies. My current performance monitor on this scoring system proves that statistically they are poor performers. Of course, there are exceptions and market conditions could change.

- Take out the following sectors: bank, mining, insurance, drug (generic ok) and biotech. The financial statements do not tell the entire story such as the quality of their loans. You need more help than a scoring system such as subscribing to a newsletter specific to the sector.

- Take out companies with low average volume (less than 8,000 shares for example). You would pay extra for the spread on low-volume stocks.

- It is a personal choice to trade penny stocks that usually have market cap less than 200 M, with prices less than $2, and are not listed in major exchanges. They are risky, but some could provide large price appreciation. There are exceptions. When I traded ALU, I should not have been a penny stock even at $1 per share; its market cap was about 2 B.

4. Analyze each stock

I prefer to analyze stocks that pass the scoring system. The number of stocks to evaluate further depends on how much time available to you. Check out the intangibles. Here are some sources to help you know the company better:

- Yahoo! Finance board. Be careful as there is a lot of bad information too and some are very biased.
- Seeking Alpha. Be warned of the author's hidden agenda. Today there are fewer articles that are free.
- Fidelity's website or your broker's website for research reports.
- Many subscription services such as Value Line and AAII. Check out whether they are available in your local library.
- Zacks for its earnings revision rating and it is free for individual stocks.

5. Buy the stock

Place a buy order close to the market price.

6. Sell the stock

Periodically (about every 6 months) evaluate your purchased stock with the same procedure you buy stocks. If it scores below the passing grade or the market is expected to dip, it could be time to sell.

Afterthoughts

- When not to use any scoring system.
  When you buy at the bottom of a sector or at the bottom of the stock market, all your stocks score low and their outlook would be bad too. When the market recovers, it could be the most profitable time to buy.

- Some stocks with the lowest score surge in a short time. As of 4/25/13, I had TAHO and WLT that had a big surge on the next day after I scored them. I did not know whether it was a dead cat bouncing, or some favorable development or event.

  They usually represent very risky stocks for stocks with lowest scores. When you find these stocks, you either ignore them as suggested by our Adaptive Stock Scoring System, or perform thorough research. Personally, I skip them and have a better sleep.

4   Get metric data from Fidelity

There are many sources to get the same fundamental metrics. This article uses Fidelity and the previous article uses Finviz.com. Other sources are Yahoo!Finance and your broker's website.

An Illustration
Use AAPL as an example and today's date is 4/19/13. Enter the value in the last column of the table and then add the individual scores to get a grand score, which is used to determine whether the stock is value or not.

No.	Metric	Good	Bad	Score	Value
1	P/E (use expected if possible)	Between 2.5 and 12.5, Score = 2	> 50 or < 0, Score = -1	2	8.9
2	Price / Cash Flow	< 12, Score = 1	>30 or < 0, Score = -1	1	8.75
3	Price / Sales[1]	< 0.8, Score = 1	< 0, Score = -1	0	2.2
4	Price / Book	< 1, Score = 1	< 0, Score = -1	0	3.2
5	Analyst's Opinion[2]	> 7, Score = 1	< 4, Score = -1	0	6
6	Short % (check reason for high %)	Between 30% & 40%, Score = 1[4]	Between 10% & 20%, Score = -1	0	2%
7	Insider Purchase[3]	Score = 1		0	Few
8	Profit Margin[3]	> 25%, Score = 1	< 5%, Score = -1	1	44%
	#9 to # 10	Compare Q to Q last year			
9	Revenue Growth[3]	> 15%, Score = 1	< 0, Score = -1	1	17.65%
10	Earning Growth[3]	> 20%, Score = 1	< 0, Score = -1	-1	-.4%
11	Intangibles	Positive, Score = 1	Negative, Score= -1	1	My view
			Grand Score	5	
	AAPL 4/19/2013[5]	$390.05	SPY = 155		

Footnote
1. If negative values for Sales (due to accounting adjustments), Equity and Book are possible but not likely.
2. It is obtained from Fidelity's website.
3. This metric can be found from many sources.
4. A short squeeze could be coming when a stock is oversold. If a critical problem of the company cannot be recovered easily, change the Score from 1 to -1.
5. The last row is for information only. SPY is used to measure whether it will beat the market by comparing the return of this stock to the return of SPY.

Step-by-step instructions

1. Log on to Fidelity.com.

2. Select Research and then Stock.

3. Enter AAPL for 'Company or Symbol'.

4. The sector is Computer, not one of the sectors (bank, insurer, mine, drug and biotech) which we want to avoid as most metrics do not apply.

5. It is not a foreign company judging by the address and the names of the officers. Needs more research on those companies that are not well-known.

6. It passes the basic criteria:
   1. Average Daily Volume is larger than 6,000.
   2. Price is greater than $2 per share.
   3. Belong to one of the three major exchanges.
   4. Market Capitalization is greater than 200M.

   Modify, define and / or add your own criteria here. If you want to be in micro-cap stocks, change your criteria accordingly.

7. Enter 0 for Equity Summary Score.

8. Its P/E is 8.9 (not the desired expected P/E). Enter 2 for its score (metric #1) as it is within the favorable range.

9. Click on Detailed Quote. The short interest (on the right side of the screen) is about 2%. Enter 0 for the score for this metric.

10. Click on Key Statistics.

11. Enter the scores for Price /Cash (metric #2), Price / Sales (metric #3) and Price / Book (metric #4).

12. Click on Ownership & Insiders, and then Insider Trends. The trend does not indicate a lot of insider purchases. Enter 0.

13. Revenue Growth (the current quarter compared to the same quarter of last year) is obtained under Growth.

14. Earning Growth (the current quarter compared to the same quarter of last year) is the same as EPS growth (last quarter vs. same quarter prior year) under Growth. It is barely negative, so I treat it as 0%.

15. Determining the intangibles is very subjective. The outlook for Apple and its industry is good, but the current (as of 4/2013) market is risky.

The Grand Score

Sum up all individual scores giving AAPL a grand score of 5. According to my passing grade of 3, AAPL as of 4/18/2013 passes our scoring system by 2.

Try it yourself with the same company or other companies. Your score may not be the same as mine as your date of performing this exercise is different from mine.

Some companies such as IBM may not score high, but they should be re-considered. Compare its score to its historical scores if it has been scored before.

The scoring system is a good guideline only.

I started with IBM instead of AAPL in writing this chapter. It scored two and the day after IBM plunged by 10%. It could be just a coincidence. From my scoring system, IBM is not deeply valued. Its earnings is expected to grow and its price had this built-in. When the earnings disappointed, the stock price plunged. That's why I prefer 'Buy Low and Sell High' than 'Buy High and Sell Higher'. Most deeply-valued stocks have nowhere to go but up.

In general, growth companies will not do well in this kind of scoring system, which is based on fundamentals. In this example, AAPL has changed to a value stock from a growth stock.

Check out the intangibles, its company's outlook, its sector's outlook and the market's outlook. If the market is risky, do not buy any stock at all.

If you trade in a shorter-term period (less than 3 months), select high-scoring stocks and time the entry and exit via technical analysis. It is better to trade stocks that are on a long-term uptrend. In this case, trend parameters such as SMA-50 are more important than most fundamental metrics.

Again, this scoring system is used to pick up good stocks based on fundamental metrics and hopefully it works most of the time.

Picture Filler:

Screenshot on research screen from Fidelity:

[Screenshot of Fidelity.com research screen showing Key Statistics for AAPL (Apple Inc.)]

Fidelity.com — Accounts & Trade | News & Insights | Search | Research | Quotes | Customer Service | Guidance & Retirement | Open an Account | Investment Products | Log Out

Saturday, May 4, 2013

Research > Stocks >

Enter Company or Symbol: AAPL [Go]

Stock Details
- Snapshot
- Detailed Quote
- Advanced Chart
- Key Statistics
- News & Events
- Compare
- Analyst Opinions
- Research Reports

Key Statistics
- Earnings & Dividends
- Ownership & Insiders
- Financial Statements
- Technical Analysis
- SEC Filings

OTHER STOCK RESEARCH
- Stock Research Overview
- Stock Screeners
- Explore Research Firms
- Watch Lists

DJIA: 14,973.96 +142.38 (0.96%) NASDAQ: 3,378.63 +38.01 (1.14%) S&P 500: 1,614.42 +16.83 (1.05%) — Markets closed

Print Format | Help/Glossary | Trading Tutorials

Key Statistics: AAPL
APPLE INC

449.98 ↑ 4.46 (1.00 %) AS OF 4:00:00 PM ET 05/03/2013

[Trade] Quotes delayed at least 15 min. Log in for real time quote.

| Add to Watch List | Set Alert | Hypothetical Trade | Option Chain | Price History ▼

Accounting and Governance Risk
Accounting and Governance Risk (AGR®) is a statistically modeled assessment of corporate integrity which can be used as a confidence level indicator in the company's management and reported financials. Log in for AGR® details

Valuation

	AAPL	Computers & Peripherals Average	Industry Average & Percentile Methodology Industry Percentile
Market Cap	$422.37B	$9.53B	100th
P/E (Trailing Twelve Months)	10.74	13.05	64th
P/E (5-Year Average)	16.19	16.99	34th
PEG Ratio (5-Year Projected)	0.51	0.96	46th
Enterprise Value	$418.46B	$282.14B	100th
Price/Cash Flow (Most Recent Quarter)	9.41	10.02	71st
Price/Cash Flow (TTM)	9.44	7.42	69th
Price/Sales (Most Recent Quarter)	2.43	2.93	89th
Price/Sales (TTM)	2.50	2.14	89th
Price/Book	3.43	3.04	82nd

Content and data provided by various third parties and Fidelity. – Terms of Use

5   Compare the two sources

The following compares the two sources for fundamental metric data: Fidelity and Finviz. You can add your source, if it is not one of the two.

Advantages of Fidelity

- Equity Summary Score.
  I rate it superior. The following are from Fidelity's website.
  "The Equity Summary Score provides a consolidated view of the ratings from a number of independent research providers on Fidelity.com. It uses the providers' relative, historical recommendation performance along with other factors to give you an aggregate, accuracy-weighted indication of the independent research firms' stock sentiment."

- Compare the metrics to the sector.
  There are many metrics such as P/S and Debt / Equity are unique to a specific industry. Super markets should have high sales with low profit margins and some industries such as utilities have high debts. Comparing the company to its peers makes a lot of sense.

- Compare the current P/E to the average P/E for the last five years. It is a sensible way to evaluate its current value. P/E is an important metric but not the sole metric to evaluate a company.

- There are decent reports available free.

Advantages of Finviz

- It is free to everyone while Fidelity allows their customers only to use the website. However, there is no balance required to open an account with Fidelity.

- It saves some time to display most of the metrics on one page.

- Forward P/E. To me, the prediction accuracy is better than the P/E based on the last twelve months.

- Easy to enter Insiders' Purchase.

- Technical analysis indicator is clear.

I use the 50-day SMA-50%, Simple Moving Average for the last 50 sessions. It is nicely expressed in percentage. I also use Elliot Wave found on Fidelity's website. The chart displays the trend of the stock clearly.

- The metrics P/C, Current Ratio and Cash /Share are readily available.

Conclusion

Both have their own strengths and weaknesses. Fidelity has been improving their website many times. More often I found more data errors in Finviz and that could be they do not update the database often enough. If you have the time, select the better metrics of the two and find out why if they are different.

Differences in the data from Finviz and Fidelity

On 6/17/2013, I used both systems to score the stock CI. Using Fidelity data, it scored 4 and using Finviz it scored 6. This is why we use the scoring system as a guideline only, and we need to evaluate the stocks further.

Most likely, one's financial data is more updated than the other and / or different evaluations such as Equity Summary Score. Let's check what metrics are identical or very close.

Metric	Finviz	Fidelity
Short %	1%	1%
PEG	1.38	1.38
P/S	0.6	0.6
P/B	2.0	2.1
Earnings growth Q to Q	-84%	-84%
Revenue growth Q to Q	21%	21%
ROE	14%	14%
Total Debt / Equity	52%	53%
Recom. / Equity Summary Score	10	8

The slight difference could be due to the daily fluctuation of the price. Once a while, I found there are big differences.

Filler: Random thoughts

High taxes have been proven bad for the economy and the stock market throughout our history. As Gandhi said, the world has enough resources for all but we're not unselfish enough to share.

6   An extension to the scoring system

The following metrics has not given me good predictive accuracy during this monitoring period. Monitor them in the future. The surprise to me is that ROE did not work this time. I remember a very popular book that just uses ROE as its sole indicator to select stocks. It may be due to too many folks using the same metric.

The following scores are optional. If they are used, add the total to the Grand Score.

No.	Metric	Good	Bad	Score
	Monitor the following			
1	EV / EBITDA			
2	Cash / Market Cap[2]			
3	Technical Analysis[3]	Bull, Score = 1	Bear, Score = -1	
4	ROE[1]	> 35%, Score = 1	< 0, Score = -1	
5	Debt / Equity[1]			
6	Dividend > 3%[4]			
7	PEG			
8	Compare P/E to its average in last 5 years			
9	Compare metrics to their industrial averages			
			Total	
			(Add Total to Grand Score)	

Footnote

1   If the value of Equity is negative, it would affect many related metrics. Price / Cash is easy to find and it is similar to Cash / Market Cap.
2   I use Fidelity's Elliot Wave.
    Finviz.com offers a good alternative. If SMA-50% is more than 10%, it is bullish and if it is less than 10%, it is bearish.
3   The market favors dividend stocks as of 4/13.

Current findings as of 10/2013

From my current monitoring (10/2013) I found the following good candidates for future conditions to add to the scoring system:

- The Total Grade and the Cash Flow Grade under Fundamental Grade Blue Chip Growth (not free now).

http://navelliergrowth.investorplace.com/bluechip/password/index.php?plocation=%2Fbluechip%2F.

- Zacks (free for individual stocks) grade for short term.
- IBD's composite grade (required a subscription).

The following three should be included for some investors.

- Stocks with dividend yields > 3% and less than 5% (trying to skip the return of capital).
- Debt / Equity.
- Earning growth (current quarter to quarter from the prior year).

Filler: The New Norm

Have you noticed that the index performance was wrong in MarketWatch on 3/1? The Arrow and Color indicated the market was down, but actually it was up. It is so basic. Recently they said the market was down by 2% but actually it was up by 2%.

Before I posted anything in Facebook, they asked me to select all the pictures of a lion. I skipped those pictures with two lions and they told me I was wrong. They need to hire someone who has at least graduated from high school.

#Filler: There is no afterlife according to me

If there is one, the Chinese ghost and the ghost from the west should be the same. Chinese ghosts jump and cannot turn; that's why some bridges are crooked in Chinese gardens. In addition, Chines ghosts stick out their tongues and are quite different from the 'foreign' ghosts.

No Chinese see the light from the endo of the tunnel in near-death conditions.

Today's population is about 8 B. From my calculation, the heaven should be very crowded with so many folks going to heaven from Adam's day to today.

#Filler: What happened to the once-great country named U.S.A.?

7 A scoring system for growth stocks

When the market favors growth stocks more than valued stocks, we would like to change our scoring system to place emphasis on growth.

In the early recovery phase of the market cycle (about one or two years after the market crash), value stocks are favorable. After this period, growth stocks are favorable in general. You can find out which of the following are favorite today: Value or Growth by:

1. Articles from many financial sites.
2. From the performance of an ETF on value stocks (SPYV for example) for the last three months and compare it to an ETF on growth stocks (SPYG for example).
3. From the change of P/E of SPY that simulates the market. If P/E is less than last 3 months, value stocks win. Use PEG (the change of P/E) if you do not keep P/E value in the last 3 months.

When you have a good size of the evaluated stocks for a long time, you can compare their performances and then adjust your scoring system accordingly. The following are the examples of suggested changes for growth stocks.

- Forward E/P. Decrease the number from 2 to 1.
- Earning Growth Q-Q. Increase the number from 1 to 2.
- Sales Growth Q-Q. Increase the number from 1 to 1.5.

8 A scoring system for momentum stocks

When you buy stocks and hold them for a month or less, you do not care about fundamentals but rather the momentum. The momentum metrics such as SMA-20 (Single Moving Average with 20 days average) would be appropriate. The other metrics are: price increases from last 15 and 30 days, earnings revisions and any catalyst (such as a new drug) and insider's purchases.

The rotation by institutional investors is a critical metric for momentum stocks.

Section II: Monitor parameters

Periodically (say half a year), we should monitor the performances of our screens, metrics and our scoring systems and adjust them accordingly. Use the better performing screens more often. Some metrics may lose their predictability due to different market conditions. For example, if value is important in the current market, increase the score value for P/E.

9   Monitor my big gainers

This chapter checks the characteristics of my big winners and the next chapter is on my big losers. The purpose of these two chapters is to demonstrate how to check out the common characteristics of the winners and losers. It also applies to the performances of strategies in the recent market.

Once the common characteristics of our big winners have been identified, search stocks with the screens that perform well. It does not always guarantee the same result. However, it would increase your trading profits more often than not.

In my system of evaluating stocks, it consists of two major parts:

1. Screen for stocks (same as search).
2. Analyze the screened stocks (scoring them to start with).

The database
The following data accounts for all the portfolio holdings and the stocks I sold this year in my largest taxable account as of 6/1/2013. My trading strategy keeps track of a lot of stocks, about 50 in this account. This monitor includes 21 stocks (CSCO bought two times), which had a greater than 25% return. The result is too small to draw a concrete conclusion. However, the result of this monitoring is quite compatible with the results of the previous monitors.

To increase your database, consider the following:

- Include the stocks that you have evaluated even if they have not been bought.
- Include the entire year of sold stocks not only YTD.
- Relax your threshold of the big gainers (use 20% instead of 25%).
- Include all accounts. I skip some accounts as they serve different purposes such as one for a momentum strategy.

The results

The results are summarized by the following four tables:

Performance

It should be compared to a market index.

Table 1: Performance Summary.

No. of stocks	Avg. Return	Avg. Annualized	Avg. Holding Period
21	50%	111%	211 days

Source

Table 2: Source of the stocks:

Sources	Web & media	Deeply valued	Acquire candidate	Misc. screens	Short squeeze
No. of stocks	4	3	3	10	1
Annual. Return	75%	53%	204%	115%	164%
Stocks	ADM, BSX, C, EMN	CSCO, CSCO, MSFT	CAMP, FFCH, ADES	ACAT,BIIB CUZ,DGI,NSIT, STRZA,USNA, OMX,DLTR	DECK

The returns are annualized for a better comparison.

Web and Publication.
There are four (from a total of 21) stocks selected from web articles, magazines and newspapers. When I was convinced that there was great appreciation potential, I bought that stock without further evaluation (not recommended). I was lazy but you should do some evaluation. Need to distinguish whether the authors are pumping-and-dumping the stocks they recommended.

Deeply-valued stocks.
I placed an order with prices about 5% lower than the market prices betting they are still on its way down a little. About three out of six orders were successfully executed. If I have a time machine, I should place market

orders on all six as the market is rising. Try to buy all the deeply-valued stocks in the future.

I doubled my normal bet on most of these stocks (CSCO about 4 times). As of 5/2013, these deeply-valued stocks have not realized its potential values and they're the under-performers in the group. However, the average 53% annualized return is nothing to sneeze at!

Update 3/2016. Both CSCO and MSFT have been doing great. From 5/1/2013 to 3/1/2016, their average annualized return is 16% vs SPY's 9%.

Candidates to be acquired.
There are quite a few candidates that would be potentially acquired by other (usually larger) companies in the early recovery of the market cycle (a phase defined by me). However, with plenty of easy money around due to low interest rates and the high corporate cash reserves, it extended the acquisition craze to 2013. This phase will end when the Fed begins to tighten the money supply. This group represents the best return. I should have doubled bet on all of them even though they normally are smaller and unknown companies.

The potential candidates to be acquired are usually smaller companies with a technological edge and/or having a valuable customer base. Sell them when they're no longer candidates.

Miscellaneous screens.
A screen consists of criteria in searching stocks such as P/E < 20. There are 10 stocks from the miscellaneous screens. The performance of each screen is further analyzed. It is better to use the screens that have had better performances recently. My screens are different from yours and some require subscription services, so they will not be disclosed here.

Short squeeze.
The short squeeze happens when the stocks that have been oversold by the shorters. When the stock is oversold, those seeking a short position cannot find the extra shares to be shorted, and sometimes the shorters are forced to cover their shorts due to the high expenses of shorting that stock (interests and dividends).

If the company is not heading towards bankruptcy, any good news would also boost the stock price. This is the typical situation, but it does not work all of the time.

Increase bets on stocks that have better appreciation potential

The confidence in my predictions for CSCO's future is so high that I have bought it four times, and then 2 times for BSX and STRZA. All scored high in my scoring system.

Table 3: Score (using the score system in my book Scoring Stocks:

Avg. Score	Foreign Country	Insider Purchase
3.00	0	1

The average score of 9 stocks is 3 and that is my passing grade in my scoring system. The scoring system is a guideline and we do not have to follow it religiously.

There is not a single foreign stock in this group. I usually do not trust the financial statements of the smaller, foreign countries. The next chapter may convince you to skip most of them at least for now or until it is proven otherwise.

Only one stock has meaningful insiders' purchases out of 21. The database is too small for any conclusion. From my past data, Insiders' Purchases with purchase prices close to the market prices is a good predictor.

By Sectors

Sectors fluctuate in performance.

Table 4: Sectors:

Sector	Tech	Health Care, equip & drug	Consumer goods	Finance	Retail	Misc.
No.	6	4	3	3	2	3
Ann.	77%	230%	102%	60%	57%	78%
Stock	CAMP, CSCO, CSCO, DGI, MSFT, NSIT	BIIB, BSX, USNA, ADES	ACAT, ADM, DECK	C, FFCH, BANR	OMX, DLTR	CUZ, STRZA, EMN

Technology companies.
Technology companies are doing fine, but some are also included in the worst performers described in the next chapter. I rate this sector neutral in this period. Just buy the tech companies with high scores and good outlooks for the company and its sector. In general, tech is doing well in a rising market as consumers have more money for high-tech toys and companies have money to invest such as upgrading their accounting software.

Mining companies.
Miners are not doing so well in this period as described in the next chapter. Monitor this sector as they may be rotated back in when the economy improves with higher demands for industrial ores. There is no miner in the winners' circle.

Health care, medical equipment and drugs.
With the aging population, the companies in health care, drugs (generic preferred), and medical equipment should be doing great. It is the best performing sector.

The last 90-day performances of ETFs specified in sectors are better predictors for sectors.

Conclusion

The database of 50 stocks is too small to make any conclusive conclusion. However, this result is pretty compatible with the previous monitor about 6 months ago that had a large database (about 200 stocks).

Personal performance monitor

There are more sophisticated ways and better tools to monitor performance. Most of them require subscriptions and most are low cost. Some are briefly described together with my experiences.

1. Searches. I have the name of the screens with their average returns. Currently I have about 20 screens I use to search for stocks.

2. Evaluate stocks. Each screened stock should be scored. The performance after 3 months should be compared to the S&P 500 or its corresponding index such as using QQQ for tech stocks. The prediction for the accuracy of each fundamental metric should also be checked periodically.

In addition, I divide the database into short term (3 to 6 months) and long term (about 12 months).

Afterthoughts

- Health care sector. Click here for a SA article. (http://seekingalpha.com/article/1503232-bull-of-the-day-biogen)

- We need to check how the portfolio performs when the market goes down. The best performance is when it beats the market in both market directions. However, there is no evergreen strategy. You should use a strategy that is supposed to be favorable in specific market conditions.

Links

Selling short:
http://en.wikipedia.org/wiki/Sell_short

Short squeeze:
http://en.wikipedia.org/wiki/Short_squeeze

Oversold:
http://www.investopedia.com/terms/o/oversold.asp

Filler

ArtGo gained 3,744% in 2019 before it lost most of the stock value in one day. Lessons are 1. Diversify, 2. Use the trailing stops, 3. Buy value and 4. Be careful on foreign stocks.

10   Monitor my big losses

This article is a repeat of the last one except with my big losers. It is more important to learn from big losers, so we will reduce buying losers that fit into a certain pattern.

The database

The database is smaller due to the current rising market. Partly, it is due to my avoiding the potential losers from previous monitors.

I delete the stocks which have less than a 25% loss. It only has 11 stocks from a total of about 50. A database of 11 stocks is too small to draw any conclusions. However, the results are compatible with my previous results. In other words, they follow similar patterns.

The results

As in the last chapter, the results are summarized by the following four tables:

Table 1: Performance Summary.

No. of stocks	Avg. Return	Avg. Annualized	Avg. Holding period
11	-43%	-163%	223 days

From here on, annualized returns will be used.

Table 2: Source of the stocks:

Sources	Deeply valued	Acquire candidates	Misc. screens	Short squeezed
No.	0	0	11	0
Annualized Return			-163%	
Stocks			BPI,NTE, SIGA,SIM, VELT,STEC, IAG, END,DEER, CRUS,HXM	

All the stocks here were from my screens. I find the screens with better recent performances perform better than the average; it means the selection of the screens work.

There is not a single stock from the categories from web & publication, deeply-valued list, being acquired or being short squeezed that we find in the last chapter.

Table 3: Score (using the score system):

Avg. Score	Foreign Country
1.86	6
Annualized	-216%

The average score is 1.86 (3 is a passing grade defined in my book Scoring Stocks). Four (out of 11) stocks have not been scored. If I scored them, I may not buy them. My mistake was not scoring them.

There is not a single stock with a meaningful insider purchase. I have encountered that the lowly-scored stocks with meaningful insider purchases appreciate more than the average. Most foreign companies do not have to list insider information.

There are too many foreign stocks in this loser group while there is not a single foreign stock among the best performers. If I skipped these six stocks, I would have saved a bundle. We cannot go back in time, but it is a strong guide for the future. I do not know why I still bought foreign stocks as they did not perform well in the last monitoring period.

Luckily, I did not place any double bets on any of these losers.

Table 4: Sectors:

Sector	Tech	Miner	Health care, equip and drug	Misc.
No.	4	3	1	2
Annual. Return	-128%	-131%	-34%	-734%
Stocks	NTE,VELT, STEC,CRUS	SIM,IAG END	SIGA	BPI,HXM

Miners are not doing well in this period. Watch out for this sector as it flows with the global economy. Most miners are foreign companies. I do not trust their financial data except from Canada and Australia.

Technology companies are not doing so well. However, we have some technology companies included as the top performers as described in the last article. The only difference is most of the losers are smaller companies and most are foreign companies. I rate Tech a neutral. Buy those tech companies with high scores, headquartered in the U.S. and good outlooks.

Performance

The combined annualized return of my big losers is 73%. It is smaller due to no double bets on losers.

Update I did another performance analysis in 1/2015 including all the stocks that had been screened but I had not bought. Except one from 25 stocks, the losers are either lowly scored, foreign companies and/or miners. Nine stocks had a grade of F from Blue Chip Growth (not free any more). Surprisingly six of them had heavy insider purchases.

Conclusion

The database of 11 stocks is too small to draw a conclusion. However, the conclusion of this monitoring is very similar to the one I did with the larger database of about 200 stocks 6 months ago.

In combining the results of the two chapters, my conclusions are:

1. The stocks with high scores perform better than those with low scores in my two monitors.

2. Screens (searches) are monitored separately with about a total of 200 stocks and from about 20 screens. Buying candidates that are acquisition prospects have been profitable for this year and 2003.

3. From this monitor and the previous, foreign companies including those companies listed in the U.S. exchanges have been underperforming compared to the U.S. stocks.

4. Miners do not perform this time. It could be due to the so-called sector rotation. When the economy improves or this sector is recognized as being oversold, most industrial metals would return to the former price levels.

5. The better performances from sector health care, medical equipment, or drugs are responding to the aging population.

6. My previous monitors had identified that foreign companies did not perform on the average. I still have several foreign companies this time. If I had omitted them, the return of this portfolio would be far better. I need to follow my recent results.

7. I bet less on the risky companies (most were small companies and /or had low scores) and bet more on better companies.

8. Read articles on this topic. Here is <u>one</u>.

#Filler: An interview of a successful fund manager

This is a typical interview of fund managers that I read in magazines. Learn from what are applicable to us and ignore most ideas that do not make sense. Let me argue for and against them. The name is withdrawn to protect the innocent.

1. "Never can predict market crashes". Look at my simple chart that has successfully detected the two crashes since 2000.

2. "No. 1 in the last 10 years, but lags the market in the last 5 years". The last five years is more important to his investors. It could also be due to his assets having grown more than 15 times. Another bad sign for his future performance.

3. "Seldom sell". Most stocks change a lot in 3 years. Portfolio churning improves the quality of a portfolio. I prefer the one that turns over in a year.

4. "Visiting many companies". It is not applicable to our retail investors. I also hear many stories that the officers set up a good show to fool the analysts. We can look at the financial sheets that cannot lie easily and legally for a long period of time.

5. "Water is a long-term trend". Yes, it is. However, I had a bad experience using this idea too early.

6. He continued to show how some of his stocks made over 100%. Let me remind you that he did not beat the market in the last five years. Hence, he was not being kind enough to show his losers, which may be more important than learning from his winners.

11 My performance monitor

This article serves as an illustration on how to do your own monitor. Most data are from 7/2015. By the time you read this article, the findings could be outdated. Hence, learn how to monitor performances from this article. In addition, it is based on my stocks actually screened and the number of stocks is too limited to draw a general conclusion.

There are two monitors, one for short term and one for long term. Score 3 is my passing score for both short term and long term.

The score results:

Score =	Avg.	< 3	3	4	5	6	7	>=8
Short	7%	2%	8%	11%	7%	14%	11%	-10%
Long	8%	4%	13%	14%	7%	21%	4%	-10%

Explanation

- The score system works if the higher the score, the better the performance. It is to some extent with the exceptions of Score 7, 7 and >=8.
- From the table, I should use 3 as the passing grade for both short term and long term.
- Do not buy stocks when the score is 8 or higher. It is consistent from my previous monitors. I do not know why. I assume that when the stock is too good to be true, most likely it is not.
- When the stock scores between 3 and 7 inclusively, it is a buy. It is quite similar to the previous monitors. It also destroys the price efficiency theory.

How reliable is the score?

As stated, it only applies to me for this test period. The reliability also depends on the size of the sample. The following shows the number of stocks.

	Total	< 3	3	4	5	6	7	>8
Short	747	397	113	97	69	41	27	3
Long	555	299	75	70	53	30	25	3

How fundamental metrics score

The following table shows us the predictability of the metrics.

Short Term: (7% return for the average)

Metric	Parm. 1	No.	%	Parm. 2	No.	%	Predict.
EY	>14	203	4%	<5	94	0%	Good
Blue Chip BC	A	150	7%	F	63	-4%	Good
BC Fundamentals	A	191	14%	F	66	-11%	Good
Fidelity Analyst	Buy	150	10%	Sell	279	3%	Good
P/B	<1	162	1%	>2	333	9%	Bad
ROE	>25	180	9%	<2	110	4%	Good
GRT	<20	71	-4%	>25	685	6%	Good
P/CF	<20	179	8%	>30	99	5%	Good
Earn Gr Q-Q	>50%	227	6%	<5%	68	0%	Good
Sales Gr Q-Q	>25%	153	7%	<5%	154	0%	Good
Debt/E	<.1	172	15%	>1.5	69	2%	Good
RSI(14)	>60	85	9%	<40	33	-2%	Good
SMA 200%	>5	94	1%	<-5	19	-4%	Good

Long Term: (8% return for the average)

Metric	Parm. 1	No.	%	Parm. 2	No.	%	Predict.
EY	>20	28	3%	<5	77	-1%	Good
Blue Chip	A	99	8%	F	62	-4%	Good
Blue Chip Fund.	A	178	15%	F	65	-11%	Good
Fidelity Analyst	Buy	90	17%	Sell	208	4%	Good
P/B	<1	15	2%	>2	227	9%	Bad
ROE	>25	135	11%	<2	93	4%	Good
GRT	<20	67	-3%	>25	488	9%	Good
P/CF	<20	133	11%	>30	54	9%	Good
Earn Gro Q-Q	>50%	141	11%	<5%	68	0%	Good
Sales Gro Q-Q	>25%	97	8%	<5%	110	2%	Good
Debt/E	<.1	168	15%	>1.5	61	4%	Good
RSI(14)	>60	27	22%	<40	7	0%	Bad

Explanation

- I skip the metrics from various subscription services I subscribed.
- The returns are used for comparison only ignoring many standard yardsticks such as comparing it to the market index, and excluding dividends.
- P/B is not a good metric from my samples. RSI(14) is fine for the short term but not useful for the long term. However, due to the limited data on RSI(14), they are not conclusive. SMA-200% is not available for the long term as it is a new one for me.
- Short term is usually about 4 months and long term is about 12 months on the average; this is just a general guideline.
- Some data are both long term and short term by playing some tricks by not updating the stock prices of some data; some data could be eligible for both short term and long term as they are close in the specified ranges.
- The predication of the metric is good if they're as expected.
- Your score is derived from the above metrics. Weigh more on the metrics with better predictability. Modify your scoring system based on your monitor.
- EY (E/P) is expected (a.k.a. forward) earnings yield. GRT is earning growth rate.
- The stock has a higher chance of appreciation if Fidelity's Equity Summary Score>7, ROE> 25%, GRT > 25%, Debt/Equity < 10% and Earnings Growth > 50% for the long term. It is quite similar to the short term which should include SMA-50.

When you cannot find any stocks, relax the selection. I would start with Earnings Growth > 30% as my primary metric.

Filler: Smart male pigs

Chinese use 'pig' as an adjective to describe stupidity such as pig brain. Pigs are smart enough to convince many religions not to eat them.

If you're in the old-fashion farm, you can see all the female pigs line up every afternoon to mate with the male pig. I bet you want to be a male pig in your next life. I must have a pig brain to say so. LOL.

12 Metric performances & market cycle

From my limited testing on the last two market cycles (2000 and 2008), some metrics perform better than others. This is for reference only. I select the following metrics. Grades are estimates from a hypothetical vendor.

- EY, Expected Earning Yield (Expected Earnings/Price).
- TG, Timing Grade. It is based on price momentum, increases in sales and profits…
- VG, Value Grade. It is based on fundamentals such as P/E, Debt/Equity…

Cycle stages	Performers	Bad Performers
Year before plunge	TG, EY	VG
Plunge to bottom	TG	EY
Early Recovery	EY, VG	
Up and Peak	EY, TG	
All stages	EY, TG, VG	

- They are in descending order. For example in All Stages, EY has better performance than TG.
- EY and TG are good in almost all phases. The exception for EP is poor performance during market plunges. Aggressive users can short the stocks that have high EY at this stage.
- EY and increasing EY turn out to be a best performer during Early Recovery, a phase in the market cycle defined by me. In this phase buy stocks with high EY and VG. It has been proven in 2003 and 2009.
- I expect EY is part of the VG. However, my tests tell me otherwise.
- EY, TG and VG are metrics close to the status of 'evergreen'.
- I also have other metrics that may not be relevant to the general discussion. They are growth of earnings, growth of E/P and growth of dividend.
- The performances of many AAII strategic screens are provided. Separate them in the phases of a market cycle and make the conclusions accordingly.
- To check performance of metrics, I use Google Finance to create a portfolio and download the current prices to a spreadsheet.

13   Investing: Long Term vs. Short Term

I claim short-term investing is not gambling. Short-term investing can make you good money, if you have the correct knowledge and discipline in this strategy. Actually, I use both a long-term strategy and a short-term strategy and monitor the performances. I would invest more on the strategy that is more profitable among the two in the current market. In general, I use taxable accounts for long term investing.

Long-term investing
Fundamentals are important. Technical Analysis may be used to time the entry and exit. Everyone has their own favorite fundamentals. Here are mine:

1. EV/EBITDA is a good way to measure the value of a company. This metric has its advantages and disadvantages over P/E. It is better as it includes cash (including short-term securities), and debts. I have seen a small company having more cash than the total market cap and total liabilities. If there are no major liabilities such as pending lawsuits, the buy decision is a no-brainer. The only disadvantage is most of them used earnings of the last twelve months, not the forward (same as expected) earnings.

    EBITDA/EV (EVEBITDA flipped over) is easier to understand and it takes care of the negative earnings if available. To illustrate, if it is 35%, you can receive your entire investment in about 3 years.

2. The next important metric is free cash flow. The company can have a lot of sales and good reported earnings, but the cash flow is poor. You have to find out the reason why. If their vendors are not paying, most likely it is a serious account payable problem; 2000 is a common problem to many companies.

3. As described in this book, many free websites evaluate the stock for you such as Fidelity's Equity Summary Score.

    Most analysts are good in estimating earnings but due to the conflict of interest, they may not publish reports for the public.

4. Let the profit rise. I usually sell my stocks when they double. I have missed many profits. I recommend using trailing stops for these rocket stocks.

5. You're swimming against the tide with value stocks. Be patient as it takes time for the market to recognize its true value. Review the purchased stocks routinely to ensure there is no major problem.

"Buy and hold" should be replaced by "Buy and monitor. Many big companies have gone bankrupt or close to such as GM and U.S. Steel. Polaroid and Kodak suffered by advance of digital cameras. Many retailers suffer from the rise of Amazon.com. The pandemic of 2020 will make some sectors poorer such as travel industries.

Short-term investing
In general, it is opposite of long-term investing. Some metrics have more weights in scoring them. Price momentum is more important than fundamentals. To illustrate, the discovery of a new drug will not be shown in their fundamentals, but the rise in the stock price will. Everyone has their own favorite technical metrics. Here are mine that can be found from Finviz.com:

1. SMA, Single Moving Average.
   It indicates the uptrend when it is positive. SMA20 is for short term (20-days average) and SMA50 for intermediate term.

2. RSI(14). When it is over 65, the stock may be overbought. Hence, the chance of reversing from the uptrend is high.

3. There are many technical patterns. Experience is important to check whether they are useful to you. I usually select both Daily and Weekly for Time Frames in Finviz.com. Personally, I prefer "Double Top" for down trend and "Double Bottom" for uptrend.

4. Daily Volume is the confirmation.

5. As opposite of Long-Term Investing, the holding period is relatively short. Mine is one or two months. I also have mental stops in case the trend is reversed. The uptrend may be reversed when the SMA and/or RSI(14) decrease.

Book 5: Trading Stocks

This section will answer some of the questions with regard to trading stocks. They are but not limited to:

- The fair price of your trade.
- Protect your profits.
- Make extra money with covered calls.
- Diversify your portfolio.
- Bonds.
- Taxes.
- Trading plan.
- Brokers.

The following link from Charles Schwab offers a lot of insightful articles on this topic. Fidelity and Investopedia have similar articles too.
http://seekingalpha.com/author/charles-schwab/articles#regular_articles

1   Chronology of a trade

This is a summary in the life of a trade as described throughout this book.

- Ensure the market is trending up before you trade (use simple market timing). You do not need charting knowledge. It is simpler than it looks.

- Beginners. If you are not ready to buy stocks, buy CDs with different maturing dates. Buy ETF(s) such as VOO, a low-fee ETF for S&P 500 index.

- Non-beginners. Screen stocks with the screens that have the best performances recently. Evaluate stocks with metrics from Finviz.com such as avoiding stocks being dumped by the insiders, negative Q-Q earnings, etc.

- Metrics are generally divided into short term and long term. For me, long term means holding the acquired stocks for more than one year.

- Consider the lower taxes on capital gains on non-retirement accounts.

- Recommend buying less than 10 stocks with less than 3 stocks in the same sector. To illustrate, for a $10,000 portfolio, buy 10 stocks with a position of $1,000 each.

- Sell stocks when your objectives are met or the market is trending down.

- The reason why investors making good profits when their success rates are only 50%: stop orders. Many recommend set stops so you can lose only 5% (or 10% for volatile stocks) of a trade. Use trailing stops for winners (i.e. periodically renew the stop based on the current price).

Everyone's situation is different, so tailor the above to your own requirements, knowledge and available time for investing. Usually, I hold more than 10 stocks and I use covered calls to maximize my profits.

Do not put new money on losers but on gainers if the trend is positive. The above are my opinions only. Read the Disclaimer in the Introduction section.

Link: Beginners: https://www.youtube.com/watch?v=aod3cyUEu4k
Trade stocks with Fidelity: https://www.youtube.com/watch?v=wMxj6iB92ZA&t=2s

Filler: Fidelity's Conditional order.
If one condition is satisfied, the order conditional will be cancelled. It is powerful and the possibilities are only limited by our imagination.

Filler: Consumer or stockholder
The more you bash the airlines, the more profit the airlines make.

How? The less service they give, the more profits they get and so are their stock prices. However, do not go to the extreme. Do you want to be a consumer or an investor?

2   Order prices

Market orders
It is simply trading the stock at the prevailing market price. Place market orders to buy only when the stock is moving up. Many winners never take a breather on their way up. Trade prices can easily be manipulated on stocks with low trading volumes. To reduce being manipulated, do not place market orders after hours.

Consider bid and ask. A 'bid' is the price a potential buyer would like to buy while the 'ask' is a potential seller would like to sell. Your market price is usually the worst price in either case, but it is a guarantee that you would trade the stock. A large spread would mean that it would take a longer time to use a limit order and/or the trade volume of the stock is small. A liquid stock usually has a spread of one penny or two.

In my momentum portfolio on 11/2013, I placed a sell price for GERN far higher than the market price. Surprisingly I sold it for this price making an annualized return of 1,176% for holding it for 21 days. When there are few or no other sellers for the stock, the market price would be the price you set. If I cannot sell it in the next 9 days (30 days is my holding period for momentum stocks), I would set it lower. Update: One year later, GERN lost 29%.

Sensible discounts
I prefer to buy the stock at the price closest to the last trade price (to most it is the market price) via a limit order. I seldom lose buying these orders. Sometimes I use the day's lowest price to buy (or the highest to sell) plus a penny (or minus a penny for sell prices to sell).

My other purchase strategy is using 0.15% or 0.25% less than the current prices for stocks I really want. For some promising stocks, I buy them at almost the market price and then place another order on the same stock at 0.5% less than the last traded price (and sometimes 2% depending on the current market trend).

We all want to buy less and sell at higher prices. However, if the trade price is too far away from the current market price (such as 5% from the market price), these trades may never be executed. I have had a long list of buy orders that were not executed and turned out to be big gainers. Learn from my bad experiences.

Use a good discount (such as 10% from the market price) if you believe the market, the sector or the stock will dip by 10%. After you bought the stock, you place a sell order 10% more than the price you paid for it hoping the stock will return to the original price and you pocket 10%. Wishful thinking! However, it has happened to me several times primarily due to temporary market dips.

It works when there is a correction and/or the stock is very volatile. It is usually within the 5% range to take advantage of these situations, not the 10% as described. For a 10% plunge, it usually is due to some serious problem of the company surfacing. One common reason is not meeting its earnings expectation and in this case it usually continues its downward trend. It is **not possible to get the best prices consistently**.

Larger discounts on a falling market
During a falling market (or a mild correction), 3% less than the current prices for buy orders may be fine for some stocks (use 5% for volatile stocks). To illustrate, I placed about 10 of these orders over the last two months during a market dip. Most of the orders were filled. When the market is plunging, do not buy any stock.

Caterpillar and Cisco were some of my buys at these discounts. They were on my watch list to buy. Initially these shares often fell even lower as the trend was downward. As of 12/18/12, CAT earned me between 3% and 14% (bought on 6/12 and 7/12) and CSCO bought on 7/14/12 returned about 34%. My original objective: Buy deeply-valued stocks, wait and sell them when the economy returns.

When you predict the market will dip by 5%, set your buy orders accordingly. Again, predictions are just educated guesses. From my experience, they work most of the time but not all of the time.

On the day of the earnings announcement, the fluctuation of the stock is usually high. Check any change in the earnings estimate before the announcement and act accordingly. Zacks is supposed to be a useful tool to predict earnings estimates. Do not leave orders during the earnings announcement dates, which can be found in Finviz. When the earning turns out to be good, the stock price surges and your order will not be executed. When the earnings is bad, the stock price will plunge usually and you most likely overpaid.

Option expiration dates usually cause more volatility. Retail investors do not have to be concerned except you may use wider stops. In theory, dividend days have little effect on the stock price as it will be lowered by the dividend amount.

High volume of a stock could mean opportunity High volume usually increases the stock price volatility. If the volatility of a stock increases substantially (such as doubling its average daily volume), there could be important news on the company, recommendation changes from a major analyst or trading by the institutional investors. It usually takes the institutional investors a week to trade a stock with their sizable positions.

Many times it is started by the insiders who know about the breaking news of a stock before it is publicized. Some investment services / sites specialize in identifying the increasing volumes on these stocks. Because day traders do not want to leave any open positions overnight, higher volatility occurs at the end of the day. It is the same on the day (usually on Friday) when the options are expiring.

Monitor your trade prices
You cannot tell whether you are paying a fair price without keeping a record. To illustrate, you're paying 1% less than the market prices in buying stocks. You may have missed buying some winners. If the 1% you saved is smaller than the appreciation of the stocks you would have bought at market prices, then you should adjust the buy prices to 0.5% less than the market price and monitor again.

Market trends make a difference too. When the market is trending up, buying any stock would most likely be profitable and usually the purchase orders with higher discounts will not be executed.

Follow the same logic on sell orders. Need to have at least 25 stock purchases (and potential purchases) to make the conclusion meaningful. If you do not trade a lot, you will not have enough data to verify. As described, I prefer not to place an order during the earnings announcement dates which can be found in Finviz.com. If you cannot buy the stock, consider using market order the next day. With most brokers offering no commission trades, the "All or none" option is not valid.

Position sizing. To illustrate, if you have $10,000 to invest, invest 5 stocks with $20,000 each. If you have more time, invest more stocks such as 10 stocks with $10,000 each. Define the maximum loss for a trade (1% of your total portfolio for example) that can be determined by position size and the stop loss.

Good prospects. When you find gems, especially those stocks that are followed by analysts, buy them at market prices and consider doubling the bet if you are really sure you have a winner. From my super stock screens, I spotted NHTC. I placed several bets and one market order. All of them were NOT executed except with the market order. At the end of the day NHTC is up 18% and my executed order is up 14%. I did not have the best buy but made a good profit. NHTC was on its way to a huge appreciation and I sold it too early. I have learned not to sell a winner and protect the profit with a stop.

Lower the buy for risky stocks (if the beta from Finviz is greater than 1 for example) even if they have good fundamentals.

Quality over quantity

If your time is limited, spend all the time on researching one stock one at a time. However, you need to own at least 3 stocks (more stocks for a large portfolio) for your diversification purposes.

Double your normal purchase position on stocks that look great after the research. For risky stocks that look good, you may want to halve your normal purchase position to cut down on the risk. If you are less risk tolerant, do not buy risky stocks at all. My results are not conclusive on risky stocks but I do get a good sleep.

A recent example

Recently I sold EA with $1 more than my order price but $2 less than the current price of the day, which was the earnings announcement day. I do recommend not placing orders right before the earnings announcement day for the stock. If the earnings is good, you do not get all the profit as in this real example; my broker did get me $1 more. If the earnings is bad, you will not sell it anyway. It is the same for buying stocks.

Afterthoughts

- Besides luck, the smart investor never sells at the peak but usually within 10% of the peak. No one can predict the peaks consistently.
- My personal experiences. I have to use market orders for stocks that are heading up. Sometimes I have two buy orders for the same stock, one has a far better price. Most likely I can get the buy orders executed by placing one cent less than the lowest price. When the market is heading down, I place buy orders more favorable to me.
- I made mistakes like most of you. One time my buy price was higher than the last price executed. Luckily my broker adjusted it to the right price but I may not be that lucky next time. Several times I switched the buy price and sell price by mistake. One time it was due to my boss coming by that forced me to enter my order hastily. Try to avoid the first hour of a trade session.
- Some experts do not suggest their clients buy stocks on the way down. With respect, I offer opposing arguments.

- It is fine to buy them on the way down, if you have the conviction that the company or the economy will recover.
- No one knows where the bottom is, but averaging down could be beneficial if the company or the economy can recover. Check why its stock price is falling and whether the company can fix its problems. Some major problems are only temporary or easy to fix.
- Most of my big profits are made by buying close to the bottom prices on stocks that have a good potential to recover.
- Many value stocks are on sale when the market dips. The most favorable time is in the Early Recovery, a phase in the market cycle defined by me.
- Most experts agree that: The best time to buy is when there is blood in the street. It is demonstrated by the years 2003 and 2009.
- Contrarians never follow the herd, but you need to have a good reason to be contrary. I recommended Apple in 2013 when every institutional investor was dumping Apple.
- Stocks are manipulated via selling shorts. When the shares of a stock to be shorted (like over 30% of shorts) are running out, there is a good chance for a short squeeze. Ensure the company being shorted heavily is not heading into bankruptcy.

* Make good money when you are right only 45% of the time by: 1. Limit your losses via stops and 2. Place higher stakes on stocks with higher appreciation potential.
* Some make money on earnings announcements (found in Finviz.com). Earnings would amplify the stock price by at least 5%. Once in a while, there are exceptions. In the last quarter of 2015, Disney posted great results, but the stock dropped. It could be that the market even expected better results or the market is not rational. I believe the latter in this case.
* Many foreign stocks that are listed in U.S. exchanges have extra hefty fees.
* As of 5/2021, the following stocks have been appreciated shortly but their buy orders have not been executed: FL (by 25%), MTZ (31%), RBNC (17%), ANIP (30%), METC (34%), etc. To avoid this from recurring, I would increase the buy prices and even use market orders if necessary

Links
Selling short:
http://en.wikipedia.org/wiki/Short_%28finance%29
Short squeeze:
http://en.wikipedia.org/wiki/Short_squeeze
Fidelity Video: Stop Loss.
https://www.fidelity.com/learning-center/trading/trailing-stops-video
https://www.youtube.com/watch?v=l7EHWyOrfu4
Order type: https://www.youtube.com/watch?v=9IMHnK9eqQw
　　　　　　https://www.youtube.com/watch?v=p9YndmEoJn0
Fidelity order: https://www.youtube.com/watch?v=wMxj6iB92ZA

3 Stop loss

What is a Stop Loss?
A stop-loss order automatically sells a stock when its price falls to a predetermined level, limiting potential losses. Variations like stop-limit orders trigger a sell at a specific price but may not execute if the stock moves rapidly beyond the limit.

Types of Stop Losses
1. **Traditional Stop Orders**:
   - Triggers a sell when the stock price falls below the set stop price.
   - Works well in stable markets but can cause issues during extreme volatility.
2. **Trailing-stop Orders**:
   It is used to protect your profitable stocks. Reset the stop order with current price periodically (weekly, be-weekly or monthly).
3. **Stop-Limit Orders**:
   - Ensures a minimum sell price, but the trade might not execute in rapidly falling markets.
4. **Mental Stops**:
   - A strategy where you manually sell a stock once it drops below a predefined price, avoiding automatic triggers during flash crashes.

Risks of Stop Losses
1. **Flash Crashes**:
   - Events like the 2010 and 2015 flash crashes converted stop orders into market orders at substantially lower prices.
   - Mitigation: Use mental stops during volatile market conditions.
2. **Post-Earnings Volatility**:
   - On earnings announcement days, stock prices may swing significantly. Avoid placing stop orders during these times.
3. **Low-Volume Stocks**:
   - Thinly traded stocks can be easily manipulated to trigger stop losses. Mental stops or manual monitoring are preferable.

Setting Stop Losses
1. **For Stable Stocks**:

- Use a 10%–12% stop-loss margin below the purchase price.
- Adjust the stop price upward as the stock appreciates to protect gains (trailing stop).
2. **For Volatile Stocks**:
    - Account for higher fluctuations by setting wider stops, e.g., 15%–20% below the purchase price.
    - Use metrics like beta (available on platforms like Finviz) to assess stock volatility.
3. **During Rising Markets**:
    - Tighten stop-loss margins to lock in gains as stocks rise steadily.
4. **Avoid Overreacting to Noise**:
    - Avoid stops too close to the stock's support line, as normal price swings might trigger unnecessary sales.

Practical Example
- **Stock Price**: $100
- **Initial Stop Loss**: $88 (12% below purchase price).
- If the stock price rises to $150:
    - Adjust the stop loss to $132 (12% below the new price).

This strategy ensures you lock in profits while limiting potential losses.

Lessons from Real-Life Events
1. **The 9/11 Market Impact**:
    - Many investors lost money as stop orders were triggered during market panic. The market recovered within days, but investors who sold missed the rebound.
2. **Flash Crashes**:
    - Use mental stops to prevent selling during artificially low prices caused by temporary market errors.

Tips for Effective Stop Loss Use
1. **Volatility Awareness**:
    - Stocks in tech, biotech, or growth sectors often experience greater price swings. Set wider stops for these.
2. **Avoid After-Hours Orders**:
    - Stop-loss orders placed after hours can be exploited by manipulators.
3. **Check Broker Policies**:
    - Ensure your broker executes stops during normal hours and offers trailing stops for convenience.

What should be the stop price?

Basically, you do not want to sell the stock via a stop order during the regular fluctuations. If it happens (sometimes stops do not work as expected), buy the stock back ensuring it is not a wash sale in taxable accounts.

Many websites have suggestions of the stop price. Usually, Finviz and Fidelity have the resistance line in the charts. You select the order price slightly below the resistance line.

For simplicity, select 12% less than your purchase price (more or less depending on the market volatility). For example, the purchase price is $100, use the stop price $88 (=100 – 12). Also, change the stop price even lower if the stock is volatile according to its beta (available in Finviz).

If your stock rises, you want to adjust the stop price higher and it should be based on the current price (not your purchase price). In this case, I would review it more often (say a month). It is similar to the trailing stop. Most brokers provide you a percent or a stop price. Personally, I use 15% and 20% for volatile stocks. You need to review it periodically as many orders could expire as the period may be determined by your broker. For shorting, you can use stops to limit your potential losses.

Links
https://www.investopedia.com/ask/answers/06/stoplossorderdetails.asp
https://www.investopedia.com/terms/t/trailingstop.asp
Fidelity: https://www.youtube.com/watch?v=6Wp4cWqFlpw&t=669s

4 Short selling

Definition and Process
Short selling involves selling a stock you do not own, with the intention of buying it back later at a lower price, thus profiting from a decline in its value. To do this, you borrow the stock from your broker, which requires a margin account with adequate collateral. The broker charges interest on the borrowed stock.

Note: Short selling is not allowed in retirement accounts, but you can use contra ETFs as an alternative.

Advantages
- Short selling is effective when you anticipate a stock or market decline.
- It is easier to profit during a market downturn compared to traditional investing.
- Many mutual funds are restricted from short selling, potentially reducing competition in identifying poor-performing companies.
- Psychological biases in retail investors, such as reluctance to sell losing stocks, may create opportunities.

Recommendations for Beginners
Start with paper trading to refine your strategy. Gradually invest small amounts once you've demonstrated consistent profitability. Seek advice from a financial advisor and review disclaimers thoroughly. For lower risk, consider contra ETFs, which are less volatile, can be used in retirement accounts, and limit losses to the initial investment.

Risks and Mitigation Strategies
- **Unlimited Loss Potential:** If a stock's price rises exponentially, losses could far exceed the initial investment. For instance, Weight Watchers' stock surged 170% in 2015 due to unexpected developments. Use stop-loss orders to manage risk.
- **Costs:** You must pay dividends and interest on borrowed stocks. Avoid high-dividend stocks unless your holding period is very short. Compare broker fees to minimize borrowing costs.

Contra ETFs and Put Options
Contra ETFs mitigate many risks associated with shorting stocks directly. Put options are another viable alternative, although they require more expertise.

Advantages and Disadvantages of Short Selling

When to Short Sell: bear market
Short selling is most effective in a plunging market. However, the market typically rises over time, so be cautious during periods of growth.

High Risks
- Theoretical losses are unlimited.
- Certain sectors (e.g., biotech, banking, or insurance) are particularly volatile, driven by earnings announcements or regulatory approvals.
- Market manipulation and insider activity may unpredictably influence stock prices.

Tax Considerations
Gains from short sales are typically taxed as short-term capital gains, which are subject to higher rates than long-term gains. Consult a tax advisor to stay compliant with current laws.

Fundamental and Technical Analyses in Short Selling

Importance of Analysis
For short-term trades, technical analysis often outweighs fundamental analysis. Identify stocks with poor fundamentals and negative technical indicators. Avoid high-risk candidates such as low-cap stocks or those with strong insider buying trends.

Key Metrics
- Negative earnings yield (EY = 1 / P/E).
- High debt-to-equity ratio (> 0.5 for most industries).
- Poor momentum indicators (e.g., negative SMA-20% or SMA-50%).

Stock Selection Tools
Platforms like Finviz and Fidelity offer valuable screening tools. Look for stocks with a poor Equity Summary Score or negative insider transaction metrics.

Common Pitfalls in Short Selling
Avoid High-Risk Stocks
Do not short stocks in trending up sectors, stocks with strong momentum,

or those driven by speculative hype (e.g., Tesla and FAANG stocks in 2015–2020).

Manage Risk with Stops
Use mental stop-loss thresholds to cap losses. For instance, close a trade if the stock rises by a predetermined percentage above your shorting price.

Short Squeezes
Stocks with over 25% of their float shorted are at high risk of short squeezes. Monitor short interest carefully.

When to Sell Short
Timing is Critical
The best time to short is during a broad market plunge. Focus on the weakest sectors and their worst-performing stocks. However, even in a downturn, avoid stocks with strong potential for acquisition or recovery.

More considerations
- Do not trade in the first hour (first half hour for me) as there may be new developments overnight.
- I use subscription services. I do not trade on Monday or the day after a holiday, as the data is at least one day late.
- Your broker may limit your short trade (limited order) to be valid for the day; check this with your broker.
- Your broker may need to approve whether you can short stocks based on your experiences.
- When you sell short and are using limit orders, enter a sell price higher than the last trade price just like selling a stock.
- Close the short position when your trade loses a predefined percentage which depends on your personal tolerance.
- Put Option is similar to shorting a company. However, it is not for beginners.

Random cases

- As of 7/2013, shorting Amazon, Netflix and Tesla as a group was not beneficial. It is best to stay away from shorting, except during the plunging (from peak to bottom) in the market cycle.
- Did you watch 60 minutes on Lumber Liquidators in 2015? That's how you short stocks. Find out why the company boosts its profit and stock price in such a short period. If it has been proven to be fishy, place a

- short position. However, when the news becomes public, it could be too late for us to act.
- As of 1/15/2015, GME had a short squeeze. The stock was up by 10% with a decent earnings announcement. I am surprised that the short % was over 45% for a decent stock with a decent P/E. It had low debts and decent cash reserves. The shorters (same as short sellers) must be losing their shirts. Even for the fundamentally sound Netflix and Tesla, the shorters (one by a famous hedge fund manager) would lose a fortune; Tesla was at one time 11 times its lowest price.
- I found out the hard way in not using stops to protect my trade.

My experience in selling short

It is easier to make money on the right side of the market. From March, 2009 to today (August, 2018), the market has been rising. Hence it is easy to make money in the stock market by buying an ETF such as SPY.

As of 2021, the market may be peaking and it may seem to be overpriced. The market is fundamentally unsound (e.g., high P/E example), but technically sound (e.g., high moving averages).

Let me examine how the SPY performs and how my short strategies (about 30) performed in recent months in 2018. As in this book, most performances are annualized without including dividends. All figures are for illustration purposes.

Perform.	May	June	July	Aug.	Sep.	Avg.
SPY	38%	-7%	40%	34%	8%	23%
Strategies	-88%	-52%	42%	-74%	66%	-21%

The averages of my short strategies are not doing well. It loses 21% while SPY gains 23% for the last 5 months. The market may be changing for shorters. If I use the top strategies, I could have achieved positive returns even in this market. It shows several promising hints for shorting the market. Use paper trading.

- The market may be declining from July in the above test dates.
- The strategies are better now with 2 months being positive out of the last 3.
- I further look at big winners and big losers. I identify timely metrics (a.k.a. momentum by some vendors) as the only one that matters.
- Several strategies use 52-week highs. They did not perform as well as I expected.
- I will exclude risky stocks such as low average volume and low cap.

- Drug companies appear to be risky but some have great returns for shorting. Use stops particularly for drug companies.
- My small tests do not show any differences in holding the stocks for 4 weeks or 6 weeks. Momentum could change in short durations.
- If you subscribe to a database that is refreshed by the end of the day, skip Monday or the day after a holiday. If not, pay attention to moving averages, RSI(14) and other technical metrics from Finviz.com.
- Some brokers may not have the stocks you want to short and/or expire your orders by the end of the day. This is an introductory guideline on how to short stocks.
- I did not short for a while as the market had been rising. In September, 2020, I started to short again as I expected the long-term rise of the market would come to an end. My broker charges about 8.5% while another one offers 2.5% interest. It took some time to switch shorting and funding to this broker and had to be familiarized with their way to trade.
- On 9/2/2020, I bought AXDX instead of shorting it due to the high insider purchases (139% from Finvix) and high shorting percent (46% that could lead to a short squeeze).
- My broker #1 has more restrictions than broker #2 such as not extending the trade to next day.
- Avoid the following conditions: turnaround, stocks with big losses, short squeeze and double bottom.
- A YouTube video on shorting:
https://www.youtube.com/watch?v=oMnmTV5HF5Y

Margin

You need a margin permission to sell short. Check out the interest you're your broker charges for selling short. Margin should not be used extensively. It is expensive and most brokers try every trick they can to squeeze profits from all transactions to subsidize their low-commission incomes. Usually, you can borrow up to 40% of your current position and the rules and the margin rates vary among brokers.

Many investors had losses during the last two market plunges. However, many including myself had made a killing in 2003 and 2009 using margin. I use it for the following reasons.

- For convenience in placing buy orders that exceed my cash position in my taxable accounts.
- I can pay back my outstanding margin loans from my home equity loan (check the current tax laws) as it is far, far lower than my broker's margin interest rates. However, I do not recommend this for conservative investors.

Links & Articles
Introduction https://www.youtube.com/watch?v=oMnmTV5HF5Y
https://www.youtube.com/watch?v=2VQp6-alQMg
Tilson
Put Options. http://en.wikipedia.org/wiki/Put_option
https://www.youtube.com/watch?v=TyZsemV_0YA
Fidelity Video: Options.https://www.fidelity.com/learning-center/options/finding-options-strategies/options-analysis-tool-video
Fidelity Video: Selling short.https://www.fidelity.com/learning-center/trading/selling-short-video
Option: https://www.youtube.com/watch?v=EfmTWu2yn5Q

Filler: How to win the Powerball
1. Go to the local lottery office and ask to buy all combinations with a check dated today when it is over 500 M. It worked yesterday. If you have more than one Powerball winner (or someone using the same trick described here), you may have to skip town.

2. Borrow my time machine which is being repaired or the car from "Back to the Future".

Filler: **On 5G**
If we chose not to use Huawei 5G, we may be 2 years behind. It is likely that we would even be behind some developing countries in Africa.

It happened before in 4G: When the Orientals were watching TV from the mobile phones during their commute, we're reading Kindle books. I bet books are more educational than movies. However, 5G changes the world and hopefully for the better.

As of this writing, ATT's 5G is just 4G with 'potential' or a marketing gimmick. VZ's 5G has used a lot of Huawei's patents even though they're not Huawei's products. Huawei asked Verizon to pay 1 billion for the patent use. If they do not pay for any 'regulations' from our government, China and many countries will not pay royalties on many U.S. patents.

Common parameters for short candidates

Two basic ways to screen (same as finding stocks) short candidates discussed here are:
- Use Fidelity.com to screen stocks with Equity Summary Score < 5.
- Use Finviz.com to screen stocks with the following parameters.

You can use one of the two screeners or other screeners to limit the number of stocks to be evaluated further. If you Finviz's screener, check out the parameters in Fidelity, and vice versa.

Here are my suggested parameters in using Finviz.com. Vary the values and parameters according to your risk tolerance and market conditions. Finviz.com is not complete in all functions, but it could be the best free screener that incorporates both the fundamental and the technical criteria. The following should screen too few or even no stocks, and you need to relax your parameters. I prefer 2 to 10 stocks for further evaluation. If you have more time, screen more by relaxing your parameters (a.k.a. metrics) and vice versa if you have less time.

Suggested screening parameters

Parameter	Value	Explanation
General		
Market Cap (M)	>300 M	Prefer larger companies. Some prefer 1B and / or stocks in S&P 500 index.
Price	>2	Skip penny stocks.
In all 3 Exchanges	In	Smaller exchanges are risky.
Avg. Volume	>100K	Or > 100 times your short position.
Country	USA	Personal preference.
Dividend%	0%	Shorters need to pay dividends.
Float Short	5 to 15	Above 20 could lead to short squeeze.
Analyst Rec	Sell	Fidelity's Equity Summary Score is better to me.
Fundamental		
Forward P/E	0 or negative	Also use Yahoo!Finance's EV/EBITDA.
ROE	< 5	
QQ earnings	< 0	Quarter to Quarter (last year)
QQ sales	< 0	
PEG	Negative	
Insider Trans. (Buy %)	< -5%	Confirm it by scrolling down to see the date and size of the selling.
Inst. Trans.	Negative	

Technical		
SMA50%	Negative	SMA-200% for long holding period.
RSI(14)	<30	Personal preference

Test out the screen(s) until it is proven. You may want to have at least four screens for 4 different stages of the market (described in Book 6: Market Timing in this book), as different market stages have different market conditions.

You want to sort the most important parameter in your screen. Starting your research on the top stocks. For example, on Fidelity's website, I would sort Equity Summary Score in ascending order.

In Finviz, there are many options for Finviz's screener such as SMA-50% in ascending order. If you use a spreadsheet, use Earnings Yield (= 1 / (Forward P/E). Be careful that Finviz and many screeners may not handle negative earnings.

What to do with the screened stocks
After you set up the screen parameters and test it until you are comfortable, you can save your screen. It only takes a minute to run the screen and it should display a number of stocks.

You need to evaluate every screened stock before you short sell a stock.

The two screeners described do not have EV/EBITDA, which is available in Yahoo!Finance. The earnings yield is better to understand and it is equal to EBITDA/EV by flipping the two numbers. It can be done easily using a spreadsheet. The more negative it is, the better it is for short selling.

Stocks screened by Fidelity.
Check out the timing score which is available from many sites; the worse the stock is, the better it is for short selling. However, do not select the worst timing grade as there is no way to go but up. If available, check out the comparison of the P/E to its five-year average ad to its average for its sector. Now check out the Finviz's parameters as described in the above table, particularly the following parameters: Debt / Equity, SMA-50%, Short percent (avoid stocks with over 20%) and Insider Trans.

Stocks screened by Finviz.
Check out the parameters available from Fidelity.

We want to use the best features of Fidelity, Finviz and Yahoo!Finance.

5   Covered calls

Covered calls are an options strategy that involves selling call options on stocks you already own. While this approach generates consistent income, it caps potential gains if the stock's price rises significantly.

It is like collecting rent from the apartment you bought. The difference is that the renter has an option to buy the apartment at a preset time and price.

The rent is quite substantial if you do good planning. To start with, you want to buy stocks that have a market to sell. Usually, they are large companies with high trading volumes.

Since one contract is for 100 shares of a stock, you cannot sell a covered call on 50 shares of a stock. On the other hand, when you have 1,000 stocks, the commission of 10 contracts would be more than the cost of 1 contract depending on your broker's schedule.

It is time consuming to keep track of the covered calls but it is well worth your time and effort. If the stock price exceeds the strike price of your covered call, you may want to buy the same shares back, so you would not miss any further appreciation of this stock.

However, if it is in a taxable account and you have a loss in a forced sell, do not buy it back otherwise the tax loss is not allowed (i.e., a wash sale) for the year as of 2016. When the contract expires, you may want to start another contract on the same stock if the stock has not been sold.

Covered calls do have their disadvantages such as losing profits for rising stocks (higher than the strike prices), higher commission rates and sometimes forcing you to sell at a higher tax rate for short-term capital gains in taxable accounts. It is avoidable by using covered calls on stocks that are qualified for long-term capital gains. In addition, you need to buy them back when they increase in price beyond your strike price or lose its potential to appreciate further. Using another put could keep you from not losing any gains beyond the strike price. However, I prefer to use my time in more productive ways and this insurance is not cheap. One's opinion.

One company advertises their techniques using covered calls which could give their users 3 to 6% monthly returns. If you believe in this fantasy, you do not need this book. There is no free lunch.

How to sell covered calls

First you need to open an account with your broker and apply to trade options including covered calls.

Check how your broker charges commissions. Ask how much they charge for one contract and 10 contracts of a stock.

The covered call is an agreement to sell the rights to the buyer of the stock at the strike price for a specific date range (a.k.a. expiration date). Typically, options expire on Fridays.

You need to write covered calls on the stocks you already own. One contract is 100 shares of stocks. Check out the option chain to select the price, expiration period and the strike price. Normally, the strike price should be higher than the current market price. You may want to have an expiration date 2 weeks or longer and better on the Friday of the third week when the volume of options is heaviest usually. When the contract is expiring in a few days, the contract has little value and most likely the small 'rent' is not worth the risk and the commission.

When the covered call is sold, you receive the 'rent' immediately and any dividend during the 'rental' period.

When the option is 'called' due to a price rise above the strike price, your stock will be sold and you will have to pay the regular commission.

At this point, evaluate the stock to check whether you want to buy it back. If the stock surges, you may have to pay a higher price – thus losing the extra appreciation. I recommend you buy back that stock. In addition, you may have to pay a higher capital gains tax if it is held less than the required period for long-term capital gains in a taxable account.

Note. Notice that some stocks are not optionable and/or not practical to write options on. Some brokers charge a flat rate for the first contract (such as $7) and an incremental fee for each additional contract. One of mine charges nothing. Shop around as the fees vary if you write a lot of covered calls.

The best stocks for covered calls are large US companies with a large average volume. The option (a.k.a. the 'rent') pays better for volatile companies such as high-tech companies. I prefer the difference between the current price and the strike price to be about 6% and the stock price is over $20,000. I do not recommend selling covered calls before the earnings date (from Finviz for example), as you may lose the appreciation when the earnings is good.

My recent experience

I sold Netflix covered calls with the strike price about 2% higher and a 3% premium (from my memory) but the price shot up 12% higher in one day, so I was potentially losing 7% profit. However, it turned out to be a good experience as Netflix went downhill later (8/2012).

Normally I prefer to sell covered options for stocks with a quantity from 100 to 600 shares (i.e., 1 to 6 contracts) for the longest time (about 2-3 months). Some non-volatile and small stocks are not candidates to write covered calls on. Some stocks are not optionable. Typically, high-tech stocks have a higher premium to be collected as their stock prices fluctuate more. The right stocks can generate 10% or even more a year in addition to the fluctuations of the stock prices.

In general, if I feel the market will be down for the period, I use covered calls especially for stocks holding over one year (unless I have short-term loss to offset any short-term gains) in taxable accounts. Watch out for any tax change that may affect your total return.

Recently I attended a sales pitch on a 3-day training course on a strategy for making 24% per year and it is quite possible especially with the S&P 500 returns about the same. I wish it were available to me 15 years ago. It seems to be too good to be true.

Links

http://en.wikipedia.org/wiki/Covered_call)
https://www.youtube.com/watch?v=dzMOnI4Eh04
https://www.youtube.com/watch?v=7a0BRIAufBA
https://www.youtube.com/watch?v=hbLp63AOceo

Filler: Recent covered call experiences
It is better to have a covered call with a Strike $102 than selling it at $102. "Call" is for covered call, so select "Call" if there is a choice of either "Call" and "Put". It should be "Sell to Open" for covered calls. My broker does not use the current account when I enter a covered call. These two 'defects' caused me hundreds of dollars. I negotiated with my second broker to give me free option trades as my other one did not charge commission.
My estimate: Make 1% or 12% more a year using covered call after considering the lost profits due to appreciation beyond the strike price. For ease to remember, "Call" up your mom, and "Put" if down. "Up" expects the stock to go up. My estimates.

6 Diversification

LTCM, a hedge fund which was run by smart people, and Isaac Newton both made one serious mistake in investing. They bet all their money in one investing vehicle and lost it all in one bet. They were the smartest folks on earth but they violated one basic principle in investing: diversification.

Another example was the potato famine. Irish people made a good living with their primary crop: potato. When a virus came, they lost all the potatoes and caused the potato famine.

Diversification improves a portfolio's performance in the long run and it reduces risk. Diversification includes other asset classes besides stocks such as oil, gold, cash (yes even cash as a safety net to grasp better opportunities ahead), real estate, etc. However, stocks historically produce the best return. In addition, most stocks are quite liquid as it takes a minute to sell them compared to selling a house for example. You can buy other assets such as gold (GLD), money market funds and real estate (via REITs) via their low-cost ETFs.

When an asset is overvalued, it will return to the average historical value with one or two exceptions. Gold is one exception, but it is partly due to the depreciation of the USD and the previous prolonged downfall of gold adjusted for inflation.

Simply put, owning 10 to 15 good stocks with less than three stocks in the same sector (which have to be good sectors to start with) achieves a diversification goal for most people. When one sector crashes, you still have two more good sectors.

Every one's situation is different:

- Depends on your wealth and your age.
  For younger folks with limited wealth (less than $50,000 to invest), a portfolio of 3 stocks (preferably most in ETFs) in different sectors or one diversified ETF could be enough. Your objective in investing is saving money for a down payment for a house, paying your loans including college loans and/or improving your earning power by taking classes.

Retirees may want to maintain a larger percentage of your holdings in cash and/or invested in bonds (long-term bonds could be very risky when the interest rates are going up). Those wealthy enough can fully invest in stocks as losing 50% of their portfolio may not alter their lifestyle. Most business owners should invest in stocks and other vehicles instead of plowing back into their businesses in order to diversify their investments.

Portfolios with more than a billion dollars such as in most large mutual funds could own 10 stocks with 100 million each, but that is just too risky for me. In this case, I prefer they own 20 stocks with 50 million each.

Holding cash is safe but it loses its value due to inflation. To illustrate this point, consider these three scenarios in 1950:

1. An apartment bought in for $10,000 in NYC or in your home town.

2. An investment in the Dow Jones 30 Industrials for $10,000.

3. A 3.5% certificate of deposit or one of the U.S. Treasuries for your $10,000.

By now, all real estate investments should have appreciated many, many times over and most stock shares value would have multiplied also. The $10,000 CD gain has lost real value due to inflation. Our capitalist system punishes us for not taking risks. In the long term, risk is smoothed out over time.

- The excessive frequency in re-balancing your portfolio for diversification takes up time from evaluating other stocks. It may cost you in transaction fees but they are low in today's self-directed brokerage accounts. In addition, it may have some tax consequences in taxable accounts.

  The advantage of churning the portfolio (but not excessively) can improve the quality of your portfolio with most updated information about the companies you invest in.

  Many brokers display your current diversification in your monthly statement summaries. If not, use a simple spreadsheet to classify the sectors and the asset classes in your portfolio.

- Diversification can easily be achieved by buying indexed funds and/or ETFs. They are less volatile. I recommend it to all folks with less than $50,000 to invest.
- Diversification does not mean to pick simply a stock in other sector that has the opposite correlation of the stock you own. The stock quality comes first.
- Diversification takes a back seat to spotting market plunges. When most stocks plunge such as during 2007-2008, diversification does not save your portfolio, but spotting and reacting to market plunges will.
- Some of our stocks will lose values. If they were due to our mistakes, write them down and learn from them. If they were frauds (not avoidable in many cases), diversification would limit our losses.
- Over diversified is not good either. It takes out our resources to 2monitor the stocks we own. I usually have a lot of candidates of stocks to buy in a rising market. To compromise, stay focus on stocks that I have heavy bets. Focus investing could be very profitable.

My suggestions on diversification

Portfolio up to	Strategy	For stock pickers
$ 50,000	ETF that simulates the market	5 stocks
$100,000	80% in ETF and 20% in a sector ETF(s)	10 stocks
$500,000	10 stocks with less than 3 in same sector.	15 stocks with less than 3 in same sector.
$1 Million	15 stocks + at least 20% in ETFs.	20 or more stocks depending on your time available and less than 4 in same sector.

As described, everyone's situation is different. If you have more time for investing, you should be able to handle more than 10 stocks. Playing market timing (i.e., switching to cash) depends on one's risk tolerance. If you are good in stock picking, you should buy stocks instead of ETFs. On a personal note, I usually have more than 10 stocks.

7 High frequency trading (HFT)

If we can adjust to HFT, we take advantage of it instead of being taken advantage of. Is the flash crash in 5/2010 caused by HFT or just an error in order entry? They could drive the market to a temporary low and hence cause all the orders traded to be at lower prices and change most stop orders to be executed as market orders.

I use market orders very infrequently and only for some good reasons. I seldom use a stop loss that can be converted into market orders that can be manipulated. If you have time, do a stop order manually by watching closely the stock price and execute a market order on the stock.

HFT represents about half of all trading I bet. When the market plunges, it will plunge deeper and faster due to HFT.

HFT will see their black swan and their fund managers will lose their shirts and out-of-work for good. If you are one of these folks, you may want to brush up your resumes and do not spend your loot as your days are numbered.

My proposal:

1. Change the SEC fee into two parts: fixed and variable depending on the size of the order. The fixed fees would eliminate the penny profits for each trade.

2. Identify the servers via their IP addresses. Make them back runners instead of front runners for these trades.

Afterthoughts

- HFT favors large cap stocks with high-volume trades and low prices. (http://money.cnn.com/2013/07/18/investing/high-speed-traders-stocks/index.html?iid=H_INV_News)

- A Seeking Alpha article. http://seekingalpha.com/article/2125833-how-to-beat-high-frequency-traders

8   Tax avoidance

Tax avoidance is a good way to save some money legally. Tax laws change all the time. Check Wikipedia on current investment taxes. Consult your tax lawyer as my knowledge in taxes is limited, and the tax laws are always changing.

In general for Federal returns on your taxable accounts (as opposed to IRA, Roth IRA, IRA-Rollover and 401K), you have to pay taxes on dividends either at the ordinary income rate or at a qualified rate which is usually lower. If the stock that was held longer than a year, you pay long-term capital tax (max. 20% as of 2020). The short-term capital tax rate at the ordinary income rate is up to 37% as of 2020. In addition, you may have to pay state and local taxes. Currently, you can offset $3,000 or up to your total losses from your regular income.

Do not implement what I did as tax laws change frequently and every one's situation is different. Here is what I did and I hope it will be applicable to you.

- Sold the most profitable stocks that I held more than a year in taxable accounts in 2021 to qualify for long-term capital gains. Usually, they have more favorable tax treatments than the short-term capital gains, which are treated as ordinary income. I bought some back. I maintained a 15% tax bracket, so the tax bill from Uncle Sam is virtually 0 (not exactly due to more tax on social security and Medicare as a result of the trades). I still had to pay state tax. As a retiree, I can control my income

- Converted part of my Rollover IRA to Roth in 2012 and 2013. I paid taxes today. However, the Roth conversion gives me tax-free appreciation for the future trades in this account and it will lower taxes and my minimum withdrawal requirement in the future. Check whether it is still available.

- The taxes from dividends in the retirement accounts are deferred but eventually they will be treated as regular income when they are withdrawn. Very few people have higher income during their retirement. If you are the lucky few due to the successful investing in your retirement accounts, you may end up with a higher tax bracket during your retirement, particularly when you are forced to withdraw at age 70 ½.

- Gifted some appreciated stocks to my children. The current price of the gifted stock is used in calculating the total cost allowed, not the price you paid for them. The long-term capital gains may be waived for adult children with incomes below a specified level. I prefer the value stocks that have potential for long-term appreciation. It is good for them and not good for Uncle Sam. You can gift up to $15,000 (in 2021) for each spouse to each child without paying any Federal tax. For a family of four, you and your spouse can gift up to $60,000 (= 15,000 * 4) a year. It is a long time before your children or grandchildren withdraw, it is better to use an ETF that stimulates the market such as SPY. Also consider the loop back period for gifts. Check out this link. https://www.irs.gov/businesses/small-businesses-self-employed/frequently-asked-questions-on-gift-taxes

The cost basis of the transferred stock is quite complicated. Check out the current tax law. The cost basis of the appreciated stocks is carried to the receiver, so it would lower your capital taxes as most of us are in higher tax brackets than our children.

From my experience, the cost basis of the depreciated stocks after the transfer is the market price on the transfer day as of 2016. I do not understand it enough to comment but just to tell you what I have experienced. I tried to offset my son's unexpected short-term capital gain by transferring a losing stock and that did not work.

- My lawyer set up trusts for me including my house. They will hopefully avoid probate. From the current tax law (as of 2016), the cost basis of your stocks will be stepped up or down to the stock prices on that day you pass away. Ask your heirs to keep a business paper for the stock prices or tell your brokers to adjust the cost basis on the day you pass away. Of course, you have to tell your heirs now to take care of these tasks. Again, ask your tax lawyer for details.

Make sure you specify the beneficiaries in your and your spouse's accounts to avoid probate. Check your local state laws. Some states take more than a year to finish the probate process for a house. As of 2014, my state (Mass.) has an exemption of 1 million, not portable to your spouse, and they calculate the entire estate when it exceeds the exemption. There is no estate tax if my estate is a million dollars. I have to pay a rate on 1,000,001 if it just exceeds it by one dollar. That's why we should move 20 miles north to New Hampshire.

I estimate that it takes about three years for the average estate to be distributed. You want to cut down the duration by having a will to start with, so you do not want to pay extra for your lawyer.

- At age 70 ½ (as of 2021), you are required to withdraw them in a schedule and it could put you in a higher tax bracket. Roth withdrawal is not counted in the mandatory withdrawal for a person's lifetime. Check the current tax laws.
- Roth IRAs, if qualified, could be the best deal for most. However, you have to use after-tax money to fund your Roth IRA.
- I simulate my next year via my tax preparation software and adjust my income accordingly.
- Most oil partnerships and many MLPs require you to file special tax forms for non-retirement accounts in 2017. I avoided most of them as my time is limited. Some ETFs require you to file the complicated K-1 (vs 1099) in your tax return. You can find this requirement in ETFdb.com. You can avoid them

- by not buying these ETFs, or buy them in my non-taxable accounts. Usually, the taxes on these dividends are lowered as they are treated as the return of investment after depreciation.
- There is a $500,000 exemption from the profits of selling your house with some restrictions.

- Harvest the tax loss for future use and take the $3,000 offset to your income. My state does not allow me to write off the $3,000. Hence, my short-term loss for the future is $3,000 more for my state than the Federal.

- Avoid wash sales in your taxable accounts
  http://en.wikipedia.org/wiki/Wash_sale

  You cannot claim the loss for the year if you buy back the stock within 30 days. Before I buy, I check whether I sold this loser in the last 30 days. Before I sell a loser, I check whether I bought it in the last 30 days.

  I placed one order to sell a loser at a higher price and another one to buy it back at a lower price. When there is a big swing in price for that stock, both orders were executed within 30 days. I cannot claim the loss of the sold stock for that year. However, the loss can be adjusted to the cost basis of the newly-acquired stock as of 2013.

  There are many ways to avoid it. Try not to buy it back within 30 days (check the current regulation) and this is the best way. IRS has more restrictions and it is better not to push it to the limit. Buy a similar stock in the same sector. Buy it in your children's account. Again, check the current tax laws.
  - I bought my annuity trying to save taxes after all retirement accounts had been fully funded. So far, it turns out my tax rate is higher after retirement. I do not recommend most annuities due to the fees. Most annuities have high commission fees and that is why most financial advisors want to sell them to you.

Afterthoughts
- Tax audit signs.
  http://money.cnn.com/gallery/pf/taxes/2014/03/14/tax-audit/index.html?iid=HP_LN
  Your business would be treated as a hobby if you do not have a profit in three out of the last five years. Day traders and businesses can deduct all the trading expenses. Some form an investing company in some Caribbean Island to avoid paying taxes. Again, check the current tax laws.
- As of 2013, the dividend tax is at 20% max. Do not believe it is no tax in tax-deferred accounts. When you withdraw, it will be treated as a regular income and it can be as high as almost 40% (as of 2013). Your dividend tax rate depends on your income.
- Some countries and some foreign stocks listed in U.S. exchanges withheld part of our dividends and gains. I avoid them if possible.

- When you trade 5 times or more a week, investigate whether you're eligible to trade as a business by the current tax rule. A business allows its owner to deduct business expenses.
- IRA Rollover to Roth: https://www.youtube.com/watch?v=BkxYuQ0Vb88
- Fidelity: Investment tax. https://www.fidelity.com/learning-center/mutual-funds/tax-implications-bond-funds

  ETF Taxes on Foreign Stocks: http://seekingalpha.com/article/2491465-foreign-withholding-taxes-in-international-equity-etfs

To gift or not to gift (2024 rules)
Advantages. Shift tax burden (capital appreciation and holding period) to one with lower tax bracket. 0% tax for long-term capital gain under $47,025 for single filers.

Disadvantages. Minor accounts are taxed at the parents' rates. It also applies to full-time students under the age of 24 with earned incomes not covering at least 50% of living expenses and education expenses. It also decreases the eligibility of financial aids.
Also, exceeding the allowed $18,000 per recipient will count as the lifetime gift and estate tax exemption ($13.61 million per individual). **Check with your lawyer** before taking any actions.

Examples search "Google estate tax 2023" from the web:
Some states do not have estate tax while some do not have inherited tax. The current step-up cost basis exempts the heirs to pay the Federal tax on the day of death.

"You cannot put your individual retirement account (IRA) in a trust while you are living. You can, however, name a trust as the beneficiary of your IRA and dictate how the assets are to be handled after your death. This applies to all types of IRAs, including traditional, Roth, SEP, and SIMPLE IRAs."

" A "step-down" occurs if someone dies owning property that has declined in value. In that case, the basis is lowered to the date-of-death value. Proper planning calls for seeking to avoid this loss of basis. Giving the property away before death won't preserve the basis"

"Estate tax in MA. About 5% estimate. Sell the house to take advantage of the life-time deduction. Federal exemption is high to be concerned to me. You do not need a lawyer who charges about $500 per hour (do not cheap talk w the lawyer)."

"If you inherit a Roth IRA, you're free of taxes. But with a traditional IRA, any amount you withdraw is subject to ordinary income taxes."
https://www.bankrate.com/retirement/inherited-ira-rules/

" certain heirs, known as "non-eligible designated beneficiaries," have to deplete inherited retirement accounts within 10 years, known as the "10-year-rule." Non-eligible designated beneficiaries are heirs who aren't a spouse, minor child, disabled, chronically ill or certain trusts."

Links
Tax Avoidance: http://en.wikipedia.org/wiki/Tax_avoidance
https://www.youtube.com/watch?v=9UV313785zc
Millionaire: https://www.youtube.com/watch?v=9UV313785zc
Tax Law: http://en.wikipedia.org/wiki/Income_tax_%28U.S.%29
Without paying (gift tax):
http://en.wikipedia.org/wiki/Gift_tax_in_the_United_States#Gift_tax_exemptions
http://www.irs.gov/Businesses/Small-Businesses-&-Self-Employed/What%27s-New---Estate-and-Gift-Tax
AMT: http://en.wikipedia.org/wiki/Alternative_minimum_tax
Estate planning fun. http://tonyp4idea.blogspot.com/2014/08/estate-planning-101-for-me.html
Taxes on stocks: https://www.youtube.com/watch?v=EKYMbsjUUtE
Tax avoidance: https://www.youtube.com/watch?v=tXou5pM7zh0
Capital gain: https://www.youtube.com/watch?v=ezPs4ibFsNU&t=2678s
How the rich avoid paying taxes
https://www.youtube.com/watch?v=-hSJWt4SwzI
https://www.youtube.com/watch?v=24804zc9RmI
Capital gain: https://www.youtube.com/watch?v=sKB_FYHB9CE
Incomes not taxed. https://www.youtube.com/watch?v=B05OtAHXuJI

9   Trading plan

A trading plan is essential for successful investing and trading. It should include the following elements:
1. **Overall Objective**: Define what you aim to achieve.
2. **Entry Criteria**: Specify when to buy, what stocks to buy, and how many.
3. **Exit Criteria**: Determine when to sell and under what conditions.
4. **Monitoring**: Establish how and when to review your strategies.

Discipline
Sticking to your plan prevents emotions from interfering with decisions. For example, check your portfolio value on a set schedule, such as once a week or month, instead of frequently throughout the day, to avoid unnecessary stress.

Setting Objectives
Define clear and realistic goals. Examples include:

- Earning 5% annual returns over 10 years with minimal risk.
- Conserving wealth rather than outperforming the market.

Example Strategies:
- **Non-Taxable Accounts**: Focus on value stocks and review them semi-annually.
- **Roth Accounts**: Seek short-term gains with momentum stocks.
- **Conservative Accounts**: Prioritize safety by investing heavily in cash and stocks during favorable markets.

Flexibility and Adaptability
Every investor's plan is unique. Start with a simple plan and adjust as needed. While maintaining discipline, adapt strategies to market conditions. For example, shift focus to growth investments during bull markets.

A sample trading plan
You can review what stocks to buy and sell once a week or once a month depending on how active you are in the market. List the criteria you buy stocks. Define your average holding period for a specific objective. Also define when and why you want to sell a stock.

Personally, I prefer to have two sections: Common Tasks and Specific Tasks. Common Tasks include 4 categories: **Weekly Tasks, Monthly Tasks, Quarterly Tasks and Yearly Tasks**. Evaluate stocks to buy on Tuesday for example. Update the portfolio and check out the chart on marketing timing on the first week of every month. Review the performance of your portfolio quarterly (or half a year). Perform year-end tasks.

Specific Tasks include tasks we have to do on specific dates such as filing tax returns, transferring stocks to my children and renewing investing subscriptions.

Weekly Tasks:

Mon	Covered calls
	IBD-50 review.
Tue	Finding momentum stocks.
Wed	Sell Momentum stocks held over 2 weeks.

Monthly Tasks:

Mon	House keep all stock transactions.
	Review market timing and any corrections.

Tue	Find stocks using selected strategies.
	Find stocks using screens.
Wed	Evaluate stocks
Thur.	Buy stocks
	Review sector rotation.
Fri	Evaluate any stocks to sell.
Any	Monitor momentum performance.

Quarterly Tasks:

1	Monthly tasks.
2	Monitor performance.

Year-end Tasks:

1	Tax adjustments for taxable accounts including selling losers in non-retirement accounts.
2	EOY purchases.
3	Fully invested on Dec. 15-Jan. 15 esp. on 2nd year of the presidential cycle.
4	Monitor performance of screens.
5	Review Dogs of the DOW.
6	Optional. Gift appreciated stocks to your heirs.

Review your performance and your trading plan

If you do not know what you did, how will you know where you're going? Review every trade transaction and monitor their performances.

Learn from your losses. Did you stick to the trading plan? If you lose too many times and/or take too much risk (evidenced by many losses and/or big losses), you may have to modify your trading plan. However, the trading plan may not be good in the current market (for example trading growth stocks in the bottom of the market cycle). If you have to let the winners get away too often, review what went wrong. Sometimes, a lesson is not a lesson but just bad luck.

Learn about yourself

Learn about your risk tolerance, how mentally prepared you are for big losses and big wins. If you have more money than you can use for the rest of your life, conserving wealth should be your primary objective.

To illustrate with a portfolio of one million dollars, your average stock position is $100,000 if you only have time to follow 10 stocks.

To many, a portfolio with 10 stocks is quite risky. You may consider having 10 stocks of $50,000 each and invest the rest ($500,000) in ETFs, mutual funds and/or bonds. Ensure that no more than three stocks (some prefer 2) are in the same sector.

Prepare for some losses. Reduce the average loss to only small amounts. I prefer to use 25% maximum loss for volatile stocks and 20% for other stocks. Some prefer using stop loss orders of 10% to 15% loss. Today's market is too volatile to stop losses less than 15%. My opinion. You should have some big winners but you may let some get away by selling them too early. One way is to use stop orders (10% less than the market price) and adjust the stops periodically (say a month) for the appreciating stocks.

Summary
Write down your objective and what tasks you do every week, month and year in the inside back cover of this book (hard copy only). If you don't do it now, you never will.

Trading journal
Keep a journal of your trades along with your ideas. Review it from time to time and look at why you bought a specific stock. It is far better than trying to recall the experiences from memory.

Your journal should be part of a trading plan. You use it to monitor the performance of your trade and how the current market conditions affect your performance. When you use a screen that is for a short term, you want to exit the trade accordingly. When the screen does not perform, it may mean the market is not favorable to this screen and you should skip using it with actual money. Here is a screenshot of mine. I group the trades under different screens.

	A	B	C	D	E	F	G	H	I	J	K	L	M	N	O	P
1	Performance			Price		$					Date			Return		Status
2	Stock	QTY	Account	B.P.	S.P.	Buy $	Sell $	Profit	Curr P.	% better	Buy Date	Sell Date	Days		Ann. Ret	
3	LAKE	2,000	401K	10.93	13.99	21,860	27,975	6,115	9.45	48%	07/15/15	11/24/15	132	28%	77%	S
4	ABTL	1,500	ROTH	16.60	18.50	24,900	27,750	2,850			07/16/15	09/10/16	422	11%	10%	B
5	ELMD	5,000	401K	4.01	4.22	20,054	21,095	1,041	4.81	-12%	03/17/16	04/07/16	21	5%	90%	S

When using an excel spreadsheet, the formulae is:
B.P. (Buy Price) =IF(B3="","",IF(D3="","",D3*B3))
% better =IF(I3="","",(E3-I3)/I3)
Days =IF(K3="","",L3-K3)
Return =IF(D3="","",(E-D3)/D3)
Ann. Ret =IF(N3="","",N3*365/M3)
Add any columns you want such as Account.

10   My A.B.C. on bonds

Bonds are categorized into various types based on duration and issuer. Examples include Treasury bonds, municipal bonds, corporate bonds, and junk bonds.

Interest Rate Risk
As of 2013, long-term Treasury bonds were considered risky due to low interest rates. When rates rise, bond prices fall, particularly for long-term bonds.

Key Insights:
- **Economic Cycles**: Bond performance often correlates with economic conditions. For instance, high-yield bonds rebounded strongly in 2009 after the financial crisis.
- **Duration and Risk**: Long-term bonds are more sensitive to interest rate changes than short-term bonds.

Here are random comments on bonds

- Japan has had almost virtually zero interest rates for a long while. If you borrow 1 M from them at almost 0% and invest in another country's bond at 8%, you may think you win. However, you need to consider the risk in converting the country's currency back to Japanese Yen, inflation, bond loss, and taxes.

- In 2008, almost all assets lost money. However, some high-yield bonds (or junk bonds) made over 40% in 2009. To illustrate, you bought these bonds yielding about an 8% dividend in the beginning of the year. The government lowered the interest rates to stimulate the economy and hence the average yield was about 1% at the end of the year. The bonds you held yielding 8% were worth far more than the current bonds yielding 1% as most likely they provide better dividends for the years to come.

- As of 4/2012, the interest rates were almost too low to invest in bonds.

    Even the king of bonds made the wrong call. Do not bet against the Fed as they control the interest rates. They will raise the interest rates when they think the economy is ready.

    Conventional wisdom tells us to balance your portfolio with a combination of bonds and stocks in proportion to your risk tolerance, which for some is determined by their age. I prefer the reward/risk ratio and only buy bonds when interest rate is expected to fall, which usually occurs after the first six months of a market plunge. The government has to stimulate the economy by lowering the interest rates in almost all recessions. When the USD loses the reserve currency status, most stocks and bonds would be losers.

Repeating the important prediction, as of 4/2013, the long-term bond crash seemed to be coming. When the economy improves, the interest rates will rise. The interest rate is so low now that it has no way to go but up. It will adversely affect the bonds you're holding, especially the ones with low interest rates and long maturity.

- The government bond prices could collapse when its issuing country is printing too much money and depreciating its currency.

  A bond at 20% yield may not be good if the company/country has more than 25% chance to default on their bonds.

- Those holding the GM bonds before the reorganization (i.e., the first bankruptcy) lost more than 40% of the bond values. Corporate junk bonds (i.e., high yield bonds) have their risk. Buy a bond fund or ETF on corporate bonds.

- I believe the Muni bonds are risky. I do not really care about the small tax advantages. Many may default. If you still want to buy them, buy a bond fund to spread out the risk instead of buying individual Muni bonds. Detroit bankruptcy is a good example of this. This article was published far earlier than the collapse of several towns in California and now Detroit.

- The long-term bond price moves in the opposite direction of the interest rate. It is about a 1 to 5 ratio by my rough estimate. If the interest rates move 5% up, then the long-term bond price would move 25% down. It is a very rough estimate as it also depends on how long until the bond matures.
- Few hold the bond and see when it matures. If you need a steady income, buy government bonds at an acceptable rate (for example, greater than 8%). 2012 was not a good year to buy bonds with low interest rates. Some bonds did default and the owner lost most or even

- the entire investment. The GM bonds before its first bankruptcy was one of them however it is quite rare.
- China has been a big buyer of our US treasury bonds. China does not want to kill the goose that lays the golden eggs. They need a good economy in the USA in order to sell their stuff, which would create jobs for its citizens.

Afterthoughts

- This article was originally written in 2012. If you followed the advice about not buying long-term bonds, you would have saved a lot of money. The traditional allocating between bonds and stocks was wrong. The decision of buying long-term bonds should be based on the current interest rates and the market direction.

- Bond ETFs: TLT (20+ years Treasury Bond).

  Contra Bond ETFs: TBF (Short of TLT). Click here for an article on contra Bond ETFs.
  http://seekingalpha.com/article/1305371-strategies-for-a-rising-rate-environment-inverse-bond-funds?v=1365862967&source=tracking_notify

  Click here for other bond and contra bond ETFs.
  http://seekingalpha.com/article/1305371-strategies-for-a-rising-rate-environment-inverse-bond-funds#comment_update_link

- To respond to my 'Edu-mercial' (my new term) on 5/29/13, JTS said, "Very educational. Thanks! I'll be out of my bond funds by the end of the day."

- Using rising interest rates as an example, the long-term Treasury bonds with lower interest rates may not fare that well rather than the newly-issued, long-term Treasury bonds with a higher rate.

- Many financial advisors are trained to sell bonds. Many split the investment into stocks and bonds according to the client's age. It makes sense to them and their clients. It does not make sense to me especially on long-term bonds which are interest sensitive.

  Bonds do not have a better record of gains rather than stocks. As in my chapter on the Market Cycle, I advise my readers to buy long-term bonds only when interest rates are high and / or the interest rates are going to plunge. Muni bonds I had been advised to stay away from more than a year ago and now we have Detroit, a major city, going into bankruptcy.

- Avani: This article is mind blowing. I read and enjoyed it. I always find this type of article as a way to learn and gather knowledge.
- Buying a bond fund and an individual bond could be quite different. Bond funds usually buy a large number of bonds maturing in different time periods. The maturing periods are according to the objective of the fund such as long-term bond funds.
- There is a way to structure buying funds varying in different maturity periods to lower your risk of the interest rate fluctuations. Check your broker to see whether they provide such a tool.

  However, I believe it could be better to buy long-term bonds when the interest rates are high (say 8%). A 3% yield does not beat inflation (which is about 3%) even without including taxes.
- Mortgage REIT is similar to a long-term bond. Click here for an article. (http://seekingalpha.com/article/1548162-mortgage-reit-meltdown-i-told-you-so?v=1373916710&source=tracking_notify)

Links

Bonds:
http://en.wikipedia.org/wiki/Bond_%28finance%29
Fidelity:
Bonds vs. Bond Funds
https://www.fidelity.com/learning-center/mutual-funds/bond-vs-bond-funds

#Filler: Double standard
We set up our standard in everything and the entire world has to follow our standard. Shooting citizens at each other, separating children from the illegals, and police brutality are fine according to our standard.

#Filler: Rocket stocks
As of 6/2017, TSLA, AMAZ, NFLX and AAPL were all overpriced by most fundamental metrics. However, they are the darlings of institutional investors. My advice is not to do anything (not to buy and not to short them) as we cannot fight the city hall and their momentum.

11 Muni bonds

Unlike the Federal government, states and Munis do have to balance the budget and we are having more cities going bankrupt than previously predicted. We have to bite the bullet somehow, otherwise we will never service our growing debts. We're running out of suckers like China to lend us money.

If you read this article on 7/2012, you should have saved a lot by selling all of your Muni bonds and long-term bonds described in the last chapter.

- States will not go bankrupt, but Muni bonds will lose a lot of their values. QEn will be used to rescue the state. Property and state taxes will be raised if they have not already been raised. A lot of foreclosures usually mean less local taxes for the local government.

- State/Muni bonds together with Federal bonds will have junk status, so in the future it is harder to raise money that will be needed for any public project.

- Need to cut down the number of state employees.
  It may be easy to cut about half of the state workers and you may not notice any loss in service (as most of them work short hours and are not motivated under the union's umbrella). I just get sick of the routine 'discoveries' on there are how few hours they have worked as reported by our local newspapers while we've about an 18% real unemployment / under-employment rate.

  However, the firemen, policemen, and teachers should be paid fairly and they should not be cut.

- Cut their pensions and increase retirement age requirements. Most state workers have just a little less than their regular salaries in retirement and they retire at a young age. Most big companies do not have pensions now.

- We could cut the entitlements/benefits that encourage folks not to work such as the generous benefits to teenage mothers. We could cut free medical care to illegal aliens. All expenditures have to be at a fair percentage of our GDP rather than not how much we can borrow as politicians look at buying votes.

- We do not need a large government, but a lean and mean government to provide us with efficient services. All those taxes are not good for the economy and businesses (how can you compete with those foreign countries with minimal taxes). Without business expanding (not government expanding), we do not have real jobs.

Afterthoughts

- Our experts told us to stay away from Munis. They're wrong in timing – well you do not want to fight the Fed in the short term. However, their arguments are not wrong. Muni government bonds seldom default as they cannot issue new bonds in the future if they do.

    The reality is: Some towns are just dying and they just cannot keep up paying the necessary interest expenses and obligations. There are simply better places to invest.

- As of 8/2012, the defaults on Muni bonds are getting to be more. Actually, we have more defaults as the defaults in the unrated bonds are not tracked. As the original post was written about a year ago, the advice still holds true. There are better investments than Muni bonds in both appreciation potential with less risk.

Filler

Pension is a two-edged sword. Retiring with pensions after 25-year service does not make sense if you are in the real world in a profit-seeking organization. It weakens our competitive edge with other countries. Losing what has been promised was tough to swallow for Detroit city employees.

12   Annuities

There are advantages and disadvantages. I use my experience for illustration, and everyone's situation is different.

Why I bought annuity
As of this writing, I made over 4 times after many years. I could have made far more if I were not too conservative in the last 3 years. As most of you, I hate paying taxes. After maxing out all retirement accounts, the only choice is annuity, and at that time it was not too popular. My investment was more than my annual salary then, and hence I am not boasting my return with a tiny investment.

I worked for Fidelity and I had to report what stocks I traded. It was very inconvenient, and by the time I got the OK I could have missed the opportunity. The only get-around is to use my wife's and/or my son's account, that I did not think it was ok with the company's policy or not. However, the company let me trade mutual funds without reporting and their annuity had a lot mutual funds including sector funds. The restriction was requiring holding period of 60 days before switching without penalty for most sector funds. In March, 2000, I switched out all my tech sectors including Biotech that I had to pay a penalty from my memory. The fees in the funds could be higher than similar funds outside the annuity.

It turns out my tax rate after retirement is higher than the ones before due to the appreciation of my retirement accounts.

Why I do not recommend annuities
When you attend 'free' financial seminars, annuity is a popular recommendation and the other one is other insurance products. Most likely it is due to the high commissions. The policy of the annuity was written by the issuer to their own benefits not yours. For decades, I know only one annuity company lost big money due to the beneficial terms to her customers and the market behaved differently from what the issuer expected. Many potential buyers think it is a good and safe deal as they will be paid for life. It is similar to a pension. When you have annualized (withdrew money), your heirs get nothing on the day you die. The only way beating annuities is a long life.

Misc.
It is better to buy an ETF such as VOO (lower fees than SPY) or RSP than let your financial advisor churn your portfolio if s/he is not honest. There have been cases the 'friendly' advisor lost more than 90% of the client's portfolio in a year or two.

13   Buyback, Diluting and Spinoffs

A buyback will not change the fundamentals of a stock. When the money is cheap such as during 2022, it is beneficial for the company borrow the money and use it to buy back its own stock.

The following are all theories. When a company buys back its own stocks to reduce the number of outstanding shares, the remaining shares should appreciate in value in this aspect. However, the company uses its own cash, and hence the stock value should remain the same. It is a no-win and no-loss situation and the Supply and Demand should not affect the stock price in a buyback.

However, the management understands the value of its company and its sector better than anyone. The buyback could be the best way to use the company's cash compared to giving dividends, plowing back to research / development, or taking advantage of the easy money available. They also in theory consider the total return for the average stock investor such as taxes.

In practice, most officers take care of themselves first (a human nature): Boosting the value of their stock options. In the last several years, boosting dividends has proven to be a good way to do so.

If the number of the outstanding shares has been reduced, many metrics with earning per share will be improved such as P/E (unless P is decreased accordingly). If the company borrows money to buy its stock, the metrics on debt will head in the other direction.

Watch out for the management buyback as it may be used to grant options to themselves. Buyback improves the EPS as E is a constant and the number of shares is decreased. Hence, I do not believe that EPS is a good metric all the time.

Stock dilution means increasing outstanding shares. In most cases, it is not good for the stock price. Sometimes the company has no better way to secure financing. **Splitting** is fine as the stock price may be too high for individuals, but reverse splitting is usually a bad sign, and some stocks want to maintain a certain stock price to avoid delisting from the exchanges. The fundamentals such as P/E may not be updated in time.

Spinoff depends on the situation. If one part of the company has a lot of liability such as a major pending lawsuit, it is better to spin it off.

14   Brokers

Protect the security of your financial transactions. Do not hit any web link that you don't know including those 'good' deals – your greed could cause you to lose millions! I use my Chrome for these transactions and I do not access my emails via this Chrome. A two-step log-in (if available) should be useful. The broker sends you a temporary log-in password to your mobile phone. Install anti-virus software such as Norton and Malwarebytes. Do not use the mobile phone for trading stocks and stay away from 'free Wi-Fi' networks. Besides your broker account, tax info, bank accounts and credit card are the next important things that you need to protect.

Today most brokers are discount brokers, and many are commission-free. Choose one to start with and two should be the maximum.

The following is for illustration purposes only as I should not recommend any broker. Fidelity offers a lot of research free of charge and commission-free trades (similar to Charles Schwab), extensive mutual funds and bank/credit card services. Interactive Broker has a low margin rate (vs. Fidelity's 9% or so today) and low commissions on some transactions. Many others have their own advantages. If you only need one broker, select the one based on your requirements.

Today many brokers offer many trading options that were not available 15 years ago such as trading a stock with specific condition(s) and canceling an order based on certain condition(s). For example, you can have a stop order and a limited sell order on the same stock.

Full-service brokers offer some services most discount brokers do not offer. One offers buying IPO stocks and selling them automatically at the end of the day. This strategy had been doing well except in 2015. Do not believe you can pay someone to manage your portfolio and you're all set. There have been cases of portfolio churning to generate income for the broker.

There are many magazine articles comparing brokers. I do not really care whether the order is executed in 1 or 5 microseconds. However, I do find some orders have been traded better by one broker over another. What do you mean 'by traded better' you may ask? The following are examples. I cannot prove whether they are true or not but to me, it seems to be true.

- I have identical buy orders placed with two brokers. Consistently one broker gets them executed more often than the other broker.
- One broker often gives me better prices than the other. For example, my sell price was $10, and many times I got more than $10 such as $10.02.
- One broker has more reversed orders than the other. For example, I was informed my order was executed but they told me it had been reversed on the second day.
- One consistently charged extra fees such as commissions on covered calls and virtually none from idle cash. I understand it is tough to make the paper-thin commissions today.
- ADR fees. Some are quite hefty. I avoid many foreign stocks. Some charge more for the gains, especially France. At one time, most ADR stocks did well, but not anymore as the US stocks have been doing well (as of 2/2017). The ADR fees are charged by your broker or bank. The following is from Kiplinger's magazine.

"ADRs, which represent shares of ownership in a foreign company, trade in the U.S. in dollars. Some ADRs come with a contractual provision that allows the broker, in this case TD Ameritrade, to levy "depositary services fees."

The charges, commonly 2 cents per share, are intended to cover the cost of coordinating overseas investments. For ADRs that include this provision, the broker can levy the charge at any time, but no more than once a year.

Margin
Margin should not be used extensively. It is expensive and most brokers try every trick to squeeze profits from all transactions to subsidize their low-commission incomes. Usually, you can borrow up to 40% of your current position and the margin rates vary among brokers. Check out your broker's margin rate. In general, margin is not allowed in your retirement accounts. You may need to file an application for margin. Your brokers ensure you meet specific requirements to lower their risk such as your income.

Many lost a lot during the last two market plunges. However, many including myself made a killing in 2003 and 2009 using margin. I use it for the following reasons. For convenience in placing buy orders that exceed my cash position in my taxable accounts.
I pay back my outstanding margin loan from my home equity loan (check the current tax law) as it is far, far lower than my broker's margin interest rate.

Tips and tricks
- Many brokers' promotions offer you cash and/or free trades (no longer needed as many brokers offer commission-free trades) if you deposit a

specific amount in your account. Without commission cost, you do not need to round up to a lot size (100 shares in most cases) nor specify "All or None". Check the details of the offers. Some give you free trades only up to 60 days while others offer up to two years. If your broker cancels your 'completed' orders or never gives you trade prices better than the ones you enter, it is time to change broker.

- Some brokers restrict withdrawal in a specific time frame such as one year or during the period of the free commission. After that, you can move it to another broker that gives you similar deals. In most cases, the offer is per social security number or per person. A bad execution of a trade is not worth the free commission and/or any goodies.
- If you need margin a lot such as shorting stocks, check out the margin rates from different brokers.
- Most brokers offer basic trading lessons and market reviews. Most are well-written.
- Most brokers offer stock evaluation. Some are really good with proven records. Take advantage of it.
- Many brokers offer two-phase logon for better security. Many send you a security code to your mobile phone or your email account. Then you enter the code.
- Ignore filling out the forms for group lawsuits unless your stock holding is large. I received $20 for spending at least 2 hours to find my statement.
- Some brokers offer free commissions for specific ETFs. For sector rotation trades, it could add up to a lot of savings. Today it is not relevant to most brokers as they are already commission-free. So is the "All but none" option during entering a trade.
- Some brokers may require you to confirm if you want to trade using margin, options, penny stocks, risky stocks and after-hour trading.
- My broker calculates my performance returns and compares them to the indexes. It is handy.
- Check out the interest rate of the core account for unused cash and compare it to the current short-term CDs
- How safe your brokers are":
https://www.youtube.com/watch?v=wz64z1YuL0A
- Interactive Broker has low margin rate. Here is a comparison of 3 major brokers. https://www.youtube.com/watch?v=rAewPVEjeLM.
- Brokers comparison: https://www.youtube.com/watch?v=Dg8OUucdM7Q
https://www.youtube.com/watch?v=wMxj6iB92ZA

Evaluate a broker company
The Shocking Collapse of Charles Schwab (SCHW) Balance Sheet - Will The Company Survive?
Broker failure: https://www.youtube.com/watch?v=kY5BswpUlf4

15   Fidelity

On 10/2019, Fidelity announced there was no commission for most trades. With this, I do not have to care about "all or none" to assume all shares traded".

I have been satisfied with the trades so far. It is more important to me than commissions. One broker offered free trades for keeping a balance. However, there are many times the orders that should be executed have not been executed. More than 2 times, the completed orders have been reversed. I have not had this with Fidelity so far and actually some orders have been executed with better prices. Fidelity passes the best price to you while some brokers keep the difference for themselves.

As with most major brokers, Turbo Tax can load all my stock transactions for the year in filing my tax returns. It saves me a lot of time. Fidelity used to have more sophisticated order options such as "Execute based on certain conditions". Most investors do not need this feature.

They require you to apply for trading options, after-hour trading, using margin and trading penny stocks. Gift appreciated stocks to your children who have a tax bracket lower than yours up to $15,000 of the current market value for each receiver ($30,000 per couple) in 2019. Gifting depreciated stocks is not recommended. Consult your tax lawyer or CPA.

Ensure all accounts have primary beneficiaries and secondary beneficiaries. I have a simple trust for my taxable account for myself and my spouse. Consult your lawyer for estate planning.

Fidelity offers CD ladders so they mature in different time frames. I prefer Fidelity rather than local banks as it saves me trips to the bank (to purchase and renew) by doing my purchasing CDs on-line. However, my state offers some tax deductions for the interests from local banks. The other advantage is the bank CDs can start right away.

Save some interest in the cash account. If you have the CASH account (FCASH), change it to Government Money Market fund FDRXX by clicking on the core account. Today I have to buy SPRXX that pays better dividends than FDRXX. Automatically SPRXX will be used when the core account is exhausted. Check the current information and dividends. SPRXX should be part of the choices.

My annuity has gained 4 times during decades. I do not recommend the use of an annuity, most of which have high commissions for the sales persons. My tax rate today is higher than during my work life. Compared to many other offers, Fidelity's annuity is better than the average.

The only negative I have found is their margin interest rates are quite high. If you use margin a lot, open a second account that has a low interest rate such as from Interactive Broker.

I transferred my appreciated stocks to my son's account as he is in lower tax bracket. The performance of my account was less while my son's increased. It may be correct, but it is not I want.
I use their two-factor log in for better security that I recommend you to use for all financial accounts if available.
Traders should use Fidelity's Active Trader Pro. Their low-cost ETFs are attractive.

My major credit card is with Fidelity that gives me 2% cash back. I have no relationship with Fidelity except being a retiree of Fidelity.

Links
Fidelity vs Vanguard. I believe Vanguard will improve to be competitive.
https://www.youtube.com/watch?v=tskh-QCCH-o
Vanguard vs Charles vs Fidelity
https://www.youtube.com/watch?v=rAewPVEjeLM&
Mutual funds vs ETFs
https://www.youtube.com/watch?v=GJkoAz7BYmU&list=PLMZa6mP7jZ2brE1g3bwiKTqcRcNsEhsHn
Fidelity Active Trader: https://www.youtube.com/watch?v=JeuqUNb6MZI

#Filler: Simple measures to reduce net security.
Do not click any links from unknown sources. Some seems to be ok but not.

"MalwareBytes", for checking viruses, is free for download (they do not pay me).

Personally, I use a Chromebook for my financial transactions and a two-factor logon for my stock trading.

Filler: The most powerful word
I was deeply moved by the family members of the church victims forgiving the shooter. I wrote a brief post: "Forgive" is the most powerful word in every language and in every culture. I forgot it until I received a response from Jim.

"Tony,
Without even knowing it, you made the greatest comment I have seen on here--and it had nothing to do with investing. You mentioned somewhere that "Forgive" is the most powerful word in every language. Wow."

Summary

First determine your trade is long-term holding (e.g., 12 months) or short-term (e.g., 1 month) or in-between. Use the screen(s) that has (have) performed well in your testing.

The screened stocks should have the second evaluation such as using Finviz or Fidelity. I normally do not buy stocks with Fidelity rating less than 7 and the following parameters from Finviz: high insider selling, low Earnings Q-Q, high debt / equity ratio, high Forward P/E (also > 0), Price < 2, Market Cap less than 200, etc. Avoid the stocks in unfavorable sectors.

Use position sizing described in this section, such as $20,000 on a $100,000 portfolio. Avoid more than 25% of the stock in the same sector.

Use stop loss for the purchased stock. Use trailing stop (replacing the stop loss with the current prices periodically (every week for example)) to let the gains rise.

For non-retirement accounts, I prefer to sell the losers less than a year and the winners more than 1 year to have better tax treatments.

Be emotionally detached. The stock market fluctuates, and market crash can have a 50% loss. Trade with the money you can afford to lose.

Afterthoughts

- If your success rate is only 50%, you still make good money as your stop loss protects you from losing more.
- Be disciplined and record your trade.
- Do not be frustrated and take illogical actions when you are losing.
- Follow simple market timing such as Death Cross and Golden Cross.
- I prefer undervalued stocks for long-term hold, and momentum stocks (high SMA-20 and SMA-50 from Finviz) for short-term hold.

Book 6: Market Timing

There is no need to time the market from 1970 to 2000. From 2000 to 2014, the market crashed two times with an average loss of about 45%. Recently, the bull has been long (more than 10 years for the current one) while the bear has been less than 2 years. However, you may gain 10% or so a year in the bull market, while lose 40% or so in the bear market.

Using picking apples as an example, sometimes they may be sour but sometimes they may be tasty. The difference is picking them at the right time. It applies to market timing.

Market timing is about educated guesses. Hopefully we will have more rights than wrongs when we follow general guidelines. It would reduce risk and could benefit us financially in the long run. Recently we have had more false signals than the period between 2000 and 2010. However, it is better to follow a proven system. The harm could be minimal except for tax consequences as the system would tell you to return to the market briefly.

I divide the market timing in three categories by durations as follows. All time durations are estimates for discussion and all markets are different.

	Duration
Secular cycle	20 years (actually less)
Market Cycle	5 years (not the current one)
Correction: 10-20%	1 per year
5-10%	2 per year (count the above as 1)

Market plunges have losses between 30% and 55% usually. There is a gray area for the 20% to 30% losses, which does not happen often. When the market plunges, it plunges hard and fast. The techniques in this book tell you to exit the market and when to return to equities. The techniques are based on falling prices, so they will not indicate peaks and bottoms, but they will help you to reduce further losses.

Within the secular market, there are market cycles. There is a super cycle that I ignore as I find it not too useful. Every market is different. Today we have excessive money printing that changes all the previous logic such as the average length of a market cycle. If the USD is not the reserved currency, the market would fall. However, the correlation of the market and the economy will correlate again. We do not know when, but it will. Otherwise, we have to rewrite all the books on investing. For instant gratification, you can read Simplest Way to Time the Market and skip the rest of this lengthy section for now.

1 Market timing example

The market is making new highs as of this writing in early 2021. There are always two camps of market timers. One camp predicts a crash is coming while the other predicts it will continue making new highs. This article includes both arguments and suggests how and what actions you need to take to protect your investments. Be warned that all market is different and predictions are just pure predictions; the more educated the guesses, the more chance they will be materialized. In 2021, the market has been flooded with cash due to the excessive printing of money.

Management summary

The market is fundamentally unsound evidenced by fundamental metrics but technically sound evidenced by technical metrics that both will be described in this article. The data were obtained on 09/22/2018. This article shows you how to evaluate the market risk. As of 8/2021, the market has not changed a lot since 01/2020 with the following exceptions: 1.The excessive printing of money that is leading to inflation and 2. The pandemic is still not fully controlled.

Suggested actions
No one predicts the market correctly and consistently. Otherwise, there are no poor folks. Moving the risky investments such as most stocks to cash too early would miss the potential profits. Moving it too late would risk the loss of your stocks.

Your actions depend on your risk tolerance. If you are conservative such as a retiree, you may want to have a larger portion of your investments in lower risk such as CDs and bonds. You can take one of the following three actions or combine all of the three actions.

1. When the market turns to technically unsound, it is time to move your stocks to cash. The market timing indicators may give false signals. In this case, the indicator would tell you to move back to stocks. Most likely you do not lose much except dealing with the consequences of taxes in non-retirement accounts.
2. Move a portion of your risky investments into cash, laddered CDs and/or short-term bonds. Again, the size of the portion depends on your risk tolerance.
3. Use stops. The sell orders would be changed to market orders when the stocks dip below prices specified by you. I prefer to use SPY or other ETF to determine the market direction. Some sectors and some stocks

move faster than others. In one crash, my energy stocks were still profitable while the market was tanking. Eventually these energy stocks caught up and fell fast. Today's highly profitable stocks are FAANG stocks as a group.

I propose and prefer 'manual stop orders' to prevent market manipulation. However, usually large ETFs cannot be manipulated easily. Manipulators try to profit from your stop orders. Set a stop order price in your mind. When the stock falls to that specified price, sell it via a market order.

My friend confirmed my "manual stop order":

"High-frequency trading via Algo Trading Strategy can see exactly where pre-set trailing stops are and sweep across them (play them) like strings on a violin. Pre-set a trailing stop and it is bound to be triggered because Algo hunt them down. Then watch the market rip higher."

Analysis: Fundamentals and Technical

The bitter lesson I learned recently: **Technical is more important** than fundamentals in market timing. It consists of Fundamental Analysis and Technical Analysis. The former measures how expensive the current market is and the latter measures the trend of the market.

Many metrics were obtained from Finviz.com as of 9/22/2018 while others are obtained from other websites. With the exception of Fidelity.com, all websites described here are free and readily available. It also serves as a guide on how you can do your own market timing especially after a few months.

The following chart uses SPY to represent the market of the top 500 stocks. It is market cap weighted. It means the higher the market cap of the stock, the higher percent of the stock is represented in the index. It turns out most are riskier FAANG stocks. Enter Finviz.com in your browser and enter SPY. I am not responsible for any errors.

Indicator	Pass	Current Value	Indicating
• Technical			
Death Cross[1]		SMA-50 = 2.3% & SMA-200 = 6.3%	Pass
Technical Analysis: 350 SMA%[2]	>0	Price above the SMA-350.	Pass
RSI(14)	<70	61	Pass

Duration (yr.)	<5	10	Fail
		Overall	**Pass**
• Fundamental Valuation			
P/E[3]	<15.7	25.4	High by 62%. Fail.
Shiller P/E[3]	<16.6	33.5	High by 102%. Fail.
P/B[3]	<2.78	3.52	High by 27%. Fail.
P/S[3]	<1.50	2.33	High by 55%. Fail.
Oil price	30-100	70.71	Pass
Interest rate[6] T-Bill 1 months[7]	<5	2.05	Pass
T-Bill 3 months[7]	Yield	2.18	
T-Bill 30 years[7]	Curve	3.20	Pass
Flow to Equity[4]		-3.371M	Fail
Flow to bond[4]		7.206M	
Corporate debt/GDP[8]	<40	45%	High by 13%. Fail.
USD[5]		Strong	Fail
Gold		High	Fail
Bubble		Several	Fail
Market experts		Fear long term	Neutral
Politics		Trump	Fail
Misc.		Trade war	Fail
		Overall	**Fail**

[1] This is the market timing technique without using a chart.

[2] I tried to use SMA-400% to reduce false signals without success.

[3] Get it from http://www.multpl.com/. Same as CAPE.

[4] Get it from https://www.ici.org/research/stats. It is based on 09-12-18. "Flow to Equity" is based on domestic ETF estimates. Treat it as two phases in moving to equity. First phase of moving excessively to equity indicates the market is peaking. The second phase indicates the market is plunging when the flow of equity is excessively negative.

[5] Global corporations will suffer in profits converted back to USD and hard to sell to foreign countries.

[4] Get it from the above link.

[6] Rising interest is bad for corporations and high-ticket products, but good for lenders.

[7] Get it from https://www.treasury.gov/resource-center/data-chart-center/interest-rates/Pages/TextView.aspx?data=yield based on 09/21/18

[8] With the low interest rate, it may not be that critical. Corporations take advantage of the low interest rate.

Overall

Overall, technical is fine as the market is making new highs. Many aggressive investors exit the market on technical indicators only as the overvalued market could linger on for a long term such as from 2009 to 2017 so far.

Overall, fundamental is not sound. The increasing market price also is decreasing the fundamental metrics such as P/E, P/B and P/S. It is bad unless there is reason to support such as the fast earnings growth in 2009.

Many metrics are deteriorating

RSI(14) is getting closer to 65 (a passing grade specified by me).

Inverse yield curve (1.5 vs. 2.33) is about 61% apart from my interpretation and calculation. It is not a warning now but we should keep an eye on it. Most market crashes have occurred when it is 0% or negative. The theory is that in a normal case the short-term interest rates should be lower than the long-term interest rate.

Another source calculates it is 1.1% and that is very close to inversion since the last recession. From MarketWatch, the 30-year fixed interest rate is 4.66% and 1-year rate is 3.96% giving an inverse yield curve 18% apart, which is quite alarming.

Mathematically incorrect, today's full employment is at 4%. Most recessions are closely preceded by troughs in unemployment and the reverse for the economy to recover.

GDP growth has been predicted from 1.8% to 3%. The 3% is from the White House for their obvious purpose. I predict it will pop up due to meeting the tariff deadlines, tax cuts and spending increases. It will then be declining to 2%. A healthy US economy should maintain 3% without special factors such as excessive immigration.

We have record debts: investors' margin, corporate debt and Federal debt. These are bubbles going to burst. Federal debt / GDP is about 95% (https://fred.stlouisfed.org/series/gfdegdq188S) today. It does not predict the market performance as this ratio was 53% and 55% before the last two market crashes. It will affect the long-term performance of the economy when we have to service the huge national debt.

We do have 10 years of stock growth at the expense of a record Federal deficit. Thanks to President Obama from investors and no thanks from next generations who have to pay back our national debt. It is overdue for a correction. Hopefully it is not a crash which has an average loss of about 45%. We did have two recent corrections losing more than 10%: 2011-12 EU debt crisis and 2014-16 oil crash. The oil price has been rising from $30 per barrel to today's $70. It is still a long way from my warning of $120.

Potential triggers
Trade wars with China, Canada or the EU will be the strongest trigger. Our most profitable companies are virtually all international companies. They need fair trade to prosper.

The other trigger is the possible impeachment of President Trump.

Check the validity of our charts
It seems some metrics vary. It could be used after hour trading. It could be the "Days" may be "Sessions" – calendar day is different from trading sessions. I selected 10 years for most of the charts and StockCharts let me select only 5 years.

Here is a list of sites for charts.
https://www.stocktrader.com/2013/12/10/best-free-stock-chart-websites/
These are the three sites I use a lot: Fidelity (customers only), StockCharts and Finviz.com (missing some metrics).

As stated before, SPY may not be the best to represent the market. I prefer an ETF for 1,000 stocks and weigh the stocks evenly (i.e., not according to the market cap). Google "market timing 2020 (or current year)" for more expert info. Here is one.

Mid-year update
Basically, nothing significant has changed recently: The market is fundamentally unsound and technically sound after the recent rally. The only update is our national debt is skyrocketing. Today's "Debt/GDP" is similar to the market height in 2000 and we know what happened afterwards. That's why Buffett has accumulated a lot of cash now.

Even with the unlimited QE (i.e., printing money excessively), the high inflation and market crash predicted by many experts have not been materialized so far. This is my third prediction in "Disaster of 2020". The status of USD as a reserve currency will be shaken; I do not know when, as I do not have a time machine.

Why does the market keep going up while the economy is going down? The Fed has provided a lot of cash and the cash is chasing a fixed number of assets such as gold and stocks. It is the simple, proven theory of demand and supply. It will continue for a while as long as there is an unlimited supply of money. At some point, it will pop. At that time, it could lead to a long recession, unless the economy improves as it did in 2009. The smart Fed chairman knows how it will harm the country by excessively printing money. However, he has to obey his boss who is seeking reelection.

I expect we are in a prolonged period of low interest rates and even negative interest rates. When the rates are negative, our Treasury bonds are no longer marketable. The foreign central banks including China would dump our national debts if it has not already started. The economy is dressed up nicely in an election year. Giving us free money is the easy way to buy votes, but the long-term effects are very harmful.

Using cheap money to buy back the company's stock would boost the stock price and hence make the management wealthier. It is a false sense of the stock value. When the company cannot pay back the debt obligations, the company would go bankrupt. If the U.S. were a company, she would have gone bankrupt already.

As of 6/15/2020, QQQ (representing NASDAQ stocks) has been up 11% YTD and it is far better than DIA (representing DOW stocks) and SPY (representing the 500 large stocks in the S&P Index and losing about 5% YTD). QQQ has a lot of tech stocks while DIA has a lot of losers including Boeing. Most FAANG stocks are making record highs and QQQ is market cap weighted.

Most of the ETFs on chips have been up more than 40% in a year. I bought Amazon and two chip ETFs. I use trailing stops to protect my portfolio. Huawei is buying a lot of U.S. chips in the 120-day relaxed period. In September this year and if there is no extension, I would sell these chip ETFs fast.

I have used the strategy described in my book "Profit from the recovery of the pandemic" to take advantage of this volatile market. I used 5% as the threshold and I had too few trades; now I changed to 3%. Expecting a market crash, I weigh more on contra ETFs. As described in the same book,

I bought a lot of contra ETFs, GLD and the stock of a gold miner. It is for insurance. Oil ETFs are my big mistake.

If the U.S.D. loses the status of reserve currency (not likely soon), it would bring prolonged depression and high inflation in the U.S. In this case, it is safer to invest in real estate, precious metals and profitable companies than in CDs and bonds that would lose value due to inflation.

Check out many articles on the status of the current market. Many have opposing views, so you have to make your own decision. In any case, play it safe with stops. Here is one article from MarketWatch.com.

Update 8/2021
Nothing has changed. The market is not sound fundamentally but fine technically. When the technical indicators tell us to exit, most likely it is right. However, the market is volatile, and hence return to the market if the indicators tell us so. Here is an argument from opposite camps.
https://www.youtube.com/watch?v=I9P9IuwuTVE

Canary warning?
When I was working on my new book "Best stocks to buy for 2021" on Dec. 10, 2020, I found something really strange. I have never rejected so many stocks that have Fidelity's Equity Summary Score higher than 9. I rejected them as there was a lot of dumping from the insiders. Insiders know their companies better than most of us. Is it the canary telling us the market is overvalued?

Initially the following stocks have been screened by my value screens. Buy any one of the following stocks, **only** if you have good reason(s).

How can HEAR score a perfect 10 while the Insiders' Transaction is -75% (to me -2% is normal). The analysts must be wrong this time, or they believe the market will continuously make new heights.

Symbol	Fidelity Score	Insider Purchase	Return[1]	Annualized
BCC	9.9	-24%	46%	126%
GPI	10.0	-17%	35%	95%
HEAR	10.0	-75%	43%	118%
HVT	9.5	-37%	53%	144%
HZO	9.5	-27%	75%	204%
Average				84%

SPY				30%
Beat SPY[2]				177%

[1] From Dec. 20, 2020 to July 1, 2021. Fees, commissions and dividends are not included.

[2] = (Average – SPY) /SPY. SPY represents the market to many of us. This concludes the Insiders are wrong in this case.

A correction or a crash?
In Dec., 2018, the S&P 500 is about 15% down and a crash is about 45% down.

If a crash is coming, there should be an additional 30% down. If it is a correction (15% average), then we have it already. Should we pick up bargains now? Or, are they bargains? It is a trillion-dollar question.

We need a trigger for a market crash like the financial crisis in 2008 and the internet bubble in 2000. Besides the record-high margin debt, the possibility of Trump's impeachment and a trade war, I do not see any.

Links
Search articles from Google and YouTube on today's market conditions.
YouTube: 1
https://www.youtube.com/watch?v=czHUI0syjKo&t=300s

Filler: CIA mistook it as a missile silo in China.

2 Another example of early 2022

This article was written in March 2022 and updated in May, 2022. The market future is a predication and no one can predict accurately. This is a guideline only and it makes sense to me using my logics. Consult your financial advisor before taking any actions. The Simple Market Technique told us to exit the market March 20, 2022. I have not exited the market completely; I am guilty as charged. Again, market timing worked this time. Unfortunately, I did not follow fully what I preached. In 2020 and 2021, the market was fundamentally unsound but technical sound. Today, they are both unsound.

VIX (the fear index) is about 20% higher than the average. Shiller P/E (based on last 10 years of S&P 500 index with inflation adjusted) is still high (about 33% compared to the about 26%, the average for the past 20 years). Buffett/s indicator (total market cap / GDP) is 180%, far higher than the benchmark of 75% (I use 100%). They are all estimates and used for education purposes only.

I predict (again, predications may not be materialized) the trend of the market is down for the next 6 months or so. Personally, I continue unloading some contra ETFs, and trade precious metals and USO; do your own homework. Even in this beaten market, they may be some value stocks with low P/E and high appreciation potentials.

From now to market recovery
I will unload some stocks even they are highly valued. However, I will buy some that could reach their bottoms or some that are highly valued such as stocks with high potential returns. Sell some of my winners such as contra ETFs and commodities including USO (ETF for oil) and the precious metals. I will trade these stocks to take advantage of the fluctuation. For every 3 stocks I short, I will buy at most one stock; that is my plan. Hence, I am still investing and trading, but not too active this time.

I have accumulated a lot of cash already waiting for the market recovery. Check the market fundamentals (the Ukraine war, super inflation, the pandemic, interest rates and the economy) and the recovery indicators: Golden Cross and SMA-350. Prepare a list of stocks that have high appreciation potentials, which are usually beaten down by the market. If you don't, just buy VTI, an ETF for total market from Vanguard.

Section I: Spotting big market plunges

1 Spotting big market plunges

This chapter is lengthy and complicated in some concepts; it also requires you to try it yourself. However, the result is far better. Make your market decision by combining all the hints described in this article. The first hint is the most important.

No one can consistently predict the correct stages of the market cycle. This chapter is intended for educational purposes only. However, if we have more rights than wrongs with our calculated and educated guesses, we should do well. As in everything in life, there is no guarantee.

These are my 11 hints to identify a market plunge. The average loss of market plunges from top to bottom for the last two crashes is about 45%. It could wipe out most gains for the entire market cycle. We target to avoid half of the loss.

Do not buy stocks during market plunge that could last for more than a year, which is defined by me from the market peak to the market bottom. It is a million-dollar decision for many including myself. This low-cost book serves as a reference and past performances do not guarantee future performances.

From 2000 to 2008, we only had one false signal for our SMA-350 out of 3 signals. Since then, we have had more false signals. To adjust to this volatility, do not move everything to cash on an exit signal. Adjust the amount of cash according to your own risk tolerance. Usually we do not lose much (sometimes we gain some) as another signal tells us to return to the market shortly. They only have tax consequences in taxable accounts.

Eleven hints of a market plunge

1. Technical analysis (TA).

    The following chart is created by Yahoo!Finance. If it does not display well on a small screen, copy the following link to your browser to display it on your PC.
    http://ebmyth.blogspot.com/2013/05/ta-graph-for-spotting-plunges-chapter.html

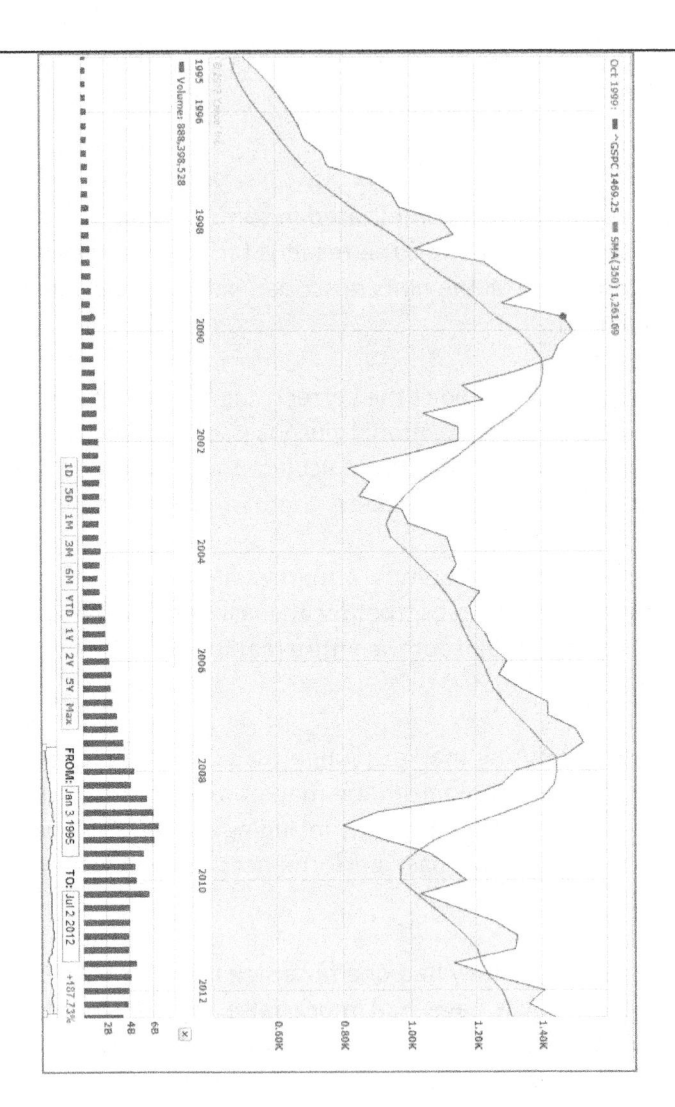

350 days simple moving average (SMA). Yahoo!Finance

The red line is the 350-day SMA, Simple Moving Average. If the stock price is below the moving average, it has detected a market plunge by this chart. Return to the market when the price is above the moving average line described as Early Recovery later. "350 days" are trading sessions. I have tried different "days" and 350 is the best fit for the last two market plunges, but it does not mean it would be the best fit for the next market plunge.

We have two cycles described in the chart. From the above, we should leave the market in the first quarter of 2000 and return to the market in the first quarter of 2003.

On the second cycle, the chart tells us to get out in Dec. 2008 and come back in July 2009 approximately. Enlarge the chart by selecting 5 years instead of the maximum or use a larger monitor for a more detailed chart. The chart sometimes gives false signals to tell us to exit but tell us to reenter briefly. In most cases, we do not lose much except the tax consequences for selling. No technical indicators are perfect.

I started to come back in Feb. 2009. It was perfect timing but most likely or partly it was due to good luck. I was partially influenced by several articles I read.

Technical Analysis is based on the past data, so you cannot avoid the initial losses but it could reduce further and larger losses. From the above, the chart detected the two big plunges nicely allowing enough time to take actions. Will the next plunge be detected? I guess it will. However, it may not allow enough time as the last two.

Sometimes, we time it wrongly or prematurely and miss some gains by leaving the market too early. We need to treat it as buying insurance; it only pays big when the worst happens. When the "reward / risk" is too low, it is better to stay in cash. One's opinion.

Return to equity when the price is above the moving average (the red line). You should profit more by following the chart than 'Buy and Hold' or keeping your money under the pillow. For the last two market cycles, I returned to equities in Early Recovery (a stage of the market cycle defined by me) and profited. Can I be 100% sure for the next market plunge and come back in a timely order? Certainly not.

If most of your stocks are in tech, use QQQ instead of SPY. In addition, QQQ is more volatile than SPY and the tech sector usually leads the market.

> It can be created by following the steps; you need to create one yourself to detect the next plunge with current data.
> - From Yahoo!Finance or any chart systems, enter SPY (or the S&P 500 index) or an ETF that represents the total market.
> - Select Interactive Chart.
> - Click Technical Indicators.
> - Select SMA (simple moving average).
> - Enter 350 days (actually it is trade sessions). Many chart systems use 'month' as a unit, enter 12 or 11.67 if decimals is allowed (=350/12) instead of 350.

- Enter 1-3-2000 on "FROM:" or any "from date" that fits your screen.
- Select Draw.

Note. I switch to Fidelity for charting now as I cannot produce the same info from Yahoo!Finance. It could be my fault or a bug that should be fixed. If you cannot use Fidelity, try StockCharts.com.

2. Do the opposite of the flow of the dumb money.

When everyone is buying recklessly, making money and proclaiming that they are geniuses, sell. In 1999, my friend told me that he should quit his job and concentrate on investing as he was making many times in the stock market over his regular salary by spending half an hour a day. I would call myself a genius by making $1,000 an hour. When AAII's bullish sentiment (a contrary indicator to me) is over 70%, watch out.

In the same year, there were so many successful IPOs with '.com' names and these companies did not know how to make profits but blindly captured their market shares at all expenses.

They gave me $20 for just registering on their site. The poor quality of their ads showing their products during the Super Bowl reflected the quality of their management. The so-called 'MBA's business model' of capturing a potential market of one million potential sales by spending five million is not Business 101 but Fool 101.

The inverse flow of money market funds is a good indicator too. The more money flowing into the equity funds by retail investors, the riskier is the market. Greed is a human nature. It is hard to resist buying stocks when your friends are all making good money in the market and you feel you do not want to miss the boat. I tried unsuccessfully to convince lottery winners not to buy lottery tickets and they showed me they had made another thousand yesterday.

3. Duration.

Cycles usually occur every four or five years. This is a very rough estimate as cycles often vary from 1 to 8 or even more years. After the market plunge in 2007-2008, we are having (as of 12/2018) one of the longest bull markets. The longer it stays at the peak, the higher the chance the market will plunge and the further it will sink. I call it Newton's Law of Gravity or

'What goes up must come down'. When we follow the charts (technical indicators), we still stay in the market most of the time.

4. Valuation.

The average historical P/E of the S&P 500 is about 15 (or 16.5 depending on when you start the data). When it is over the average, be careful. Obtain the P/E of SPY (an ETF for the S&P 500) from Yahoo!Finance and confirm it in many other sources. When the average P/E of a sector is over 35, most likely there will be a fierce correction for that sector. When it is over 40, the market most likely has peaked. When you find fewer value stocks than before, it means the market is riskier now.

The P/E of the S&P 500 index was 28 in 2000. It was 18 in 2007 and 16 in 2015. Both are over 15, the average value for the last five years.

The value of the average P/E has to be adjusted as the market conditions are not the same 10 or so years ago. Today (2016) part of the earning (the E in P/E) is due to the low cost in borrowing and less wage cost due to hiring overseas. Most global corporations can offshore jobs to reduce expenses. The global economies are interconnected far better than before. When the global economies fall, we will fall too.

5. Triggers to burst a bubble.
In 2000, the trigger was the tech bubble. In 2007 it was the housing (or financing) bubble. It was easy to spot a massive tech bubble in 2000. I moved most of my tech sector funds to traditional sectors (cash for 20-20 hindsight) in the beginning of April, 2000, which was too close for comfort to this market plunge.

Most investors including myself did not understand the workings of the derivatives of the mortgage loans and could not recognize the bubble. I made good money in the oil sector in 2007. However, in 2008 most of my investments were losers including the investment in the oil sector. If I followed the hints described in this chapter, I would have avoided heavy losses.

6. Rising interest rates.

It is more expensive for investors using margin to buy stocks, for companies to borrow money and for consumers to buy high ticket items and houses.

A related hint is rising margin debt (the debt used to buy stocks backed up by the current stock holdings). When we have a record of margin debt as in 2016, the chance of a market plunge is high when the Fed hikes the interest rates.

When the Fed discount rate is 5% or above, be careful. This is also the time to buy long-term bonds. When it is 1% or less, most likely the market starts to recover. This is also the time NOT to buy long-term bonds. This strategy was proven in market cycles in 2000 and 2008.

7. Yield Curve.

When the short-term (say 3 month) interest rates are higher than the long term (say 30 years), it is abnormal and a bearish signal. Click here to check the yield curve.

Many use two-year Treasury and ten-year Treasury. As of Oct. 15, 2018, they were 2.82% and 3.09% and it was very close to being equal and gave us some warning of a potential recession. You may want to move some of your risky investments such as stocks to safer investments such as CDs and short-term bonds. As of 2018, only two false warnings from the last seven recessions when an inverted yield occurred. Again, your action depends on your risk tolerance.

http://www.treasury.gov/resource-center/data-chart-center/interest-rates/Pages/TextView.aspx?data=yield
http://blogs.marketwatch.com/thetell/2014/05/13/bear-market-wont-come-until-the-yield-curve-says-so-kleintop/

8. Rising oil price.

It is the same as the above as rising oil prices will make everything more expensive. However, today (2015-2016) is an exception. The falling oil price correlates with the market. It is due to falling too much and the oil-producing countries have to dump the stocks to rescue their economies. If I have to put a number, I would say the market is risky when the oil price is below $30 or above $120.

9. Market experts.

There are always two camps predicting the market trend. Check out those that make sense and ignore those who try to sell you books or their services. The media try to scare you to improve the circulation. The reason I exited the market in April, 2000 is the result of reading an article that said the entire company of an internet company could fit into a conference room of a company with the same market cap. Good seeds that fall on fertile soil will prosper. The opposite is true when bad seeds fall on poor soil.

10. Politics.
The long market rise from 2009 to 2016 is due to the low interest rates even though the economy is not doing well. The interest rate is controlled by the Federal Reserve Bank, which is an agent of the government. As of 2016, the low interest rate saved the market at the expense of our national debt which was at the recent peak. Trump's proposed 45% tariff could bring global recession starting in the US and China.

11. Miscellaneous.
In 2000, I exited the market after reading an article describing how the entire corporation could fit into a big conference of a large corporation. In 2008, we had a "Double Top" technical indicator that correctly told us of a market plunge.

Be conservative
As in any new strategy, test it out and try it out gradually with real money. Most of you paid less than $25 for this book and most likely you do not want to risk all your money based on a $25 advice, so consult your financial advisors. You should not lose money by exiting the market too early, but miss the opportunity to make more money. If the market does not crash, treat it as insurance. No one can predict market directions consistently and correctly. This article gives you better hints to time the market and all markets are different.

The chart worked fine for the last two crashes, but as in life there is no guarantee to detect the next market crash for the following reasons:

- It may not give us ample time to react as the last two. The current market is high and is caused by excessive money supply. When the money supply is reduced (or no more QEn), the market will react negatively.
- When too many folks buy my books and use the same chart, it will lose its effectiveness. It is most likely not, but there is always a chance.
- Past performances do not guarantee future performance.
- The market is not always rational.

- There are more noises (crossing the red line and backing again briefly) since 2011. The chart is not the only indicator I follow. Adjust it according to your risk tolerance.

Since 2011, there have been several exits/entries as the market is not rational. However, if you follow it, you're still faring well as they tell you reentry very quickly. You do not lose or gain a lot by doing so. Even if you lose a little, it could be the best insurance you bought.

The noises would be increased if we use 200 days in SMA in the chart instead of 350. For the same reason, they will be decreased if I use 400 days but the signal will be later delayed.

As in life, there is nothing guaranteed, the chart is far better than market timing without charts and/or no market timing at all since 2000. Start looking at the charts more frequently when you feel the market is risky.

Conclusion

This article provides my basic tools and my views on market timing. Market is not always rational otherwise there are no poor folks as stated before. When the market is about to plunge, run the chart more frequently and read more articles written by market experts.

Market timing is not an exact science but it is based on educated guesses. The better guesses should have more rights than wrongs in the long term. Your actions depend on your risk tolerance. Initially you should be careful on using any strategy that you do not have full understanding and enough proven record.

Technical analysis (SMA-350) is more important than fundamentals as an overvalued market could linger for years as in 2009 to 2017. Also recommend to read articles on experts on the current market. There are always two camps.

Links:
Market crash
https://www.youtube.com/watch?v=GJD2BYhVyrM

6 Signs of market crash
https://www.youtube.com/watch?v=ynCXHgeZ_K8

2 More tools

Using VIX as a timing model

When I overlapped VIX and the S&P 500 index, I found a consistent pattern. However, it has not been conclusive to me. Try to enter VIX in any chart system such as Yahoo!Finance with the S&P 500 overlaid. In the summer of 2008, VIX jumped about 500% from about 15 to 89.

\# VIX
http://en.wikipedia.org/wiki/VIX
\# VIX from Yahoo!Finance.
http://finance.yahoo.com/echarts?s=^VIX+Interactive#
\# There are several articles on the topic.
http://seekingalpha.com/instablog/434935-south-gent/3373095-vix-asset-allocation-model.
\# Ted Talk: 1
http://www.ted.com/talks/didier_sornette_how_we_can_predict_the_next_financial_crisis

Other technical indicators
- Head and Shoulder would predict a market plunge as evidenced in 2007. The reverse pattern would predict a market surge as indicated in 2009.
- Double Top is a bearish signal and double bottom is a bullish signal.
- Death Cross is used to detect large plunges and it does not require charting via Finviz.com. Golden Cross detects when to return.
- MACD (Moving Average Convergence Divergence). When the indicator is below the zero line, it is bearish and vice versa. Use it as a secondary indicator to detect the market direction.
- When RSI (14) is over 65%, the market is most likely overbought (i.e., overvalued).
- Use the following SMA-20 as a secondary indicator as an alternative to the SMA-350. When the stock price is below SMA-20 (Single Moving Average for the last 20 sessions) for three consecutive days, it indicates a possible market plunge. In theory, the institutional investors dump the stock on the first day and then the retail investors follow on the second day. If it continues on the third day, most likely it is not the trick of the institutional investors to take advantage of the retail investors.

Sound Advice Risk Indicator
We only invest in stocks or real estates in a crude sense. This indicator comparing the allocations between these two investments has been quite

successful. When we invest too much in the stock market instead of real estate, we will expect a market crash. When this index hit 2 as in 1906, 1928, 1937 and 1965, we had market crashes at all these times. Today (12/2018), we have a similar warning. Use Google to search for articles mentioning this indicator. Here is one of many.

Buffett's Equity to GDP
It measures the value of the market. It has been quite successful. Google for the current value. Advisor Perspectives may have this value and many insights on the current market. It will not detect the peaks and bottoms as no one can consistently. About a third of the earnings of the S&P 500 companies come from abroad. Hence it boosts market cap but doesn't include those countries' GDP. This is a major fault.
https://www.youtube.com/watch?v=dexOhg3pYa0

3 Related topics

Other related hints on value

The oil and industrial commodities (copper, steel...) are within 20% of their record highs. From my memory, it is the first time that oil is in sync with the market due to the dumping of stocks by the oil-producing countries today.

The total market cap is higher than the GDP. As of Nov., 2013, "Market Cap / GDP" is about 110% (fair value at 85%) and hence it is overvalued. Daily ratios can be obtained from GuruFocus.com, a paid subscription service. It does not work in the current cycle from 2008. It may be today because most large companies are multinational. However, today most large companies are global companies, so it loses some luster in using this ratio.

Dow Theory and many similar market timing strategies may become less effective as every market is different. Many ignore the service industries such as selling music and games via downloading.

From my observation, the higher the interest rates are, the higher the chance that a market plunge will be. The companies will have less earnings due to the higher borrowing costs especially in businesses that require a lot of borrowing and/or most of their customers' purchases are via financing. The stocks are more expensive to buy using margin accounts. Hence, the market will not fare well when the Fed hikes the interest rate.

Q including intangible assets is with P/E in evaluating the value of the market. It is harder to calculate.

Shiller P/E (same as CAPE or PE10)

It can be used to detect the valuation of the market. The P is the S&P 500 (or use SPY) and E is the average earnings of the last 10 years. It can also be used on sector ETFs and stocks. Use it as one of the hints. The major flaw is 10 years is too long of a time.

To simplify, most likely the market valuation is low (good to buy) when the P/E is below 15. The market valuation is high when it is above 20. As of 2014, it is far above 20 (17 in 2/2016). CAPE (cyclically adjusted price/earnings ratio) is available from the web by searching "CAPE P/E" to get the current reading.

Shiller's P/E   http://www.gurufocus.com/shiller-PE.php
From the above links, CAPE has been pretty decent. The reason why it does not work in 2014 is the excessive money printing that makes the market not act rationally. Treat it as a secondary yardstick at best. Here is a good article on P/E and PE10.
https://www.advisorperspectives.com/dshort/updates/2016/11/01/is-the-stock-market-cheap

He has been wrong since 2011 for calling recession every year. Here is his 2020 prediction. A best seller has been preaching similar ideas of bubbles since 2009.

Fear and Greed
This index from cnnFn.com is a similar contrary index. Leave the market when Greed is high and vice versa.

Many high-flying internet stocks lost more than 95% of their peak values. As in any bubble, the last ones to get into the bubble suffer most. The investors make out pretty nicely if they use the strategies below:

- Use a stop loss to protect your profits. Periodically adjust the order when the stock appreciates.
- Use SMA-20% (from Finviz.com). When the stock falls below the Simple Moving Average for the last 20 sessions, sell it. Use SMA-50 instead if you have a higher risk tolerance.

Lazy man's market timing
Sound Advice Risk Indicator, Equality to GDP, Inverted Interest Curve and Death Cross make up the lazy man's market timing. Google for the current values of the four. If you cannot get the last one, calculate it from Finviz.com.

Fear of recession: https://www.youtube.com/watch?v=g_LeWSl2nJc

Fidelity
From Fidelity.com, click on "News & Research" and then "Stock Market & Sector Performance" for Equity Market Commentary.

My experiences

I did not time the market seriously until 2008.

- 2000 Exit. I moved most of my sector funds (most in tech) to traditional sectors after reading articles on how overpriced the internet stocks were. It would be more profitable if I moved them to cash. They did not have contra ETFs then. I could not short stocks in my retirement accounts and I did not have experience in options.
- 2003 Return. I bet the market would return in two years. I bought many stocks which could survive in two years with the cash they had. I was lucky that the market returned in the same year. One stock was acquired by IBM with a huge gain.
- 2008 Exit. I did have the chart but I did not follow it. My big wins in energy stocks in 2007 gave me false security. When the market crashed, the energy stocks crashed too. I sold some stocks during the crash. I should have bought contra ETFs.
- 2009 Return. My chart told me to return in mid-March, 2009. I started buying in Feb., 2009. With the accumulated short-term capital losses, I traded stocks. I used my home equity loan that has far lower interest rates than my margin account – not recommended. I used the margin account only to fill up the gaps between trades. Most of the time, the margin and the loan were zero. It could be my best year with making about 80% profit in my largest taxable account.
- Search the current YouTube video for "Market Sense" or search it within Fidelity.

False alarm
From 2000 to 2010, there is only one false alarm. From 2011 to 2016, there were more false alarms. We can change the parameter from SMA-350 to SMA-400 to reduce the number of false alarms at the expense of detecting the plunge a little late. The market before 2000 is quite different from the market today. Hence, I do not use the data before 2000.

4   Why the market fluctuates

The following chart uses SPY (simulating the market) with SMA-350 for the year of 2020 using Fidelity's charting function. It will be used to demonstrate how SMA-350 worked for 2020; the dates may be several days off. This article is written on 1/1/2021.

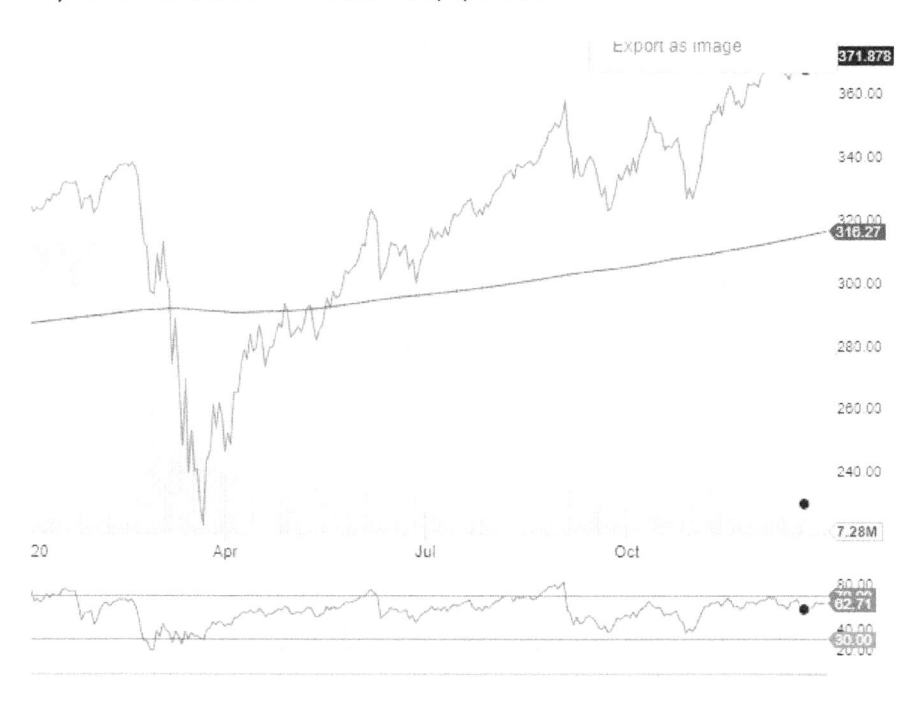

Market Timing

SMA-350 (Simple Moving Average for the last 350 sessions), described in this book, worked fine in 2020. It told us to exit the market on about 3/11/2020 and return on about the beginning of June. There were two false signals (on about 4/28 and 5/8) that told you to exit but return to the market shortly.

The other indicators are RSI(14) and P/E. Fidelity's chart uses 80 for overbought and 30 for under-bought for RSI(14). The market has been overpriced for a long while. In this case, technical analysis (SMA-350 I used in my example) works better than fundamental (P/E as one of the metrics); It has been sold for the entire 2020.

Why there is a big drop in late March and why it comes back

The trigger is the pandemic.

The market came back for many reasons:
- We understood the pandemic better.
- A lot of money on the sideline.
- The government supplies more money by printing it excessively.
- The government lowers the interest rate (almost to zero).

2021 prediction

It is quite hard to predict the market. Here are my thoughts. The market is not rational (fundamentally speaking).

For:

- The government keeps on excessively supplying money.
- With easy credit, the rising housing market leads to many profitable sectors such as furniture.
- Due to easy credit and recovery, many companies buy back their own stocks.
- Low margin interest rate usually boosts the stock market.
- If the vaccines can control this pandemic, many sectors will recover. As I demonstrated before, we have to wait one more year for some sectors such as airlines, restaurants and cruise lines.
- Trade war with China could be reduced under Biden.

Against:
- The pandemic has not been stopped.
- Unemployment is breaking the previous record.
- Small businesses continue to go bankrupt.
- Complete decoupling with China.
- The government tools do not work anymore such as lowering interest rate.
- Super inflation is due to ample supply of money chasing a fixed amount of assets (stocks for example). It would also shake the status of the USD as a reserve currency.

As in any market, there are two camps opposite to each other. Need to watch the market like a hawk and take actions accordingly (talk to your financial advisor first). I expect the plunge would cause the market to lose about 40% if it happens.

5   Double tops & a faster indicator

The following is the chart to use double tops to detect the last market peak in 2007.

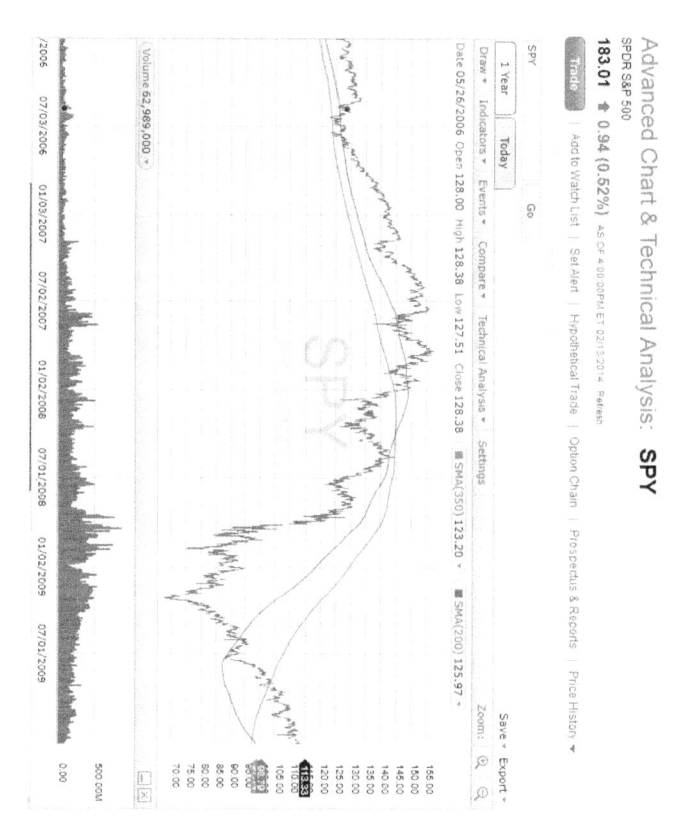

SPY: SMA.   Source: Fidelity

If you have a small screen on your e-reader, produce a similar graph using Yahoo!Finance. Enter SPY and select Technical Indicator. Select SMA and 350 days. Select the date from 1/3/2006 to 1/3/2010. Do another graph with SMA-200 as an overlay.

Critical dates

Table: Vital Dates

Market Plunge	Peak	Bottom	Indicator Exit	Indicator Reenter
2007	10/12/07	03/06/09	01/03/08	09/08/09

The following were obtained from my naked eyes to obtain the data from the graph. They are not accurate but are fine for discussion.

Top	Date	SPY
First	07/17/07	155
Second	10/11/07	157
Difference	86	1%
Selected	10/11/07	
Peak	10/12/07	

The SMA-350 indicator suggested us to exit the market on 01/03/08, about 83 days past the peak (10/12/07). Double Top is a better indicator here as it told us only one day before the peak. Will it happen again? Only time can tell.

Double Bottom

Again, the following is from my naked eyes to obtain the data from the graph.

Bottom	Date	SPY
First	03/17/08	127
Second	07/15/08	122
Difference	120	-4%
Selected	07/15/08	
Bottom	03/06/09	

Arbitrarily, I use the absolute difference of 5% or less to determine the double bottom condition (the absolute % of the second bottom to the first bottom).

The SMA-350 indicator suggests us to reenter the market on 09/08/09, about 186 days past the bottom (03/06/09). Double Bottom tells us to reenter the market about 234 days after the bottom. Hence, double bottom as defined here is not a good indicator.

It is interesting that the difference of days is 120. If we use 100 days as the threshold, then it is not qualified to be a double bottom.

We may want to use the earlier of either the chart or the double bottom to determine when to reenter the market.

Is SMA-350 better than SMA-200?
From the graph in this article, I conclude that SMA-200 has more noise that tells you to exit and reenter (or the other way) more often than SMA-350. It is logical as SMA-350 uses a longer duration (350 days vs. 200 days) for the moving average.

However, SMA-200 tells you to reenter the market earlier from the actual bottom in my limited tests. Hence, it is more profitable at least for the market plunge in 2007. For the next plunge, I would use SMA-350 to exit the market and SMA-200 to reenter the market. Is it just coincidental?

A faster, confirming indicator

In case you do not exit the market on the first sign, another faster technical indicator (SMA-50) would confirm the market plunge when it crosses over the SMA-350 downwards on Jan. 18, 2008 as an indicator in the following graph. The reentry using cross-over does not fare that well as expected.

In addition, high volume (compared to the average volume is a confirmation. To illustrate, if today's volume of SPY doubles its average daily volume, then it is a good confirmation.

Link
Double Tops: http://www.investopedia.com/terms/d/doubletop.asp
Double Tops Video.
https://www.YouTube.com/watch?v=b-PaSDJiG2U

Illogical English

How can you "flying on a jet plane" (only Afghans can do so, which is a sad joke)? It should be "in". Did Peter, Paul and Mary screw it up?

6   Retail investors and market timing

The average retail investor has advantages over the fund managers. However, the average retail investor does worse than the market. They buy high and sell low - a kind of herd mentality.

In quarterly summaries, Fidelity demonstrated this more than one time. It shows that most retail investors moved their stocks to money market funds when the market was at temporary bottoms (or close to it), and moved them to equities when the market was at temporary peaks (or close to it).

It could be a good contradictory indicator if Fidelity or any fund company publishes this money market flow.

Morningstar has similar proof. From 2000 to 2010, equity funds earned an annualized return 1.6% while an average investor captured a .2% return due to moving in and out of the funds at the wrong time.

From my own observation, investors' sentiment works in the short term, but not in the long term.

It makes 'Buy and Hold' look great. The best strategy is 'Buy at the bottom and sell at the top'. It is easier to preach than practice. Can we overcome the human nature of 'Fear and Greed'?

The majority of retail investors do worse than the market and so are most fund managers. Logically, a group of investors must beat the market. They are the institutional investors besides the fund managers. We try to be as good as this group. It is achievable if you read the chapters on market timing, stock selection and strategies in this book. Most institutional investors do not time the market and we, the retail investors, have an advantage.

Do not act right away on the financial news you hear. A lot of the time, they're contradictive, sometimes manipulative and always too late to be useful. Reading WSJ or Baron's is more useful.

Cramer will tell you how the market is manipulated.
https://www.YouTube.com/watch?v=GOS8QgAQO-k

Afterthoughts

- Searcher said:
  Guess it is a given that I, as a proxy for the average investor, am very likely to buy high and sell low because I become giddy, or at least complacent, at higher highs and frozen with fear and indecisive at a declining market until the psychic pain forces capitulation. Should I have the good fortune to encounter this article and divest, I'm not sure that I'll have the same fortune to overcome my fear and general malaise in avoiding a bear 'fake out'. Thus, riding the market up looking for confirmation until, guess what? I'm buying at the top.

- Clay said:
  In my nearly 40 years in the investment mgt. arena, I find that a very small percent sells at the tops and buy at the bottoms and it is the same ones over and over. The long-term investor, from my experience, has been the clear winner in holding good stocks through thick and then. The trader may miss a bear market, but usually leaves very early, and comes back in very late. There's the formula for subpar performance.

- DanT, an x-stock analyst, said:
  The retail investor has every advantage over the institutional investor. You might not know just how right you are.
  Needless to say, it's also true that many retail investors (especially untutored ones) shoot themselves in the foot by reacting emotionally to market fluctuations. To augment what you said about Fidelity's research regarding money markets, did you know that under Peter Lynch, most of Fidelity Magellan's shareholders in fact lost money during Mr. Lynch's tenure? Guess how they lost it -- selling low and buying high.

  Very dubious am I, however that anyone can time the market, and the more confident one is in one's self-regarded timing "skills" or the level of technical research they engage in, the greater the danger there is. For the individual investor - any individual investor - it's the best answer to the vicissitudes of the market, in all applications.

  The trick then, if you're still concerned with buying at too high a price, is to scale back during boom times and establish more conservative positions while throwing a little more money around after panics or flash crashes. The problem many people have, I've found, is that the money burns a hole in their pocket and they lack the discipline to maintain a cash reserve. A cash reserve isn't sexy, you can brag about the returns you get on your money market or savings acct..., but when you can scoop up a few thousand shares of XOM after the Dow falls a few hundred points, you feel better about it.

- With skills in market timing, one can beat the 'Buy and Hold' strategy. However, for the majority, 'Buy and Hold' is not a bad strategy.

- The retail investors moved billions to cash in 2009, the market bottom. Who are the lucky buyers? Institutional investors of course and hopefully my readers next time!

Links

Old links with the basic ideas never fade.
Advantages:
http://www.tonyp4idea.blogspot.com/2011/11/no-more-investing-hero.html
Herd mentality:
http://www.tonyp4idea.blogspot.com/2011/12/fool-of-all-fools.html
Crash of 1987: https://www.youtube.com/watch?v=jLfjEMDJubg

Fillers
Cocktail parties in 1999
I had a hard time convincing my friends and coworkers in 2000. How can you tell the lottery winners not to buy lottery tickets? We do have many rocket stocks today. From my books, I recommend you use trailing stops.

Deflation
Deflation is worse than inflation for companies. When the company finds they have to sell the products at lower prices than expected, they have to cut down some products and lay off employees.

The main job of the Federal Reserve Bank is adjusting inflation/deflation to some acceptable levels.

Section II: Market cycle

1   Market cycle

"Bull markets are born on pessimism, grow on skepticism, mature on optimism, and die on euphoria" - Sir John Templeton

The stock market has cycles as our practical interpretation of the above. It is about five years apart, but it fluctuates widely. I divide it into four stages: Bottom, Early Recovery, Up and Peak.

My defined four stages of a market cycle

We need to apply the right investing strategies to each of the four stages of the cycle.

- **Bottom**

    I would not invest for at least the first six months (or even a year) after the big plunge starts, which could lose over 25% in a few months. The exceptions are investing in contra ETFs and selling short for aggressive investors.

    I estimate it will take a year from the start of the plunge to the bottom, so I will normally sell stocks early in the plunge and do not buy stocks that are in the sector (sometimes sectors) that cause the bubble for about two years after the plunge.

    At the bottom, the high-yield corporate bonds (i.e., junk bonds) would prosper when the interest rate is decreasing to stimulate the economy.

    From mid-2007 to mid-2008, bonds suffered as the investors thought the sky was falling down - it was to those who lost their jobs and/or their houses. After that, some bonds, especially the long-term bonds, could appreciate about 50% in the following year.

    The government lowered the interest rates and these bond prices with high interest rates surged. Correct timing in buying bonds could be very profitable.

    Long-term bonds have more impact by the interest rate: The lower the interest rate, the higher the bond prices of higher-yield bonds. The older bonds with higher interest rates are more valuable to the newer bonds with lower interest rates.

I define this period of the bottom from the start of the plunge to the start of Early Recovery.

- **Early Recovery**
  It usually starts after one year from the plunge; no one can pinpoint the exact time consistently. By this time preferably earlier, we should have closed out all positions in contra ETFs and shorts.

  Roughly speaking, October, 2007 (some use 2008) is the start of the market plunge. March, 2009 is the end of the bottom stage and the start of the early recovery stage of the 2007 cycle. However, every market cycle is different in where it starts and ends.

  The one-year gain from the bottom is most profitable. It usually gains over 25% in a year from the market bottom. I, a conservative investor, had huge gains using some leverage in my largest taxable account in 2009. From my memory, I had a similar return in 2003 but I had not saved the statement as in 2009.

  In this phase, value is a better parameter than growth in searching for stocks. If your investment subscription provides a composite value score and a composite timing score, the sort parameter of your screened stocks could be "Composite Value / Composite Timing" in descending order. Select the top stocks in this order. You still have to analyze the top-screened stocks.

  Forward (same as Expected) P/E is a good metric. However, most companies may be losing money at this stage. Those companies that can last for more than one year with its cash reserve are potential good buys. The best appreciated stocks are beaten companies that have precious technologies and good customer bases. They could be candidates to be acquired if they are small enough.

- **Up**
  Usually, the growth metrics such as PEG could be better than the value metrics such as expected P/E during this phase. Most stocks are winners except contra ETFs and shorting stocks. When the growth stocks are making headlines and the defensive stocks are being

dumped, this is the hint that we're well into the Up phase of the market cycle.

Locate stocks with growth metrics such as favorable PEG and high SMA-200% (from Finviz.com). Do not be scared of how much they have already appreciated. The strategy "Buy High and Sell Higher" works in this phase. Protect your profits with stops.

Ensure that they have value too. Skip the stocks with expected P/Es higher than 35 unless there are good reasons. Most stocks will gain due to the tide of the market. However, when they're overbought (RSI(14) over 65), be careful. When institutional investors sell these stocks, they will crash.

- **Peak**
When everyone makes easy money and the interest rates are high, watch out. Stop loss and/or stop limit should be used to protect your investment. Check out whether there is any bubble that would burst like the internet in 2000 and finance (and housing) in 2007.

The internet crisis is easy to spot, but not the financial crisis. In 2007 we had a cycle longer than the average which is about 5 years. The plunge is very fast and very steep – thanks to the institutional investors who drive the market down.

Run the technical analysis chart described in the Chapter on Spotting Big Market Plunges at least monthly (weekly if you have time). Protect your investment. Do not fall in love with any stock (you can buy it back later at a deep discount). Making the last buck is a fool's game.

Accumulate cash according to your risk tolerance. A retiree or a conservative investor would accumulate from 25% to 50% and should be ready to move to all cash when the plunge starts.

We can lower the cash percent if we use enough stop loss protection. Be psychologically prepared because the stock market may still rise for a while. There is no perfect market timing.

The 2007 Cycle
The market plunged starting in 10-2007 and ending in 3-2009 (bottom), started to recover in 3-2009 (early recovery), and trended up from 2010

to 1-2013 (the up phase of the market cycle). As of 3/2016, it is the peak phase defined by me.

As of 1/2013, we have recovered all the market losses since 2007. However, as of 7/2014, the economy has not fully recovered compared to the economy before the plunge. The employment judging by the medium salary has not fully recovered and the economy is not expanding. It is uncommon that the economy does not follow the market. It is due to the excessive supply of money by the government and partly due to globalization to allow companies to hire overseas.

Although a W-shaped recession seldom happens, we have a chance today. We hope we do not have a depression and/or the similar lost decades that Japan has been experiencing. Some may conclude we are close to completing a market cycle from 2007 to 2016. As of 2016, the economy is recovering slowly and we're better than most other global economies.

Again, market timing is not an exact science as it involves irrational human beings and government interventions. The timing using the market cycle described here is a guideline as it is hard to time it exactly.

The average market cycle is about 5 years, but they fluctuate. If we consider 2007 as the plunge, we have about 8 years of this cycle as of 2015.

In a typical cycle (few are typical), we have about one year in each of the 4 phases I defined (plunge, early recovery, up and peak).

Events/Triggers

There are financial events and triggers that cause the transition of one phase of the market cycle to another. They usually do not change the sequence of the phases (say not from Peak to Early Recovery), but they may change the duration of the phase. Examples are:

- The government announcing change of the interest rate,
- Change of employment, and
- Change of GNP.

Sectors in a market cycle (my suggestion)

Market Phase	Favorable	Unfavorable

Early Recovery	Financial, Technology, Industrial	Energy, Telecom, Utilities
Up	Technology, Industrial, Housing	
Peak	Mineral, Health Care, Energy, Long-Term Bond, Consumer Discretionary	
Bottom	Consumer Staples, Utilities	Consumer Discretionary, Technology, Industrial, Long-Term & high-yield Bond

The sectors that cause the recession usually take a longer time to recover. In 2000, the technology sector was not favorable in the Early Recovery phase, contrary to the above table. In 2007, the financial sector was not favorable in the Early Recovery phase. These are the "offending" sectors that cause the plunges.

In a recession, we usually cannot cut down on consumer staples and utilities, but we can cut down on buying consumer gadgets. Companies usually postpone investing in equipment and systems during a recession and expand when the economy is humming. The government usually lowers the interest rates right after the plunge to stimulate the economy.

Conclusion

When the market is about to plunge or change from one stage to another, run the described chart more frequently and read more articles written by the experts.

Again, market timing is not an exact science but it is based on educated guesses. The better guesses should have more rights than wrongs in the long term. Our actions depend on our risk tolerance. Be careful of using any new strategy that has not been fully understood and proven. Since 2000, market timing is very important to your financial health with two market plunges with an average of about 45% loss.

Afterthoughts

- The Dow Theory has a lot of followers in detecting market directions. In a nutshell, the market heading upwards is confirmed by the Industrial Index and the Transportation Index (less important in today's market especially with internet sales such as songs and movies), and vice versa. As of 4/2014, the two indexes are not in uniform.

http://finance.yahoo.com/blogs/talking-numbers/this-is-a-130-year-old-warning-sign-for-stocks-231901097.html

- The bear market has the following three phases.
1. The market is overvalued.
2. Corporations are not doing well with decreasing earnings and sales.
3. Investors are selling due to fears.

It is the reverse for a bull market: 1.The market is under-valued. 2. The market increases due to increasing corporate profits/sales and 3. Investors are buying due to greed.
- Investopedia has several articles on this topic.
  http://www.investopedia.com/terms/b/businesscycle.asp
- The yield curve could predict the interest rates change and hence the economy. There are three main types of yield curve shapes: normal, flat and inverted.

  A normal yield curve is one in which longer maturity bonds have a higher yield. Similarly, the long-term CD should have a higher interest rate than the short-term CD.

  When the shorter-term yields are higher than the longer-term yields, it indicates an upcoming recession. A flat yield curve indicates the economy is transiting. Now, you've read the essence of a book on this topic costing about $50 to buy.

  However, especially today, it does not mean anything as the government supplies too much money to stimulate the economy unsuccessfully. My simple chart described using SMA-350 (Simple Moving Average for 350 trading sessions) which depends on the stock price works better. Click here for "The dynamic yield curve" (http://stockcharts.com/freecharts/yieldcurve.php).

  The interest rate plays a role too. The easy money encourages folks to borrow money to buy stocks and companies to acquire other companies.
- As of Feb., 2013, I believe we're in the Up stage of the market cycle. I checked the performances of my top screens from each stage (a.k.a. phase) of the market cycle for the last 60 days. The best performance as a group belongs to the screens for the Up stage. Controversial! Always use the screens (same as searches) that perform well recently.

In addition, the market has recovered 120% of the loss of 2007-2008. Hence the duration for an average Up stage of the market is quite close.
- Total Market Cap / GNP ratio is hotly debated on the market value. Different from the traditional 100%, I would suggest that the boundary ratio should be 130%. If it is over 130%, the market is overvalued and vice versa.
http://www.investopedia.com/terms/m/marketcapgdp.asp
Market cycle: https://www.youtube.com/watch?v=ebWL2TrIssA
Bull market: https://www.investopedia.com/terms/b/bullmarket.asp

2   Bull / Bear market

This is a summary of my views. In short, most investments appreciate in a bull market, and vice versa in a bear market. It is indicated by the described Golden Cross and Death Cross. In 2022's bear market, even the bonds did not fare well. It is partly due to raising the interest rates too fast to counter inflation. If inflation is under control, the Fed would not have another interest hike.

The market cycle is usually ahead of the economy cycle. When conditions such as low interest rates, companies make easy money and hence boost the general economy. When the economy is overheated, the Federal Reserve has to increase interest rates to cool down the economy and prevent the formation of a bubble. At that time, most companies suffer and lay off workers. At the end of this cycle, the Federal Reserve most likely lowers the interest rates to stimulate the economy and start the cycle again.

Investors should be very careful in investing during the bear market and avoid failing companies. In the beginning of the bull market, invest in companies that their stock prices have been beaten up but have a good chance to survive. Many S&P 500 companies were formed during the bear market. The lack of venture capital is offset by lower expenses and fewer competitions.

#Filler: Destruction of a country

Is the membership of NATO worth the destruction of a country? Definitely not. A good politician should get the membership before his announcement. Murdering citizens is a war crime to me.

2 Actions for different stages of a market cycle

There are different strategies for the different stages of the market cycle.

Strategies during market plunges

The market plunge is defined as the period between the market peak and the market bottom. It usually lasts for one year or two.

When you spot the potential plunge, consider the following actions. It depends on your risk tolerance and your investment style.

1. Contrary to popular belief, parking cash is a strategy too. Cash is needed later to move back to equities.

2. Be conservative: Buy stocks based on value and not based on momentum. Reduce your new purchases and take profits especially on momentum stocks. I buy one stock for every two or three stocks I sold during this stage.

3. Protect your portfolio with stop orders. It is one of the few times I recommend stop orders. If you watch the market every day, just place market orders when your stock falls to a specific price.

4. Buy contra ETFs for aggressive investors.

5. Sell cover calls. I prefer to sell the stocks I own.

6. Older folks may not want to sell the stocks with huge gains (due to tax consideration) or stocks that give them an income stream of dividends. They can use options to protect potential losses for the stocks they own.

What to do after the plunge

In the first year after the start of the plunge, do not start to buy unless they are very good values. Aggressive investors should start closing their short positions/put options and selling contra ETFs.

When the market plunges, it usually takes at least one year to recover as investors believe they have to sell to protect their remaining nest eggs. Those sectors that cause the bubble will take even longer to recover.

After the plunge, watch out for the interest rate. If it is still high, it is the best time to buy high-yield bonds (i.e., junk bonds). Ensure that the corporation issuing the bonds would not bankrupt; the bonds from the old GM in 2007 lost most of their values. They will appreciate when the interest rate drops that the government would routinely do to stimulate the economy. 2008 is not a good year to invest in stocks and bonds except the contra ETFs and selling shorts, but 2009 definitely is (it is my Early Recovery phase of the market cycle).

Personally, I prefer not to buy any stocks until the chart tells us to reenter the market. It is the fear that investors do not want to reenter the market. The market will always recover as in the past.

Even before the recovery, some sectors (called consumer staple) are doing better such as health care, foodstuff, utilities and pharmaceuticals that are always in demand. Interest-sensitive sectors such as housing and auto will suffer disproportionately. They are also called cyclical stocks. Consumer Discretionary are sectors that suffer a lot in a recession such as high-tech products.

What to do in early recovery and after

When the market is starting to recover (2003 and 2009 in the last two market cycles), the potential profit is the highest. Buy deeply-valued stocks on companies that have been beaten down. They will recover with the highest appreciation potential. I call it the bottom fishing strategy.

Larger companies are fishing too to acquire smaller companies that fit into their corporate synergy or small companies with the technology and/or the customer base they need.

Valued stocks could be defined a little differently in this phase. Many times P/E is not a good metric as most companies are losing money. 2003 is such a year. If you expect the recession to end in 2 years and the company has enough cash to survive in two years based on its annual burn rate, then it would be a buy candidate.

In both 2003 and 2009, I spotted at least one company that was acquired by a larger company. From my memory, one company in 2003 was acquired by IBM giving me more than 2 times return. In 2009, at least three companies were acquired giving me an average annualized return of over 200%.

Momentum strategy rewards us best from the end of the early recovery phase to the peak phase. The up phase started in 2004 for the 2000 market cycle and 2010 in the 2007 market cycle.

Note. The parameters of SMA-200, SMA-350, SMA-90, etc. and RSI are different for market exit/reentry, correction exit and individual stocks. These are the guidelines only. Stocks are more volatile than the market and are very different among them. Hence, define the 'days' according to the historical pattern of the individual stock and how often you trade them.

Filler: My translation from my Chinese friend's poem

When you understand "everything is changing", you won't be boosting your achievements. Today's splendid life could be a mess tomorrow.

When you understand "everything is changing", you won't be sad. Today's gloom could turn into sunshine tomorrow.

When you understand "everything is changing", you know today's gain could be tomorrow's loss and vice versa.

When you understand "everything is changing", there is no need to react to today's loss, gain, happiness and sadness.

Link: Making money during a crash.
https://www.youtube.com/watch?v=DjDCg4750dw

Sectors for market stages:
https://www.youtube.com/watch?v=FRdeXgf0rN8

#Filler: Do not speculate
Many speculators made big and then lost it all. There are many examples from hedge funds.
Do not use leverage too much including the leveraged ETFs and margin accounts. Do time the market in a logical way. Stay in the market as we have more bullish years than bearish years if you do not time the market.

3   Profitable Early Recovery

I had about 80% return in 2009 in my largest taxable account. I did not include it in my other books before as I just found the statement. Early Recovery, a phase of the market cycle defined by me, is the best time to make a profit. My chart told me to start to move to equity in September, 2009. I did it in March, 2009 for other reasons. It could be luck, technique or both.

I did dip into the credit line of my equity loan (not recommended to most) due to lower interest rates than a margin interest. I paid back the loan right after I sold some stocks. The turnaround was high until I exhausted my short-term losses (tax loss harvest). The strategy is bottom fishing. Some sectors described are better in this stage of the market cycle.

I had similar success in 2003. I did not have a defined bottom fishing technique at that time. I expected the market to fully recover in two years. From Value Line, I selected stocks with high "Projected 3–5-year returns" and the short-term assets can last for two more years (judged by the burnt rates).

As the stocks are recovering earnings (E), the trailing P/E may not be a good indicator, but the Forward P/E may be. Most sites on evaluating stocks such as Fidelity have a value grade. Also look for candidates for acquisition. From the last recoveries, I spotted at least one such candidate. They are usually small companies (50 to 300M market cap) and have valuable assets such as customer base and patents. Aggressive investors should buy stocks with the worst timing grades and this the only time to do so; these beaten-up stocks could be big winners.

An article stated that the entire company of an internet company can fit into the conference room of Exxon, and it had the same market cap as Exxon if my memory serves me right. In early April, 2000, I switched all my tech mutual funds in my annuity into traditional sectors (better to cash in hindsight) to avoid the crash. Fishing in the market bottom is risky but very profitable. The Golden Cross could miss the bottom as it depends on past data. Other hints are Buy / Sell ratio is less than 0.2, RSI(14) for SPY is less than 25 and the market has more than 40% lower from the peak.

The stocks that have been beaten down badly and have poor timing scores could be the stocks that have the highest appreciation potential. It is different from the traditional evaluation. I prefer those stocks with positive earnings or at least not losing a lot. The appreciation periods for most of these stocks may not last long. Hence, I recommend using trailing stops (and reviewing the stops periodically) for appreciating stocks. To illustrate, you do not want to lose more than 10% from the peak of a stock and do not take profit prematurely.

My predictions for 2023. If the market recovers in 2023, it could be the beginning of a new cycle. We can use the market timing indicator to confirm it. If there is a serious recession, all bets would be off.

I invested a lot of defensive stocks such as consumer staples, healthcare and utilities. The stocks I recommended in 79% or my book "Best stocks for 2022" has a return of 4% beating RSP by 153% from Dec. 15, 2021 to Dec. 1, 2022. Not counting market timing and the acquired USAK that gained 79% and annualized to 105%.
http://tonyp4idea.blogspot.com/2022/12/best-stocks-series.html

During market recovery, usually the beat-up stocks recover first. Usually, the small stocks gain larger profit in the short term and then the large caps. Ensure the stocks are profitable or at least Forward P/E is positive.

Links:
Bottom fishing: https://www.youtube.com/watch?v=hANAn9szRBA
Recommended stocks for Q3 2022. Understand why.
https://www.youtube.com/watch?v=4IxS7pfGukM

4   A non-correlation of the market and business

The Business Cycle (same as the Economic Cycle) is supposed to lag the Market Cycle[1] by about 6 months as the stock market is a leading indicator of the economy. As of May of 2013, this has not occurred. The U.S. economy does not correlate to the stock market. It seldom happens. The market has recovered most of its losses from 2007-2008 and actually is making new heights.

The economy is still in a recession considering the high unemployment / under-employment and the poor GDP growth. The global economies are more interconnected than before, and our trade partners are also not doing well. Though there have been some recent signs of recovery in the U.S. economy, the job employment may never reach its previous peak. As of 3/2016, the non-correlation continues.

Is this non-correlation important to us, the retail investors?

For an economist, the Economic Cycle is important. For an investor, the Market Cycle is important. Economists forecast business growth, GDP growth, job growth, housing start, etc., and plan accordingly. Investors care about the potential appreciation of their portfolios.

It could be the beginning of this non-correlation for the coming decade. There is a good chance economists can no longer depend on the previous correlation to use the market to predict the economy at least for a while. As long as the market is moving up, investors are not concerned with the non-correlation.

However, most likely the market will correlate again in the future with the economy as there has always been a correlation as far as I can remember. Until the following reasons for this non-correlation change, the correlation will continue.

The reasons for this non-correlation
1. Most big companies are now global companies.
   Hiring at these multinational corporations (MNCs) depends on where the offer is for the greatest benefits including low workforce salary, educated workers, tax credits, less taxes, stable government, good infrastructure, etc. A good portion of MNCs' incomes are from foreign countries. Hence the U.S. market is getting less correlated with the U.S. economy which uses local employment as a measurement.
2. Too many government interventions.
   The government bailed out too many companies that should have failed. No companies are too big to fail. It has not punished the executives/bankers to get us into this recession through their greed. The market may falsely expect that future failing companies will be bailed out. Hence, the stock market is expected to be protected by the government.
3. There is still a lot of easy money.
   Since the recession, banks are flooded with government money to invest. They loan out money to investors instead of loaning it to small businesses and house buyers to stimulate the economy. In addition, the demands from businesses and potential house buyers have been reduced. The cash reserves if not loaned out must be very high.
   Corporations now have the highest cash reserves for a long while. They use their cash reserves to buy back their own stocks, acquire companies and increase dividends. All these actions increase their stock values. Dividend stocks are flocked by income seekers especially with low bond yields.
   When the government borrows a lot of money (to the ceiling literally), everything including the market looks good. However, somehow and sometimes the taxpayers will pay for those debts to China, Japan and whatever other treasury buyers. Today the U.S. has a benefit: It will repay the debtors with depreciated dollars (not true if 2016). A country

loses its competitive edge if a good percentage of the GDP is used for servicing those debts. If the USA were a company that could not service its debts, it would be bankrupt. Most believe this is the primary reason.
4. Government regulations typically do not help the economy. To illustrate, the expected Obamacare is discouraging small businesses from hiring.
5. Today's market may not be a good indicator of its value, if this were considered to be a commodity unit (a combination of natural resources including gold) instead of the USD.
6. There are too many factors that influence both the market and the economy in separate directions. Examples include the recent shale energy discovery which could improve the economy. A new war would do the opposite.

What should be done
1. The government cannot pump that much cash into the economy.

   Depreciating our currency is a short-term solution at best as it would improve our trade both ways. The status of being a reserve currency is shaken.
2. The United States government must address how to service its debt! The high debt will deteriorate the United States' competitive edge in the global markets. A high percentage of our GDP to service the debts will not help the economy.
3. We and the government need to bite the bullet with more taxes, more incentives to create jobs, less entitlements, less welfare... Ending the current two wars and avoiding future wars are almost mandatory to improve the economy.
4. The U.S. economy cannot be recovered without job recovery. The money spent in creating jobs will be better spent than on welfare and unemployment benefits. Hiring more government employees is the problem, not a solution.

Conclusion
It may be better to invest in a rising market than holding the depreciating cash. However, this non-correlation will not continue forever. The basic reason that stock appreciates is the company's ability to improve its earning. P/E is still the best yardstick on how fairly a company stock is priced. With a fixed 'E' for example and a rising 'P', the company's stock will be overpriced and will return to its average value (the average P/E for the last five years). The correlation will be back again in a matter of time.

Footnote
[1]The market can only act as a leading indicator or proxy of economic activity if there is consensus on the direction. Sometimes what is coming in six months is fairly predictable but at other times when pundits are at odds the future course is fuzzy. So, market indices are really tracking where consensus "thinks" GDP is going'.

To be clear a market index is a summary of where consensus believes the economy is headed and this sentiment is a proxy for forward earnings. For the playing stocks and not the index, it is their cumulative sentiment which acts as a guide.

Afterthoughts
- There are many other correlations. The following should correlate with the economy: construction industry, employment, commodity /commodity-related currency and oil. Once a while and for a good reason, they do not.
- QE, printing money, foreign loans (to China...), reserve currency, debt ceiling all mean the same: Live in a higher standard of living than we can afford.
  When Uncle Sam unsuccessfully uses all the tools to maintain our living standard and being the world's policeman, he runs out of tools. That will build a higher cliff for us to fall. Hopefully, shale energy will save our economy.
- The global economy still has not recovered as of July, 2013 according to this article.
(http://www.telegraph.co.uk/finance/economics/10174862/Renewed-fear-of-global-recession-as-companies-rein-in-spending-plans.html)
- Here are some economic indicators.
  http://en.wikipedia.org/wiki/Economic_indicator
- This time is REALLY different. Your Dad's generation does not have the internet, powerful PC, low-interest commission, trading at a click of the mouse... Global economies are better connected via the internet, shipping... All these affect our lives and economies.

5   A tale of two market plunges

I gather the data of the last two plunges (2000 and 2007) and check out what they have in common.

All the data are for information and education purposes only and so are the conclusions. All market plunges are different but some common characteristics do exist. Market plunges older than 2000 may not be useful as the market conditions then were very different from today's market.

Charts

The first one is for 2007 and the next one for 2000.

The following charts are also saved in the following link in case you read this book on a small screen. Type the following link in your browser to display the graph on your PC if desirable.

http://ebmyth.blogspot.com/2013/07/chart-market-plunge-2007.html

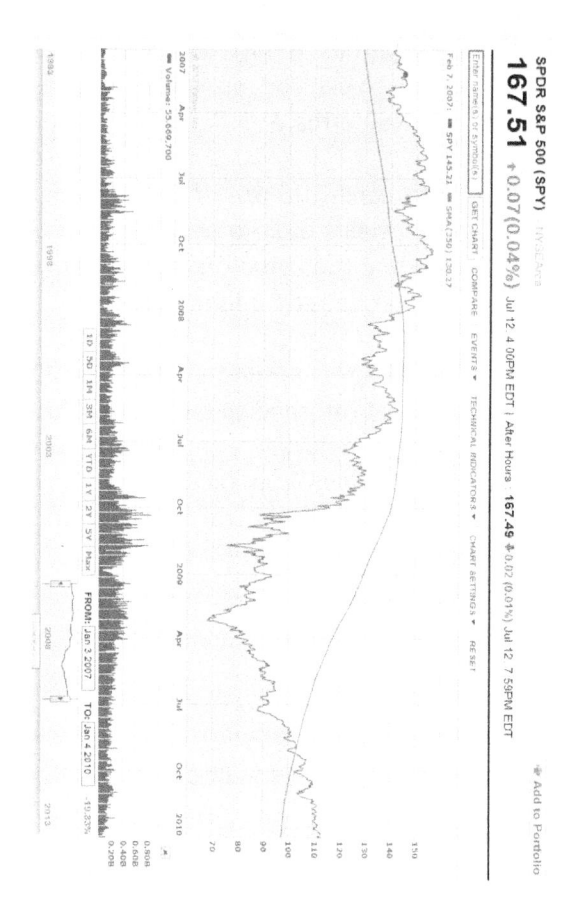

2007 Market Plunge Chart from Yahoo!Finance

Explanations:

- The red line is the 350-day SMA (simple moving average for the last 350 trade sessions). Sell when the price is below the SMA and buy when it is above the SMA. It gives us the exit point from the market and the reentry point to the market
.
- This chart uses SPY, an ETF simulating the S&P 500 index. A total market ETF would be a better choice unless you only trade the S&P 500 stocks. If most of your stocks are in small caps, use an index ETF for small caps. Instead of using an ETF, you can use any market index.

- The exit point is Jan. 7, 2008 (a brief indicator in Nov., 2007). Either exit point is fine. We should start to exit the market on Nov. 26, 2007 and this market plunge was nice to give us one more exit point. In reality, it takes us more time to exit the market totally. It looks like a double peak to me in technical terms.

- It is not possible to catch the peak from the chart (July – October, 2007), but this chart helps us to prevent further and bigger losses. I have researched to find the common metrics for peaks and bottoms. They have not been proven so far in my tests.

- The return to the market is around September, 2009 from the chart (above the 350 SMA). I returned to stocks in February, 2009, right at the bottom. It is just pure luck, my timing was based on the duration after the plunge, or many other factors that I may have forgotten. That's one reason we should take notes and learn from our experiences.

- Enlarge the chart by selecting a shorter date range or using a larger screen.

The following graph displays the same for the 2000 market plunge. If you have a problem in viewing it on the small screen, display it on your PC screen via the same link above. It is better to produce it yourself using Yahoo!Finance or one of the many sites to produce SMA charts.

#Filler: Why the market rises in 2019 and 2023

Since the end of WW2 and as of this writing in 2024, the market seems to be positive on the year before the election.

First the corporate tax has been cut deeply and it makes the corporate rise. Secondly, the interest rate has been maintained very low. It stimulates the economy, especially the housing sector. It also encourages buy-back to make the stock look better. However, it may not work in the long term.

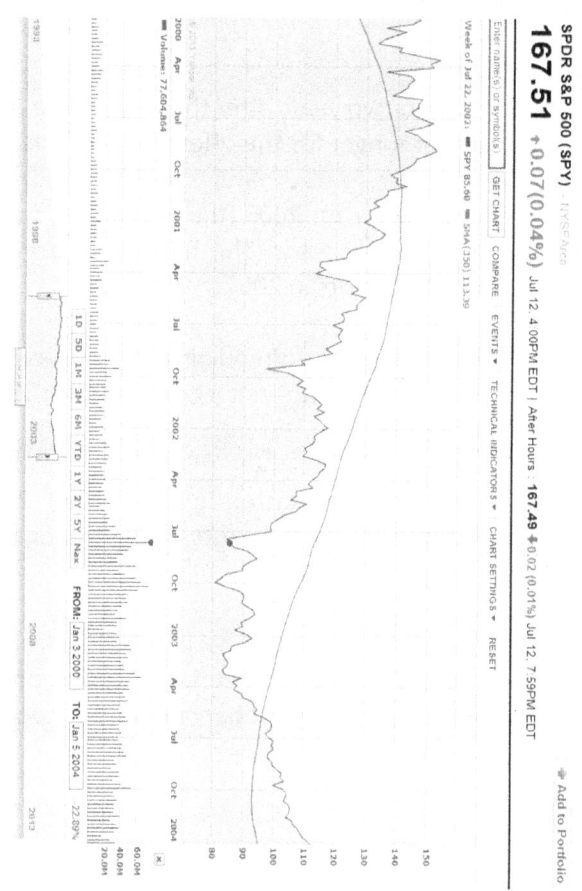

2000 Market Plunge Chart from Yahoo!Finance

Significant Periods

All the durations are estimates. They are different in each market plunge.

- Plunging period.
  It is the period between the start of the plunge (i.e., the peak) and the bottom. On the average, the duration of the plunge is about a year. Do not buy stocks during this period except selling shorts and buying contra ETFs to the market for aggressive investors.

- Early Recovery.
  It is the period between the market bottom and the mid part of the recovery and usually it starts one and a half year after the plunge.

Detecting the bottom

1. **By the duration.**
   It is about one to two years after the start of the plunge. It takes at least half a year longer for the offending sector(s) to recover.

   The offending sector for 2000 (the sector that caused the plunge) was the technology sector. The housing sector and the finance sector were the culprits in 2007.

   Some of the stocks in the offending sectors lose most or all of their values such as many internet companies in 2000 and Lehman Brothers in 2007.

   The market recovered faster in 2007 than 2000 due to the government intervention by excessively printing money.

2. **By the total loss.**
   Another hint is how much the market has lost from the peak. From the next table, 45% is a good bet. I start buying on 40% loss instead of 45%. There are many great bargains and we do not want to miss the opportunities.

3. **By the 350-day SMA.**
   For more conservative investors, wait for the stock price to pass the 350-day SMA (or other SMA such as the 200-day SMA). The 'day' is the last trade session.

All the market stages can seldom be predicted precisely. We are responsible for our own actions. Your actions also depend on your risk tolerance. A conservative investor would leave the market entirely on the first hint and return to the market slowly and gradually after the first hint.

Offending Sectors

Usually the offending sectors (the sectors that cause the bubble to burst) take at least 2 years to recover. Try out the SMA-350 and SMA-200 charts on the ETFs of these offending sectors.

ETFs and more articles on the offending sectors:

2007:   Housing ETF XHB and Financial ETF XLF.
        Housing bubble.

(http://en.wikipedia.org/wiki/United_States_housing_bubble)

2000:   Technology ETF XLK and Telecommunication IYZ.
        Internet bubble.
(http://en.wikipedia.org/wiki/Dot-com_bubble)

Depending on which report you read, the dates will not be exact. Some claim the housing crisis started in 2008 instead of 2007 and the internet crisis started in 2001 instead of 2000.

Summary by tables

Again, the dates are not exact and they depend on an individual interpretation. My table indicates 51% average loss and I use 45% as a more conservative number. I use my own dates and interpretations on the following tables.

Table: Market Plunges

Market Plunge	Months (Peak to Bottom)	Loss	Annualized loss
2000	17	56%	40%
2007	25	47%	23%
Average	21	51%	31%

Table: Vital Dates

Market Plunge	Peak	Bottom	Indicator Exit	Indicator Reenter
2000	08/28/00	09/20/02	10/30/00	05/26/03
2007	10/12/07	03/06/09	01/03/08	09/08/09

Most investors were fully invested in 2007 and 2008 and NOT fully invested in 2009. If you followed the exit indicator and reenter indicator, you should do far better than the average investor.

Afterthoughts
- Many including myself do not believe a market plunge is coming as of 7/2014. However, we have to be careful with the following analysis. Run the simple chart to spot any indication of a market plunge at least once a month. The following are from my experiences.

- o   Among my top-performing screens for the last 3 months, many top-performing screens are from the peak stage (defined by me) rather than other stages in a market cycle.

- o   The typical market cycle is about 5 years. It has been about 6 years since 2007.

- o   The stock market has not reached the bubble stage yet. It will if it continues to rise at this pace in 2014.

- On 6/20/2013, the market lost more than 2% in a day due to the Fed indicating no more easy money. The bond yield jumped. The Fed has been dumping about 1 trillion a year. When the money stops, the market would crash and the 2% loss seems to be a canary. Hopefully the current correction would be less than 10%

  [Update: only 6%]. Wall Street depends on the government handouts and the government is running out of tools to fix the economy.

- Some REITs are inversely affected by the rising interest rate.
  http://seekingalpha.com/article/1570772-american-capital-mortgage-investment-was-the-baby-thrown-out-with-the-bathwater

- Will the market go even higher as of 6/2014? We have to compare the risk / reward ratio. If the risk is too high, we may want to take some chips off the table.

- To me, there are 4 groups of investors.
    1. Institutional investors. Their performances vary. In short, hedge funds as a group have not beaten the market in the last 5 years.
    2. Mutual funds. Most cannot do market timing from their own regulations and as a group they do not beat the market after expenses.
    3. Retail investors are always on the wrong side of the market via fear and greed.
    4. While investors from #1 to #3 are losers, there must be some winners beating the market as a trade is a zero-sum game. In theory, we cannot beat the mutual fund managers who have better resources. However, we can use market timing to our advantage.

6   Secular bull market is coming!

My definitions

A secular stock market is a prolonged period (about 12 to 22 years) that the market is heading in one particular direction. There have been secular bear markets and secular bull markets depending on the direction of the stock market.

Market cycles exist within a secular market. Market cycles last for about 5 years. The market cycle of 2000-2007 lasted for about 7 years and the current one from 2007-to now (2016) for about 8 years so far.

Within a year there are usually two mini market cycles (I call them 5% corrections or dips/surges and sometimes one 5% and one 5-15% correction). The surges provide the best time to sell stocks and the dips provide the best time to buy stocks if there is no market plunge.

The secular market cycle, market cycle and yearly corrections (also defined by me as mini market cycles) are not scientific concepts. Hence, their average durations are very rough estimates. I use 20 years for the secular market cycle for the ease to memorize while 15 could be a better average.

Market Cycle vs. Economic Cycle

Understanding the Market Cycle is important to investors and the Economic Cycle (also known as the Business Cycle) is important to economists and businessmen. Do not be confused with the two. The secular economic cycle usually follows the secular market cycle as indicated in the last 60 years. With the obvious exception of the current one (2007-2016), the economic cycle usually lags the market cycle by an average of 6 months.

My prediction: The secular bull will start in 2018

Whenever a famous person predicts with any certainty that the end of the world is coming or the Dow will double next year, it is loudly broadcasted over the news. I predict that the next secular bull market will start as early as in 2018. Who would take me, a nobody, and his prediction seriously? If it does not happen, check out which ones of my many arguments are wrong and/or any unpredictable event or events have happened.

This is a bold prediction! There are reasons why it might happen and also reasons why it might not happen. I could write a book on this topic but I will spare you the details. However, let us carefully scrutinize the coming events to better clarify my prediction.

Timing is everything even though there is nothing truly considered as perfect timing. But be aware that reacting too early to a secular bull market can cost you money, and reacting too late to a secular bull market can miss the profit opportunity. Vice versa for a secular bear market.

Past secular markets

If the market is good, the economy would be good and every person would have a job in theory. Even the poor would benefit from the more generous government benefits and the increased individual generosity. Today, global corporations can hire any worker in any place in the world at the least cost to change the US employment picture.

I have identified the last three secular bull and bear markets (again they are rough estimates):

Secular bear market: 1960-1980
Secular bull market: 1980-2000
Secular bear market: 2000-2020

I did not include secular markets before 1960 as these times did not resemble today's market conditions.

In a secular bull market, every investor is a genius. Most of our stocks rise with the tide in a bull market. With the profits from the market, we spend more on disposable consumer products. During wars, most sectors fall except those making bombs, jets and tanks.

The cause of secular markets: War or lack of war

What causes the secular markets that usually last for about 20 years? My contribution to this theory is that war is the major common denominator to the secular bear markets. Though I have not read any article that distinguishes it out, I am sure the concept is so obvious that someone would have reached the same conclusion.

In the 1960s, it was the Vietnam War and the effects after this war. Today it is the two wars in the Middle East. Wars cost us a lot of resources. When these resources are devoted to the economy after the wars, the economy would grow.

After each major war, our leaders do not forget the harmful effects at least for a while. They cannot get re-elected with a new war, so there will be no major war for a long while. That's my explanation of the secular bull market from 1980-2000. After the year 2000, our leaders forgot the harmful effects of wars and history repeated itself.

Wars are the primary cause of a secular bear market and bubbles are the triggers to market plunges. Usually, recessions follow market plunges. In 2000, we had the internet bubble and in 2007 we had the housing bubble. With minor exceptions, all bubbles are caused by excessive valuation and they will come back to the average value eventually.

In 2000, many internet companies had no profits or their P/Es were very high (some over 40) from the average P/E of about 15. In 2007, the market housing value was too high due to the availability of easy credit. The only exception of the bubbles is the recent price of gold which does not really appreciate that much but the dollar depreciates. The two wars partly contributed to its appreciation.

If the government concentrates its efforts on the economy rather than wars, it could detect the bubble earlier before its burst and at least the economy would have had a soft landing rather than the hard landing in 2008. Remind the politicians to avoid any future war and use your voting power to enforce it.

We should have learned from the French before we participated in the Vietnam War or the Russians before we did the same in Afghanistan. We have been dragged many times by Israel to the Middle East wars but we have no business there.

We cannot afford to be the global policeman. Our youth should enjoy the best time of their lives in colleges or new jobs instead of being sent to the front line. The National Guard should guard in case of emergency and natural disasters, not to be sent to the front line.

I expect we'll have a prolonged bull market as early as in 2018 after ending the two wars completely; still there is no sign it will end soon as of 3/2016. By 2015 and hopefully earlier, the housing problem should be resolved by absorbing the inventory and the Euro crisis should also be resolved (as of 3/2016, it is not). The politicians will not forget the harmful effects from the wars, the secular bull market will hopefully continue for the next 15 to 20 years.

War and the lack of war determines the secular market to me. However, there are many other factors playing an important role. In 1974, the oil crisis made the secular bear market even worse.

Secular bull market could be postponed to 2020

The following events may prevent a secular bull market from starting in 2018 and postpone it to 2020 and hopefully earlier:

1. A possible war with China due to protecting Taiwan from invasion.

   When the Chinese government cannot suppress the internal unrest and to detract attention from its own inability, it would force itself to invade Taiwan. More likely, a trade blockage by China would be more effective with the tight economic ties between each other.

2. Another probable cause for a war is the U.S. military backing of Japan and other Asian countries on the disputes of the islands near Japan or the Philippines.

   It is illogical to borrow more money from China to contain China.

3. World climate change adversely affects the food supply. If technology has not improved the production of food in the last 50 years, there would be a famine in poor countries today.

   Global warming leads to many problems such as the shortage of drinking water. India would suffer most when China, the owner of the water source in Tibet, would redirect the water flow for its own citizens.

4. Natural disasters such as earthquakes and hurricanes. California is long overdue for a big one. Japan suffered its worst Tsunami in recent history.

5. Huge budget deficit.

   If the government continues to spend at the current rate, the prolonged unbalanced budget could never get us out of the recession. In addition, the government's excessive obligations on generous welfare, social security, Medicare and other entitlement budgetary obligations are growing too quickly and lead to imminent bankruptcy. We would already be bankrupt if the US government were a company.

The Fiscal Cliff has not really been fixed and we are still too deep into debts. We cannot pass our debt obligations onto the next generation forever.

6. The trapped gas and oil could provide us with enough energy for the next 50 years. The successful extraction could accelerate the start of the secular bull market one year earlier. We're facing oil dumping by oil-producing countries as of 2015.

Conclusion

Be realistic, check out these developments and adjust such predictions accordingly. An accurate prediction based on current events would better assess the risk of the market.

I do not suggest staying away from the market until 2018. As before, there will be market cycles within a secular market and yearly corrections. When we are in a secular bull market, we should be more aggressive, and vice versa in a secular bear market.

Statistically, there are three recessions in a secular bear market. Is it coincidental? As of January of 2014, there were two so far.

Is 2009 to 2016 a secular bull market? No, the bull market has to be correlated with the economy and the economy has not been fully recovered as of 2016. This exception is due to the excessive money supply. The money has to be paid back. Before we have our debts under control and balance our budget, our economy has not been recovered.

Afterthoughts

- I predicted a market top on April, 2012 within days.

- Signs of an economy recovery:

    1. Increase corporate profits.
    2. Increase employment.
    3. Increase housing starts.

4. Decrease Federal deficit.
5. Increase the growth of GDP.
6. Rising values in some sectors such as consumers, high tech., housing, etc.

As of 1/2014, #2 and #3 seem to be improving. #1 is OK. However, #4 is not.

When you borrow money (#4) and use it productively, you can improve #1 to #3. I have strong doubts about this economic recovery.

We're having a non-correlation in the Economy and the market.

The following information is supplied by my friend Norman.

- Traditional theory would say a 20-years secular cycle with 10 years between the major pullbacks. The first major pullback was called the Capital Crisis (1997-2003). The second major pullback was called the Real Estate Crisis (2007-2009). According to this theory, the next major pullback will be 2017 (Capital Crisis).

- In between major crises are business cycle pullbacks (Kitchen Cycle) approximately 5 years each. These are also called inventory cycles.

  It should be noted that these have always existed, even before Capitalism in 1720. During the secular bull market, they are muted by the positive market trend. However, they still exist.

- Norman believes we have started the secular bull market on Jan. 1, 2013. The secular 20-year cycle is based on the generations. The X generation has just moved into old age and the millennials are becoming mid-life consumers--This is a huge generation, similar to the Baby Boomers and demand for everything is going up.

- Nikolai Kondratiev would say the generational economic cycle has 4 seasons. He said it lasted 50-60 years.
  http://en.wikipedia.org/wiki/Nikolai_Kondratiev

7   Market prediction for a new year

This article demonstrates how I predict the market to be. It is for 2013, but the logic is valid for predictions about the future market.

In the article "My prediction for 2013 – all other predictions will be wrong", Larry Smith, a respected contributor at Seeking Alpha, suggested that many yearly predictions on 2012 by known organizations and famed individuals are often wrong.

Larry said,

"To prove my point, I thought I would look at some of the 2012 market forecasts that were made at the end of 2011. Let's start by looking at some of the S&P 500 forecasts that were made by the leading Wall Street firms. **Morgan Stanley** (MS) takes the worst prediction prize by forecasting an end-of-year the S&P 500 closing price of 1167, off by almost 300 points. **Goldman Sachs** (GS) predicted 1250 as the closing price of the S&P 500 price and **Seabreeze Partners** misfired on the high end by forecasting the S&P 500 closing price of 1527. Click here to see all the major brokerage firms' predictions for 2012. Most of the firms underestimated the size of the stock market rise.

Individual forecasters were not any better; here are some quotes from relatively well-known investors."

I agree with him completely, but there are exceptions and I try to be one of them. We can profit a lot from an accurate prediction. We need a prediction to be a framework on how we want to invest for the year and adjust the prediction as events surface.

My past prediction

Why should you want to follow a prediction from a nobody like me? My predictions have been on track many times, particularly for the year 2000, 2003 and 2009. In 2012, SPY (similar to the S&P 500 index) had a return of 13%. My prediction is 10%, off by 3%.

2013 is harder to predict and it depends on whether we have a QEn and the interest rates that have no way to go but up. We've been up too much since 2009 and the economy is still off with poor employment rates.

8   What to do in mid-year

The following may work or may not work in the future. It could fit into a data-fitting category. I include it here and will update whether it works in the coming years. From my observation, when the market over-reacts in the first half of the year, it will usually (but not all the time) correct itself in the second half of the year.

There are two camps on what you should do in mid-year.

1. If the market has moved far more than its predicted share (such as double the predicted return), act opposite for the rest of the year. I belong to this camp.
2. Flow with the market's momentum.

Basically, they are opposite of each other. Portfolios need constant manipulations as my mid-year action adjustment for 2012. It depends on a good prediction at the beginning of the year. I did not adjust mine in 2012, but it might provide valuable lessons. The rear mirror is always clearer.

2012 as an example

I predicted 10% for 2012. SPY was about 13%, so it is quite good.

At mid-year, we calculate how much it will still go up by the formula (predicted percent – actual YTD percent).

As of July, 2012, the SPY's return is 7% YTD, and it is better than expected. From the above formula (10% - 7%), we should still have 3% gain to go. Hence, we do not change our investment in stocks. In reality, it gained another 6% from July to the end of 2012, so the action is correct.

Inconclusive conclusion

To conclude, if the market has substantially gained its share of the predicted return, it is time to be conservative. Be more aggressive when the first half of the year loses more than its predicted return. It is a very rough and inconclusive guideline and I will test it out more in the future.

In any case, in mid-year we should make some adjustments such as balancing the sectors, monitor the risk of a market plunge and detect yearly dips especially if there is no dip so far.

Again, it is just a prediction and hopefully we have more rights than wrongs in the long run.

9 The worst scenario

From the described hints, you move all your stocks to cash but the market may keep on climbing and making new heights. You would be frustrated on how much you would have gained and hence move back to stocks. Then the market plunges. It is the worst in market timing. My suggestion:

- In the first hint of a market plunge, move a percentage of your stocks (preferably the risky stocks first) to cash. The percentage depends on your personal risk tolerance.

- Gradually move more to cash when the market is still climbing. If I expect the market to move up 2% more, I place sell orders at 2% more than the market prices.

- When the market plunges or the hints are all indicative of a market plunge, sell all. Personally, my 'sell all' is about 50% of my portfolio. It is not because I do not trust my strategy, but I do not bet all in either direction. That is just me.

No one can tell you what to do as everyone's situation is different. If you depend on your investments for daily income, be more conservative.

The most conservative investor can stay close to 100% in cash during the entire peak stage of the market cycle and invest in long-term bond funds when the interest rates are high. He has to ignore the excitement in the market. He only buys stocks at the bottom. I bet he is doing better than most retail investors with the least risk.

This scenario may not happen as our charts also tell us to return to the market – we call it a false signal.

10   Market timing from 2008 to 2015

Produce the SMA-350 chart using any chart system. This time I switched to my Fidelity broker as I cannot produce the same chart with the new version of Yahoo!Finance. It could be my fault.

Specify SPY, an ETF to simulate the market, SMA (Simple Moving Average), 350 sessions and the period from Dec. 1, 2008 to Dec. 1, 2015. The following are my findings.

- In my previous chart from 2000 to 2009, we only had one false signal. False signals tell us to exit the market but tell us to reenter the market shortly. In most cases, it does not change much in our portfolio except some tax consequences for taxable accounts.
- Between 2010 and 2015, we had several false signals. It tells us the market is more volatile than the period from 2000 to 2010. There could be too many followers on this technical indicator.
- I could reduce this number of false signals by using SMA-400 (400 sessions instead of 350). I do not as I predict 2016 could be more dangerous with possible interest rate hikes. "SMA-350" alarms us earlier than "SMA-400".
- Again, market timing is not a science. It is only a prediction. It has been proven from 2000 to 2010, but I do not expect it will always work. Otherwise, we will have poor folks.
- I had about 50% in cash before the August, 2015 correction. If I followed the chart, I should have 100% in cash. I could not conquer my greed.
- Even today (12/1/2015) when the stock price of SPY is above the SMA-350, I still want to have about 50% in cash as the market is risky to me.

I will have less cash after I buy stocks using my year-end loser strategy. You have to decide the percentage of cash you want to hold based on your risk tolerance. The less risk tolerance you have, the higher is the percentage of cash you want to hold.

11   Market timing of 2022

As of this writing (2/2023), fundamentals of the market had been poor for the past few years, but the market had been rising until 2022. It confirms again that technical analysis is more important than fundamentals in market timing. Our simplest technical analysis that does not require charting told us to leave the market in March, 2022. Most of us did not follow it – I am guilty as charged. We should at least move some of the risky stocks such as the FAANG stocks to cash.

All markets are different. The fast recovery of the 2008's market is due to China's purchase of a lot of our debts at the request of the chairman of the Federal Reserve Bank. Now we treat China as our enemy and China is having their own financial problems, and hence they will not help us again. Many 'experts' expected the market would not recover even in 2015.

The culprit of our market has been printing too much money. It is the trick of buying votes, especially during Trump and now Biden's eras. Our national debt is about 129% to GDP in 2022. Our government spending seems to be limitless, as they do not know how to fix our problems.

The government has given out a lot of money to our citizens. Many low-wage workers do not work with free money. It leads to hyperinflation (as high as 9.1% at one time in 2022). The government is forced to hike interest rates to fight inflation, and in turn it leads to a poor economic outlook. Consequently, the bubble of the booming house market (also affecting many companies selling big-ticket items) would burst in 2023. The high-tech companies suffer most as we do not need to upgrade our iPhones or buy any gadgets. Those companies depending on advertising such as Facebook and YouTube suffer too. Many high-tech companies are laying off high-salary employees. The only bright area is AI with the amazing ChatGDT that would affect many companies including NVDA producing AI chips.

Use the Golden Cross in the described market timing in this book to re-enter the market slowly and gradually. Personally, I am looking for fundamentally sound companies that will prosper in the future. Again, consult your financial planner before taking any actions.

Links
How the market works: https://www.youtube.com/watch?v=IsM0huAyyw0

12   2023 Market Outlook

This article was written in Feb., 2023, and it discussed some highpoints of the following 3-hour YouTube from Yahoo!Finance outlook forum. If you read this article after 2023, you can check out how accurate the predictions are. For future years, you can select similar YouTube videos or articles by searching "market outlook for 202X" (2024 for the next year for example).

https://www.youtube.com/watch?v=VaO1WF1P6ns

In general, there are two camps: one on a mild recession with a soft landing and the other on a hard landing.

One analyst recommended switching conservative sectors (Utilities, Consumer Staples, etc.) to beaten-up sectors (Technology, Drug, etc.). He also thought Energy was too high. I prefer using SMA-50% (from Finviz) to ensure they are in uptrend.

From my memory, we have not had a down market a year before the presidential election from the end of WW2 to 2024. Will it repeat history? Only time can tell.

Many stocks in artificial intelligence (AI) have risen in early 2023. They include NVDA and MSFT. My NVDA was up about 40% at one time. MSFT was up by 15% in a month by the time it was in my radar. The following describes the wonderful ChatGPT that would help high technology in the years to come.

ChatGPT recommendation

You can create a free account. I asked "best stocks for now", and it gave me the following stocks. It gave me FB instead of the new name META and made me suspicious of the accuracy of the rest of its database. The current database was updated to 2021. Most of the recommended stocks are high-tech and all are large companies. It could lead to many asking the same questions and it would result in these stocks rising consequently.

ChatGPT's recommendation is based on 01/03/2022. My estimate on the performance.

Stock	6 Months	12 Months	18 months
AAPL	-22%	-31%	6%
AMZN	-33%	-50%	-23%

GOOGL	-22%	-39%	-17%
JPM	-30%	-16%	-9%
META	-50%	-63%	-16%
MSFT	-21%	-28%	1%
NVDA	-50%	-52%	41%
TSLA	-42%	-72%	-30%
XOM	33%	68%	69%
Avg	-26%	-32%	2%
SPY	-21%	-20%	-7%

Only XOM passed my proprietary score, and the above proves my scoring system works at least this time. Oil prices affecting XOM would be reduced in demand when electric vehicles replace combustion cars. JPM would suffer from the reduced number of IPOs in the current market conditions. The recent rise of NVDA and MSFT is due to ChatGPT. GOOG would benefit using AI in their products.

More info from ChatGPT

Use MSFT for illustration. Type "Microsoft MSFT stock", then "Fundamental Analysis", "Technical Analysis" and lastly "Buy or sell".

Links

How to invest in 2023's recession
https://www.youtube.com/watch?v=ALjWkfJjGUA

Section III: Correction

1   Correction

Market timing has been judged wrongly by many. Just check out how the two major plunges can be detected easily by my simple chart.

Corrections are harder to detect. So far, I have more rights than wrongs in detecting corrections.

Everyone has its own definition of a correction and mine is as follows. A correction is a 10% or more down from the peak of the last 180 days or more than 5% down in a month. Sometimes, corrections continue to 20% loss. My definition of a market plunge is the loss of 40% or more from the recent peak to the bottom. There is a gray area between a 20% to 40% loss.

From my definition, there is no correction in 2013 and that is quite rare. On the average it happens at least once every year since 2000 depending on my interpretation. I also estimate two minor corrections of 5% every year if we do not have a 10% correction.

Corrections provide us opportunities to enter the market. Temporary peaks provide us opportunities to sell. They happen about one to two times a year on the average but their frequencies fluctuate widely. I usually start selling at the expected peaks, and buying at the expected bottoms. Your cash position depends on your risk tolerance. 'Buy-and-hold' investors can just ignore corrections and this chapter.

Some hints (not always reliable) predict the temporary market peak:

- Up more than 10% of the expected gain. To illustrate, you predicted this year's total return is 12% in the beginning of the year. In March, the market has already gained 12%, there is a good chance it is close to the yearly peak and you should act accordingly. Review the stocks you own and sell those with less appreciation potential first.
- The market has exceeded a good percent over the last peak. Define this percent based on your risk tolerance.
- Compare the annualized market P/E (SPY or any market index ETF) to its 5-year average (10-year average is fine too).
- Foreign markets are down and ours are up by a good margin.
- The interest rate. When it rises, the market will be down.

- It happens more than three consecutive days that there are more stocks advancing than retreating.
- It happens more than three consecutive days that the number of new highs is more than the number of new lows.
- From Finviz.com, SPY's SMA200 exceeds 10% (= (Price − SMA)/SMA). SMA-200 is Single Moving Average for the last 200 sessions. It indicates it may be temporarily peaking. Use it for reference only as it is not always reliable.
- From Finviz.com, SPY's RSI(14), the relative strength index based on the last 14 days, exceeds 55%. It indicates that it may be overbought. This is for reference only as it is not always reliable.
- There are always reasons for corrections such as the market is overvalued, rising interest rates, degrading corporation earnings and trade wars.

Conclusion

Corrections are harder to detect compared to the market plunges which we have excellent results so far from 2000.

Do not bet the entire farm on corrections especially when the market is risky. Keep less than 25% of your portfolio in cash on the expected peaks.

When the market corrects, it is a buying opportunity. However, when the market starts to plunge, we should exit the market as the losses could be high. If all the conditions in the following table are exceeded, most likely the market is peaking. One's opinion.

SMA-50%	SMA-200%	SMA-350%	Avg. of the 3 the SMA%	RSI(14)
4%	6%	11%	9%	65%

2 Six signs of a correction

Six signs of a correction:

1. All my technical indicators show the market is peaking and overbought. SPY is an ETF simulating the market of the S&P 500 stocks. As of 6/29/2014, the RSI(14) is at 67% and the SMA-200% is at 8.35%. SMA-200% measures how far away the stock price is from its simple moving average of the last 200 trade sessions.

   You may argue that you do not believe in technical analysis. However, many institutional fund managers learn technical analysis and they will act accordingly. It is one of the many tools that hedge fund managers use to 'hedge'. Most mutual fund managers cannot practice market timing bound by the rules and regulations.

2. Newton's Law of Gravity has never been proven wrong (some humor to get your attention). What goes up must come down. The market has been up even after inflation. However, it takes a breather from time to time. A small one is called a correction and a big one is called a market plunge.
3. We did not have one such correction of 10% in 2013, so the time is ripe. The average is about one correction of 10% or more and about 1.5 corrections for 5% in a year. Many experts predicted wrongly on a correction in 2013. I do not bet against them to be wrong two times in a row.
4. There are more articles predicting a correction than articles arguing against it. It could be a self-fulfilling prophecy. It is the herd mentality. One's opinion.
5. The market has low volumes and narrow ranges for many days may indicate that the market is changing direction. The sea is calmest before a storm.
6. I am not convinced that I can make a lot of profit even if there is no correction. To me, the market is fully valued. It is my reward / risk ratio. I prefer not to make the last buck and have a good sleep.

How to protect yourself

It depends on your risk tolerance.

1. Accumulate cash from 0% to 50%. I recommend 15% for most. 0% is for those who ignore the signs. It was a great selection for 2013. I select 50% as I'm more conservative than most.
2. Place stop orders. Adjust them when they have appreciated in price. Some stocks are more volatile than others. I prefer to use stop orders in market plunges rather than corrections, as corrections are too brief to be effective.
3. Short the market. I do not recommend shorting in most cases. Buying a contra ETF may help. In any case, do not risk money you cannot afford to lose.
4. Use options to protect your portfolio.
5. Prepare a list of stocks to buy when there is a correction, and wait for a better time to invest.

Do not treat my (or all others') predictions as gospel. Predictions are just predictions. It is like buying insurance that we do not expect to collect from.

I have to admit market timing is not an exact science. Hopefully we are more right than wrong.

Summary of comments on the article

There are two camps: one who believes and one who does not believe. It is as expected. I will not take credit if there will be a correction within a month, or take the blame if there will be none in the next 3 months. From my record, I have more right than wrong predictions, but it may have nothing to do with future market predictions. Here is my summary:

1. I did think of other signs as mentioned by some of my readers: interest rate, oil price, current events... I expect interest rates will start rising by the end of the year. The recent rise in oil price is due to the turmoil in the Middle East. The current events including Ukraine and the Middle East seem not to be a factor as our leader does not want to participate in this.

2. I do not expect a market plunge (over 30% down) as I do not see any bubbles (those bubble stocks are too few). My prediction: These bubble stocks will be half the peaks achieved in 2013 and 2014 by the end of 2014. To me, all stock trades are predictions. Some materialize and some do not.

3. Corrections are harder to detect than market plunges. After I detect a plunge, I will spend most of my time in protecting my portfolio.

3 Anticipating a correction

'Buy-and-hold' investors can ignore this chapter. This chapter enhances the last one.

You should try to sell as many stocks as you own before the correction comes and buy them back during and after the expected correction. It does not always work. However, it is good to churn your portfolio to ensure it has better appreciation potential at the expense of capital gain taxes in non-retirement accounts.

Signs of a market top (same as correction is coming)

- The market has been up for over 4 months from the last dip.
- The market has gained more than the predicted share.
- If most of your stocks are at the peak, take some profits.
- Use Technical Analysis (via use of charts) as below.

    Here is one of the charts that could predict temporary market dips and surges. Buy when the price is above the SMA (simple moving average) and sell when it is below. This example uses 50 days for SMA for 2012. SMA-50% is also available from Finviz.com.

    Vary the number of days and/or use other indicators to reduce noise or improve the trading frequency to fit your individual needs.

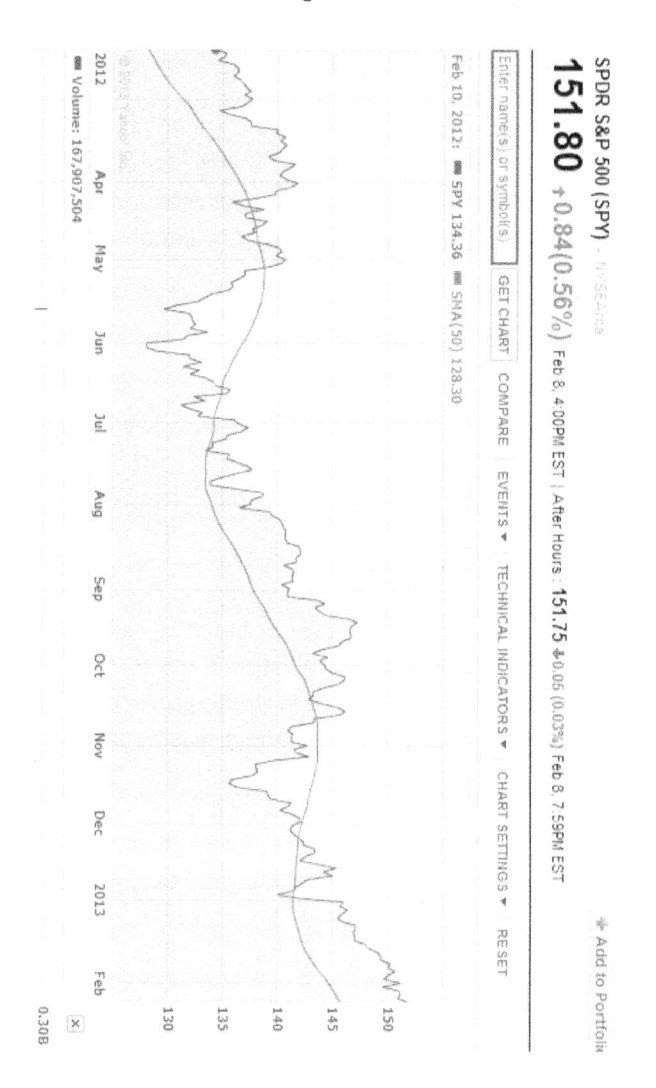

Source: Yahoo!Finance.

If you are reading this book on a small screen and cannot see the chart, type the following into your browser.
http://ebmyth.blogspot.com/2013/09/correction-example.html

There are too many trades in the above chart especially in the month of April. The period from July 1 to Oct. 15 is a good capture of the upward trend. It is useful but not perfect. Try to use SMA-100 instead of the above SMA-50.

Example of a market top

The following is from my blog written on May 19, 2011 and it turned out to be quite accurate. Check why I expected a correction would be coming. Hopefully we can spot the next one with similar reasoning. However, there is no guarantee for future performance and predictions.

Click here on the actual blog and the summary follows.
http://www.tonyp4idea.blogspot.com/2011/05/anticipating-correction.html

As of May 19, 2011, the market had been up by about 9% YTD. The experts were divided on whether the market would take a correction with convincing arguments for and against.

I had been selling stocks several weeks before and moved most of my Annuity positions to a money market fund. My total cash was 25% and I was still selling. I tried to sell most of my stocks at 5 to 10% higher than the market prices. Hence, even if there were no correction, I was still selling far better than my current prices and it was a reasonable insurance policy. I predicted that the market was risky at that time; you have to trust your prediction and act accordingly as it did.

After I had accumulated more than 30% in cash, I played the 'Buy one and Sell two' strategy betting I could spot stocks better than others. I tried to sell the stocks I bought right away for a small profit as I still expected a correction.

* Arguments for no correction:

- QE3 would materialize (even it will not amount to a lot of cash due to the debt ceiling).
- Corporate profits are still rising.
- The economy is improving.

* Arguments for correction:

- QE3 will not be materialized and no money will be used to stimulate the economy.
- The market is taking a breather after 9% YTD (I expect 5% rise in mid-year).

- Slim chance for the rule 'Stay away in May' as it had not been working for the two consecutive years except in today's extended bull market.
- There are financial problems from China, EU, Japan and N. Africa.
- With tightening margin requirements on commodities, oil…, speculative trades will be reduced (good for the long term).

The above is a summary of what the experts said. I did not do any research (as it is already available from the web). I summarized their opinions, selected what made sense to me, and acted accordingly.

I chose the middle road by not taking extreme actions such as selling all my holdings and heavily investing in contra ETFs.

Afterthoughts

- My Elastic Band Theory.
  The more you stretch an elastic band, the more it will rebound. When a stock's timing score is 10 (the best), it has no way to go but down. That is similar to the general market.

  The risk/reward ratio is too high as of 4/2013. Unless you have a time machine, you may not want to make the last buck.
- A related article from SA.
  (http://seekingalpha.com/article/1344071-5-reasons-why-i-am-shorting-the-market)

Links
Original blog:
http://www.tonyp4idea.blogspot.com/2011/05/anticipating-correction.html
An article on preparing for a correction.
http://www.forbes.com/sites/investor/2014/05/19/five-things-to-do-in-a-stock-market-correction/

#Filler: Roadblocks to progress

We use privacy to stop facial recognition. The device from Ring has reduced a lot of thefts and possibly crimes. Similar to stem cell research. That's why China is passing us in these areas.

4 Market correction example

I have 50% in cash before the August (2015) correction. I should have 100% if I followed my chart. However, we are just human beings blinded by our greed / fears and emotional attachment.

Stocks	Buy Price	Buy Date	Return	Sold date
Apple (AAPL)	107.20	08/26/15	12%	10/19/15
Gilead Sciences (GILD)	105.94	08/26/15	-4%	
General Motors (GM)	27.69	08/26/15	12%	09/17/15
Genwealth Financial (GNW)	4.54	08/26/15	10%	08/27/15

Section IV: Market timing by Calendar

1 Market timing by calendar

The following predictions are based on historical data. You may have slightly different findings depending on when you start and when you end your testing.

You can load the historical data of SPY via Yahoo!Finance and check out how close you are or different from my own predictions. They are my predictions based on historical data. Use it as a reference only.

- Presidential cycle.
  Usually, the market performs worse in the first two years after the election than the next two. During the **3rd year** the president has to make the economy look rosy in order to buy votes. Statistically it is the best year for the market and is followed by a good year (the election year). The government may stimulate the economy, the stock market and employment by printing more money, lowering interest rates and lowering taxes. The market in the 100 days before the election should be positive and less volatile according to 40 years of data. The next 100 days after the inauguration should be good for the market (termed as the honeymoon period).

  Democratic presidents have better market performance statistically than Republican presidents. This is not too logical as though Republicans are more pro-business traditionally.

- Olympics.
  It has been proven that the host country has a better chance that its stock market appreciates the year after the Olympics. It could be due to the exposure from the Olympics and / or the huge expenses in preparing for the Olympics.

  The last two Olympics follow this pattern as of 12/23/2013:

Olympics Country / Year	ETF	Period	Return
United Kingdom / 2012	EWU	Jan. 3, 2013 - Dec. 23,2013	11%
China / 2008	FXI	Jan. 3, 2009 - Dec. 31, 2009	43%

Greece could be an exception. It is too small a country to host this world-class event and it has wasted too many resources by building too many white elephants that the country can never justify. Brazil depends on its export of natural resources to China, so I do not count on the Olympics effect there. Japan 2020 was adversely affected by the pandemic.

Winning a lot of Olympic medals has no prediction for the stock markets. Both the Russian Empire and E. Germany were winners but disappeared in their original forms afterwards.

- Seasonal.
  Best profitable investment period is: Nov. 1 to April 30 of the following year. It is similar to the saying 'Sell in May and Go away'. It has not worked since 2009 as it was an Early Recovery (defined by me) in the market cycle.

  The market does not always happen as predicted. However, when more folks follow this, it becomes a self-fulfilling prophecy. I prefer "Sell on April 15 and come back on Oct. 15" to act before the herd. The more practical strategy is to start selling on April 1 and become more aggressive (selling at closer to the market prices) when it is close to May 1. For the last five years, I did not find this prediction reliable.

  The explanation of the 'summer doldrums' could be that the investors cash their stocks for vacations and college tuition in the fall. Buying quality companies at the dips could be profitable.

- The worst month: September.
  The next worst month is October. However, if there is no serious market crash during October (and this month has more than its shares of crashes), it could be the best month to buy stocks.

- The best month for the bull: November.
  However, several market bottoms occurred in October and November. The next strong month is December. Most experts believe the best 3 months of the year starts in November.

- Best 30 days: Dec. 15 to Jan. 15, next year.
  It was correct for the period of 2012-2013.

- Window dressing.

Institutional investors sell their losers and buy winners around Nov. 1. From my rough estimate and on the average, the winners have a 2% percentage point gain better than the market and the losers have 1% worse than the market.

I recommend that you evaluate the top 10 winners from the last 10 months or YTD on Oct. 15 and sell them at 3% gain or two months later.

I recommend that you buy in Dec. and sell them 3 months later. Include the stocks with more than 30% loss for the last 11 months or YTD, sort them by Earning Yield in descending order and evaluate the top 10 stocks.

In both cases, do not buy foreign stocks and stocks with return of capital. Ignore stocks not in the three major exchanges, with low volumes and stock prices less than $2. Do not buy in losing years such as 2007 and 2008. I have my tests with my own assumptions and I use tools not available to most readers. From my own experiences, I made more money by buying the losers from Dec. 15 to end of Dec. than buying the window dressers.

This is a guideline only. Do not buy any stocks during market plunges. Current events should be considered first such as a potential war and the hiking of interest rates.

Afterthoughts

- I predict it will be a sideways market in the later part of 2013. I am following the sideways strategy: Buy on dips and sell when the market is up. One's prediction.

- Why September has a bad reputation?
  http://www.marketwatch.com/story/betting-on-septembers-terrible-odds-2013-08-27?dist=beforebell

  September of 2013 (2 days away at the time of this writing) may have more problems. Check out how many of the following are correct on Oc. 1, 2013. Use it as a future guideline to predict the next September using the current market conditions then:

  1. The market is not excessively expensive, but it is not cheap. It is due for a 5% correction.

2. Unrest in Syria (check any unrest in your next prediction in September).
3. High oil prices due to Syria.
4. September is statistically a bad month for the stock market. However, it could be an opportunity to invest after the correction if any.
5. Interest rates are rising.
6. All the above indicate the market will dip. However, the rosier outlook is that the global economies are improving even slowly.

- January effect.
  The performance of January may determine how the entire year performs. I cannot find any rationale but it has been proven right statistically.

- Earnings period announced in Jan., April, July and Oct. would cause big swings in stocks when they have surprises. Earning revisions could be a good predictor.
  http://www.investopedia.com/terms/e/earningsseason.asp

Links
Presidential Cycle:
http://www.investopedia.com/articles/financial-theory/08/presidential-election-cycle.asp
Calendar-based market timing:
http://stock-chartist.com/2010/10/calendar-based-market-timing/
Calendar market timing for 2013:
http://www.investorecho.com/archives/8047

Filler: Golden Gate
Just minutes ago, my mail system asked me to sign in. I did and repeatedly they asked me to sign in again and again. I closed down everything and followed Gates' golden rule: If everything does not work, just power down everything and power it up again. I did this and prayed too. It works. Thanks, Gates, for fixing my problem.

There is NO one doing BASIC quality control. If it happened in my generation, many guys would be fired. Mediocrity is the new norm?

2   Summary

I made the following charts so it is easier to time the market by the calendar.

All dates are inclusive.

No.	Metric		Score
1	Seasonal	Nov. - April, Score = 1	
2	Best Month	Nov., Score = 1	
		Sep., Score = -1	
3	Best Days	Dec. 15 – Jan.15 Score = 1	
4	Presidential Cycle	Election Year, Score = 1	
		1st Year in Office, Score = -1	
		2nd year, Score = -1	
		3rd year, Score = 2	
5	Presidential[3]	Democratic = 1 Republican = -1	
6	Market Cycle	Early Recovery, Score = 3	
		Up, Score = 2	
		Peak, Score = 1	
7	SPY (Finviz.com)	SMA200% > 8%[2] Score = -1	
		SMA200% < 0 Score = -1	
		RSI(14) > 65% Score = -1	
		Grand Score	

Footnote.
1   Refer to the Market Cycle chapter on how I define phases of a cycle.
2   For simplicity, use Finviz.com. Enter SPY and you will find SMA200% and RSI(14) to predict whether the market is peaking and overbought.
3   I'm politically neutral. The selection is based on historical statistics.

Add up all the scores. The passing grade is 0. According to my table which is based on my personal selections/preferences, the market is favorable when the grand score is 1 or higher. I bet it is the first time you see such a scoring system for market timing.

Sectors for market cycle

Market Phase[1]	Favorable	Unfavorable
Early Recovery	Financial, Technology, Industrial	Energy, Telecom, Utilities
Up	Technology, Industrial	
Peak	Mineral, Health Care, Energy	
Bottom	Consumer Staples, Utilities	Consumer Discretionary, Technology, Industrial

Seasonal	Favorable	Unfavorable
Winter	Energy, Utilities	
End of year	QQQ, EWG	

Olympics	ETF for host country[2]	

Footnote.
1. Refer to the Market Cycle chapter on how I define phases of a cycle.
2. Buy it next year after the Olympics. It could be due to higher GDP or the publicity. However, be selective. Greece is too small a country to host an Olympics.

Section V: Peaks and bottoms

It will be great when we can sell at peaks and buy at bottoms. It is not that easy. However, I try to find the common characteristics of peaks and bottoms. No tools can detect them. Otherwise, there would be no poor folks. The following are my suggestions.

1 Market peaks / bottoms

Summary by tables from my findings

The dates could be a little different from my similar tables as I use monthly data instead of daily data. The data are subject to my interpretations and the tables are used for illustration purposes only.

Table: Market Plunges

Market Plunge	Months (Peak to Bottom)	Loss	Annualized Loss
2000	17	56%	40%
2007	25	47%	23%
Average	21	51%	31%

Table: Vital Dates

Market Plunge	Peak	Bottom	Indicator Exit	Indicator Reentry
2000	08/28/00	09/20/02	10/30/00	05/26/03
2007	10/12/07	03/06/09	01/03/08	09/08/09

Most investors were fully invested in 2007 and 2008 and NOT fully invested in 2009. It proves the majority of us are performing worse than the market. If you followed the exit indicator and the reentry indicator, you should do far better than the average investor. A brief exit and reentry in the 2007 market cycle is skipped for simplicity (I call it a false signal).

Market plunges

The SMA-350 (Single Moving Average for 350 trade sessions) has detected the last two crashes (2000 and 2007) correctly leaving us a lot of time to prepare. It is based on the falling market, so it will detect the next market plunge. However, we may not be that lucky to have plenty of time to prepare for it (selling most of our positions) as in the last two (2000 and 2007).

Market peaks and bottoms
From the above table, the chart does not spot the peak and the bottom as expected. We would make far more money when selling at the peak and buying at the bottom. A dream perhaps?

SMA and/or RSI would confirm that the market is close to its peak or bottom. I gathered their values for the last two peaks and bottoms and I summarized them in this article. It is based on limited data and we treat the conclusions as nothing more than useful guidelines.

SMA, SMA% and RSI

SMA-20 (Single Moving Average for the last 20 trade days), SMA-50, SMA-200 and RSI(14) are the indicators I used. Look them up on Investopedia.com if you are not familiar with how they are used. Most are available in Finviz.com by specifying SPY as the stock symbol.

SMA percentages measure how far away is the market from their respective moving average. If the SPY's SMA-200 is 100 and the stock price is 200, the SMA-200% is 100% over the moving average. It would indicate that the market may be peaking.

$$SMA\text{-}200\% = (\text{Stock Price} - SMA) / SMA$$
$$= (200 - 100) / 100 = 100\%$$

RSI(14) measures whether the market is over or under bought using the last 14 trade sessions.

For detecting market crashes, I still prefer SMA-350. SMA-20 is good for predicting the short-term trend of a stock, but not for the entire market.

Bring Finviz.com up from your browser and enter SPY (or any market ETF representing the majority of your stocks). The SMA-n percentages and RSI(14) are displayed.

Misc.

Advance / Decline (AD or Buy/Sell ration). When it is below 1, be careful that the market could be near the top even if the S&P 500 index is rising. The theory is that fund managers (who drive the market) believe the market is risky, they want to unload the small stocks. They still want to keep or even add the investment on blue chips, which they are easier to unload when the market crashes. It indicates the market could be near the top. It is similar to (# of stocks making new heights) – (# of stocks making new lows). If it is positive and the market is rising, the market could be still fine.

The market could be heading up from the bottom as indicated by the following technical indicators.

- RSI(14) from SPY or RSP is less than 30%.
- AD is less than .2
- With the previous sessions mostly in red candles, the market changes to a long green candle.
- Both SMA-20% and SMA-50% for the market index are positive, and SMA-20% is more positive than SMA-50%.

Findings

I include my findings in 3 sections: market timing for crashes, market timing for corrections and briefly on individual stocks, which have many other factors to consider.

I try to exit the market during market plunges (i.e., the stock price of SPY is below its SMA-350). My greed does not always allow me to do so entirely.

Market corrections provide opportunities to buy stocks. However, you need to accumulate cash in advance to take advantage of the temporary dips and prepare a list of stocks to buy at specified prices. For market plunges, we should not buy any stocks.

Market corrections of 5% happen about twice a year (or a 10% correction once a year), but its frequency varies. They are harder to detect, so do not leave the market totally. I prefer to keep less than 15% in cash to buy in the expected market dips. 2013 is a good year for stocks and in preparing for the corrections you could miss the opportunity of making more money.

Conclusion via a table

My test data are using SPY from 1-2000 to 2-2014. The following is from my own interpretation. Again, past information does not guarantee future performance. It just serves as a guideline.

	SMA-50	SMA-200	SMA-350	SMA50/SMA200	RSI (14)
Market					
Peak		5%	9%	101%	65%
Bottom		-32%	-31%	78%	25%
Correction					
Peak	4%	6%	11%	102%	65%
Bottom	-5%	-6%	-7%	97%	26%
Stock					
Peak					70%
Bottom					30%

As explained, the market is plunging when the stock price of SPY is below its SMA-350 (i.e., the SMA-350% is negative). From my table, the market could be peaking when SMA-350 is 9% or above.

From the first glance, it is quite logical. At market peaks or temporary peaks, the SMA% is substantially over 0% and RSI(14) is far higher than the RSI(14) in the market bottoms.

Corrections are harder to determine. I have tested two times in different ways to determine corrections and the results are a little different.

The first method is to identify the peaks of the corrections and then get the averages of SMA-50%, SMA-200%, SMA-350% and the RSI(14).

The second approach is more complicated and more subjective to describe here. The above table is a combination of the two approaches.

The market is not always rational. Today's market is influenced by the low interest rates.

What to act

Everyone wants to sell at the peak and buy at the bottom. However, these technical indicators and my interpretation may not always work.

When the market is peaking

To illustrate, when SMA-350 is over 9% (i.e., SPY's stock price is 9% over its SMA for the last 350 trade sessions) and/or RSI(14) is over 65%, it may indicate the market is peaking and overbought. I recommend:

- Accumulate cash but less than 15% of your portfolio. The actual percent depends on your risk tolerance. For those who do not care much about market fluctuations or do not have the time to trade stocks, do not play market timing on corrections.

- Sell the stocks that have appreciated enough to meet your objectives and/or their appreciation potentials are less than the average of your portfolio. Preferably, sell the stock with less tax implications (such as those qualifying for long term capital gain in your taxable accounts).

  Alternatively, buy one stock for every two stocks you sell when the peak drags on.

- Do not buy any new stocks with the above exception.

- Enforce stop loss that turns your sell orders to market orders when they fall below specific prices. Adjust the stop orders when the stocks appreciate (but do nothing when they depreciate).

  My suggestion is using 5% stop loss and 10% stop loss for volatile stocks. To reduce excessive trading, you can use 10% and 15% instead. After the earnings announcement (available in Finviz), the stock would fluctuate far more than 5%, so adjust them before their earnings announcement dates.

When the market is bottoming

You want to reenter the market when the stock price for SPY (or other ETF simulating the market) is above the SMA-350. The following two suggestions when to reenter the market earlier. They are riskier but have better rewards if the guess is correct.

- Start to reenter the market when SMA-200% (the stock price is above the SMA-200) is positive.
- Start to reenter the market when SMA-350% is less than -31% and/or RSI(14) is less than 25%, it may indicate the market is bottoming and under-bought.

Do the following:
- Buy the stocks that have the best appreciation potential and most are fundamentally sound and beaten up badly by the general market. Alternatively, buy two stocks for every stock you sell.

- Do not sell any stocks with the above exception.
- You need to prepare a list of stocks to buy and at what prices when the market is plunging. If you do not have such a list, buy ETFs.

What to do in a market correction
It is very similar to market timing on crashes as above. However, I recommend keeping cash to less than 15% of your portfolio. Again, corrections are far harder to detect. 2013 has fewer and smaller corrections due to the excessive supply of money.

Stocks

Stocks are treated as overbought when the RSI(14) is over 70% and under-bought when it is below 30%; most stocks fluctuate more than the market. Some may use 65% for overbought and 35% for under-bought.

Depending on how long you usually keep a stock, you select the number of days in SMA. For example, if you keep most stocks for 200 days, use SMA-200. Buy when the range of its SMA-200% is ranging from 0 to 10% and the RSI is less than 60% as a rough guideline. Some stocks may just shoot up disregarding their fundamental and technical metrics. One's opinion. Selecting the SMA percent also depends on your risk tolerance. There are many other factors to consider on individual stocks such as a major lawsuit(s), losing/gaining market share... Again, use the above as a very rough guideline for the stocks.

Afterthoughts
- You will find many related articles on this topic by searching using Google.
- As of 3/5/2014, the market was supposed to be peaking as SMA-350% was 15% and RSI(14) was 73%. The historical data for these metrics can be shown on charts.
- Articles on market top.
  Business Insider.
  The flow to equity is a good contrary indicator (the more money goes to equity funds by retail investors, the more chance the market will plunge).
  http://www.businessinsider.com/signs-this-is-not-a-market-peak-2013-12
  The 15 signs. http://theeconomiccollapseblog.com/archives/15-signs-that-we-are-near-the-peak-of-an-absolutely-massive-stock-market-bubble

2 Peaking and Overbought

This chapter is an extension of the last one. The following indicators are not very reliable and they should be used as secondary indicators. However, exiting from the peak could make you more money if the signal is correct. When the price is 9% over the simple moving average SMA-350, the market may be peaking. This ratio is defined by:

(Price − Moving Average) / Moving Average.

When the RSI(14) is over 65%, the market could be overbought (i.e., highly valued). This ratio can be found in Finviz.com with SPY or another ETF that represents the market as the stock symbol. It is defined as:

RSI = 100 - 100/(1 + RS)

where RS = Average of x days' up closes / Average of x sessions
RSI(14) is the relative strength index using the last 14 trade sessions.

The reentry point is less than -31% for the SMA-350 ratio and less than 25% for the RSI(14). Again, they are used for a guideline only.

Suggested Actions

Peaking and overbought conditions indicate the market is overvalued. My suggestion is not to sell all positions except those stocks that are overvalued or have met your objectives. Place stop orders to protect profits. I recommend 5% below the current price and 10% for volatile stocks (10% and 15% are fine in today's volatile market). When the stock price rises, change the stop orders accordingly. When the stock is sold, accumulate cash until these conditions change.

I recommend using the cash to buy CDs and short-term, bonds that are investment grade. Save some cash to buy contra ETFs when the market is plunging. 2008 was not a good year for bonds, but 2009 was. Based on this, I would sell the bonds when the market is crashing. Investing is not a 100% sure thing. These are my recommendations and you need to modify the plan according to your risk tolerance.

3   Design a test for market peaks/bottoms

This article describes how to set up a test for the last article on detecting market peaks/bottoms by using SMA and RSI. There is no need to understand how I derived the results and it could serve as a model for designing a test for another strategy.

Objective
To find out any common values of SMA and RSI when the market plunges, corrects or surges.

The data for this test are obtained from Yahoo!Finance and/or charts available from many other free sites.

How to get data

From Yahoo!Finance, enter SPY for the stock. Select historical prices from 1/3/96 to 2/5/14 in my example. Use the prices adjusted for splits and dividends; in this case it may not make any difference. Load it to Excel. Sort the date in the ascending order. Delete the columns I do not need.

Adjusted Close Price is mostly the one you want to use for testing to compensate for the split and dividend.
https://help.yahoo.com/kb/finance/SLN2311.html?impressions=true

Most historical databases do not include dividends but handle splits. Hence, we have to adjust accordingly. Add the dividend rate (about 1.75%) to the annualized return rate where appropriate.

Get critical dates

I limited my test data to the last two crashes (2000 and 2007). The test data before 2000 may not reflect today's market. Here are the critical dates from my other book.

Table: Vital Dates

Market Plunge	Peak	Bottom	Indicator Exit	Indicator Reenter
2000	08/28/00	09/20/02	10/30/00	05/26/03
2007	10/12/07	03/06/09	01/03/08	09/08/09

Get statistics on previous peaks and bottoms

To illustrate, the peak in 2000 is 08/28/00, calculate the SMA-200, SMA-350, SMA-50 and SM50/SMA200 for this date. Actually, I included 4 days before and 4 days after and averaged all the mentioned parameters for a total of 9 days. Try to automate this procedure as much as possible.

Repeat the above for 2007. Average the parameters in the two market plunges.

Repeat the same for the two market bottoms.

RSI(14)

There is too much logic to calculate this indicator. I used the RSI from charts for the critical dates. Select RSI in the chart.

Filler: OTC, cars and filthy rich in 5 seconds

OTC, over-the-counter stocks, are risky as many do not have information required by SEC and the major exchanges. They are traded over the counter, OTC. They cannot be shorted (and most likely you do not want to do so even if it was allowed). Pier 1, Ford, American Airlines and many others were all penny stocks.

Expect one winner for several losers. However, the total profit could outpace the total loss if the strategy is properly implemented.

Filler: Advances in cars
I have not used cruise control even ONCE. I could be the exception. The more complex the car, the more chance it breaks down.

A few years ago, I got an on-line statement from my broker saying I had over 10M. I took a screenshot. When I logged off and logged on again, my millions were gone and so were many better things in life I planned to buy. What a tough life! I try to say the car computer could break down too and it may cause lives.

4 Market peak example

It is hard to determine market peaks and bottoms. Otherwise, there would be no poor folks. Based on data from 7/4/2017, I tried to predict (again predict) whether the market is peaking. From my previous findings:

Table: Market Plunges

Market Plunge	Months (Peak to Bottom)	Loss	Annualized Loss
2000	17	56%	40%
2007	25	47%	23%
Average	21	51%	31%

Table: Vital Dates

Market Plunge	Peak	Bottom	Indicator Exit	Indicator Reentry
2000	08/28/00	09/20/02	10/30/00	05/26/03
2007	10/12/07	03/06/09	01/03/08	09/08/09

My test data uses the SPY from 1-2000 to 2-2014 to get the averages of the peaks. The following is from my own interpretation. Again, past information does not guarantee future performance. It just serves as a guideline.

	SMA-50	SMA-200	SMA-350	SMA50/SMA200	RSI (14)
Market (SPY)					
Peak (avg.)		5%	9%	101%	65%
7/4/2017	0%	6%	10%	N/A	50%

Both SMA-200% and SMA-350% are on par with the averages of the previous two market peaks. RSI(14) shows the market is overbought but it is 15% less than the average. I missed some parameters such as P/E. The P/E as of 7/4/17 is 25.69 and is about 71% more expensive assuming the average is 15. The average of 11 stocks from Fidelity's best sector list increased by only 0.35% for last month. So, it is not a good sign.

Fundamental metrics (07/20/2017)

	L.T. Avg.	7/20/17	High by[1]	Min	On	Max	On
P/E[2]	15.66	26.17	67%	5.31	12-1917	123.73	05-2017
Shiller P/E[2]	16.76	30.12	80%	4.78	12-1920	44.19	12-1999
P/Sales[2]	1.45	2.15	48%	0.8	03-2009	2.15	07-2017
P/Book[2]	2.75	3.22	17%	4.78	12-1920	44.19	12-1999

[1] High by = (Current – Mean) /Mean

[2] From http://www.multpl.com/.

The market is fundamentally overvalued as indicated in 07/04/2017.

The transport index (DJT) could be an indicator too. It loses its luster due to web sales not depending on rails and trucks.

Read articles on the current market such as this one. https://www.marketwatch.com/story/the-biggest-problem-in-the-stock-market-bullishness-is-clouding-investors-thinking-2020-08-27?mod=home-page

Section VI: Miscellaneous

1   A sideways market

The market moves up or down. Usually, it dances sideways when switching from one trend to the other. When it moves down, it moves at a faster speed. When the volume is unusually low, it could be a hint that the market is changing direction on me.

Market movements could be predicted by moving averages (30-days moving average is one for dips and 52 weeks for plunges for example). When it moves above the average line, most likely it will move up and vice versa.

For volatile markets, the last time it peaks and the last time it bottoms are termed as **resistance lines and support lines** respectively. In theory and theory only, a sideways market never breaks out from these two lines. It is a prediction only and many other factors should be considered. Even with all the right educated guesses, the market is not always rational.

Take advantage of the sideways movements by buying at small dips (the support line) and selling at small peaks (the resistance line).

You can take advantage of market timing by not holding a stock forever and by buying and selling the same stock or an ETF. I believe the 'buy-and-hold' idea has been dead since 2000. I cannot find too many articles praising this strategy with data after 2000.

Market plunges are usually fast and steep.

2015 Update. From my memory the last time we had a down year in a year before the election year was 1939, the start of WW2. Even 2007 was an up year. I had posted this info for 2015 even during the fierce correction in August, 2015. Adding the 1.9% dividend, the market beats the one-year CD by a good margin in 2015. To profit in this market, buy at temporary dips and sell at temporary surges.

Links

Resistance line and support line:
http://en.wikipedia.org/wiki/Support_and_resistance

Filler: Insider trading

First, the stocks are bought or sold by insiders and their relatives, then followed by programmed computers, institutional investors, technicians and then retail investors.

2 Market timing by asset class

Two major trading strategies are:
1. Buy high and sell higher.
   It is a kind of momentum play. You may keep these stocks for less time (say, less than three months). The momentum could change very fast. In my momentum portfolio, I keep most of my stocks for less than a month.
2. Buy low and sell high.
   When the asset class is totally out-of-favor and it has high value, buy it. It is a value play. You are swimming against the tide. You need to hold these stocks longer (say, longer than 6 months) for the market to realize its value.

It is not possible to predict correctly the peaks and bottoms of any asset class consistently. However, #1 usually starts first and is followed by #2. The holding period is just a suggestion.

Your success will be improved by using technical analysis correctly. Try the 50-day moving average (actually the last 50 trade sessions) to start with. Buy when it is above the moving average and sell when it is below. Next, try the 20-day moving average and many other technical analysis indicators such as exponential moving average and different days for the moving averages. The moving averages are available from Finviz.com without charting.

Basically, there is a tradeoff on switching too frequently and reacting too late. Some stocks are more volatile than others.

Try out different asset classes such as gold and oil. To illustrate, no one can predict that a gold price at $1800 is the peak. If you buy gold coins at $1000 and ride the gold wagon to $1600, you're doing quite well. In this case, trade GLD, the ETF fund for gold for technical analysis. The way to protect your profit and let the profit rise is using stops. Adjust the stop when the asset appreciates.

My experience in gold

I had gold coins bought at about $400 each many years ago. Gold did not appreciate much for over 20 years. When its price rose to $800, I sold some. I made a 100% return, but it may not even beat inflation. If I invested in stocks instead of gold coins, I would be far better off in total return (appreciation plus dividends). When gold rose to $1000, I sold more. Our rational thinking (part of human nature) would not allow us to hold these coins until $1,800. The moral is no one can predict the peak value of an asset and act accordingly.

Trading coins in your local shops would cost you a lot (commission and the spread) but it is safer. The coin shops do report your sales to the IRS if the sell is below a certain amount. Check the current rules.

Links
Disadvantages of gold ETFs:
https://www.youtube.com/watch?v=wMxj6iB92ZA

3   My predictions

Recently I read several books on how several authors claimed their correct predictions on the housing bubble in 2007. I do not know whether it is before the fact or after the fact. At least two authors made similar predictions on the bubbles of the stock market after 2008.

So far, they have either not materialized or have been just wrong. If you followed them to move all the stocks into cash, you have missed the biggest recovery of the stock market from 2009 to today (12-2015). The excessive printing of money boosts the stock market even though the economy has not been totally recovered.

It taught us:

- The correct prediction of one major event does not mean his/her future predictions will be correct even with good arguments.
- Even authors of best-seller books could be just a one-trick pony. I was amused that at least two authors blamed other authors of being a one-trick pony while they were one themselves.

I had the best performance in 2009 and recovered most if not all of my loss in 2007. I was too conservative after 2009. As of 7/2013, I would like to review which of my predictions are right.

This chapter is for information and education purposes. I have not spent enough time to evaluate every one of my predictions. The primary purpose is:

- With educated guesses, we should have more right than wrong. A win percentage of over 50% can make you a lot of money.
- Buying stocks or any investment is a prediction for better profit potential. Hence, there are risks that the prediction will not materialize.
- Learn from good experiences and bad experiences. However, ensure the lesson is not due to an irrational market, luck and conditions you cannot control.
- Even with the best arguments, the prediction may never materialize. Do not bet the entire farm on it.
- Your actions depend on your risk tolerance.

Correct or close to correct predictions

- 2000 market plunge. Moved most of my high-tech sectors to traditional industries. It could be better to move them to cash or contra ETFs (I believe they were not available in 2000).
- 2003. Moved back to stocks for better profit in Early Recovery.
- 2009. Moved back to stocks in Early Recovery. I had my best return in my largest taxable account by dipping into my credit line (not recommended).
- 2011. My prediction was very close and better than most other predictions for that year. Same for 2012.
- April, 2012 Correction. Quite close.
- June, 2013 Correction. It was a 6% correction, not the predicted 10%.
- Some stock winners (more winners due to the rising market and scoring system). Scoring System works by beating the market for the test period.
- Recommended Apple at 390.50 (before the split) on 5-2013.

Incorrect predictions

- 2008 market plunge.
  It was due to my false security on huge profits from energy stocks. When the economy continued heading south in 2008, everything including my energy stocks plunged. The simple chart from the chapter on Spotting Big Plunges should help. I did not use it as I had not discovered and refined this simple technique.

- Correction on Q1 2013.
  There was no correction. It could be due to the pumping of too much money in the market by the government. As of 8/2013, my stocks performed quite well. However, I've been keeping too much cash expecting a serious correction. It is a case of winning the battles but losing a war.

- Some stocks were losers. I did not learn from my previous findings to avoid these stocks.

The prediction for all predictions

The chart in Detecting Market Plunges shows you how to follow the moving average to exit the market and reenter the market. It works splendidly in the last two market plunges (2000 to 2015). It will work for the future plunges. However, the charts may not provide plenty of time to react as the last two; only time can tell.

Summary

It is not important about how many times we have predicted right, but what we have learned from our good and bad predictions. Learn from our experience and that would help us to make better future predictions. All our stock trading decisions are based on predictions. Some will materialize and some will not. Diversify your portfolio.

#Filler:

The golden rules on market plunges heard from the street:

Rule #1: Anything can go wrong; the market is irrational.

Rule #2: The market falls 3 times faster than it rises most of the time.

Rule #3: You have to gain 100% to rectify a 50% loss.

Rule #4: The easier the rules of the market game, the fewer will want to play.

Rule #5. Retail investors buy at the top due to greed.

Rule #6. Retail investors sell at the bottom due to the fear that the market will never return but it always does.

Fidelity

Click on "News & Research" and then "Stock Market & Sector Performance" for Equity Market Commentary. The advantage is Fidelity does not require paid subscriptions to see the entire articles.

4 Reasons for the coming market crash

This is an **example** for 2021 and 2022 only. For the last few years, most market predictors have had their crystal balls broken. It is due to the excessive supply of money that leads to a non-correlation of the economy and the stock market. It cannot last forever. It will correlate again when the money supply is reduced.

The incredible recovery of the market from 2007-8 is due to the excessive printing of money (i.e. money supply). History is repeated again in 2020. It leads to easy credit to buy stock (margin debt) and buyouts/corporate profits. With more money to buy stocks and fewer stocks to buy (buyouts), it is a simple case of Supply and Demand.

Since World War II, we never had a down year in a year just before the election including 2007 and 2019. However, 2021 could be a tough year and the market bubble may finally burst. As usual, there are two camps arguing in opposite directions for predicting the market direction of 2021. I recommend my readers to take some actions, the same as buying insurance. As of 1/2021, the market is unsound fundamentally but sound technically. When the technical is unsound, it is the time to leave the market as indicated by the simple market timing illustrated in this book.

Consult your financial advisor before taking any actions, and I am not responsible for your gains or losses.

Good News

- We have hopes on the ending of this pandemic at least reducing the impact in 2021.
- The economy is improving slowly except in some sectors that are affected immensely by the pandemic.
- Energy cost could be bottom that is good for the energy sector. Judging by the forward P/Es of many energy companies, I do not believe green energy would take over in 2021.
- The interest rate is almost zero and that is good for the housing sector and related sectors, buybacks, margin interest rate and investing by the corporations.

Bad News
- It has been one of the longest bull markets.

- The economy is poor compared to one year ago with a high unemployment rate.
- Many small businesses such as restaurants will be closed forever.
- The record-high market is a bubble to many.
- Margin debt is at a record high.
- The government is running out of tools to revive the economy such as lowering interest rates. Excessive supply of money will hurt the economy in the longer term.
- The national debts (partly due to our endless wars) and obligations (partly due to our aging population) are high as a percentage of the GDP.
- Most foreign countries except Japan have been reducing buying our national debt. Most of the debts were purchased by the Fed by printing money excessively.
- Many retailers that cannot service their debts will go bankrupt if not already.
- The USD is weak and the status of a reserve currency is shaken. However, a weak USD is good for export, but not good for the profit for global companies.
- I expect higher inflation is coming.

Summary

2021 could be very risky. We're living dangerously on borrowed time. Hence, be conservative. The recent rise of the market is due to supply (excessive printing of money) and the demand (fixed number of assets). The market is not rational compared to the economy.

5   A simple but risky strategy on market timing

Follow the article "Simplest Market Timing" to time the market. If it tells you the market is going down, buy contra ETFs and/or move stocks to cash depending on your risk tolerance.

Recommended ETFs (5 total)
SPY
PSQ
SEF
GLD
Money Market / CD

My reasons

Contra ETFs are betting the sectors represented to go down. During a market downturn, I would bet against bank/financial stocks (SEF, a contra ETF for the financial sector) and tech stocks (PSQ, a contra ETF for NASDAQ which includes a lot of tech stocks).

GLD is an ETF for gold. During a recession, gold should fare better than stocks, but it may not perform most of the contra ETFs. If the value of the USD depreciates, gold would fare better. Every portfolio should have 2 to 10% in gold depending on your risk tolerance. If you are conservative, move everything to Money Market fund / CD instead of the contra ETFs when the market is crashing.

We have only one false alarm from 2000 to 2010 but more after 2010. The false alarm tells you to exit the market and then tells you to reenter the market shortly. If you do not buy any contra ETFs, most likely you do not lose much.

After the crash

When the market timing tells you to return to the market, sell contra ETFs and buy SPY (or any ETF that simulates the market) and value stocks. You need more time to find and evaluate value stocks, so buy SPY first. Use stops to protect your portfolio.

Read the Disclaimer in the Introduction section of this book. Again, all investor's opinions are different. Check with your financial advisor before you invest.

6   Navigate in a stormy market

Disclaimer. Consult your financial advisor before taking actions. Past performances and predictions may not be indicative of future performances.

As of 2024, if you followed my book stating "Since the end of WW2 and as of this writing in 2024, the market seems to be positive on the year before the election.", you should be doing great so far. 2024 could be a stormy market: 1. Excessive printing of money and 2. Possible war with China. The following are my suggestions.

Ultra conservative investors should invest in broker's money market funds, CDs and short-term bond funds and skip the rest of this article. I would buy longer term CDs when the interest rate is high such as 8%. Laddering CDs would not tie up cash when you return to the market.

Recommend buying value stocks. Avoid companies with high debts and insider dumping (from Finviz.com). Use stops to limit losses and trailing stops to protect profits. Trailing stops should be entered periodically such as every week when the stock rises. For simplicity, I use 5% for non-volatile stocks and 10% otherwise – they are my lazy steps and figure the stops yourself . There are web sites to give you better stop values, and some recommend using resistance line as a reference.

Have the same stops for momentum stops. Make sure they are replaced or closed in a short holding period (one month for me).

Use simple market timing described in this book. Reentering the market is as important as existing the market. There could be false signals, and usually they do not affect your portfolio except some tax implications.

When you exit the market, you can park the cash in CDs, short-term bond funds, etc.

Aggressive investors can buy contra ETFs and even short stocks. Stops can also be used to protect your portfolio even in shorting stocks.

There are many articles on the current market via web articles (including Fidelity's) and YouTubes. There are always two opposing camps; use them are reference.

Book 7: Investing Strategies

A strategy is a method or a procedure in when and how to find stocks (usually via screens, also known as searches), analyze the stocks, buy them and when / why sell them.

I categorize strategies into long term and short term by the holding periods (a year or longer for long term and one to three months for short term). There are some other different strategies: day trading, swing strategies (about 2 to 6 months) and shorting strategies (about 1 month).

Usually, you do not use a long-term strategy (which is based on fundamentals) for holding stocks for less than a month; you are swimming against the tide and it usually takes longer for the market to realize about the stock's value. Examples: "Redefined Dogs of the Dow", year-end strategies and dividend strategies.

For the same reason, a short-term strategy (which is based on momentum) is usually most profitable in less than 3 months as the momentum may change. Examples: Momentum strategies, Sector Rotation and Insider Trading.

Within the category, I sub categorize them into safer and riskier strategies. Choose them according to your risk tolerance.

The following few books describe different strategies or styles of investing such as Swing Trading, Sector Rotation, Insider Trading, Penny Stocks, Micro Cap, Momentum Investing and Dividend Investing. I have included many other miscellaneous strategies.

It is not possible for one individual to specialize in all the different styles described above. Typically, I have read about two books on each of the strategies. I include their ideas and my ideas in this book. All these books share many common topics such as market timing and evaluating stocks. These topics have been described elsewhere in this book, so they will not be duplicated here.

I have not tested out all the strategies (as I have a life too), but they have to be proven profitable by someone at least in one market condition. We have to match the strategy or strategies to the current market. For example, the strategy should have a high chance of success if the market is trending up and the stock has high insider purchases. **Consult your investing advisor before committing real money**.

You may want to paper trade each of the strategies. Select the one that is favorable to the current market (i.e., it performs best in the last three months). In addition, it has to fit your risk tolerance and your own requirements. In addition, different phases of the market cycle favor specific sectors and investing styles. For example, market bottoms favor value stocks while the Up phase (defined by me) of a market cycle favors growth stocks.

The article "Dividend better?" in Book 5 serves as a procedure to evaluate a strategy with a historical database. There are two ways to test some strategies such as "Sideways Strategy" and its opposite strategy "Momentum" without a historical database:

- Load the historical price data of SPY for example from Yahoo!Finance to a spreadsheet.
- Many charts provide many historical data right on the charts. However, typically they do not provide most fundamental metrics such as Debt/Equity.
- Update the stock prices for your strategy weekly or monthly - it will take time to collect all the data. Hence, you cannot draw your conclusions readily as the last two described.

We can divide strategies into short-term (for traders) and long-term (for investors). However, you can be both. Personally, I allocated about 80% for long-term investing and 20% for short-term trading; it fluctuates depending on the current market conditions. To start, I recommend Long-Term Swing trading. Find sound fundamental stocks. Evaluate them every 6 months and sell them if their fundamentals deteriorate. Briefly I outline some of the shortcomings of the following strategies first as they all have their strengths in certain market conditions.

- Sector Rotation - Be prepared to spend more time and paper trade it. Also, sectors can reverse direction.
- Insider Trading - Do not treat it as a value play (i.e., do not depend on fundamentals). Sometimes the insiders are wrong.
- Penny and Micro Cap - I prefer micro-cap stocks over the risky penny stocks. Ensure the volume is at least 10 times larger than your potential buy position.

- Momentum - Do not hold the momentum stocks too long as momentum can reverse very fast.
- Dividend - Do not buy a stock solely on the dividend yield. Today it is very popular and profitable when the bond yield is low. Watch out for the changing interest rate.

The average return of each strategy serves as a guideline only due to my limited data and the specific parameters I use in screening and evaluating stocks. When you're making money in one strategy, stick with it until the performance deteriorates. When you lose money in one strategy, find out why and return to paper trading at least until you are comfortable with the strategy.

#Filler: lessons from a strategy named Turtle with my inputs
The experiment to train students who have no experience in two weeks worked. The technical analysis strategy would not work today for many reasons. However, the concepts are still good and explained here.

Do not time the market (not agree totally). Find a good strategy (easier said than done) and stick with it consistently. Cash management (agree with stops from 5% to 15% depending on your risk tolerance and the volatility of the stocks). Do not use leverage that could wipe out your entire portfolio. Follow the trend of the stock with higher positions.

1   Introduction

A strategy is a method or a procedure in how to find stocks (usually via screens, also known as searches), analyze the stocks, buy them and sell them. This section concentrates on screening for stocks.

I prefer value stocks (i.e., based on fundamentals). However, fundamentals are secondary for some strategies such as momentum. This book uses the same techniques in Finding Stocks and Scoring Stocks, so they will not be repeated here.

This book describes some simpler strategies and leaves the complicated ones in their own books that follow.

I read the book "What Works on Wall Street" by James O'Shaughnessy blaming many other strategies for non-performance. Later I read another book mentioning that O'Shaughnessy did not work after he published his book.

As mentioned previously, the strategy will not be effective when there are too many followers. That's the reason I provide you with many strategies and you should explore newer strategies yourself. The market favors different groups of strategies in different stages of the market cycle.

The best way to check what is the favorable strategy is to test the performances of your different strategies for the last three to six months. Several low-cost subscription services provide a historical database to make this task simple and feasible.

Traders and hedge fund managers change their strategies frequently. Retail investors should do the same.

One strategy was the poster boy for a subscription service. It worked well before. I tested it recently and it was one of the worst strategies. The lesson is: There are no evergreen strategies. Test out whether they still work in the last 90 days.

It is not possible for an individual to test out of the strategies described in this book. I try to find the best strategy to fit the current market. During a market crash, shorting stocks is the best. During a recovery, value stocks are the best. When the market is bullish, momentum stocks are most profitable. Year-end investing is profitable so far.

Select a strategy and stay with it until you are ready for real money. Always use stops to reduce your losses and trailing stops (adjusted to the current prices periodically) for appreciated trades.

A Sample Strategy

It is an example. Adjust it to your preferences and requirements. Instead of buying stocks, just save them in a watch list and buy them when the entire market is on sale. It consists of the following three steps.

1. When to search stocks to be traded. For example, it is once a month when the market is not risky.
2. What to buy. It will be described in more detail later.
3. Sell the stock(s). When the market is plunging, your objectives have been satisfied, or the bought stock(s) does not satisfy most criteria described in #2.

Step #2. There are several steps: Fundamental Analysis, Intangible Analysis, Qualitative Analysis and Technical Analysis.

For simplicity, stick with Fundamental Analysis here. The stocks have to satisfy most of the following criteria. Try to use a screener to limit your selection. If you do not find any stock, relax the criteria or do nothing as the market may be peaking and/or expensive. Skip those criteria that you do not have a subscription to access to.

- It must be in one of the three major U.S. exchanges. No ADRs and partnerships (unless you're an expert in the countries/fields).
- Market Cap is over 100 M (or over 10B for blue chips).
- Price is over $2.
- Average daily volume must be at least 20 times more than your potential position.
- Expected P/E is less than 20 and E must be positive.
- P/Cash Flow is less than 25 and Cash Flow must be positive.
- Debt/Equity is less than 1 (preferable .5; also depending on specific industry).
- Blue Chip Growth: A or B in both Total Score and Fundamental Score.
- Fidelity's Analyst Opinion is 7 or higher.
- Piotroski's (from GuruFocus or other sources) F-Score is 7 or higher.

Testing strategies

You can use the free screener in many sites including your broker's website and Finviz.com. However, most do not provide a historical database for back testing. Some include historical data for technical indicators such as SMA (Simple Moving Average) and/or P/E.

Here are some services that have historical data for back testing: VectorVest, Zacks and Portfolio 123 at low prices. This article outlines some of the hints for evaluating their services. You should list your requirements. They are expensive and time-consuming to learn. However, they should give you valuable tools if they are properly used.

- Price. Most would charge $500 and up for a yearly subscription. If you cannot afford it, use Finviz.com which is free. It does not have a historical database for fundamental data and you need to save the test results.
- Most sites do not compensate for survivorship bias by taking out the unlisted companies. There are more bankrupt companies than merged or acquired companies hence making your strategy looking better than it actually is. If you take out Enron and/or Lehman Brothers, your test would look better.
  Since more small companies go bankrupt than large companies, try to include companies with a market cap greater than 500 million (100 million for strategies for small companies) to reduce this bias.
- I prefer the historical database which starts from the year 2000 so we have two full market cycles from 2000 to 2019.
- I prefer dividing the test periods into phases of the market cycle. Some screens perform better in the down market than the up market for example.
- Most have a comparison to the S&P 500 index or SPY for simplicity. In the last few years (as of 2019) SPY has been doing great because SPY is weighted by market cap with a lot of high-flyers. If these high-flyers fall, this index and SPY would fall accordingly. Use related ETF for comparison. For example, if you are testing a strategy on dividend stocks, your yardstick should be one related to dividend stocks and most likely you need to add dividends to your results and the ETF. Personally, I would buy SPY for the money left over, and hence SPY is a logical choice for me. Do not use DOW index: 1. It has only 30 stocks, and 2. It is price weighted and that is not practical.
- I prefer to enter the filter parameters via 'click-and-select'.
- It is easier to understand annualized return; a 1% return per month is equivalent to 12% in a year, especially for short-term trades. However, if the period is less than 15 days, the annualized return would be amplified too much.
- Most do not include dividends and it is fine when you do not include the same in your benchmark such as the SPY. For screens specialized on dividends, add the extra dividends to the performance.

- Many vendors group several parameters such as P/E and Debt/Equity into a value score. The other popular score is momentum score with the simple moving average for example. The combining of these two scores is a summary score. There are many other scores such as a safety score using beta.
- Determine that whether the search is for value stocks or momentum stocks. You need to hold value stocks longer (one year for me) and momentum stocks shorter (1 month for me). Then do the same for testing.

  To illustrate, SMA-20, Sales Q-to-Q and Earnings Q-to-Q are momentum parameters while P/E, Debt/Equity and P/B are value parameters. If you test a value strategy, the holding period should be more than 6 months.
- Some screens find more volatile stocks than others. It is measured by the maximum drawback, which is defined as the loss from the recent peak. For stocks from volatile screens, use a higher stop loss otherwise they would be stopped out during stock price fluctuations.
- Read the evaluations of the service you are interested in by googling it. It could save you a lot of money by learning from others' experiences.
- A screen has many criteria such as P/E. My basic parameters are: in one of the 3 major exchanges, U.S. stocks, Market Cap within a specified range, Earnings Yield > 5% and Stock Price > 1. Vary it for your requirements for the specific screen.
- Sorting. You may want to sort Earnings Yield (E/P) in descending order.
- Testing. You may want to test the top 5 stocks according to your sort specified.
- Testing period. For value screens, you may want to hold the stocks for 6 months or a year.

  The following uses the Year-End screen as an example. You have the following start date: 11/1, 11/15, 12/1, 12/15, 1/15 and 1/30 and hold the screened stocks for 1, 2, 4 and 6 months.

  The number of simulations from 2007 to 2017: 10 years * 6 start dates * 4 (1, 2, 4 and 6 months holding) = 240 simulations. For each sort variation, you double the number of simulations to 480.

  Adding every variation to the screen such as Market Cap > 1000 would again double the number of simulations to 960.

  It is a time-consuming process. Some sites may have strategies simulating what gurus such as Buffett would buy.
- In reality, after you have found a handful of stocks, be sure to start further research using Debt/Equity, Q-Q sales / earnings, short % and Insider Transaction from Finviz.com; also use Fidelity.com's Equity Summary Score and average 5-year P/E and Yahoo!Finance.com's EV/EBITDA.
- If you have found too many stocks, restrict your criteria and vice versa for too few stocks.
- Ensure the calculations are correct. When you compare the returns to SPY, the negative values could give you wrong interpretations.

- Define your tests according to the phases of the market cycle. Market Peak (a phase defined by me) should have different strategies rather than Early Recovery.
- The last 5 years is better than the last 10 years as it is more similar to the current market.
- A spreadsheet is the tool to summarize all your test results.
- Short-term strategies should use a holding period of one to three months, while long-term strategies should use 1 year (6 months when appropriate) or annualized.
- A strategy with more losses than wins could be profitable depending on the positions (such as higher position for stocks with better scores) and/or stops (such as 50% for gains and 15% for losses).
- There has been no evergreen strategy, which is defined as a strategy that works well in all market conditions. High Insider Purchases is close to one. Recently, the following were the actual averages for my six strategies. I interpret that the period "2007 to 2014" does not favor stock pickers.

	Beat SPY by
From 2000 – 2006	490%
From 2007 – 2014	-96%
From 2000 – 2014	180%

Fidelity Video:
Trading strategies
https://www.fidelity.com/learning-center/trading/types-of-trading-strategies/overview
Top swing pattern: https://www.youtube.com/watch?v=wH8GnsjoFb0

Monitor performances of strategies

Need to monitor the recent performances of your strategies. Do not invest in the strategies that do not perform well recently. It can be done easily with a service (usually costs) that has a historical database. However, most of them do not take care of the survival bias – they take out the stocks from the database when they are delisted, bankrupt or merged. You just create a watchlist.

For example, the watchlist name is "YearEnd 20211215" keeping track of the stocks screened by your year-end strategy on 12/15/2021. Check out the performance from 12/15/2021 to a month later, and compare it to SPY (an ETF simulating the S&P 500 Index). I usually have 3 watchlists: a primary one, one that has deleted the duplicate stocks in the last month and one that I trade. You do not want to waste time in analyzing the stocks that have been evaluated recently. After the screened stocks, analyze them using tools such as Finviz and Fidelity for example ignoring the foreign stocks selectively or high dumping by insiders.

It is possible but more tedious without a historical database such as Finviz and Fidelity. From our example, just save the stocks in a spreadsheet on 12/15/2021 and enter the stock prices a month later. Besides the strategy, you may want to test the performances of individual metrics such as P/E.

Execution of a strategy
Be disciplined
You need to execute your strategy in a disciplined way. Set up a trade plan. The best time to buy is when the market is uptrend. It is uptrend when the SMA-20, SMA-50 and SMA-200 are all positive from Finviz.

Your screen from the strategy may have too many stocks. It would be too time-consuming to evaluate too many stocks. You need to narrow your search by:
- Select the top 5 stocks such as EP (E/P for long-term strategies and SMA-50 for momentum strategies).
- Change the criteria.
- Do a quick analysis to discard stocks such as high Debt/Share (for most industries for long-term strategies.

If you cannot find any stock or too few stocks for comparison, either skip this session or relax the search criteria

Filler: Max. drawdown. 'Max. drawdown' should be understood for short-term investors. It is the maximum money you can lose. If your tested strategy tells you that you can lose 40% in this strategy, then you should place the stops accordingly. To illustrate, you bought MSFT for $100, and it dipped to $50, your max. drawdown is $50 or 50%. If you use margin, your broker would issue a margin call on its way to the $50 drop. Eventually the stock would recover and hit the $200 mark, and the long-term holders are glad that they did not close the position.

.

More on strategies

A strategy tells you how to find a stock and when to sell a stock. The most important task is how to screen potentially profitable stocks to limit your selection and then evaluate each screened stock.

Today, there are many predefined screens available and we can define our own screens. Most of the financial ratios such as P/E have been defined for us to reduce the need for the time-consuming task of finding them from the financial statements. There are certain items in the financial statements that we should be concerned with after the initial evaluation.

To me, the most important advance for retail investors is the availability of historical databases at prices we can afford. It shows us the performance of our strategies for the last 10 or so years in an hour or two. The following are my suggestions to make a better use of the findings from these databases and their pitfalls.

- Start with proven metrics as demonstrated by research (the metrics used in this book and other sources such as from SSRN.com) and your own trading.
- Select parameters as close to your trading style as possible. For example, if you only deal with small stocks, select market caps from 100 M to 500 M.
- Some screens perform better in the short term while some perform better in the long term. I recommend testing the performances for 3 months, 6 months, 12 months and 18 months for short-term screens (1 month for momentum stocks). If you believe the strategy is for a long term only, get the performances for 6, 12 and 18 months.
- In 2015 (use a date more current), I start with the year 2000 and end with 2014 for a total of 15 sets. It covers the two market cycles. The market before 2000 may not be relevant as today's market is quite different from that time. Actually, I prefer the tests for the last 10 years.
- Run the screen in the first part of the year and test the performance at year end. Repeat the test for the rest of the intervals: 3, 6, 12 and 18 (adding 1 for momentum and 2 years for long term).
- I do not start with an amount (say $10,000) and see the results at the end of a period (say 10 years). It could be misleading when your screen performs exceptionally well (or bad) in the first few years. I call the one I use "window testing" for lack of a better term. To illustrate this, the start date is Jan. 1, 2000 (actually Jan. 2 due to holiday) and end date is Jan. 1, 2001. The next set is Feb. 1, 2000 to the start, the next set is Feb. 1, 2001 and so on.
- I use the next available date if the date falls on a weekend or a holiday for consistency. If you have more time, try another set starting in mid-year. For some strategies and when time allows, I test the strategy monthly.
- If my screen makes 10% and the market makes 20%, it is 100% worse off. I compare how much it beats the market.
- For simplicity I use the SPY to simulate the market. No index is ideal. The S&P 500 is capitalization cap weighted. In 2015, the bubble stocks dominated this index. The better selection is to choose the index according to the type of stocks that you usually have such as the Russell 2000 for small stocks. Russell 1000 has 500 more stocks than S&P 500, and hence the first 500 should be the same as S&P 500.
- Consider safety such as the Sharpe ratio, maximum drawdown (peak-to-trough loss) and a winner percent. A winning percentage of 55% (target for 52%) is very good. If your strategy has a very high winner percent, most likely it is safe but just not only performing.
- Why your actual performance with real money may be worse than the tested strategy:
    - Survivor bias. Most databases take out the stock when they're bankrupt, merged or acquired. Hence the performance of the screen is better than it really is as there are more bankrupt companies than merged/acquired. From my experience I have at least one such stock in a year. Hence, the test results are not correct if the database does not take care of this bias.
    - Emotions do not allow you to stick with the strategy.

- The strategy does not work in the current market; that's why we need to test the performance of the last 6 months.
- There is idle money between trades.

- I use the top 5 stocks (hence sorting is important). In addition, if you do not buy foreign stocks, deselect them. I use the top 2 for some strategies such as sector rotation.
- If you cannot find data in some screens in any month, just leave it blank (actually null), which will not be included in calculating averages / totals. If the market is risky, you may not find any value stocks.
- The most recent tests would resemble the performance of the strategy better. Hence, I have an extra average of performance on more recent tests.
- Return = (B-A)/A, while A is the return of SPY for me. It does not handle the negative numbers. Use (B-A)/ABS(A). In any case, check the results to see they make sense. When B or A is zero or a very small number, the results could be misleading. I usually delete the test results on huge returns in both directions.
- Using sector rotation strategy as an example, the holding periods are 1, 2 and 3 months.
- Some strategies work better on different phases of the market cycle such as growth stocks in the market trending up and staple stocks during market plunges.

Section I: Common strategy ideas

2 Screening stocks

A screen is part of a strategy to find potential stocks to buy. It limits the number of stocks to evaluate. Evaluate the screened stocks to find the better ones. Buy them for the right prices. Set the exit procedure such as losing 12% or making over 25%. The optimal performance of holding the stock is 6 months for the Insider strategy for example. When you have the stock for 6 months, do another evaluation to determine your buy/hold decision. Monitor your performance.

It works for me with about 40 screens. I check out the recent performances periodically and select the top screens (about 4 usually).

Before looking for stocks, check out whether the market is risky. After screening, I score the screened stocks and do some further evaluation before I purchase any stock.

When we follow all the above, there is still no guarantee that we'll make money. In the long run, we do and it is far better to follow a proven strategy than not to.

Here are some free sites for screens.

More description: article
http://stocks.about.com/od/researchtools/a/071909screenlist.htm

Swing trading: https://www.youtube.com/watch?v=ldDsi8F4ZeA

Filler: Happy Mother's Day Poem

The following is my translation from poet Yu's work in Chinese. I changed some words as some could not be translated effectively. I added the title "Two Cries".

-------- Two Cries -----------

I cried at two unforgettable times in my life.

The first time when I came to this world.
The second time when you left this world.

The first time I did not know but from your mouth.
The second time you did not know but from my heart.

Between these two crises, we had endless laughs.
For the last 30 years, we had joyful laughs that had been repeated, repeated...

You treasured every laugh.
I cherish every laugh for the rest of my life.

A simple tutorial

This tutorial is for beginners using Finviz's Screener to screen value stocks of large companies with my own preferences. Bring up Finviz, and select Screener, which has 3 sections: Descriptive, Fundamental and Technical.

- **Index**. S&P 500.
- **Country**. USA (my personal reference).

Select the second section (Fundamental).
- **Forward P/E**. Under 25. I prefer under 15 for non-tech stocks.
- **Price/Free Cash Flow**. Under 25. This metric had been ignored by many.
- **Debt / Equity**. Under 1.

Select the last section (Technical)
- **200-Day SMA**. Above SMA200.

The number of screen stocks is still too many for individual evaluation. Ignore the stocks Insiders are dumping (more than negative 10% for me). Ignore all stocks with negative earnings (i.e., Forward P/E = '-'). You can sort Forward P/E in ascending order and evaluate the first 10 stocks (or more depending how much time you have).

Alternatively, add the following to reduce the number to the one you desire: RSI(14) (less than 50 for example), Return of Equity (more than 15 for example) and EPS Growth Qtr over Qtr (over 5% or example).

You can save this screen for future use. Evaluate each screened stock. Start with Fidelity's Equity Summary Score (prefer over 7) and Yahoo!Finance's (under Statistics) Enterprise Value / EBITDA (EBITDA/ Enterprise Value should be over 5%).

As in most screeners, this one has many limitations. The number of limitations has been reduced with the paid subscription. Many can be resolved by using multiple screens such as different Market Cap and higher debt for some sectors.

Screening momentum stocks uses different metrics such as high 50-SMA.

Since Finviz does not have a historical database for fundamental metrics, you cannot test how your screen performs. Save the evaluated stocks in a watch list and update the performance periodically (a year for value screens and 1 to 3 months for momentum screens).

Buy the stock and set your exit policy to complete the strategy.

3 Experiences in strategies

A strategy tells you what stocks to buy, what and when to sell.

We should use one or a few of the proven strategies that match well with the current market conditions. It is not an easy job and not an exact science especially when human emotions are involved. A perfect match seldom happens. However, when it does, it can be fireworks and your pocket will be over-stuffed with money.

The following strategies are for illustration purposes only. Test them out before you use them with real money.

- We usually ignore when to sell. If the strategy such as the "Year-End Loser" shows statistically that the best holding period is 4 months, sell them before May. That's why we should have the performances at short-term, mid-term and long-term in testing strategies.

- Sideways market (such as 2015).

    Buy at dips and sell at temporary highs and vice versa. It is a correction of about 5% by my definition. The market may just fluctuate in a small range.

    The hard part is to determine what these dips and bottoms are. Here are my suggestions and how we need to adjust the percentages to the volatility of the current market. To me, if it is 2% lower than the last session (or 5% lower than the highest price in the last 5 sessions), it is a temporary bottom. The definitions vary based on your personal tolerance and time for investing. To benefit from this small fluctuation, buy stocks from your watch list or any ETF that represents the market such as SPY or IWM.

    The holding period could be one day to two weeks depending on your risk tolerance. It takes advantage of the fluctuation of prices due to the good news and bad news scenario typically.

    Alternatively, you determine when to sell by how much it would rise, such as 2% higher than the last session (or 5% higher than the lowest price in the last 5 sessions). The disadvantage is you may never be able to sell stocks that are continuously heading down. The stop orders would prevent further losses.

In reality, the market does not behave the way we expected it to. You need to protect your loss (say sell it when it is over 15% loss). In the long run and if the market fits this sideways market, you SHOULD make money. As in life, there are no guarantees. You can load the historical price of SPY (or another ETF) to stimulate this strategy using different percentages and holding periods.

- The market is up or down steadily.

    The profits form momentum strategies are usually better than buying value stocks in a bull market. "Buy high and sell higher" is a good strategy in a rising market.

    Use contra ETFs on a downward market. The average holding period for me is 1 month (some may use 3 months). I stop using momentum when the market is too risky as I do not usually short stocks. It takes several weeks of small profits to recover from one big loss in one day even if it recovers.

- Buy value.

    The average holding period could be more than one year. You're betting against the tide, so it will take a longer time for the value to be 'discovered' by the market. When the institution retailers are selling, find out their reasons. Buy what they are selling if they are wrong (rarely but it has happened many times). It is similar to "Buy low and sell high" and "Contrary Strategy". It seems to be easier said than done, as our emotions do not allow us to act rationally. The typical retail investor usually buys at peaks and sells at bottoms.

    My examples. I sold 2/3 of SMCI for 300% profit and my wife asked me why I did not sell them at 1,200% profit. I am no God and I do not have a time machine. I sold the stock for fundamentals and I should use trailing stops. Similarly, I made big profits in Game Stop but I sold it far too early. I still have TTWO and it is having 50% annualized return from 2015 to today (4, 2024).

- Turnaround and breakup of a company.

    When the company fixes its major problem(s), its stock price could skyrocket.

A company may be worth more by adding up the pieces. The recent example is ALU when I bought it at $1 in 2013. At the time, the company had a market cap of around two billion but the debt was about the same. However, their patents could be worth far more than two billion.

- Follow talented investors.

    First, you need to find talented investors who have good recent performance records. GuruFocus.com (subscription is required) shows what stocks the gurus recently traded. 2015 is not a good year for gurus.

    Check out this article.
    http://seekingalpha.com/article/2762935-a-wisdom-of-experts-portfolio

- Follow what insiders buy.
    There are many tricks to separate the gems from garbage.

- Emotionally detached from market's (and also personal portfolio's) ups and downs. We all make mistakes in investing. My common mistake is to invest too early based on fundamentals. Many times I was right, but I ignored the momentum.

- Buy at the bottom.
    2009 is one bottom. In my definition, it is Early Recovery (usually about one year from the plunge or indicated by the chart described in this book). This bottom fishing strategy buys beaten down stocks that are fundamentally sound. The average holding time is about one year (less if there are better bargains).

    My best returns are from the last two bottoms in 2003 and 2009. At these times, there were more potential stocks for huge profits and my average holding period was about 6 months. 2009 was the only time I dipped into my credit line on my house - **not recommended to most investors**.

- Market Neutral.
    If you are a good stock picker (or believe you're one), treat the market as neutral (i.e., ignoring the market timing). For example, you pick five

stocks to buy and five stocks to sell short. You make money due to your skill in picking the right stocks no matter how the market moves. In theory, you should make good money without betting on the market direction.

- Sector Neutral.
  If you specialize in a specific sector such as airlines, you may buy 2 good stocks and short 2 bad stocks in that sector. You can make good money because of your knowledge in the sector. In this strategy, compare stocks to its sector averages. You can use options to do the same if your cash position is limited.

  Trading drug stocks could bring you huge profits. To improve your odds, you need to be an expert in this field. If you're not, subscribe to a specific newsletter that specializes in this industry and has a proven track record. Weigh more on the buy side when the sector is heading up, and vice versa.

- Sector Rotation.
  Investing in a sector or shorting the entire sector could add more profit. To illustrate, the tech sector may be a laggard during a recession as most consumers will not have the spare money to buy consumer electronics, and many companies would postpone their investment in enhancing productivity and development. Every month or two, rotate to the sector that is in an uptrend. Protect your profit when the sector reverses its direction.

- Theme investing.
  When China is moving up, FXI (an ETF) would be a buy. Other examples are OIL and GLD (for gold).

- Strong USD.
  It would be bad for global companies when the profits from foreign investments would be reduced when they are converted to a strong USD. The other bet is on USD itself.

- Super stocks.
  Most are small companies with increasing sales and earnings. It is a little different from the conventional stock analysis. They are riskier but the profits could be huge. Expect one big winner for several small losers. These stocks of small companies are not followed by analysts.

- The winners are already in your portfolio.
  Do not sell your winners as they may turn into bigger winners unless you have a good reason. Do not sell them if they still pass your recent stock analysis. During any market plunge, you may want to sell them but you should buy them back when the market recovers.

When you mismatch the strategy with the market conditions, you lose the opportunity for profit or even lose money. If the market is up or down steadily, a sideways strategy will not work for example. Matching the strategy to the current market conditions is not an easy job and sometimes it takes some luck. However, when it matches it, there could be fireworks. If you match it more times than you miss it, you should make good money.

Afterthoughts
"Buy and hold" needs no explanation. You just buy the stock and hold it forever. It is a good strategy in a secular bull market such as 1970-2000. After 2000, there were better strategies than "Buy and Hold".

A better way is "Buy and monitor" to ensure the stock you bought still has an appreciation potential.

"Buy and forget" is my term and it could be a good strategy in 2012. Buy the deeply-valued stocks (i.e., big bargains for quality stocks) and forget it until the economy comes back. I have made some profits in established companies such as MSFT, CAT and CSCO during this period.

Links
Market Neutral http://en.wikipedia.org/wiki/Market_neutral
Sector Rotation http://en.wikipedia.org/wiki/Sector_rotation

Filler: "First" as of 4/2016

This time could make some history at least for one of the following:
1. First woman president.
2. First spouse stays in the white house two times. "Buy one get one free" or give Bill another chance with the interns.
3. First non-politician president.
4. First president spending less in campaign.

So far, they try to satisfy every group (such as the Great Wall of the US, free tuition...) without telling us how to finance them.

4   The best strategy

Note. Most parameters described here such as SMA-20% and Short% can be found from Finviz.com

It is Buy Low and Sell High.

It is simple but most retail investors just do the opposite: Buy High and Sell Low. The flow of money to/from money market funds turns out to be a reliable contrary indicator.

The Early Recovery in 2003 and 2009 and the later part of June, 2012 could be the best time to buy.

The above represents buying at low prices and selling at high prices. Considering P/E (positive 'E' only), buy at low P/E of a stock, a sector and the market (via an ETF) and sell them respectively at high P/E.

Here are some hints when to buy and sell with this strategy:

- Sell when everyone including your silly mother-in-law is making good money and all participants think they're financial geniuses. It could be the riskiest time. The high interest rates (my yardstick is over 5% for Fed Discount rate, the best rate the Fed lends to the banks) usually confirms this as folks falsely expect better returns even though they pay more on interest to borrow money to buy stocks.

- Do not buy the stocks that formed the bubble(s), such as the technology stocks in 2001-2002 and the bank stocks in 2008-2009 as some 'optimists' think it is time to return and usually they're wrong.

    Do not think the stock is a good deal when it loses half of its value. Buy them only when the root problem has been fixed. The best time to return to the market after a market plunge is usually two years after the market plunge (2003 for the market plunge in 2000 and 2009 for the market plunge in 2007/2008). Many bubble stocks never recover and many of these stocks take more than 3 years to recover. Their prices appear to be low, but no one can predict the bottom unless it goes to zero.

- Be careful in the sectors or group of stocks that have a winning streak for more than two years. Most likely they will correct. Use a stop loss to protect your profits if you want to keep them.

    You could have saved a lot if you used this strategy on tech stocks in 2000. As of 2015, dividend stocks could be the next sector to burst, but only time can tell. Do not fall in love with a stock. Yesterday's winners could be tomorrow's losers, and vice versa.

    'Buy and hold' has been dead since 2000. We have two market plunges with an average loss of about 45% from their peaks.

- Do not buy dividend stocks solely for their dividends. Most of them are matured companies; most have less growth and hence less appreciation potential. They usually lose less value in a recession after dividends. Income investors are chasing them for higher dividends than bonds.

    Except from Roth accounts, when you withdraw from your retirement accounts, your dividends will be treated as income. Check the current tax rates for income and dividend from taxable accounts.

- Buy value stocks that seem to be bottomed. It is hard to identify the bottom. When the appreciation potential outweighs the risk, it could be a buy.

- No one can predict consistently the market bottom. However, use your better judgment with educated guesses to gain an edge. Refer to the exit point using the 350-day SMA from the chapter on detecting market plunges.

- Buy the stocks that have been losing money but their burn rates can last for the entire recession. They're risky but the potential profits are great. There were many in 2003 and 2009. Even in a bad economy in 2012, a few corporations had historically low P/Es.

- Buy value stocks with a turnaround sign such as when the SMA-50% is positive.

- Buy against the experts who have unconvincing predictions. They usually exaggerate the rosy outlooks of the companies in order to sell the stocks they own. This is one of the few times you should bet against them. Use your better judgment to ensure how false their predications could be.

Using Citicorp (symbol C) as an example

Following the chapter on avoiding bank stocks, buying this stock at $550 a share could be avoided. After the big plunge in 2008, I believe it has long-term profit potential. Accumulate this stock if you believe C will be profitable in 10 years (2024) or so. Do not sell it unless there is potential for a market plunge. If so, buy it back after the plunge. One's opinion.

With our market timing (defending sector may return in two years), I checked it in mid 2009, about 2 years after the start of the market plunge. Optionally I could use the SMA-350 of the stock to determine the reentry point. However, it had no meaning due to the big plunge from $550. On 8/2009, C's P/E was negative, so I did not buy it.

Alternatively buy it for when there is a big drop in P/E regardless of the current price as follows. We started when the P/E was about 40. Normally I buy it when the P/E is at around 20. Take an exception for turnaround stocks.

Date	P/E	Price
06/2010	40	40
01/2011	13	49
08/2011	9	32

The above is for illustration purposes only, so the numbers are not precise.

As of 6/12/2014, I expected a correction, so I sold it at about $48. I only trade these kinds of stocks when I see long-term appreciation potential. The other three important metrics are P/B, P/S and RSI(14). Use Forward (same as Expected) P/E if possible. The most important metric for lenders is the quality of the loans, which is hard to evaluate for retail investors. The other factor is any serious, pending lawsuits. When Lehman Brothers was gone, the governments will chase after the institutions that sold the derivatives.
Update 8/2019. C's stock price is $62.

The second-best strategy

Buy high and sell higher.

When everyone is looking for stocks with the highest value, there may not be any such stocks available. It seems to contradict with my best strategy but it is not intended to. Fundamentals may not show everything about the company such as a new drug, a new product… The all-time high prices usually show that. Buy the stock when it is over the 50-day simple moving average (50 or 200 days depending on how long you usually hold a stock) via Finviz.com.

Buying fully-priced stocks is dangerous even if it may be profitable. To protect your profits:

- Be extra careful in risky markets; I prefer not to buy any stock when the market is risky.

- Set stop loss orders. Recommend 10% (or 15% for volatile stocks) less than the current price. If you set a 5% stop, it would be stopped out by normal fluctuations especially for volatile stocks.

- Use Technical Analysis. When the price drops below the moving average you used, sell it. When RSI (14) is high (over 70), check out the reason as it could be overbought.

If you are not very sure, sell half of it. You will not go broke for taking profits.

As in life, there are no guarantees, but using a proven technique / discipline is far better than trading without one. Paper trading ensures the strategy fits the current market conditions, your personal tolerance and requirements.

The third best strategy

Buy very high and sell even higher.

It is the riskiest. These stocks could be bubble stocks moved by institutional investors and then moved even higher by retail investors. It may take a while before the institutional investors rotate to other sectors / stocks and/or take profit.

My strategy is to follow the herd but ensure you're ready to exit.

- Find them. Usually they have break-outs. They pass the resistance, a technical term. Now, they are in the low point of the support line, so they have a long way to go to the next resistance line. It has to be confirmed with its daily volume such as 3 times or more than the average daily volume. Usually they are in the 52-week highs.

- Usually, they are large caps with high trade volumes. My range is 100M to 5B. Be careful on stocks ranging from 100M to 500M. They may appreciate a lot on the positive side; they are risky and they can be manipulated easier. Stocks from 1B to 5B appreciation potential is lesser than 100M to 500M.

- Do not short them.
- Buy them ignoring the fundamentals as they are moving up with the herd sometimes for a reason and sometimes not. Alternatively, use options.

- Set mental stop losses. Adjust the stops periodically after they have been appreciated.

Watch them every day. Bring up Finviz.com and enter the sector ETF the stock belongs to and the stocks. Pay attention to SMA200%: The higher it is, the higher chance it is peaking. When RSI(14) is over 70% (65% for sectors), most likely it is overbought. When SMA-20% is negative, there is a good chance of reversing the trend downward.

Buy and Monitor

I usually sell my stocks that have fulfilled my objectives or admitted I have made a mistake. However, some stocks keep on rising and I may miss many 3 or more baggers.

I gifted many appreciated stocks to my family members. My grandchildren will keep them for a long while. Here are the stocks I gave on 5/1/2015 (the date I gifted them) and the performances today (5/12/2018).

Stock	Total Return	Annualized return
CSCO	58%	19%
STX	88%	29%
TTWO	377%	124%
Average	174%	57%
Compare to:		
SPY	29%	10%

My point is "buy and hold" is still valid for many stocks. Buy low when they have been temporarily ignored. These stocks should have long-term potential as they will be held for a long while. My actual performance is substantially more as I bet at least double more in TTWO.

Instead of "Buy and Hold", you need to buy and monitor. When they have serious problems such as Circuit City, Radio Shack, Sears…, do not hesitate to sell them.

When you time the market, ensure buy back the stocks you sold during the recovery phase of the market cycle.

My long-term grade

They are composed of the following (using metrics from Finviz.com): low Forward P/E (5 to 25), low Debt/Equity (less than .25), high Cash/Share, larger Market Cap (> 200M), high ROE (>15%), low RSI(14) (less than 35), high Insider Own/Purchase, Sales Q/Q (>15%), EPS Q/Q (>10%) and SMA200% (>0). In addition, they have competitive products, invest heavily in research (except for established companies), and there are no serious lawsuits pending.

#Filler: Depending whom you talk to
"White lives matter" is racial remark from a white guy.
"Black lives matter" is not from a black guy.

Same for "white power", "black power" and "yellow power".

#Filler: Life guarantee
Eat vegetables, small portions of meat without skin, exercise, do not drink and smoke. No buffets. I guarantee you live two years longer and it is a lifetime guarantee. Of course, it is your life not mine.

#Filler: I do not have a life

I do not smoke, do not drink a lot, do not gamble and do not chase wild women. The beautiful hostess in the restaurant I used to work at asked me, "What do you do for fun?" Nothing!

5 Different investment styles

There are three major styles to evaluate stocks: Fundamental, Growth and Technical Analysis (TA).

The debate on their benefits could be endless. I believe TA is good for short term (1 month for stocks), growth for intermediate term (say 3 months) and fundamental is good for longer term (say 6 months). Here is my summary of the two (I place Fundamental and Growth into the same group for discussion here). Market sometimes favors value (i.e., fundamentals) and sometimes growth.

TA depends mostly on the stock price and hence it predicts the trend better; it also can track oversold conditions. TA would catch the stock movement, but not by fundamental or growth metrics.

- TA.
  Most TAers (those who practice technical analysis) do not care about fundamentals, but price and volume. They do have good arguments. A lot of data about the stock are not available or too late to be effective such as a new drug discovery, being acquired, or a serious lawsuit pending.

  The following are two illustrations on how TAers can benefit.

  When the insiders and/or analysts know about some promising new products or positive unexpected earnings, they buy and tell their families to buy. I do not judge whether it is Illegal insider trading or not. TAers notice the rise of the stock price with increasing volume and they buy. Many times, the last ones to buy may end up losing money as the insiders would unload them especially when the stock prices are overvalued.

  When the institutional investors (pension fund managers and fund managers) are buying a specific stock, the stock volume and its price will both rise. TAers would notice them from the charts and jump on the wagon. To me, this is the basic reason on how good day traders make money. It usually takes a week for an institutional investor to finish trading a stock.

'Max. drawdown' should be understood for short-term investors. It is the maximum money you can lose. If your tested strategy tells you that you can lose 40% in this strategy, then you should place the stops accordingly. To illustrate, you bought MSFT for $100, and it dipped to $50, your max. drawdown is $50 or 50%. If you use margin, your broker would issue a margin call on its way to the $50 drop. Eventually the stock would recover and hit the $200 mark, and the long-term holders are glad that they did not close the position.

- Fundamentals.
  They look at the companies' metrics such as P/E, expected P/E, PEG, debt, sales growth, etc. A good company's stock price with rising profit and rising sales should appreciate in the long term. Some short the stocks of companies with bad fundamentals. In some cases, data is hidden in the financial statements that most metrics do not detect.

To conclude, the best TAers and the best fundamentalists usually make money in either market in the long run. However, fundamental analysis is easier to master and they have made more money than TAers in the long run. You find a lot of successful fundamentalists from Buffett and his followers, but not too many successful TAers. Some successful TAers even lose their accumulated fortunes. Be warned that if you do not know what you're doing in either discipline, you will lose money. Learn it and trade it on paper before committing even small amounts of real money to it.

The best way is using both disciplines in selecting stocks as described below.

- When your chart(s) displays a candidate to buy, take a look at the fundamentals. If the fundamentals are bad, be cautious. Some screens can search for the stocks with good technical patterns (Finviz.com is one).

- After you spot a bargain stock to buy via the fundamental metrics, check out its SMA-200 (Simple Moving Average for the last 200 trade sessions) or any duration that fits your purpose. If the price is above the moving average, it could be a buy.

Afterthoughts

- Try the following to see whether fundamental works better if you have a historical database.

Fundamentals

1. Include all stocks that are below the 200-day SMA (Simple Moving Average) - opposite of what a TAer would do.
2. The expected positive P/Es have to be between 4 and 15. In addition, both profits and sales are rising by 5%.
3. Exclude financial companies like banks and insurance, miners, bio companies and drug companies that are hard to evaluate.

TA

1. Buy stocks that cross over the 50-day, simple moving averages.
2. Never buy stocks when the market is below 200-day, simple moving average.

Check the result in 1-month intervals and 6 months intervals. My own simple test favors the fundamentals in 6 months intervals and favors TA in 1-month intervals. You may need more exhaustive testing to draw a good conclusion in different phases of a market cycle for at least 2 market cycles.

- SMA-200 (from Finviz.com without charts) and its variations are the ones most TAers use and even most experienced fundamentalists know how to use it if they want to. It is also a good indicator for the general market by using an ETF that simulates the market.
There are many sophisticated TA indicators in Yahoo!Finance. For qualified clients, Fidelity provides a tool to back test your TA strategies.
- It may be beneficial to use fundamentals to look for stocks and use TA to find the entry and exit points. Today's screens can do it in the reverse order, or both in the same screen.

- Fundamentals can be divided into Value and Growth.
Value. I use it mostly. Especially good in the early recovery phase of the market cycle.

6   Summary on value investing

When the market is plunging, most stocks will lose in prices. Hence, it is not a good time to buy stocks. The best time to buy stocks is when the market is recovering. I call it Early Recovery as described in my articles on market timing. I had about 80%

return in my largest taxable account in 2009. During this stage, the average P/E is high but the PEG is improving.

Similar to the Early Recovery of the 2000 market crash, I had good results but I did not keep good records. At that time, I expected the market would recover in two years. I scanned stocks that had enough cash to last for the two years and evaluate them further.

From about Dec. 15, 2018 to early January, 2019, I made over 50% in one month on quite a number of stocks. I bought stocks that had lost about 50% but were profitable. This is a perfect screen to this market conditions. I bought many stocks during the temporary dip in December. It is partly luck and partly skill.

The following is my recommendation to a sideways market. First, we want to avoid companies that would go bankrupt. Skip companies that have negative earnings especially those with high debts unless they have good reasons and/or belong to specific industries that require heavy borrowing. The reason could be a new drug, a new product and/or are settling a major lawsuit. Check out the Free Cash Flow / Share and Insider Transactions to start. Experienced investors may consider to short these stocks; do not short them if their trends are up such as SHOP and ZM in 6/2020.

The most popular P/E may not tell the entire story. EV/EBITDA from Yahoo!Finance takes debt and cash into consideration. Check out free evaluations from several websites such as Finviz.com, Seeking Alpha (which currently has fewer articles for non-subscribers) and Fidelity.com.

Need patience as the value stocks are swimming against the tide. It may take a year or two for the market to recognize their true values. Even so, I have value stocks that stay low forever. They may be 'value traps'. You may want to enter a position when the stock starts moving up as evidenced by the positive SMA-20% or SMA-50% in Finviz.com.

We have been surrounded by new gadgets in our daily life. Most are technical companies and they are not value stocks in most of our definitions. We have to relax the definitions such as changing the upper limit of the P/E from 20 to 25.

As in life there is no guarantee that it will increase in value. That's why we need to diversify (i.e., not putting all eggs in one basket). However, the chance of appreciation is substantially increased if you do all the homework described here.

Value investing. The primary aim is to buy stocks at good prices, and wait patiently for the market to realize their values. Their characteristics are:
- Low P/B. This metric is not valid for mature companies as the book value does not include many important assets such as brand name and customers. We need to include many other metrics.

- **High Yield (E/P).** EV/EBITDA from Yahoo!Finance takes debt and cash **into** consideration.

On 5/2021, I spotted some stocks with Cash/Share higher than the Share price. The investor would receive more in cash if you give away the company for free. In some cases, they are the ultimate bargains. However, some companies may be heading to bankruptcy, having high burn rate, facing a serious lawsuit(s), or any of the above. From Finviz.com, you can spot these companies by specifying Price/Cash under 1. Ignore sectors: Banks and Asset Management. I found ASMB, VYGR, ADVM, ODT and YELL (not from this screen). You can further evaluate them. ODT declared the termination of their major drug for cancer. I placed a small order on YELL.

A good Link: Peter Lynch:
https://www.youtube.com/watch?v=J1DFMXL2kXE&t=2304s
I have proven market timing worked fine in the 2000 and 2008 market crashes. I bought many products from BBB, and they are close to bankruptcy. Buffett was late in buying Apple, as he did not use a smartphone. New drugs may not be understood by most investors and they could lose some buying opportunities. Hence, they have many exceptions.

7   AAII, a source for strategies

AAII has many nice stock screens. Check out their performance summaries. You can divide the screens and their performances into groups according to the different stages of a market cycle and rank the performances. Some screens perform better in certain stage(s) of the market cycle. Most likely, the value screens should do better in the market bottom (Early Recovery defined by me) and growth screens do better in a bull market (Up and Peak phases defined by me).

As a regular subscriber, the screen stock recommendations are about 15 days old (check the current policy) and the most updated screens require extra cost. Their strategy for most screens is: Sell all stocks that do not meet the criteria of the screen and buy new stocks that meet the criteria every month. This trading strategy would require a lot of trades and you need to consider their tax consequences (none for non-taxable accounts) and commissions. Trade on paper before you commit to their recommendations with real money similar to many strategies described in this book.

The basic membership with a decent magazine-publication is a good deal. If you are new to investing, there are many basic books provided on their website.

Update 2/2016

AAII publishes its screen performance every year. Here are some pointers.

- Do not follow last year's winners. I predicted 2015 was a sideways market and 2016 is a risky market that has a good chance to turn into a bear market.
- During bear markets, the screens had lost from 10% to 83% without a single winner here. When the technical indicator SMA-350 or Death Cross tells you to exit, exit as there is no screen that would find winners.
- Every year from 2011 to 2015, the return of the market is positive after adding dividends. When the technical indicator SMA-350 or Death Cross tells you to invest, invest if you trust the charts.
- Some screens work great in one year and become big losers in another year. To conclude, there is no evergreen screen.
- It does not go earlier than 2009 in the summaries, the last Early Recovery that has the best profit potential. I recommend value stocks for this stage of the market cycle.
- For the same reason above, it does not show performances in the bear market of 2007-2008.
- I would select the screens that have a good five-year average. However, the last five years is a typical bull market. Most screens do not beat the S&P 500's 12% average for the last five years. You're better off buying SPY, an ETF simulating the S&P 500 index.
- AAII screens have high turnovers as they replace the stocks when they do not meet the screen criteria.

8   Profit from a proven strategy

This chapter illustrates how to use a subscription and even makes it work better for you. We use AAII's shadow screen as an example but it will apply to most other subscription services.

Does it perform?
From AAII's website, the shadow strategy performs quite well as of this writing. However, it has not performed well recently (as of 1/2016). It uses

cash, so there can be no cheating. However, you have to concern yourself with the following.

- Check out the performance of the last 10 years only, not the system's entire long history. The market has changed a lot in the last 10 years. Hence any performance data from 10 years ago would not predict any better than the more recent data.

- Can you simulate the same performance? You cannot if the selection of stocks is distributed to others before you. I have treated it as a general alarm and not specific to AAII.

  First, ensure that the insiders from the subscription service do not have this selection and are able to act on them first; some subscription services enforce it. Second, check whether you have to pay extra to be the first group to receive the selection list before other members. Most gurus do not perform. Google on the reviews of their past performance and it could save you a lot of money.

- In general, I prefer they give me the tool to select stocks myself as there are too many pitfalls especially on low-volume stocks. However, this requires less effort.

- Actually, they provide the database and the screens at an extra cost. It may be worth it as you will be ahead of the general subscribers. The large number of subscribers could drive up the prices of the recommended stocks initially.

  There is a better way is to modify the screens so that they do not produce the identical lists of screened stocks.

Once you get the selection list, analyze the stocks and perform paper trading. If the performances during the up market and the down market both beat the general market, then the service performs well.

Improve the performance

We would improve the performance from what we have learned in this book:

- Market timing by cycle.

Close all stock positions before and during the market plunge. Hopefully the market plunge can be detected correctly and we can act accordingly.
- Market by calendar.
  For example, select the favorable (by statistics) holding period of a stock from Nov. 1 to May 1 of next year for non-taxable accounts.
- Diversification- In general, do not have more than 25% of your portfolio in the same sector.
- Skip the sectors that require an expertise unless you have the expertise such as in banking, insurance, miners and drugs.
- Common criteria that may not be included in this strategy such as large stocks only.
- Modify the strategy. The purpose is not to trade the same stocks as everyone else is doing. When you do, the herd theory would apply – the leaders of the investors on the same stock would profit more than the rest.

This strategy suggests that you sell all the stocks that do not meet the filter criteria. The following may not apply to this strategy. However, you may want to be ahead of the herd by selling most of them earlier than most others by setting more criteria for selling such as reaching a price objective and close to a fixed holding period.

1. Try to sell before the herd. If the strategy asks you to review the stock positions in 6 months, do it in 5 months.
2. Modify the selection criteria. If it asks you to have a market cap less than 150, try the market cap between 100 and 300 – just for illustration purposes.

- Analyze the stock.

- Second opinions:

  1. Use Fidelity. Only select stocks with the Equity Summary Score 8 or higher.

  2. If the screen is for value stocks, buy the stocks and hold them for at least 6 months. Usually, they have fundamental metrics such as P/E. If the screen is for momentum stocks, do not hold them more than a month. The momentum metrics includes SMA (Single Moving Average) and other technical metrics.

- Buy the stock.
- Sell the stock. Analyze the stock. If it has met your objectives or the fundamentals are deteriorating, sell it.

Links
Gurus are not gurus: https://www.cbsnews.com/news/who-are-the-most-least-accurate-stock-gurus/

#Filler: The other side of a story
The security guard slams the child in a mall or in a school all the time. The other side of the story is the bad behavior of today's children. The retail stores have to protect themselves as shoplifting by teenagers is quite common. Where were the parents? Education starts at home.

9   An illustration of testing strategies

The following is an illustration in testing three related strategies: Growth, Russell and Russell without S&P 500 stocks. A strategy usually includes a screen (finding stocks) the holding period (a year in this illustration for a long-term hold for value stocks) and an exit strategy (that is not described here). They both share a few common parameters such as EY (Earnings Yield). "Russell" only includes Russell 1000 stocks (the largest 1,000 stocks) and the other "Russell" excludes S&P 500 stocks (for potential candidates to be included in S&P 500).

For this testing I used a system that has historical data. The test starts on 1/1/2021 and ends on 6/1/2023 (today is 9/7/2023) with a new test every month. Each test starts on the first day of the month (or next trade day) and ends about a year away. The following table includes only 2 out of 29 tests and the summary results.

Start Date	RSP[1]	Growth	Russell	Russell wo S&P500
...				
09/1/21	-16%	-36%	No data	No Data
10/1/21	-14%	-18%	-10%	-19%
...				
Summary				
Average	-2%	16%	10%	7%
Beat RSP		807%	523%	404%
2021	-8%	2%	-11%	-17%
Beat RSP		122%	-40%	-122%
2022	-1%	19%	9%	6%
Beat RSP		3850%	1800%	1383%

2023	2%	28%	29%	37%
Beat RSP		1675%	1725%	2213%
Bear[2]	-11%	-8%	-1%	-9%
Beat RSP		24%	93%	12%
Bull[2]	3%	28%	20%	23%
Beat RSP		724%	471%	571%

[1] RSP represents the S&P 500 (the market for most) better than the weighted SPY.

[2] RSP have negative returns in most of these months from 7/1/21 to 4/1/22(as opposed to the Bull market from 7/1/22 to today).

Explanation
- These three strategies all beat the market (-2% in my tests): 16%, 10% and 7% in my tests.
- In the bear market (market timing could give some hints too) should give better results as most of the strategies selected few or even no stocks during these periods.
- I skipped tests when there is screened stock for all three strategies.
- The strategy without screened stocks I enter "null", which will not be included in averages.
- I screened producing a maximum of 20 stocks, then sorted them by a metric, and use the top five for tests. In actual trading, I further evaluate each screened stock as potential lawsuits, sector direction, politics... are not included in strategies.
- Sometimes you may want to exclude stocks that appear from several consecutive months as they would distort the performance results. For diversification, I do not buy stocks I already owned, but there are exceptions.
- 2021 is not a good year for Russell strategies and they both do not beat the market in this year.
- The strategies are long term. For short term such as strategies based on momentum, use 1, 2, or 3 months for durations.
- Your tests should reflect as closely on what you do in actual trading.
- The calculations can be easily done using a spreadsheet.
- I should also include the most favorable sectors for the periods.
- As in my convention in this book, all the returns do not include dividends, fees and commissions. Making the tests perfect could be too time consuming.
- This is a suggestion of what I test strategies. Personalize your own testing. Few successful investors would show you their secrets similar to here. To speed up testing, I used annualized returns and some end dates were within 6 months (not recommended if you have time for testing).

Section II: Safer strategies

Super safe strategies

These strategies are for orphans and widows. The common theme is that you want to spend very little time investing. There are better things to do than investing. You may not have the knowledge in investing or the desire to learn about investing. However, most likely the safe strategies do not beat inflation except the last strategy described in this article.

Strategy #1: CD and long-term treasury bills

They are virtually risk-free. Even if it takes almost no-effort for the strategy except in renewing the expired CDs, I still recommend some actions:

- Do not invest in a CD with a bank that you have already exceeded the government's limit on insurance. As of 2019, the standard deposit insurance coverage limit is **$250,000** per depositor, per FDIC-insured bank and per ownership category.
- Today's CDs do not beat inflation. It is our capitalist system that punishes us for not taking any risk and effort in investing.
- Some mortgage-backed bonds or similar offerings could lose all their potential value as many found out the hard way from Lehman Brothers bonds disguised as safe CDs.
- Do not buy callable CDs. They will be called to the bank's advantage.
- Buy long-term treasury bills when the interest rates are high (say 5% or higher). Buy short-term treasury bills when the interest rates are low (say less than 2%). Although you can receive your entire principal plus interest when they mature, the value of the bond fluctuates in opposite directions to the current rate. When the current interest rates are better than the one in your treasury bill, your bill will depreciate.
- Most folks buy the treasury bills via mutual funds and/or ETFs.

Strategy #2: Annuity

When you retire, it seems to be a good vehicle to buy an annuity to provide income for life. However, you have to understand the annuities' terms are defined by the sellers with their own agenda. If you believe they're in business to make you a comfortable retirement at their own expense, think again. Very few if any are low-expense operations. Ask how much the salesman would make to sell you the annuity, and most likely you would run to the door for a quick exit.

I invested in an annuity when I was working to postpone my taxes for the gains. It could be a mistake for me even though it was made over 4 times during several decades. My taxes after 70 ½ (the age for mandatory withdrawal of retirement accounts) will be higher than my working years. I did well in rotating sectors (offered in my annuity) partly due to luck. The total expenses (the trading fees and the management fees) are not cheap compared to most ETFs.

It is good when you have better things to do in your life than worrying about the market. It would save some taxes if your tax bracket is lowered after retirement (as most folks do). If we have a market plunge, then these two strategies would be a winner. As of 4/2024, my Fidelity's annuities for these volatile markets are in Consumer Staples, Energy, Value Strategies and Materials,

Strategy #3: Rotation of an ETF and cash

Rotate between SPY (or any ETF that simulates the market) and cash (or a short-term treasury bond ETF). When the market is risky, rotate your investment into cash and vice versa for SPY. This book describes market timing; it is quite simple.

For beginners, it appears more complicated than it is. You only spend several minutes every month. You will beat most mutual fund managers as most of them are not allowed to play market timing. To start, allocate a small percentage of your investing to this strategy or test the strategy on paper. There is some risk due to false signals. However, "nothing risked, nothing gained" is quite true, especially for the long term.

Filler: Black swan
No EU countries want the war in Ukraine for their own benefits. No politicians, even comedians, want to confront an enemy with tanks at the gate. It turns a rich country into the poorest country in the region.

10   Tom's conservative strategy

The following is a summary of Tom's conservative strategy as described in his profile on Seeking Alpha website. Use it as an example and modify it to fit your investing philosophy. You need to ignore your friends telling you how much money he is making when the market is up. You also need not tell them how much money you're not losing, otherwise you will not have any friends.

Click here (for Kindle readers) for Tom's strategy.
(http://tonyp4idea.blogspot.com/2012/05/tom-armisteads-investment-strategy.html)

Ignore the date posted as this is one of the very few strategies that are evergreen. As of 12/2015, it did not perform well during 2009 (or 2010) to 2015 due to the long, unexpected rising market. However, it should beat the above two strategies by good margins in the long run.

A winning strategy for couch potatoes

My friend John has a very similar strategy to Tom's. My friend is making money with the least risk. He only buys stocks after the market crashes and sells stocks when the market rises. Ignore all market pundits. This is recommended to anyone who does not have time to monitor his/her investment.

He bought stocks in 2008-2010 and sold them after 2010. It was very profitable for him in 2000-2008 using this simple strategy. However, he missed the gains from 2010 to 2018. It is unusual that we have such a long bull market. I bet he is still beating most mutual fund managers with this simple strategy that does not require much work.

Enhance a good strategy

Following the favorable stages to trade in the market cycle described in this book:
- Buy SPY in the Early Recovery phase (about 1 ½ year after the crash or use the entry point described in Market Timing in this book.
- Sell SPY in one or two years after the buy.

Here are some options if you have time to watch the market.

- Buy stocks (or an ETF that simulates the market) on Nov. 1 and sell them on May 1. I prefer to buy stocks on Oct. 15 and sell them on April 15 to avoid the herd.
- Buy stocks on Dec. 1 and sell them on Feb. 1 to take advantage of the best (statistically) period of the year.
- Buy stocks in the year before the election and sell them after a year.
- Add long-term bonds when the interest rates are high (say more than 5%). Switch to short-term bonds or cash when the interest rate is low (say less than 2%).
- If you have time, time the market by following my simple technique to exit and reenter the market.

Spend the rest of the time on your comfortable couch (i.e., enjoying life) or sip some fancy tropical drink served by some beautiful tropical lady on some nice tropical island. Not a bad strategy! Of course, the market is not always rational and there is always risk involved.

An alternative to Tom's strategy

Have a list of value stocks to buy and update the list periodically (say every 3 months).

When the market loses 5%, buy them at 2% less than the market prices or alternatively 5% less than the prices on your list.

Decide when to sell such as making 12% profit or losing 12%. If the market is not risky, you may want to keep them longer. It should work in a sideways market but not during market plunges.

John's Strategy

John maintains about 75% cash and only buys blue chip stocks at 52-week low. He ignores friends telling him about making good money when the market is up.

Here are my changes for better returns at the expense of taking more risk. I would maintain 50% cash and 0% in Early Recovery, a phase in the market cycle defined by me. I would also include all stocks with market cap over 1 billion and stocks close to 5% of their bottoms. In addition, I would evaluate the stocks before I buy as some stocks may go to zero.

Jill's Strategy

Jill does not have time for investing. She subscribes to an investing service. She prepares a list of stocks to buy. For illustration purposes only, the stocks should have Safety of 1 or 2 in Value Line or VST grade higher than 1.25 in VectorVest. When the price reaches the price she is willing to pay, she does second research with her subscription service and checks the fundamental rating at Fidelity.com. If they are good, she buys it and usually keeps it until the market is risky.

#Filler: Miss Mia

In my first job and just after the Vietnam War, everyone (yes, guys and ladies) tried to date my beautiful officemate Mia except me. If we married, then her name would be Mia Pow ('missing-in-action' and 'prisoner-of-war'). She would be very popular or very unpopular without showing her beautiful face. In any case, when she becomes a mother, she will be Mamma Mia.

11   Define Swing trading

The definition varies from different folks. Basically, it is not "Buy and Hold". Most well-known companies have great returns in the first ten years, but not the second ten years. If you follow this strategy, use "Buy but Not Forget". Holding index ETFs is better than "Buy and Hold" as they replace better stocks once or so a year. However, an index ETF may hold too many bubble stocks.

We exit the market when the market is plunging and reenter afterwards as indicated by my simple technique. To me, "Buy and Hold" has been dead since 2000 as illustrated by the fewer articles praising it after 2000. The average loss of the last two major market crashes is 45%.

Evaluate your requirements, your time available for investing and the size of your portfolio, and then decide which style would fit your requirements.

I further subdivide swing trading into long-term (6-12 months), short-term (1-6 months) according to your average holding period. This book describes both strategies. Many tools are common to all the strategies. However, long-term swing stresses more on fundamental metrics than momentum metrics. P/E (Price / Earnings) is a fundamental metric and SMA-20 (Simple Moving Average for the last 20 sessions) is a momentum metric.

The following belongs to even shorter terms: Momentum (less than 1 month), Rotation (1 – 2 month), Insider (3 months), Headlines (1 – 3 months), and Day trading (1 day, not discussed in this book). The holding periods are for guidelines only.

First do not buy any stocks if the market is risky. Value stocks are important for long-term swing trading.

1. **Long-term swing (trading about 6 to 12 months)**

Most of my profits are made using this strategy. It is simple and effective.

Buy a stock with favorable fundamental metrics. When you buy value stocks, you're swimming against the tide. Hence, it will take at least 6 months for the market to realize its value.

After 6 months or sometimes less from the initial purchase, evaluate the stocks that you bought again based on the same fundamental metrics used. If the company's outlook and/or the fundamentals changes for the worse, sell it. If not, keep on holding the stock for another 6 months and repeat the same evaluation. We would like to keep the stocks longer than a year for better tax treatment on long-term capital gains; check the current tax laws.

We have to be flexible in the holding period. If there is any major event such as a major lawsuit or a new fierce competitor or a new competing product, evaluate the situation and decide whether you should sell the stock. To keep you informed, enter the bought stocks into the portfolio in Seeking Alpha and check the articles under the Portfolio tab. In addition, use Finviz.com to check articles on the stocks you own.

Most of the wealthiest investors use this or a similar method. Buffett holds his stocks far longer. Soros and Jim Rogers bet on a longer-term development of the economy.

2. Short-Term (3 months) Swing.

Most associate it with swing trading. Contrary to popular belief, it is the hardest way to make money while #1 is the easiest and requires less work. If you believe you can learn it by studying several books, most likely you will lose your shirt. Most beginners cannot compete with the experienced, disciplined professional traders.

This book includes many chapters on technical analysis (a.k.a. charting) to get you started.

Books are no substitute for the experience in actual trading with real money. The following is my recommendation to pursue using technical analysis for swing investing:

Study one or two indicators (SMA is a good one) thoroughly. The most common mistake for beginners is using several technical indicators that they do not understand completely. Try out Finviz.com to screen stocks based on technical parameters.

Read books or take classes from experienced traders. One class charges several thousands of dollars but it lets you trade with real money provided by the company.

Using SMA (Simple Moving Average) as an example, the experienced can find a buy signal when the stock price, or a sector ETF moves above its moving average and then sell it when it moves below the moving average.

It is quite simple, but it works for most stocks and probably it is better than most other technical indicators.

The common number of days (actually sessions) affects how you want to keep the stock. For example, use SMA-20 (20 sessions) if you keep stocks for an average of 20 sessions. SMA-50 and SMA-200 are common parameters. For starters, you do not need to learn charting by entering the stock symbol in Finviz.com and it will display the three common parameters. To illustrate, if SMA-50% is positive, it is normally a buy signal for a positive short-term trend.

The stocks that are usually better fitted for technical analysis are large cap stocks with high volume. I prefer stocks that are fundamentally sound and do not short them at least initially. For volatile stocks, I prefer higher percent such as SMA-50% > 10% instead of > 0%.

Try the stock in its historical chart and decide the best parameters for charting this stock. Past behavior does not guarantee future behavior, but it is better to have a guideline than do without.

Be aware that this discipline requires that you spend a lot of time on the screen. The shorter the duration (hence the faster the parameter such as 20 instead of 50 in SMA), the more time you need to check your stocks. That's the reason you do not want to keep more than 15 stocks for this style of investing at a time.

I use technical analysis more frequently to detect market crashes and sectors as it proves to be a better indicator than on stocks. Technical indicators usually work better in shorter durations than fundamental metrics.

When the market is safe, the sector the stock belongs to is favorable and the stock is favorable as measured by SMA, then the chance of its appreciation is high.

Besides charting and many sites providing technical indicators and patterns, use Finviz.com to specify them in the screener. Besides SMA, the following are quite useful: Bollinger Bands, MACD and SMA: RSI(14), Double Bottom, Golden Cross and Inverted Head & Shoulder. Use Wikipedia, Investopedia, StockCharts, Stockpedia or Google to find out about their descriptions and examples on how to use them.

Again, it is better to start with one or two indicators/patterns and thoroughly test out their performances before committing real money. Day trading is not covered in this book as it is too risky and my knowledge on this topic is minimal. Basically, it is riding on the wagon of the institutional investors as detected by the huge volume.

Day trading: https://www.youtube.com/watch?v=wruCNVSq608

This book serves to be a strong introduction to swing trading using technical analysis. More hints are:

- Buy at the support line and sell at the resistance line. It is important to have stops reducing short-term losses and let the winners run higher. Even with a 40%-win percent, you could make huge profits with the above strategy.

- There are many strategies for short-term swings. This book describes Simple Moving Average (SMA-50), Bollinger Bands, RSI(14) for over/under bought... Stick with one instead of jumping from one strategy to another.

- The size of the trade is important. I recommend to reduce the size of the trade when it is risky and/or the potential appreciation is low.

3. Momentum

I also call it short-term swing (1 month for me).

Buy the momentum stocks and sell them within a month.

I use subscription services and select the momentum stocks before my own evaluation. Most of my subscription services assign a timely score. It only takes less than an hour a week.

Alternatively, and for those who do not subscribe to investment services, use momentum metrics and technical indicators to spot the trend. Use the technical screen of the free Finviz.com to screen stocks.

I have pretty good luck so far in using this strategy. I abandoned it later when I felt the market was risky. The annualized return is about 100% from Dec. 2012 and the annualized return this year (as of 3/2014) is about 50%. They are inflated due to not considering the idle cash.

4. Trading by headlines

Headlines usually drive the market briefly. Need to evaluate the headline news and trade fast. Depending on the news, I trade sector ETFs, market ETFs and sometimes stocks. Personally, I have not practiced enough to draw a conclusion due to my limited time, but I have had pretty good returns so far.

5. Sector momentum / bottom / rotation

It is hard to detect the bottom of a sector, but it is easy to track the trend. I rotate ETFs and my annuity funds monthly based on momentum when the market is safe. In a nutshell, I buy the winner from last month.

6. Following insiders

Purchases by CEO and CFO at the market prices in substantial quantities is a good sign. Do not forget to evaluate the fundamentals and avoid many traps. Charts usually can identify the trend after these purchases especially on the rising volumes. Check out the website Open Insider. I check out insider purchases once a month.

Summary table for Swing strategies

	Long Term	Short Term	Moment.	Headline	Sector Rotation	Insider
Avg. Duration	6 - 12	3	1	Vary	1 - 2	1 – 3
Fundamental	100%	50%	20%	10%	10%	50%
Technical	0%	50%	80%	90%	90%	50%

Explanation

The above are guidelines only.

- For Long Term Swing Trading. Evaluate the stock every 6 months and decide the hold and sell action.
- The average hold time for headlines depends on the news. You have to react to it fast. It is similar to the insider strategy.

- In general fundamentals are important for stocks you intend to hold for a long term. For other strategies I still prefer value stocks. However, when you only keep the stock for a month or so, I prefer momentum metrics such as SMA-20. The percentages indicate the balance between the two categories of the metrics.

My additions

Hopefully my additions improve the performance of a strategy that already works.

- I add market timing to Swing Trading. You need to sell most stocks during a market plunge. Of course, it is better to sell them at the peak but that is hard or even impossible to detect. Buy the stocks back when the chart indicates so. It worked during the market plunge of 2000 and 2008. However, no markets are identical. From time to time, we do have false signals.

- Diversify your portfolio. Keep less than 15 stocks for a portfolio less than a million. Ensure that no more than 3 stocks are in the same sector. Keep 20 stocks for a portfolio over a million. Too many stocks would require more of your time that would be better spent in evaluating stocks. Too few stocks would impact your portfolio when one stock has a big loss.
- Stick with stocks with a stock price over $2, average daily volume over 10,000 shares (or 8,000 shares for price over $20), market cap over 200 million, and listed in one of the three major exchanges.

  Most big winners usually are in the price range between $2 and $12 price, and market cap between 200 million to 800 million. These stocks are usually ignored by the institutional investors due to their restrictions. There are exceptions. Adjust the criteria according to your requirements.
- Ignore the subscription services that claim making more than 30% profit consistently. Some even have examples of making 5,000%. Most likely they tell you the winners but not their losers. When they back test their strategies, they cheat on their performances with survivorship bias (i.e., those bankrupt stocks are not included in the historical database). If their returns are that great, do you think they will share their secrets with you? Some made a big fortune and lost it all. So, the turtles that make small profits consistently and keep all the wins fare far better.

12   Top-down investing

The nutshell is described here. Only buy stocks when the market is favorable. Find the best industry (a subsector) and then find the best stock(s) within the selected industry. In doing so, our chances of successful investing are substantially increased.

It is so simple and it has been proven by many including myself. I just wonder why it has not been extensively practiced. I offer a simple trade plan as follows:

1. Do not invest when the market is plunging. I have a simple way to detect market plunges without any expensive subscriptions or tools.

2. Select the best industry (most are represented by an ETF or ETFs specific for the industry or sector). For example, Technology is a sector. Computer and Software are industries (subsector under Technology). From time to time, I use sectors for simplicity and most free sites do not subdivide the sectors into industries. Check out the best-performing industry or sector from last month in many sites including SeekingAlpha and CNNfn.

   If you're a value investor, you may not want to choose the timeliest sector but the most under-valued sector. Value investors should hold the sectors/stocks longer (such as 6 months or even longer) for the market to recognize their values.

   In addition, you need to detect the sector/stock rotation by the institutional investors who control over 75% of all trades (i.e., smart money). They will rotate sector/stock when they find better profit potential in another sector/stock. Use stops to prevent further losses.

   If you do not have time to research stocks, trade ETFs for sectors and skip the next step.

3. The final step is to select the best stock(s) within the sector via fundamental analysis (including intangible analysis), insider trading analysis, institution trading analysis and technical analysis.

Do not let these terms scare you. We will start with the simplest approach without any subscription and a lot of effort.

4. The next step is when to reevaluate and sell the stocks when conditions change or they meet your objectives. If the market is plunging, sell all stocks.

Stick with and repeat the entire process.

The easiest retirement planning system
Have a budget and live within your means. Buy good stuff that lasts for a long time. After saving enough cash for emergency and planned expenses such as vacation, new car, college, etc., invest your extra money in a retirement account (Roth IRA if allowable) with 80% in a market ETF and 20% in a short-term bond ETF.

Run the chart described in the market cycle chapters once a month. If the chart tells you to exit the market, move all to cash. Reenter the market when the chart tells you to do so. It beats most if not all of your financial plans from the best experts money can buy.

From my book "Best stocks for 2022"
They are actual, verifiable recommendations from a published book.

Symbol (11)	Return	Annualized
ADES	-54%	-56%
AOSL	-34%	-35%
BLDR	-18%	-19%
BZH	-37%	-39%
DVN	73%	76%
MLI	19%	20%
MTDR	81%	84%
NUE	40%	41%
SCHN	-30%	-31%
UFPI	-5%	-5%
USAK	See below	
Average	4%	4%
RSP	-6%	-7%
Beat RSP by	153%	

USAK has not been shown in my historical database that has a survival bias. The recommended price as of 12/15/21 was $17.74 and the last price (09/14/2022) was $31.71 gaining 79% and annualized to 105%.

The performance could be boosted if we selected only the rising sectors: energy (DVN 76%, MTDR 84%) and trucking (USAK 79%).

Click the following link for more detail.
http://tonyp4idea.blogspot.com/2022/12/best-stocks-series.html

Afterthoughts

My late friend had a 'buy and hold strategy' that worked pretty well. Most of his stocks were big companies. He died with a house worth more than a million and many millions in stocks. His only mistake was not to transfer more of his stocks to his heirs before his death. He died in the year when the estate exemption returned back to a million. Uncle Sam was the biggest winner and won big without any effort.

Link: Finviz: https://www.youtube.com/watch?v=M8sNMhPJINU

Section III: Riskier strategies

"Nothing risked, nothing gained."

From my book "Best Stocks to Buy for July, 2021", Sub List of risky stocks:

Commodity (3)	Return	Ann.
EVC	16%	43%
NUE	10%	26%
YELL	108%	283%
Average	45%	117%
RSP	1%	2%
Beat RSP by	5,275%	

The details can be found in the following link.
http://tonyp4idea.blogspot.com/2022/12/best-stocks-series.html

---

13 The contrarian

Contrarians invest in the manner opposite of the crowd. Look for extremes in the market sentiment and investing activities and do the opposite.

However, timing is everything. You want to follow the herd and switch gears when the market or the asset is overpriced.

When an asset or a strategy is overbought, it will return to the normal price. There are one or two exceptions. Gold is one but it is not due to gold alone, but the depreciating USD and the long-term depreciating of gold after inflation.

Blindly taking contrarian actions could cost you. You need to analyze and determine whether the herd is wrong.

To illustrate, do you want to move to equities when their prices have been down as of 7/2012? It really depends on the following factors.

- If the long-term trend is down (i.e., moving to a W-shaped recession), we want to wait longer before we move back in.
- If we're heading to the same path as Japan's lost decades, we may want to wait even longer.

- If we're heading to a secular bull market (not today), then waiting too long will be bad.
- The counter argument is the excessive printing of money that could lead to a rising market.

Do we want to buy bank stocks after 2008 or tech stocks after 2001?
- With the rear mirror now, the answer is 'No' even if some of these stocks had lost half of their value. As long as the root problems have not been fixed, they might fall further and some companies may even go bankrupt. Do not invest in equities one year after a market plunge and two years in the sector that caused the bubble in general. They are quite correct in the last two bottoms (2000 and 2007). It has more chances to be right than wrong in the future, but as in life nothing is 100% sure.

Individual analysis

Ignore what the media says. A lot of time the 'news' is obsolete by the time it reaches us. It is the group thinking. Sometimes they magnify the news in order to sell their ads. The worst is that the smart money manipulates the news which tells us to trade while they're doing the exact opposite.

Buffett told us to ignore airline stocks. However, many airline stocks made over 4 times their stock prices in the last few years. Popular books are no different. One predicts the Dow at 40,000 and one predicts a market plunge in 2009. As of 2016, they're all wrong. When they are right, they will tell the world.

Links

Contrarian
(http://en.wikipedia.org/wiki/Contrarian_investing)

#Filler: Tips
- When you have a lot of money to invest and you're not using a financial adviser and/or not subscribing to any investment service, it could be a big financial mistake.
- LTCM, with two Nobel-prize winners, best supporting team and best technologies then, ran their hedge funds into the ground.
- The so-called modern portfolio theory is most likely based on the wrong and/or insufficient testing parameters / assumptions.

14 Refined "Dogs of the Dow"

The Dogs of Dow is quite popular and even some mutual fund managers are using it exclusively. In a nutshell, you buy the ten Dow stocks that pay the highest dividend rates at year end and repeat the process every year. Ignore the stocks whose dividends are returns of capital. Click the above hyperlink or enter the following link into your browser for more info on this strategy.

(http://en.wikipedia.org/wiki/The_Dogs_of_the_Dow)

Past Performance

As of 2014, it just beat the Dow and the S&P 500 by a small margin in the last decade. It worked quite well in the last four years. It could be due to the recent mild bubble on dividend growth stocks. Hence, be alert to when the dividend bubble bursts.

From Wikipedia,

"In fact, the Dogs of the Dow and Small Dogs of the Dow struggled to keep up with the Dow during latter stages of the dot-com boom (1998 and 1999) as well as during the financial crisis (2007-2009)."

My suggestion to improve the performance

1. Avoid stocks with high expected P/Es (i.e., > 35) or P <= 0 such as most dot-com stocks in 2000.

2. Avoid specific sectors such as banks in 2007 and any sectors on travelling during the pandemic of 2020.

3. Practice market timing. Do not buy most stocks during market plunges and move back to equities in Early Recovery, a phase of the market cycle defined by me.

Improve the performance by customizing

When a strategy becomes popular, it will not perform.

Customize the strategy so we do not pick up the same stocks as everyone else does. Instead of buying the ten dogs, buy the first five dogs sorted by the forward (same as expected) P/E in ascending order ignoring stocks with zero or negative earnings.

This variation has an average annualized return of 15% (= 12% appreciation + estimated 3% dividend) from Nov. 1, 2000 to Nov. 1, 2010 from my testing. It is better than the original strategy already. The testing is for educational purposes only.

Another variation is: Buy the top five candidates on Nov. 1 and sell them on May 1 next year to take advantage of the statistically favorable period.

Further Refining Dogs of Dow

The following are more variations to the original Dogs of Dow. Try them out with different combinations.

1. Include the stocks in the S&P 500 and NASDAQ, so there are more stocks to choose from than just from the DOW.

2. Adjust the time between Dec. 1 and Dec. 15 (a little earlier is fine) instead of the start of the year to avoid the herd who follows the same strategy and performs the same task at the beginning of the year.

3. For retirement accounts or offsetting the short-term losers, buy on Nov.1 and sell on May 1 to take advantage of this statistically favorable period.

4. Sort the selected top 10 with positive earnings by P/E in ascending order and buy the top 5. A value play. I prefer to skip P/E less than 4 as there could be something really wrong with too low of a P/E. Skip stocks with high Debt/Equity ratio unless the sector requires high debts.

5. Avoid stocks in the following sectors: lenders, drug companies, miners and insurers. Avoid emerging countries.

6. Skip the companies that have serious lawsuits against them. Minor lawsuits are fine.

7. Avoid stocks that are being shorted in the range of 10% to 20%. The short % is defined by: No. of shares being shorted/Total floating shares. Stocks with short percent over 30% could trigger a short squeeze that could have good appreciation potential.

8. Do not buy in the first year after the market plunge.

It is a lazy man's stock picking and market timing. I bet it performs better than the original strategy.

Link: https://www.youtube.com/watch?v=Jwf8wrtDKGo

Afterthoughts
*

When you test out the above strategy, try different parameters. If possible, use the most recent data (such as the last ten years) to check out whether your strategy still works. If you are less risk tolerant, select the screened stocks with P/E between 4 and 12 only.

The following are some of the variances and can be combined into this strategy for testing out the performances.

- Holding periods. Try 6 months, 11 months and 12 months.
- Buy contra ETFs during the unfavorable stock period such as May 1 to Nov. 1. It is not recommended in a secular bull market.
- Automate your test as much as possible, so you can add other parameters such as different holding periods.
- Avoid data fitting to obtain better results.
- Test for each stage of the market cycle.
- Annualize the return if it is not 12 months to make it easier to compare. Do not get too excited on great returns. When you implement your strategy with real money, expect less performance than the performance from your test.

Review your test procedures when the return is excessive such as 60%. However, when you find one strategy yielding 60% and another one yielding 20% with the same testing conditions, stick with the winner for real money.

Start with paper trading and then commit cash slowly. There is no Holy Grail in investing. The market changes and it is not rational all the time. Investing with a good and proven strategy is better than investing without one.

Link: 1 https://www.youtube.com/watch?v=9icBf8iZXbc

15 Multi baggers

It is very rewarding to find the next Apple making many times profits over the original investment. It is possible, but it is not everyone's cup of tea. For every winner found, there would be ten losers.

How to find them

I developed a screen to find potential multi baggers. Basically, these stocks double in sales and profits (prefer to compare the quarter of prior year to avoid seasonal fluctuations). Initially most are penny stocks with small market caps and are not listed in the three major exchanges. When they move up to a major exchange, it is a good sign. Usually, they do not pay dividends as most of the profits have to be plowed back to research and development in the initial years.

Most likely, the screen would find them at least one year after their IPOs as we need the financial data. It is a good starting point to take out the companies that do not survive in the first year, and there are many.

Many of these stocks are traded in the $2 to $10 range. Most stocks below $5 are not 'marginable', which is important to boost its rising. These stocks usually trade within a low-price range for a while before they breakout (i.e., surge in price).

When the breakout is supported with high volume, the price will tend to rocket even higher. I do not want to hold a triple bagger unless there is a good reason to do so. Need to calculate the reward / risk ratio. If it is the same chance to double as losing half of the value, I would hold or sell half of it. No one goes broke for taking profit.

When these stocks take off, most are overbought with RSI(14) above 65 for a few years to come.

IPO

There are two kinds of IPOs: from established products such as Facebook and from companies without established products. The former is less risky. Roughly, about 60% lose money in the first year while 40% make up the loss. IPOs are the best way to fund research and/or marketing of new products/services. Investors have to analyze whether the new product(s) is/are innovative enough and profitable to pay back their investments.

There are many investors specialized in new companies. Most IPOs make money on the first day with the recent exception of Facebook. Buy in the morning and sell at the end of the day. Most retail investors cannot participate in IPOs without connection with some brokers. However, there are successful investors spotting Microsoft, Wal-Mart, Tesla and companies involved in 3D printing in its early stage after IPO.

As of this writing, I do not find too many potential profitable companies with the exception of 3D printers. Zynga is a typical example. It seems it is repeating the usual sad chronology of a hot IPO:

1. Founders and the initial investors make a fortune on a good idea or a product.
2. Most initial investors make money.
3. The stock skyrockets. The insiders cash in after the restricted period that they cannot sell after the IPO. Usually, most retail investors do not sell.
4. The stock purges. Most losers are retail investors.

You're buying for the company's new vision and/or the innovative products. However, many of these new companies do not make it as expected. You have to evaluate their product potential and review the progress of the company periodically. Innovative products that everyone wants may not be able to bring to the market due to regulations and the opposition from its potential competitors.

The first year will be a honeymoon period when most investors ignore the fundamental metrics. The second year on, evaluate the company again with fundamental metrics. For example, if the P/E is over 50, most likely the company's stock will be in danger or the investors have been moving the price too fast and too high. Check out Debt/Equity. If the company cannot pay back the loan, it may go bankrupt.

Cisco was one of top-valued companies. It went down and then in the first half of 2013 it recovered. Again, fundamental metrics (such as P/E) and technical analysis guide us better as to when to trade Cisco. The long-term outlook of Cisco is good envisioning more devices connected to the routers. However, we need to examine its future offerings and its competitors.

The second phase
The initial investors before the IPO are not allowed to sell the stock. When it expires, the stock price may fall. When the stock price keeps on climbing,

evaluate the appreciation potential. When they reach the peaks, sell. When the expected P/E is still reasonable (such as less than 35), check the PEG (P/E growth). If they are reasonable, hold on to the stock, but I would use a stop loss to protect profit. From my limited statistics, successful companies are usually less successful in the stock price after the first 10 years. It could be that their peaks may have come.

It is a balancing act: sitting on a winning horse on its way up and selling the winning horse at its peak. No one can find the peak consistently. Use technical analysis's SMA (Simple Moving Average) to determine the enter/exit points. If you're not too sure, sell half of your holding.

Company turnaround

When a stock loses most of its value, it could go to zero or it could turn around. Check the possibilities in both scenarios. Sometimes the chart together with insider purchases could indicate a turnaround.

The staircase pattern described next is a good sign. The stock stays in the current value for a while before it moves up to the next peak. It then stays there for a while and moves up to the next peak again.

More losers than winners

I suspect many small companies fail for each of the multi baggers found. The losers may not show up in the database as they're taken away from the database when the stock price goes to 0 (termed as survival bias) or the stock is delisted from the exchange. If your test database does not take care of survival bias, your test result will appear far better than your strategy really is.

You need to have cash that you do not need for a long while, a lot of patience and the mental power to experience many losses.

Apple, Microsoft and Oracle all have the right products in this generation. Judging from the recent IPOs including Zynga and Groupon, I do not think that we have too many potential multi baggers from the current offerings, but I could be wrong. No stocks can justify a forward P/E over 40 unless they have very high potential like a promising new drug.

Many big winners can shoot up 200% in 6 months. It needs one or more catalysts to boost this kind of performance. It could be a new product that could change the world, a potential acquirer (very seldom the acquirer pays more than 50% of the current price). Fundamental analysis seldom finds these stocks, but technical analysis can.

2015 IPO

2015 is a loser year for IPOs especially compared to the better years in 2013 and 2014. The tiny Hong Kong was number one in IPOs in terms of the total market value for IPOs and most of them are Chinese companies. NYC took a back seat for the first time in what I can remember.

Shenzhen Exchange was even crazier than Hong Kong with its volatility and huge price fluctuations. It supports financially the growing high-tech companies in South China. If you have a new high-tech gadget such as a drone, it is the best place to build it. Most of your component suppliers are close by.

The average NYSE stock price lost about 15% at the close of the first day in 2015. Is it a trend? Only time can tell.

Tax considerations
You may want to sell a loser when it does not show any future promise to offset any gain from other stocks. When you find a big winner and you're not young, you can keep it until you die so the cost basis will be stepped up and your heirs do not pay the tax on the capital gain according to the tax law of 2016. Alternatively, give it to a charity for an extra deduction. Tax law changes and I'm not a tax professional, so ask your lawyer for advice.

My personal experience
I sell most stocks when they double. Very seldom do I keep a stock long enough to be a triple bagger. Most of my double (and once in a blue moon triple) baggers were acquired by larger companies, or I need to hold them longer to be eligible for long-term capital gain. One's opinion. However, I recommend keeping rising stocks and protecting the profits by periodically adjusting stops on the current prices.

Finding the next wave

You can make more than 10 times your investment when you invest early in the companies that can change the world. Some are started via IPOs. Many others are initially invested by venture capitalists, then they are listed in small exchanges and eventually are moved to one of the three major exchanges. By the time these companies are noticed by the market, they usually are already fully valued.

I saw many in the last 30 years, and unfortunately, I did not act on many of them or did not buy them early enough. It is primarily due to my conservative nature. The examples are:

- Apple in its early stage and so are many high-tech companies such as Microsoft, Google and Cisco. When I see my stock prices doubled, I am tempted to sell them and would miss the opportunity of its doubling again.

    Use technical analysis and fundamental analysis to determine the exit and reentry points. To protect the profit, use stop orders and adjust the stop price when the stock appreciates by more than 10% (more frequently if you have time).

- Drug companies discovering new drugs. I had some successes via a subscribed newsletter and followed insider trading from public information.

- Change of the retail business by Wal-Mart via importing products from China especially after Sam Walton who incorrectly estimated the difference between the Chinese and American prices on similar products. It is similar to Amazon creating a new channel for retailing.

- Change of policy such as one allowing GPS for public use or banning importing of Chinese solar panels. GPS devices are eventually obsoleted by smartphones that provide the same function. Solar panels are still not ready economically without cheap Chinese imports. The recent legalizing of a drug is a good example. I knew about it and I did not act on it due to my ethical reasons. Fidelity has a social score.

Currently we have some new drugs, cloud computing (too cloudy for my taste as I cannot figure out how they can make money as of today), 3D printing... Amazon revolutionizes digital publishing and internet retailing. Amazon's stock skyrockets even though the fundamentals look bad. Amazon invests its money for the future.

There are many small companies that would offer products that would change the world. However, most of them will be acquired by larger corporations as it is too expensive to launch these new products / services unless their IPOs provide a lot of cash.

In ten years or so, China would have more of these innovative companies for the following reasons. However, I do not trust the financial data of most developing countries, especially small companies.

1. There are many educated scientists and engineers. Contrary to popular belief, they do have genius schools that will produce more geniuses such as Gates and Jobs.

2. The government encourages science and technology and has long-term objectives. However, they need to set up regulations to protect intelligence properties.

3. Chinese engineers' wages are only a fraction of ours. A typical Chinese engineer works far more hours than our engineers. When a Chinese engineer works 10 hours a day while the US engineer works 8 hours, it is more than the 2-hour difference in productivity.

4. They have a large internal market.

Profit from IPOs

If your broker does not have the connection, most likely you cannot buy them on the first day of the IPOs. Skip trading the stock for the first few days. When it makes a new high, consider buying it. Unless the fundamentals/outlooks are good, sell it before the insiders are allowed to sell (6 to 12 months after the IPO depending on the company).

Filler: I have a dream

Two unrealistic (realistic hopefully in the future) proposals:

1. Change the constitution to require the president to balance the budget as most states do.

2. Allow the voters to assign a % to each category of the budget. Also, the ones who pay no Federal income tax cannot vote on this. Representation without taxation is worse than taxation without representation

IPO Calendar: https://www.nasdaq.com/market-activity/ipos

16   Trading by headlines

On 6/29/2019, Trump and Xi seemed to settle a trade war in the G20. The market would likely rise on the coming Monday. Luckily, I had closed a short position. Many chip stocks would rise as they can sell their products to Huawei. I have several of these stocks expecting the trade war would be settled. The farmers and their supporting industry would breathe easier.

I bet the shipping companies would be more profitable from the news. Without doing further research, I checked out this shipping sector and found the following stocks had been up more than 4%: DHT, NM, SBLK, STNG, TNK and ASC. It was during the weekend, so your trade account should be able to trade after hours and you need to act right after the news.

I exchanged comments with Andrew McElroy, a sector rotation expert. He does not have the rules set up as in this book but he makes great trades by 'seeing' the market and using technical analysis. The following is from his article.

"The idea is fairly simple. There is more potential for profit (and loss) in individual sectors, especially when the index is trading sideways. I try to buy strong sectors which have pulled back onto support and avoid overbought sectors at resistance. I also use Elliott Wave to identify cycles of buying and selling and stages in trends."

I would like to include headlines such as Trump's election, interest rates hikes and new regulations.

When it rains in Brazil, buy coffee futures

Recently it rained too much in SE Asia, so buying rice futures was a good idea. I did not trade futures, so I missed out on the opportunity and unfortunately there is no equivalent ETF for rice. In the beginning of 2012, we should know the farming crops, especially that corn will not be good due to the flooding and drought in different parts of the world. Act accordingly for the profit potentials.

When a war is starting in the Middle East, most likely the oil price will rise. Buy the oil ETF and sell it when the chance of the war is reduced. Many tiny drops of profit could turn into a river of profit.

Trading by headlines is profitable, but it is hard to master and is very time-consuming. Test this strategy on paper for years before you commit real money as in most strategies. Most couch potatoes read the newspaper and watch TV all day long without making a penny. He could be a couch potato millionaire if he read this article, paper traded/refined the strategy and acted on it!

However, the media tend to exaggerate headlines in order to sell their ads. Ignore all the recommendations on stocks. Most likely they are outdated information and some may be used to manipulate others. Do your own research as your mother taught you that there is no free lunch.

Rules of the game

1. Do not be too emotional; ignore your past wins and losses except when using them as lessons if they are valid (i.e., educated guesses).

2. Do not trade the entire farm. Consider options, ETFs and/or small trade on stocks, which have too many other factors to be considered.

3. Trade it fast – today's headlines will not be headlines tomorrow. There are very few exceptions.

4. Where there is a winner, there is always a loser. For example, Apple was a winner with the iPhone and BlackBerry was a loser. Same for Best Buy and Circuit City.

5. Ensure you can trade after hours from your broker.

6. Do not forget when to exit for either a small profit or a small loss.

7. Quick evaluation. The headline will be gone if you do not act fast. Skip companies with poor metrics such as high debt and low earnings yield. Prefer to buy an ETF related to the headline.

8. Most likely someone has used the information before you get it. However, some info can be deducted before it occurs. Insider purchases is a good guide.

9. I recommended crude oil at $30 per barrel on Jan. 15, 2016 as the price was at rock bottom. For value sectors, you may have to wait for a long time for the market to realize its value.

10. Sometimes you ignore stock evaluations as the headline news is more important. Learn my 5-minute evaluation process of a stock (a quick way but not recommended if you have time to do thorough research):
    - From Finviz.com, enter the stock or ETF symbol. Look at how many greens in metrics over reds.
    - Check out Forward P/E (E>0 and P/E < 20), Debut / Equity (< 50%) and P/FCF (not in red color).
    - SMA20 (or SMA50 for longer holding period). If SMA20 is > 10%, it is trending up.
    - Scroll down for Insider Trade. It usually is a good buy if insiders are buying recently and heavily with market prices.
    - Be cautious on foreign and low-volume stocks.
    - If most of the above are positive, it is likely a buy. As in life, nothing is 100% certain.

    If you have a hard time following the above, most likely this strategy is not for you and it is better to return to your couch. No offense.

Volatile market and headlines

As of 7/2012 (2015 too and historically a positive market in a year right before the election), the market went sideways and was influenced by headlines. 2013 had been volatile with dips and surges influenced by daily news. The trend was up though. The Federal debt problem, EU crisis... had not been resolved. Every time we had good news, the market rose, and vice versa. In this market, buy on dips (3% down from last temporary peak) and sell on temporary surges (3% up from last temporary bottom). Some use 5% instead of 3% depending on one's risk tolerance.

Trend and calendar timing

Usually following the trend is better than ignoring it.

- Many retail investors want to get rid of the losers for year-end tax planning. Buy them at year-end and sell them early next year. In the year end of 2012, it acted the opposite as folks were selling their winners expecting a larger tax bite next year but that turned out to be false.

    This could be the reason for a sell-off of Apple in the year-end of 2012 and it gave us a good entry point. To me, Apple's fundamentals were sound though the media said otherwise. In a few months, Apple became a value stock from a growth stock according to the press.

- Investors are not rational and follow the market blindly. The strategy 'Buy low and sell high' works.

- We have so much good news and bad news in the same year. Ensure the bad news will not extend to worse news. Timing is everything. Buy on bad news and sell on good news; it does not work when the market plunges.

- The media influences the market. Analyze their arguments. If they exaggerate them, do the opposite.

- Over-reaction to earnings missed or gained. When the company missed the earnings by 5%, there is a very good chance the stock will be down in a year, and vice versa. However, when it missed by 1% and the stock lost by 10%, it could be a buying opportunity, particularly when it was a temporary condition and the company is fundamentally sound.

- Buy the stock at dip when a solvable problem surfaces. Sell after the problem has been resolved. Ceiling debt is such a solvable problem and it is caused by politics. In the beginning of 2013, I mentioned that the debt problem had not been resolved and we would have this ceiling debt problem periodically until it will be eventually resolved.

Scheduled events

Some events are scheduled such as earnings announcements, unemployment reports, etc. Most likely educated guesses of the outcomes have already been circulated on the web.

The last five events on the Federal debt handling (using fancy names such as sequester and debt ceiling) were scheduled such as the government shutdown. They drove the market down by about an average of 5% each time. Sell before the event and buy back afterward. The Congress has cancelled these debt deadlines as of 1/2014.

Many sectors are impacted by events such as Trump's success in election, hikes of interest rates and trade wars.

Follow the institutional investors

They drive the market. When they see the sector is overvalued or the peak has been reached, they rotate sectors.

Use deduction

In 2014, China had a great harvest on wheat, corn and rice. China's population is #1 in the world and its middle class is growing. The farmers in the US will be hurt as they cannot export these products to their number one customer. Use the same logic to deduce that there will be problems in the companies that supply products and services to the farmers. They are combines, fertilizer companies and seed companies. It further translates into Deere, Potash, Monsanto and AGCO.

Due to increasing wealth in 2017, the Chinese demanded more meat. It takes a lot of corn to produce one pound of meat and in turn corn needs fertilizers. Hence, you can expect the companies producing fertilizers will increase their profits.

Geopolitical crisis

Many times, no action is the best action. It applies here. I had my experience in selling too many stocks via stops in 911. The market returned in a few days and I did not buy them back.

An analysis from Ned David Research covers 51 events from 1900 to 2014. My interpretation for actions: Trade the affected sector (via sector ETF) in the first few days and reverse the trade 2 months after. Many times, it means the oil price and gold price would rise.

I bought SH (a contra ETF to SPY) in August, 2017 as August and September are statistically the worst months in addition to the high risk in the current market. It is expected to be sold on Nov. 1. The North Korea crisis did not do much to the market on the first day but the market (the S&P 500) lost 1.45% and the risky NASDAQ lost 2.13% (see my blog on FAANG) on the second day.

If there is a hint of war or conflict, buy gold (GLD, gold trusts and gold coins) and defense stocks such as Northrop Grumman (NOC), L3 (LHX), Raytheon (RTN) and Lockheed Martin (LMT). I stayed away from Boeing (BA) in early 2020. If the conflict may disrupt oil transportation and/or production, buy oil such as (OIL and USO) and oil stocks.

Caveat. Need to understand the crisis. If it leads to World War 3, most sectors will not recover for a long while. Again, there is no sure thing in investing otherwise there would be no poor folks. However, educated guesses should materialize more often than not.

My experiences
- When the interest rates are expected to rise, plan on investments that are favorable to it and vice versa.
- In the same week, CROX lost almost 40% in one day. I bought some and made about 10% profit in a week. CROX's fundamentals were no good and it did have a history of a roller coaster ride in its stock price. After a year, I found out that I sold it too early as the stock price doubled. Better to buy a stock on its way up than down unless we identify that the bottom has been reached.
- I was on vacation while the second incident of the Boeing Max happened. Should have shorted the stock. In addition, Boeing's suppliers would suffer similarly to Apple's suppliers on Apple.

  https://www.barrons.com/articles/boeing-737-max-jet-production-cut-suppliers-stocks-51554499957?siteid=yhoof2&yptr=yahoo

- I missed applying the same trick to the rise of Apple when Apple announced its new iPod. I should at least buy the stocks of its suppliers. I hope to learn from this lesson and take advantage of future similar circumstances.
  I missed the opportunity to buy uranium stocks. It should be bought after Japan's disaster. When Japan approved the reopening of nuclear reactors today, these stocks including CCJ, DNN, LEU, URRE, UEC, URZ, URG and UUUU surged. When China's new nuclear reactors are on-line, they will surge again.
- Experiences in early 2014.
  Recently and in a short time, I made a good profit on BBY and a tiny profit on TGT. Both were bought due to headlines.

17 Earnings season overreactions

AAII has some screens for stocks with pleasant earnings surprises and bad earnings surprises (Jan., April, July and Oct.). The pleasant surprise screen always beats the other screens from the last time I checked.

Zacks ranks stocks with positive earnings revisions. As of this writing, their stocks ranked #1 have an amazing average annual return of 26% according to them. In 2019, the performance of recent tests did not hold up that well.

As with all vendors, we should check their recent performance (say, the last 5 years). If the strategy is proven to be effective, more investors will follow and usually make it less effective. It is usually a bearish sign and the peak may have been reached, when a rising stock falls upon a good earnings report, and vice versa.

It usually starts on the first two weeks after the ending of quarters (Dec., March, June and September) as indicated in the following link.
http://www.investopedia.com/ask/answers/08/earnings-season.asp

My experience

Contrary to the conventional wisdom, I enjoy the negative surprises more. If the company has a reason to come back or its problem is only temporary, I buy the stock. Sometimes it takes a few months and sometimes even a year for the stock to come back. The strategy of 'Buying low and selling high' works more often than it does not. However, avoid the stocks that start their long-term plunge.

Missing expected earnings by 1% and causing the stock to drop by 10% is a buy to me. Heading to bankruptcy is a different story though.

My momentum strategy buys stocks with positive earnings revisions. I usually do not keep these stocks for over a month.

As of today (4/6/2016), the quarter earnings season is starting. This year I am worried about the earnings due to the strong USD. It would impact the earnings as about 40% (my rough estimate) of the incomes of global companies are from foreign countries. If we feel there will be more disappointments, we should short the stocks that are expected to have poor earnings.

My lesson
Take advantage of the irrational human reactions. Retail investors and institutional investors are both human beings. Fund managers have more pressure to sell a loser to keep their jobs. Retail investors usually sell after the big institutional investors. Try to find out whether it is just a sentimental reaction or the stock is going to fall further.

How to hedge your stocks from earning surprises
Stocks might have a wide swing after the earnings announcements. Hedge the unfavorable announcements by the following three methods:

1. Stop loss.
   Usually, the swing is steeper than your stop price. When the price reaches or goes below a specific price, it will be turned into a market sell order. Institutional investors usually unload the stocks faster than the retail investors, opposite of buying. However, their positions are huge. We can tell they are unloading (or loading) from the unusual high trading volumes of the stocks. Ensure that your trades are allowed after hours.

2. Option.
   It is like buying insurance to protect your loss. Protect yourself from large losses as insurance is not cheap and smaller losses could be due to volatility.

3. Earnings prediction.
   They are also known as whispers or educated guesses. Zacks has a grading system.

   Also, insiders know the earnings before their announcements. However, it is illegal to use this information before its announcement.

Earnings revisions will be available before the announcement and they would provide better guesses to the announcement. With today's dividend chasers, the announcement of dividends or its increase would boost the stock price.

Personally, I do not do a lot to protect my stocks from earnings announcements. I have too many stocks. However, when we have evaluated the stocks correctly and monitor them regularly, we should have more pleasant surprises.

Profit from earnings surprises

The stock price usually rises on positive earnings surprises and falls otherwise. Sometimes they are not rational such as 1% miss in earnings that causes 10% loss in the stock price. In some rare cases, the positive earnings causes the stock to plunge as the investors expected better earnings even better than consensus. Here is an example of looking for tocks with positive earnings (you can profit by buying puts or shorting the stocks for stocks with negative earnings).

- Find stocks that have earnings announcements next week or month. Sources are Finviz.com's screener and SeekingAlpha.
- The screened stocks should fit some basic criteria. My criteria are: Market Cap > 200M, stock price > $2, average volume > 10,000 shares...
- If you subscribe to Zacks, check out the earnings grade. Stocks with Grade 1 and Grade 2 deserve our time for further research.
- If there are meaningful insiders' purchases, the chance of positive earnings is high.
- A positive short-term trend (SMA-20% from Finviz.com) is a plus.
- A positive short-term trend for the sector that stock belongs to is a plus. The sector can be represented by an ETF for that sector and use SMA-20%.
- Read articles on the stock for a qualitative analysis. Find these articles from many sources including SeekingAlpha. Today they have fewer articles for free.

Be warned that we do not expect all wins. When we achieve more than 50% wins, we should fare very well financially. When the market is falling or the earnings are expected to be poor, do not buy stocks except those that are fundamentally sound.

Take advantage of others' orders

1. Ensure your account can trade after hours.
2. Use Finviz.com to look for stocks announcing earnings this week. Prefer fundamentally sound stocks with a market cap greater than 500 (100 for smaller stocks).
3. Check out earningswhispers.com. They have two estimates: the consensus and the one from this website. Write down the exact time too.

4. If you subscribe Zacks.com, use its rating too as a reference.
5. Be at least 15 minutes earlier than the announcement date and time.
6. Google the stock and EPS from Google News. Refresh the search every 2 minutes. Check related articles.
7. If it beats the estimates, buy it at least one penny less than the last trade price and sell it within a day or two. The logic is to take advantage of all those orders that have not considered earnings in a timely fashion. It does not always work.
8. To improve performance, include Revenue with EPS.

Personally, I do not do it as it is too time-consuming for me; my beauty sleep is more important than money. Again, test it out before committing real money. There are many parameters that can be tuned to adjust to your personal preferences and the current market conditions. This is the essence of an entire book. I read with my own enhancements such as using Finviz.com.

18 Strategies on earnings

Here are two strategies on earnings. It is supposed to make millions for my children but they are not interested in investing. You either hate or love what your old man does.

1. Buy the stocks with earnings announcement soon with a Zacks rating 1 (the best) and short those with a Zacks rating 5 (the worst). BTW, Zacks rating is free so far for individual stocks.

2. After the earnings announcement, Google the company every second or so. If the earnings is good, buy it fast with market order. If it is bad, short it.

Do not be greedy and set a limit on loss. Do not call me if the trade is good or bad. In addition, check insider transactions and SMA-20%. I use Finviz.com.

I have tried #1 once a long while ago. I have not tried #2 as I have a life too. In the long haul, these strategies should make you some money.

19   Strategies that worked before

The following are three popular strategies that worked before but not too well recently. I try to see whether I can revive them to return to their former glory.

1.   O'Shaughnessy's Strategy
(http://en.wikipedia.org/wiki/James_O%27Shaughnessy)

It made a stunning return from 1954 through 1994. His strategy is:

Buy the 50 DOW stocks that have the highest one-year returns, five consecutive years of rising earnings and share prices less than 1.5 times their corporate rate of revenues.

After he publicized his strategy in a book, it was no longer effective. It was his tradeoff to make a lot of money from his book and his personal prestige to make money in his mutual funds. It fits my saying: When too many folks follow the same strategy, it will no longer be useful.

2.   The Foolish Four
(http://en.wikipedia.org/wiki/Foolish_Four)

From Wikipedia: "The "Foolish Four" is a discredited[1] mechanical investing technique that, like the Dogs of the Dow, attempts to select the number of stocks of the Dow Jones Industrial Average that will outperform the average in the near future.

To identify the "Foolish Four," an investor determines the current dividend yield and current price for each of the 30 stocks comprising the Dow Jones Industrial Average. Then, the yield for each stock is divided by the square root of the stock's price. The stocks are ranked from highest to lowest using the number resulting from the division. The stocks ranking the second highest, third highest, fourth highest, and fifth highest in equal dollar amounts are bought. The highest-ranking stock is not bought."

3.   Buy the highest ROE stocks

It has been described in a popular book. I do not believe that it still works but the book is still popular. I do not think I can revive this strategy and it is NOT the Holy Grail in investing as blindly followed by many. The followers should replace this strategy with better strategies.

My take

The above three strategies work at one time. After the authors publicized their strategies, they did not work anymore.

The ROE strategy will not work consistently as it is only one of the many fundamental metrics the value investor should consider. The Foolish Four seems to be similar to the Dog of the Dows. Hence, the only serious modification is on O'Shaughnessy's strategy.

Modify O'Shaughnessy's Strategy

I would take another look at O'Shaughnessy's Strategy. It is a long-term momentum strategy with some protection of not buying overpriced stocks. It will be effective again when fewer folks use it. Check its current performance. Many stock screens such as AAII's simulate this strategy. The following modifications apply to similar screens for this strategy.

What to include:

- Include the S&P 500 stocks, so you have more stocks to select from besides the Dow stocks.
- Alternatively, include stocks in all three major exchanges.
- Optionally select stocks with prices greater than $2 (or $5 for conservative investors), and daily average volumes greater than 10,000 shares. It would effectively eliminate most penny stocks.
- Use the expected earnings which predicts better instead of the last twelve month's earnings.
- Skip the stocks from most if not all emerging foreign countries (at least for today).
- Score each stock fundamentally such as using my Scoring System described in my books. Discard all the stocks that do not pass the scoring system.
- Analyze each stock fully.

Timing:
- Buy on November 1 and sell on May 1 for retirement accounts; alternatively start buying on October 15 and sell on April 15 for better choices and avoid the herd.

- Buy in November and December for non-retirement accounts to avoid the crowd. Sell losers after holding them less than a year and winners over a year in non-retirement accounts. Long-term capital gains have better tax treatments - check the current tax laws for both Federal and the state you reside in.
- When the market has a high chance of plunging or is plunging, close out all positions.
- Consider covered calls on stocks that are qualified for lower long-term capital gain taxes.

Optimal number of stocks:

- If you cannot find enough stocks to buy, relax your selection criteria such as 3 consecutive years of rising earnings instead of 5 years. If you still cannot find many good stocks, it could mean the market is fully valued and / or there are few bargains. It could also be due to too many folks following the same strategy.
- If you find too many stocks, sort them in descending order of the expected yields (E/P) and select the top stocks. Omit stocks with yields higher than 35% as they may sound fishy for such high returns. Alternatively, consider the stocks with high scores in my scoring system.
- 50 stocks is too large a number for most retail investors. Cut it to 25 (and even 10 if you have less than $50,000 to invest). Ensure that there is no sector having its total value more than 25% of the portfolio for better diversification.

Adjust the strategy to your risk tolerance and requirements. If you do not have a lot of time, five stocks in different sectors should be diversified enough.

Paper trade the strategy before you commit with real money. If you have a historical database, test it and tune it for better results.

Links
https://www.youtube.com/watch?v=zlYJ1eRjXvA
https://www.youtube.com/watch?v=uGUIUg_617o

20   Short Squeeze

When there is a short squeeze (i.e., over shorted), the stock may appreciate due to the shorters unable to find more stocks to short. The candidates can be found in Finviz.com. I use 35%. However, there may be valid reasons for the shorts such as a lawsuit pending, losing sales... Select the stocks with sound fundamentals.

The following are tests (not real trades) and many tests will be added. As of 09/04/15, the returns are:

Stock	Buy Date	Return	Annualized	SPY return
CALM	07/16/15	-3%	-33%	-1%
GME	07/16/15	-1%	-7%	-1%

The following are real trades as of 09/04/15.

Stock	Buy Date	Return	Sold date
CALM	03/11/15	47%	N/A
GME	04/06/15	8%	N/A

CALM, a candidate

Cal-Maine Foods Inc. (CALM) had fallen from over $60 to $46 recently and it was my heavy bet. The opening price on 12/15/2015 was $46.76. Readers might wonder why I still recommended accumulating a falling stock. Simply put, the race is not over and this horse has a lot of potential (i.e., fundamentally sound). The payout would be huge as it has been ignored (the short float is over 55%). Let me show you my evaluation process, so that you may use it to enhance your strategy if you have one.

Currently, this stock was screened by my Short screen that spots fundamentally-sound companies with short floats over 35%. Most of the screened stocks deserve to be shorted, but I cannot find any justification for this stock.

Technically speaking
First, this stock has been hated as described by the following table with the exception of Finviz's "Recom". Most of the data in this article were derived

from the free Finviz.com on Dec. 15, 2015. The 'Conditions' are my personal preferences.

	Condition	Indicate	12/15/2015
Short Float	>35%	Short squeeze	55%
RSI(14)	<30%	Oversold	31%
SMA-20	<0	Short-term down	-13%
SMA-50	<0	Mid-term down	-17%
SMA-200	<0	Long-term down	-9%
Recom.	1 - Buy & 5 – Sell	3 – Neutral	2

Fundamentally speaking
Did this stock deserve this hatred? From the following table, it is a big NO.

	Condition	Indicate	12/15/2015
Forward P/E	>0 and < 20	Favorable	7
ROE	>20%	Favorable	40%
Profit Margin	>8%	Favorable	15%
EPS Q/Q	>15%	Favorable	418%
Sales Q/Q	>10%	Favorable	71%
P/FCF	<15	Favorable	12
Debt / Equity	<.5 (industry related)	Favorable	.05

One or two favorable metrics do not mean a 'Buy' or great fundamentals. However, all these metrics all yell 'Buy'. They are my major fundamental metrics that have recently proven my predictability.

I combined all these metrics and scored CALM in 3 scoring systems plus PEY described below. As of this writing, CALM passed all my scoring systems with flying colors. Actually, when stocks exceed the passing score by that much, I have a little concern; I cannot find any problem with this stock.

	Passing Score	Score
P-Score	3	6
Short-term score	15	40
Long-term score	15	24
PEY	5%	23%

Explanation
- P-Score, Pow's Score. It uses the metrics available in the free Finviz.com with the exception of using Fidelity's Analyst Opinion instead of Finviz's "Recom". This score system is described in my book "Scoring Stocks".
- The other two systems use additional metrics and/or scores I subscribe to. I monitor these two scoring systems periodically and adjust the scores accordingly. My Short-Term Score is used for holding stocks for less than 6 months.
- PEY, Pow's Earnings Yield. It is similar to EV/EBIT (5 from GuruFocus or 1/5 = 20% for Earning Yield). Both consider debt and cash. The advantage of PEY is all the metrics are readily available for calculation if using Cash/Share instead of Short-term Liability. PEY also uses expected earnings.

Intangibles
From Seeking Alpha, enter CALM and you should find many articles. I have not found any alarms on CALM. Some farms that are affected by the bird flu will return if not already to production and eat into CALM's market. It is always a possibility that CALM will be infected by bird flu. However, with most chickens staying inside the farm and the extra precautions, the chance is slim. Let me share three scenarios below.

Say if there is another bird flu (not in CALM) that happens, the egg prices would rocket up and also is the profit of CALM.

Let's say if that happens to CALM, it will affect the location involved. As I stated, the management (they had been great) should have taken precautions to minimize the chance of a bird flu.

Then what if it happens in Hong Kong or another Chinese city, they would ban chicken from local farms and bring the frozen chickens from the unaffected countries such as the US. It would bring profits to CALM.

The egg price is returning to its normal price. Hence, the EPS will be lowered. With a Forward P/E less than 7 and PEY greater than 23%, the stock price would have to fall a lot to cause any great alarm.

Bonus metrics
From GuruFocus.com (a paid subscription), F-Score was 7 and Z-Score was 8; both are favorable.

Summary
This stock is technically unsound but fundamentally sound. It may still trend downward, but when it shoots back up, it would be like fireworks on display. Most value stocks are swimming against the tide, so we have to be patient for the market to realize its real value.

No one can identify the bottom precisely and consistently. I expect a short squeeze is coming when the shorters cannot find more shares to short. The interest rate hike could trigger some covering of the shorts. The shorters are paying about an 8% dividend; I do recommend not to short high-dividend stocks. With this price, the risk is low and the potential appreciation is high. When one or two institutional investors move in, the price will surge. I bought it on 3/11/15 and sold it on 10/28/15 making a profit of 48% or an annualized return of 77%.

Links
Timing: https://www.youtube.com/watch?v=XexaKTJ-qQU
Short squeeze: https://www.youtube.com/watch?v=XAyaQaWajpl
https://www.youtube.com/watch?v=T5MmthJgwSU

#Filler: No free lunch

Many commercials on YouTube show you how to make big money by following their recommendations. Some tell you how many times you would profit from their recommended stocks such as Apple and Amazon. However, they did not tell you how many stocks they recommended had lost all their value.

It is similar to some trading systems. It seems it works and they can prove it. However, the bankrupted stocks have been taken out from the test database (termed as survival bias). You need to follow the right strategies. I do not promise you the sky, but in the long run, most of my techniques in this book should work. As in life, there is no guarantee. Otherwise, there are no poor folks.

21   Year-end strategies

I have two: 1. Buy the current year winners (YEW) and 2. Buy the current year losers (YEL).

The first strategy is riding the institutional investors' window dressing to include the winners in their funds to make them look better. It did not work well in 2018, so I skipped it in 2019.

The second strategy takes advantage of selling losers for tax purposes. We need to find value stocks, but not stocks that are heading into bankruptcy. I had amazing returns in 2018 and will continue this strategy in 2019.

The following describes how to create your own testing if you have a historical database. It would be a frame for testing other strategies.

- Define the starting date. For the first strategy, I would use 9/1, 10/1 and 11/1 for two sets of test data. For the second strategy, I would use 12/1 and 12/15. Check to see which starting date is better for the specific strategy.
- Define the durations, the number of months before you sell the purchased stocks. I use 1 months, 2 months, 3 months and 6 months for my designated durations.
- Define the number of tests. I would start from the year 2000, one or two years older if your historical database allows for that. Actually, I started in the last 3 years or so to save time. However, do not use dates older than 1995 as the market was quite different then.
- Compare your results to SPY (or the S&P 500 index).
- Ignore dividends for simplicity.
- Use annualized rates for a better comparison.
- If the date has no data such as during holidays and weekends, use the date after it for consistency.
- Take out stocks that would not be the stocks you usually would buy, such as penny stocks (that likely boost the performance due to survivorship bias), small foreign companies and/or stocks giving huge dividends or giving a return of capital.
- Use different metrics to sort, such as Expected Earning Yield (E/P) or a composite grade. Use the top 5 (or 2) stocks to calculate performances.

- Include the maximum drawdown (the maximum loss from recent height) from many selected time frames (i.e., durations described). My maximum loss is -52% from 12/1/2007 to one year later in my Year-End Loss strategy, but followed by a 256% gain in the next year.
- Negative percent numbers could give you wrong calculations when comparing to an index. Check them out manually if your formula has not taken care of the negative numbers.
- A year-end winner strategy should include large companies (traded by fund managers) and stocks that have increased in values year-to-date.
- From my limited testing, my small-cap stocks that were profitable performed better than other stocks.
- Here are my best results for the two strategies. Again, my results will not be the same as yours due to different selection criteria. Past performance may not have anything to do with future performances.

The year-end loser strategy in 2015 does not work that well as I screened many stocks that were scored very low. I found out many screened stocks were from foreign countries. Many emerging countries have had problems and I do not trust most of their financial info. Besides that, many were energy companies which I already had too many of.

Many have Expected Earning Yields over 35%. However, most have very high debts such as Debt/Equity is over 1 (i.e., 100%). If I bought them, I would unload them within 3 months fearing a market crash in 2016 [Update. As of 2019, we do not have one]. Historically, it is profitable, but I may skip most YEL stocks this year as most were deserved losers. The lesson is: Adjust to the current market conditions.

Strategy	Starting Date	Duration	Avg. Annual. %	Max. Drawn Down
YE Winners	10/1	4 months	40%	-36%
YE Losers	12/1	6 months	42%	-28%

My experience. When trying to make good money, you need to find a strategy that matches the current market. Here are my recent strategies I actually tried with real money in 2018.

* You usually see window dressing from institutional investors from Nov. 1 to Dec. 1 (some use dates earlier than Nov. 1). Buy the current winners and sell the current losers of stocks with a large market cap.

The market was risky so I did not buy winners but shorted some losers.

* Buy year-end losers from Nov. 1 to Dec. 31 (some use dates earlier than Nov.1). The companies have to be profitable (>15%), big losers (most having over 50% yearly loss) and small companies (preferred).

Incorporate the strategy with today's volatile market (i.e., buy when they plunge and sell when they rise). You need to determine what is a "plunge" and a "rise". For me, it is short-term and the percent is 5% from a recent high or low.

There is a selling part of these strategies I have not included here. Most of my strategies are based on exhaustive tests from historical data with a lot of work.

Every market is different. We need to make a lot of adjustments. From my experiences, the best research may not make you money all the time. In the long run, the more educated you become, the better chance for you to make money.

Year-End 2018

This was one of my best monthly returns. The average purchase date is 12/27/2018 and the current prices were based on 1/28/2019. The return is 53% or 648% annualized. Most likely the performance will not be repeated. However, it serves as a procedure for coming years.

I change the quantity Q to 1. Several stocks have been purchased more than once. I sold 3 stocks already indicated by the Status = 'Sold'. 'JT' is my own taxable account described here.

Account	Screen	Year-end loser	Start	12/21/19	End	1/8/2019	Today	1/28/19		
Stock	Q	Buy	Sell	Buy $	Sell $	Buy Date	Sell Date	# Days	Profit $	Profit %	Ann %	Status

Stock	Q	Buy	Sell	Buy $	Sell $	Buy Date	Sell Date	# Days	Profit $	Profit %	Ann %	Status
401KC												
CHK	1	2.13	2.99	2	3	01/03/19	01/18/19	15	1	40%	982%	Sold
MNK	1	16.41	21.45	16	21	01/03/19	01/25/19	22	5	31%	510%	Sold
MNK	1	16.43	21.45	16	21	01/03/19	01/25/19	22	5	31%	507%	Sold
NNBR	1	5.68	8.58	6	9	12/26/18	01/28/19	33	3	51%	565%	
NNBR	1	5.72	8.58	6	9	12/26/18	01/28/19	33	3	66%	727%	
ESTE	1	4.35	6.45	4	6	12/26/18	01/18/19	23	2	48%	766%	Sold
JT												
LCI	1	4.61	8.29	5	8	12/21/18	01/28/19	38	4	80%	767%	
MDR	1	8.01	9.13	8	9	01/08/19	01/28/19	20	1	14%	255%	
YRCW	1	3.29	5.78	3	6	12/21/18	01/28/19	38	2	76%	727%	
YRCW	1	3.26	5.78	3	6	12/21/18	01/28/19	38	3	77%	742%	
401K												
ASRT	1	3.56	4.18	4	4	12/26/18	01/28/19	33	1	17%	193%	
UTCC	1	7.13	11.00	7	11	12/26/18	01/28/19	33	4	54%	600%	
YRCW	1	2.92	5.78	3	6	12/26/18	01/28/19	33	3	98%	1083%	
Tot/avg				84	119	12/27/18		29	36	53%	648%	

I sold my YRCW (not shown above) on the earnings date that can be found on Finviz.com. When the earnings are positive, it will be sold for my asking price plus a little more. If it is negative, it will not be sold. I recommend cancelling any trade order before the earnings date.

As of 09/07/2019, LCI is up by 185% and YRCW is down by 27% (I sold one position in my retirement account for about 100% gain).

Year-End 2019

As expected, I did not gain 50% in a month but I made a decent profit. The "Gain %" are good based on data on 1/18/2020 and no dividends and fees are considered. HOFT has been bought two times. If the "Sell Date" is blank, it means I still own the stock on 1/18/2020. This portfolio is heavily weighted in energy stocks.

My own trades that have an average of 4.7% for the month:

Stocks (11)	Buy Date	Sell Date	Gain %
HOFT	12/04/19	01/14/20	4%
HOFT	12/06/19	01/15/20	11%
METC	12/03/19	01/02/20	14%
REI	12/09/19	01/03/20	35%
EGY	12/10/19		25%
SND	12/10/19		0%
SBOW	12/17/19		-19%

SD	12/17/19		-17%
URBN	12/20/19		3%
GT	12/11/19		-8%
CAL	12/11/19		-4%

The performance of the stocks listed in my book "Best Stocks for Year End 2019" is 4.6%. The 2018 result of 53% in a month is not sustainable, but beating the SPY (without considering fees and dividends) by 19% is nothing to sneeze at.

If I only include the 4 stocks from the recommended 9 that have Earnings Yield (forward earnings) more than 20%, I would have a return of 10%. I went back to 2018-year end. If I selected the top 4 highest Earnings Yield, I would get about 40% (vs. about 30% for all 8 stocks). I will select stocks according to this finding in the next book titled "Best Stocks to Buy in 2021" shortly available after Dec. 15, 2020. It is not a promise for the book. There are some stocks not included in my actual trades.

Stocks (9)	Gain %
CAL	-4%
EGY	25%
HOFT	0%
METC	17%
REI	10%
SCOR	6%
SND	-12%
URBN	-2%
ZAGG	2%
Avg.	4.6%
SPY	3.87%
Beat SPY	19.1%

How long should we hold these screened stocks? Except those in my taxable account, I sold all of them in the first two months. The following is the annualized returns for holding 1 month, 2 months, 3 months and 5 months (as of 6/22/2019). From my previous testing, I should have held the stocks for 6 months. However, I have made my objective already and I want to take advantage of this volatile market. I could not find UTCC in my historical database. I sold it with an annualized return of 572%. It could be acquired or merged.

The following tries to determine what would be the best holding period for these stocks. For simplicity, I used 12/27/2018 as the purchase date for all stocks. I consider one position for each stock even though I bought it several times. Hence, my three purchases of YRCW are considered as one purchase here. Again, I do not include dividends, the bid spread and commissions.

	1 Month	2 Months	3 Months	5 Months
Ann. Return	497%	366%	178%	17%
SPY	72%	74%	52%	31%

2020 result

The following recommendation is one of the three lists from my book "Best Stocks for 2021". As in most if not all performance calculations in this book, dividends and fees are not included. The date range is from 12/10/2020 (the publish date) to 01/9/2021 (about a month later). SPY, an ETF simulating S&P 500 index, is used as a yardstick.

The current revision of this book has a new list of recommended stocks. The next book with a list of Year-End Losers may be in mid Dec. of 2021– not a promise.

Symbol	Return	Annualized
BCOR	20%	224%
CEPU	-10%	-114%
EEX	-8%	-94%
FANG	17%	191%
STFC	9%	105%
AVG	5%	63%
SPY	3%	37%
BEAT SPY		**48%**

22   Rocket stocks

There are stocks making yearly highs and continue to do so for a while. They defy fundamental rules. Among many examples, Tesla appreciated about 400% from 4/2013 to 10/2013. However, when they reverse direction, they may lose more than they have gained. BBRY lost 95% of its value in 4 years after gaining about 30 times in 5 years. Some are manipulated by institutional investors. Most have new products that could change the world. When they have unfixable problems such as competing products and/or major pending lawsuits, they will tend to plunge. I call them rocket stocks and they may plunge at the speed they surge.

From my tests on these stocks, they share common metrics. Most of these stocks are hitting 52-week highs or close to them, and they can be found in your stock section of the newspaper and many investing sites. Usually their SMA-50% is higher than their SMA-200%, which are both available from Finviz.com.

The other metrics are stock prices greater than $10 and the market cap is between 3 billion and 8 billion. I would also include 100M to 500M stocks for a larger appreciation potential although they are riskier. They should be listed in the major 3 exchanges. These are the stocks institutional investors would evaluate (greater than 4B); institutional investors drive the market. The volume should be at least double the average volume; it is a confirmation. Their rating grade on timing from many investing sites (some are free) are high.

You can alter the above criteria especially on many small drug companies and small high-tech companies. Insider purchases are another good criterion to search for rocket stocks. Avoid bankrupting stocks no matter how high they surge.

Do not be greedy as some will return to the original prices and even go to zero. When the institutional investors switch to the next rocket stock or sector, these rocket stocks will plunge in their prices. As recommended on how to sell rising stocks, use mental (a.k.a. trailing) stops such as 10%. When it falls to 10% of the last time you set the stop, sell it and **do not look back**. The average holding period of 3 months is the best in my limited testing. However, some rocket stocks do not obey the law of gravity. No one can time the peaks and bottoms consistently. Never buy a growth stock in a downward trend.XOM
Link: 52-week high:
  https://www.barchart.com/stocks/highs-lows/highs?timeFrame=1y

FAANG stocks

To many investors, FAANG stocks define the market. To me, as a conservative investor, it is not. For market-cap ETFs such as SPY, FAANG has more weight than other stocks. As a group, FAANG has been very profitable for the last year. To me they seem to be risky today. The following tables summarize these stocks, and I'll check them again in a year and/or after September (usually the worst month) to confirm my findings. It is also a case of momentum vs. value.

All the info is available free on websites such as Finviz.com. All data is from 8/5/2017. These are for info only and I'm not liable for any errors. Returns are annualized and dividends are not included.

Stocks	Current Price 8/5/17	From 8/5/16 to 8/7/17	From 8/7/17 to 8/7/18	From 8/7/18 to 10/7/18	From 01/03/22 to 1/03/23
FB (Meta)	169.62	37%	7%	-84%	-63%
AMZN	173.85	29%	88%	2%	-50%
AAPL	156.39	48%	30%	48%	-31%
NFLX	180.27	48%	94%	-4%	-51%
GOOGL	945.79	17%	33%	-47%	-39%
Avg.[1]	247.41	44%	50%	-17%	-47%
Beat SPY by		214%[2]	233%	-440%	-130%
SPY		14%	15%	5%	-20%

[1] All averages in this article are estimates. Fees and dividends are not included.
[2] Beat = (44% - 14%) /14=214%. Similar to other calculations for "Beat".

From the above and assuming using the recommended trailing stops, you should have exited your positions of FAANG before 2022 and saved the loss of about 50% in 2022.

Fundamentals as of 8/5/2017 (recommend to do the same analysis whether they good buys now.

Stocks	P/E	P/E FWD	P/S	P/B	Debt/ Eq.	Sales Q/Q	EPS Q/Q	ROE
FB	37	26	15	7	0.00	45	69	23
AMZN	16	14	6	4	1.11	2	18	27
AAPL	18	15	4	6	0.73	5	10	35
NFLX	221	90	8	25	1.55	32	58	13
GOOGL	34	24	7	4	0.03	21	-28	14
Avg.	65	34	8	9	0.68	21	25	22
Beat SPY [1]	164%		277%	186%				
SPY[2]	25		2	3				

[1] Very rough estimate.
[2] Most fundamental metrics are from other sources than Finviz.com, so there may be small discrepancies.

Technical as of 8/5/2017

Stocks	SMA50%	SMA200%	RSI(14)	52-week height	Short%	Insider Trans.
FB	8%	23%	67	-3%	1%	-86%
AMZN[1]	35%	8%	51	-6%	1%	0%
AAPL	5%	17%	63	-2%	1%	-31%
NFLX	10%	26%	59	-6%	6%	-69%
GOOGL[2]	-2%	8%	41	-6%	0%	0%
Avg.	11%	16%	56	-5%	2%	-37%
Beat [3] SPY by	1020%	173%	-9%			

[1] Recent double top. Bearish.
[2] Multiple tops.
[3] Very rough estimates.
The two SMA (Simple Moving Averages) technical metrics are positive.

Summary
As a group, FAANG is fundamentally unsound but technically sound compared to SPY. I said the same about the market. As suggested, use trailing stops if you own any of these stocks. When they turn to be technically unsound, this is the time to exit. They could stay in the current valuations for a long time. However, when the institutional investors are dumping them, they will fall very fast and steep. SMA-20% would be a good indicator for an exit. NFLX is the most fundamentally unsound stock.

The rosy pictures of these stocks have been priced in. I recommend that you sell the stocks with a P/E over 35 unless you have a good reason not to. It is insurance to protect your profits. Even if they still rocket higher, you still will have a good sleep. When any bad news occurs, they may rocket back to earth. Newton's Law of Gravity? If you are one of the lucky owners of these stocks, use trailing stops (i.e., stops from the current prices instead of your buy prices) to protect your profits. As 1/2020, most of these stocks are still not fundamentally sound but technically sound.

23   Small caps vs. big caps

Sometimes small caps are better than larger caps, and sometimes the opposite. We use the Russell 2000 (or the ETF IWM) to represent small caps and the Russell 1000 (or ETF IWB) to represent large caps. Every year, there are many better stocks within small caps move up to large caps and vice versa. When the ETF representing them is better than the other one in one month and also in three months, most likely the current market favors that index.

Try the same with value stocks and growth stocks.

Actually, they are part of the sector rotation: the rotation between small and large stocks and the rotation between value and growth stocks.

A growth stock with less than 5 billion market cap has a better chance of appreciation potential for the following reasons: 1. It is easier to move a 5 billion stock than a 50 billion stock, and 2. Many institutional investors (who move the market) do not look at stocks with market caps less than 5 billion.

24   An aggressive strategy

I use a similar strategy that includes metrics and composite grades from vendors that I subscribe to their services. The following is a brief description. As in life, there is no guarantee.

The basic major steps are:

- Use market timing to determine when to buy and sell.
- How to screen stocks.
- How to modify the screen to fit the current market conditions.
- Score the stock fundamentally.
- Intangible analysis.
- Qualitative analysis.
- Optionally, technical analysis.

Market Timing

Refer to the chapters on this topic described in this book.

Screen stocks

Most small cap stocks are not followed by analysts, so we can find some gems. The common screening criteria will be mentioned briefly here.

- Skip the following sectors and countries: financial companies (banks, loaners), miners, drug (generic OK), insurance, emerging countries including China, India and Mexico.

- Ensure the company is not heading into bankruptcy. "Price / Free Cash Flow" cannot be manipulated easily. Profit growth and sales growth compared to the last quarter are good indicators too. Massive insider dumping is another one.

- Common filter criteria:

    1. Listed in one of the three major exchanges, or specific exchange(s) for your country.

    2. Market cap > 200 million and < 800 million.

    3. Price > 2 and less than 20.

    4. Average daily volume > 8,000 (some use 10,000) shares.

    5. Short % less than 15% (some use 10%).

    6. Expected earning yield (E/P, reversal of P/E) > 5% and < 30%.

    7. Ensure the SMA%-200 (simple moving average for the last 200 trade sessions) is positive. In other words, the stock price is above the SMA-200 line. You can obtain this value from Finviz.com.

    The above information can be easily obtained from Finviz.com. Try any extras criteria your broker offers. Use the Equity Summary Score from Fidelity and ignore stocks with ranks less than 6.

    The next useful comparisons are the averages of its industry or sector. The common parameters are: Price / Cash Flow, Debt percent, P/E (also its own 5-year average), Price / Sales, etc.

Sorting the screened stocks
If you have too few stocks from your screen, the market may be risky. If not, ease up on your filter criteria.

If you have too many stocks, sort them in descending order by the expected earnings yield. Select the top stocks for further evaluation.

What the current market favors
If the market favors growth, sort them in descending order of the SMA % (use 50 or 200 depending on how long you expect to keep the stock) from Finviz.com, or any growth metric such as earning quarter-to-quarter growth rate. The higher the SMA % indicates the higher chance the stock is moving up, but it should not be excessive as that could indicate a peak. Also determine whether the stock is over-bought indicated by the RSI(14) indicator.

If the market favors value, sort the screened stocks in descending order of the expected E/P.

Qualitative analysis
Most of the above information or criteria belongs to quantitative analysis. Check out the tangibles and qualitative analysis.

Use screens to select a handful of stocks for your further evaluation as it saves time.

Screen sites

There are many sites to screen stocks and many have built-in screens for immediate use. Your stock broker may provide you with screens. There are many good ones that are free including Finviz.com, Fidelity.com and Yahoo!Finance.com. AAII provides screened stocks from the basic subscription and provides screens that you can modify for an extra fee.

Some vendors provide a historical database and/or better tools at an extra cost: AAII, Stock 123, Zacks, VectorVest... It would be useful to test screens with past data. Some sites provide back testing features for technical analysis. Validea (http://www.validea.com/home/home.asp) has some promising screens at a cost, and so is GuruFocus.com.

Interesting screens

- There are screens that simulate what the gurus such as what Buffett would buy. They may beat the market but not by a wide margin. It could be too many followers using these screens.

- Include stocks that were not in any major exchanges one year ago. It includes the companies that started in the basements, moved to a local exchange, and now have moved to a major exchange. Most major companies such as Apple and Microsoft belong to this group at one time. Some may skip the local exchange as Facebook did.

- Sort PEG and select the stocks with the best PEGs such as lower than 1. It is a growth strategy.

- Select stocks that have been increasing in prices in the last 3 months. It is a momentum strategy.

- Stocks with better metrics compared to companies in the same industry sector. Compare Apples to Apples.

- Combine growth metrics and value metrics. It is the Growth with a Value strategy. It is also known as "Growth with a realistic price".

- Candidates for being acquired.
  Usually, they are small companies in specific markets and / or having specific technologies. 2009 was a good year for acquisitions, especially when there was a lot of corporate cash and the interest rates were low.

- Candidates to be listed in the three major exchanges.
  Usually they are gaining in profits, market shares and/or market capitalizations. When they are listed, some ETFs are required to buy them.

- Sell last year's big gainers and buy last year's big losers. It is contrarian's strategy. Need to ensure they can turn around and are fundamentally sound.

- Select the best stocks from the top 5 sectors (I prefer industries) when the market in rising. It is a top-down approach.

- Stocks with favorable earnings revisions. This strategy works better before the earnings announcements.

- Stocks with high insiders' purchases.

- Dividend growth stocks.

They perform very well in the last few years as of 1-2014. Income seekers flock to dividend stocks when CDs and bonds cannot give them equivalent incomes.

- Besides from your broker's site on screening tools, Kapitall has a lot of ideas on building screens and the stock recommendations. Check his articles in Seeking Alpha or their website (http://seekingalpha.com/author/kapitall).

- Garbage in and garbage out. I do not trust the financial statements from most emerging countries. If your screening tools do not provide this filter, check the company's profile and skip these companies that you may not trust.

- Fidelity's Predefined screens.
http://research2.fidelity.com/fidelity/screeners/commonstock/strategies.asp?

- Many sites provide guru screens to simulate what gurus would buy. GuruFocus.com is one of them.

Back testing

If your screening service does not provide a historical database, you may have limited testing capability. However, you can still compare the screened stocks six months later. To simplify, use a virtual portfolio for each strategy.

Find out why your screen does not work when you invest with real money:

1. Survivorship bias. The historical database you use may have taken out all the stocks that have been delisted and they're usually bad.

   Stocks with less than $1 have a higher chance of survivorship bias.

   Most of them bankrupted, so your performance of a screen looks better as you have avoided these stocks unknowingly. A small percent of the 'disappeared' stocks are merged, acquired, or spin-offs and usually they're doing well. However, there are far more bankrupt companies than the above.
2. Humans are not rational. We usually buy high and sell low. Sticking with a strategy will take out this aspect.

3. Use the wrong screen for the current market conditions. A value screen should not be used when the market is trending up.
4. Market conditions change. Many years ago, selecting low P/E and foreign companies listed in the US exchanges provided above-average returns. However, it was not true in 2011 to 2014.

Conclusion
The four steps of investing are: 1. Market Timing, 2. Screening, 3. Analysis and 4. When and what to sell.

Links
SA article:
(http://seekingalpha.com/article/1806542-a-dividend-portfolio-built-using-the-piotroski-f-score

25 A turnaround strategy for value stocks

Many value stocks tend to stay in this phase for a long time. When the turnaround starts, it could be very profitable.

Market Timing
Do not buy any stock when the market is risky as described elsewhere in the book. Actually, you should sell most of the stocks when the market is risky.

Metrics

Metric	Value	Conservative	Aggressive
General			
Market Cap	>300 M	>1,000 M	>100 M
Price	> 2	>10	>1
Avg. Volume	>20,000	>50,000	>10,000
USA	Only	Only	Foreign but listed in USA
Fundamental			
Forward P/E	<15	<10	<25
Earning Gr Q-Q	>5%	>8%	>3%
ROE	>10	>15	>5
P / FCF	<10	<8	<15
Debt / Equity	<.5	<.25	<1
Technical			
SMA-50%	>10	>15	>5

Misc.			
Blue Chip Growth	A or B	A	A or B
Fidelity	>6	>8	>5
IBD	>60	>90	>50
VectorVest	>=1	>=0.8	>=12
Value Line Proj. 3-5% return	>5%	>10%	>5%
Zacks	>=4	5	>=4
ASSS	>=2	>=5	>=2

The assignment values for the metrics are not fixed; feel free to change it according to your own risk level. I do have suggestions for conservative investors and aggressive investors.

Some of the metrics are not readily available in Finviz.com and the following describes how to modify them.

Explanation
- Market Cap- The free version of Finviz.com does not allow you to specify the range. Use 'Any' and then select the stocks according to the specified values. Average Volume has a similar restriction.
- The conservative values for Market Cap, Price and Average Volume try to select larger companies. The aggressive values try to select smaller companies, which historically are riskier but perform better.
- I prefer 'USA' for Country. Stay away from small companies from developing countries unless you can trust their financial statements.
- Forward P/E measures the value of the stock. Ensure "E" (Earnings) is positive. I prefer it over P/E (from the last twelve months).
- Earnings Growth Quarter to last Quarter is preferred to be positive unless it is during a recession.
- ROE measures how well the company has been managed.
- P/FCF. "Price / Free Cash Flow" cannot be manipulated easily. Together with low "Debt / Equity", it measures whether the company would go bankrupt.
- SMA-50%- Some stocks tend to stay in a value stage for a long while (termed value trap). We like to select stocks that start getting out of this stage.

- Misc. Many sites have evaluated the stocks for us. Some only let their customers access such information, some are available for a free trial, or are available from the library.
- ASSS is my scoring system. Try it out and check the performance.

With the above, I had 35 stocks on 10/28/16 and that was too many stocks to evaluate. If you have time for 10 stocks for further evaluation, try to sort Forward P/E (P/E is the second choice) in ascending order and select the top 10 after skipping the stocks that have P/E less than 2. If you cannot find any or substantially less than the normal, the stocks you selected may not work, take a break as the market conditions do not favor the value metrics you specified.

Qualitative analysis
Double click on the stock and read as many articles described on the stock as possible. If it meets all the criteria, buy the stock. I recommend that you use market orders for large companies in a non-volatile market (when the average daily fluctuation is less than 0.5%). If the selected stock is the one you just sold for a loss, make sure you only buy it back after 31 days to avoid the Wash Sale penalty.

Keeping informed
Check the company updates/news on the stock you owned every month. One easy way is to enter the stocks in a model portfolio in SeekingAlpha.com and they would inform you on any articles/news on your owned stocks.

Sell the stock
Re-evaluate your stocks every 6 months. If it does not meet the criteria or the market is risky, sell it. If it is only a few days (currently it is 365) away from a long-term capital gain, sell the losers right away or hold on to the winners for a few more days.

Rebalance the portfolio after a stock has been sold. Ensure it has been diversified enough into market cap and sectors.

Top-down Investing
It is similar to the above. Find the sectors that performed the best last month. Under Finviz.com, select the best sector under 'sector' one at a time. Several sites such as Fidelity compare a stock to the averages of stocks in the same sector.

My recent recommended stocks being delisted

There should be more of these stocks when the market recovers from crashes. From my last books in my "Best Stocks" series, which are verifiable, my shares are quite a lot. Again, fees, dividends and commissions are not included,

Stock	Rec. Date	Date delisted	Days held	Return	Ann. Return
USAK	12/15/21	09/14/22	273	79%	105%
BDSI	12/15/21	03/22/22	97	116%	436%
CTB	02/08/21	06/17/22	129	15%	41%
Average			71	70%	194%

Book 8: Sector Rotation: The Basics

1 Sector rotation in a nutshell

How to start

I have been rotating sectors in my annuity investments for quite a long time with a sum of more than my annual salary at the time. As of 1/2020, it had increased about four times. My mutual fund employer had a lot of restrictions for me trading stocks, so rotating sector funds in my annuity was the best investment tool for me.

Starters should paper trade their strategies first. Use Finviz.com, SeekingAlpha.com and/or Fidelity.com to select the best performing sector and/or use my quick analysis of ETFs. Switch it every month (or two) to the ETF corresponding to the best sector. Again, switch to cash when the market is risky. You may consider sector mutual funds which are managed, but most have restrictions such as holding periods and fees. Most if not all sector mutual funds do not have contra funds that expect the sector to go down in value. Sector mutual funds cannot be shorted.

After the basics, this book provides many features to further refine your strategy such as technical Analysis. Beginners should use Strategy 1 in Book 2. After that, start with the technical indicators such as SMA-50% and RSI(14) with a handful of sector ETFs to rotate (suggested sectors are technology, bank, health care, housing, consumer and material).

In addition, some sectors are more profitable in different phases of a market cycle. We will examine several industry sectors and country sectors in more detail. China is affecting the global economies including ours. When the interest rates are low, it would affect bonds and stocks yielding high dividends. Many books ignore market timing. It turns out to be the most important technique as the last market plunges have had an average loss of 45%!

The keys to profitable sector rotation

Sector rotation could be very profitable and less risky than most of us may expect. However, it is volatile and risky if not properly implemented. There are two ways to profit from the following:

1. Buy the sector when it is trending up and sell when the sector is trending down. It is the common approach to sector rotation.

2. Buy at the bottom or close to of a sector and sell at the peak or close to. It is hard to detect the bottom/peak.

As described, using sector rotation, you never buy at the peak and sell at the bottom, as you need the price trend. Sometimes, the trend lasts for less than a month and sometimes it lasts for years.

Many investment subscriptions and free sites such as Finviz.com select favorable sectors every month. We assume the best-performing sector last month will perform better in the coming month or months. It does not always happen such as the tech sector in April, 2000 and the reversed direction of the drug sector in 2015. To protect your investments, use stops.

Alternatively, we can select them via simple charts as described in this book. Beginners should start with Single Moving Average (SMA-20 and SMA-50 for 20 sessions and 50 sessions respectively) provided by Finviz.com without charting.

Detecting the bottom of a sector

It is not easy and no one can detect the bottom or the peak of a sector consistently but easier with trends. Enter the ETF for a specific sector or the SPY for the market in Finviz. Use a short-term SMA such as SMA-20 and SMA-50 (expressed in percent), and check these two parameters every week. If both SMA-20% and SMA-50% are positive, most likely the market or a sector is trending up.

For market timing, the SMA-350 (Single Moving Average with 350 sessions) detects the market quite accurately for the last two market plunges. I have tested out the "days" with different numbers and 350 is the best fit for the last two market plunges. In recent days, 400 could be a better choice to reduce the number of false alarms.

Besides technical indicators, there are hints that indicate a sector is close to the bottom. Using the ETF for the sector and check out the fundamental metrics similar to evaluating a stock. To illustrate, enter XLE in Yahoo!Finance or Finviz.com to get the current price and other info about this sector. Sites specializing in ETFs such as ETFdb that will give you more information about ETFs.

The intangibles for stocks and ETFs should be considered too. For example, in 2020, the potential decoupling with China would make a lot of U.S. chip companies less profitable.

Detecting the trend

Detecting the trend is easier than detecting the bottom/peak. To illustrate, bring up Finviz.com from your browser and enter XLE. For most sectors, I use the SMA-50 (single moving average for the last 50 days), which is readily available as one of the metrics. When the stock price is 3% above this SMA, it is most likely a buy. When it is 3% below this SMA, sell. It is simple, and it has been proven many times. Currently Finviz.com provides SMA-20% and SMA-50% only for short-term averages. For other durations, you can construct charts.

You can adjust the 50-day and the 3% (some use 1% or 5%) on how long your average holding period of an ETF or a stock that also depends on how often you want to trade). If your holding period is longer, use a higher number such as 90 days; use SMA-20 if it is shorter. If you want to trade more often use 2% instead of 3% (or use 5% if you want to trade less often).

Personally, I use 60 days if I use charts (from Yahoo!Finance among one of the many free sites that provide charts). One of my sector fund accounts requires 60 days for a minimum holding period without incurring a fee.

To detect a market crash and when to reenter the market, I use 350 days (some use 300 or 400 days). The 'days' are actually trade sessions.

The RSI(14) indicates whether the sector is overbought or oversold. RSI oscillates between zero and 100. Traditionally, and according to Wilder, the creator, RSI is considered overbought with a value above 70 and oversold with a value below 30 as described in the article. This indicator is available from Finviz.com.

(http://stockcharts.com/school/doku.php?id=chart_school:technical_indicators:relative_strength_index_rsi)

A simple way is to buy last month's winner(s). Ensure your ETFs are not leveraged if you are conservative. Include contra ETFs when the market is risky for aggressive investors. Here are the links to the websites that keep track of top performers varying from 1 to 3 months.

Seeking Alpha's ETF Hub.
http://seekingalpha.com/insight/etf-hub/asset_class_performance/key_markets
Morning Star. Select the period (1 month for example).
http://news.morningstar.com/etf/Lists/ETFReturns.htm

What to buy

I prefer ETFs for specific sectors and the second choice is sector funds (check out the holding period to exit without penalties). With good analysts, most sector funds are better than ETFs in specific sectors such as banking, drug companies and mining. Compare their performances.

ETFs charge less for maintaining and they have all the advantages of a stock. However, mutual funds select the stocks within a sector selectively. Fidelity offers the most complete list of sector mutual funds. Again, compare the 3- or 5-year performance between the ETF and the fund in this same sector.

The third option is a top-down approach. First, when the market is not plunging, select the most favorable sector and then the best stocks within the sector. Many free sites provide a filter to find favorable sectors.

Here is a list of sector ETFs.
(http://www.bloomberg.com/markets/etfs/)

Here is a list of commission-free ETFs from Fidelity.

(https://www.fidelity.com/etfs/ishares)

Some funds automatically switch sectors for you. From my experience so far, they have not proved to be very profitable. You should check out their past performances.

Favorable sectors according to the market cycle
Refer to the chapter on Market Timing and Spotting a Market Plunge for specific strategies. Close and/or adjust your positions when the market is plunging.

Favorable sectors according to the interest rate
It is similar to the above. Retailing, auto and housing are usually hurt by high interest rates. An improving economy would do the opposite.

Favorable sectors according to geography
It is not an easy task. China and India had their best performing years. The trade war with the U.S. may favor India as of 2020. Japan had one of the best years in 2013 during the last two decades. For foreign countries, currency fluctuation should be considered. Most emerging countries have their ups and downs. Most ETFs and sector funds in emerging countries buy larger companies that are more trustworthy as noted with their financial statements.

Global economies have never been that tightly connected. When the U.S. economy is down, China is affected and so are the resource-rich countries that China depends on.

Favorable and unfavorable events
The EU crisis has taken more than three years as of 4/2016 and the EU stocks are still close to the bottom. I prefer to buy ETFs or mutual funds which specialize in EU stocks, when the trend is up.

When the head of our Treasury says the interest will be lower, the market and the long-term bond funds will move up, and vice versa. To me, the interest rates will move up slowly from the 1/2014 bottom.

Recent favorable and unfavorable sectors
There are many sources to check which sectors performed best recently. Finviz.com is one of them. From the top menu bar, select Group, and the best and worst sectors will be displayed. Skip one day or one week unless you have a special interest in these short durations. Select the duration depending on your purposes. Personally, I would use one month (or two)

for my monthly rotation strategy assuming the momentum would pass to the next month.

Technical analysis would help to spot the trend. Select the Simple Moving Average. It is similar to the TA used in the chapter spotting a market crash. Instead of using SPY or another ETF market index, use an ETF that represents the sector.

Sector rotation by fund managers
We cannot beat these institutional investors. We need to follow them, or be one step ahead of them. They rotate sectors when they find another sector that has better appreciation potential, or the current favorable sector has reached its peak.

When to rotate
Rotate for the following reasons:

1. When the market is plunging, rotate the sector ETFs and/or mutual funds to cash. Aggressive investors would rotate their equities to contra ETFs. The average loss of the last two market plunges had been about 45%. This chart will not determine the peak (or bottom) as it depends on the falling data. However, it will tell you when to exit to prevent a further loss and tell you when to reenter the market.
2. When the fundamentals of the current sector you owned are turning bad.
3. When there is another sector that has better appreciation potential. Finviz.com tells you the rankings of the sectors.
4. When the sector is overbought or peaking, and / or has met our objective.

Do not forget about market timing
Do NOT buy any stocks except the contra ETFs for an aggressive investor, when the market is plunging. Playing defense usually wins the game more often than playing offense. When the market is peaking, protect your profits by placing stop loss orders.

Positions and how often to switch
It depends on the size of your portfolio and how much time you can afford to monitor your portfolio. To me, it varies from 2 to 6 positions and 20 to 90 days to monitor these switches.

Statistics show that a portfolio with 5 positions rotating in 20 days gives you slightly better performance and less drawback (maximum loss for the period). I recommend 4 (2 for a portfolio of less than $20,000) and 30 days (and 60 days for Fidelity sector funds). You determine according to your portfolio size and the time available to you for investing.

Conclusion

Sector rotation is described in very basic terms here. The links in Afterthoughts provide additional information.

As a reminder, **roughly half of a stock's price movement can be attributed to the sector** it is in.

Afterthoughts
- There are many articles on this topic. They are:
  Sector rotation strategies ETF investors must know. There are many useful links.
  http://www.bloomberg.com/markets/etfs/
  Sector rotation based on performance.
  http://stockcharts.com/school/doku.php?id=chart_school:trading_strategies:sector_rotation_roc
  Fidelity on Sectors.
  https://www.fidelity.com/sector-investing/overview
  Video instruction.
  http://www.YouTube.com/watch?v=j5yYoOoATRM
- No one can consistently predict the bottom or the peak of any sector. Sometimes we move in too early and lose another 25% or so, or we leave the sector too early to lose another 25% or so potential gain. It is quite normal. Learn why we move within the wrong time frame, and a lot of times it may be just bad luck or other events that are beyond our control.
- A free (as of this writing) service on sector rotation.
  http://www.gosector.com/

More links from YouTube
Simple sector rotation, 2, another 3
https://www.youtube.com/watch?v=FOKTFFabpL8
https://www.youtube.com/watch?v=85IRL_3oR8&t=219s
https://www.youtube.com/watch?v=gu-46zcBwsI&t=177s
https://www.youtube.com/watch?v=MFVmEcRHpnk
Stock reversal https://www.youtube.com/watch?v=uO4yJGSz1vU
Sector rotation Profit by being early.
https://www.youtube.com/watch?v=MFVmEcRHpnk

2   Outline on how to start sector rotation

As with everything in life, there is no guarantee that this book will make you a lot of money. However, the chance of success will be substantially improved especially when you practice with most of the ideas presented in this book. Always start with paper trading first.

1. First determine your objectives. Retirees select safer strategies. Millionaires can afford to select riskier strategies for larger returns.

2. Determine your risk tolerance, how much time you have for investing, your knowledge of investing, and your desire to continue to learn about investing and your portfolio size.

   To illustrate, when the market is risky, do not buy any stock. However, for investors who can tolerate higher risk, buy contra ETFs as a hedge against the market for larger returns. Retirees may be less risk tolerant unless they're rich.

   If your job is very demanding, you should spend less time in investing even if you're knowledgeable on investing and have a desire to learn about investing.

   Check your net worth (= what you own – what you owe) and cash flow (incomes – debt payments). Reserve your emergency cash equal to your expenses for at least 3 months.

   If the above is limited, SPY or any ETF simulating the market is your only sector and market timing is your primary tool (Book 2, Strategy 1, Chapter 2). You can stop here for now, and continue reading the rest of the book when the limitations change.

3. When the market is peaking, invest cautiously. Use trailing stops described in this book. The same for your sector ETFs / funds that have appreciated a lot.

4. When you have lost two trades in a row, take a break and return to paper trading until you're comfortable.

5. Test your strategies on paper. This book requires you to try out the various strategies, and select the one you are comfortable with. All theories may not always work for real trading.

6. When a strategy has been thoroughly tested out recently and the results are good, use real money slowly and gradually. Then monitor your performance.

7. When you have a new strategy or you need to test a strategy whether it works in the current market.

Not all of the predictions (mine or others) have materialized, and no strategy is evergreen. Always use stops to protect your portfolio. Learn from your arguments for the predictions, not merely the accuracy of the predictions. Predictions are based on educated guesses, and hence hopefully more of them will materialize in the long run. Consult your financial advisor before investing with real money.

The rest of this book describes the other aspects of sector rotation such as Top-Down Investing (in case you prefer to find the stocks in the favorable sector), country sectors, specific industry sectors... Many investing ideas described here are applicable to other investing strategies.

Links: https://www.youtube.com/watch?v=uO4yJGSz1vU
https://www.youtube.com/watch?v=evgsloYNsek

#Filler: lessons from a strategy named Turtle with my inputs

The experiment to train students who have no experience in two weeks worked. The technical analysis strategy would not work today for many reasons. However, the concepts are still good and explained here.

Do not time the market (not agree totally). Find a good strategy (easier said than done) and stick with it consistently. Cash management (agree with stops from 5% to 15% depending on your risk tolerance and the volatility of the stocks). Do not use leverage that could wipe out your entire portfolio. Follow the trend of the stock with higher positions.

3   The 5G revolution

During the pandemic, it is easy to find the importance of 5G to enable us to work and study at home and also the inequality of the poor. That is the primary reason for the U.S. trying to suppress Huawei as they are passing us in 5G technology.

Many potentially profitable companies on 5G are in the Far East including China, Taiwan, South Korea and Japan. Some companies in Taiwan and some acquired candidates have seen their stocks doubled; they are very risky though. I hope the following ETFs would contain some of these companies: FIVG, NXTG and SNSR; use ETFdb.com for more info.

This article concentrates on U.S. companies. They can be classified in the following categories:

Network provider: Verizon (VZ) and all others. VZ started earlier.

Network builder: Huawei (a private-owned Chinese company), Ericsson (ERIC) and Nokia (NOK). As of 2021, Ericsson is not doing well because China is cutting down their sales there.

Equipment/Infrastructure: Corning (GLW), Ciena (CIEN) and American Tower (AMT), which is a REIT.

Chips: Qualcomm (QCOM), Skyworks Solutions (SWKS), NVIDIA (NVDA) and Xilinx (XLNX). Some of these stocks may suffer due to the export restrictions to China in early September, 2020.

Most of the info are from this link. Search for other articles from the web.
https://www.fool.com/investing/stock-market/market-sectors/communication/5g-stocks/

The following is my simple evaluation of selected stocks on 8/1/2020. Before you invest, do your own research and consult your financial advisor. I am not responsible for any errors.

The list

Symbol	Fidelity's Score[1]	Cheaper By[2]	True EY[3]	Debt/ Equity[4]	Insider Trans.[4]	Short %[4]
VZ	8.8	1%	12%	1.96	0%	1%
GLW	2.8	-876%	6%	0.79	-20%	3%
CIEN	9.9	44%	6%	0.34	-13%	3%
AMT	9.6	-3%	3%	6.76	-2%	1%
QCOM	9.1	-102%	5%	5.24	-18%	2%
SWKS	6.3	-78%	6%	0.00	-9%	2%
XLNX	4.8	-43%	3%	0.54	-8%	3%
NVDA	9.4	-110%	2%	0.00	-23%	1%
Symbol	Fidelity's ESS	Cheaper by	True EY	Debt/ Equity	Insider Trans.	Short %

[1] Equity Summary Score. This and "Cheaper by" can be obtained from Fidelity's website requiring free registration.

[2] Cheaper by % based on the current P/E (PE) for the last twelve months and compared to its 5-year average (PE5). If it is negative, it means it is more expensive. Cheaper % = -(PE – PE5) /PE5.

[3] True EY is the earnings yield considering debts and cash. Compare it to one-year Treasuries and CDs which are basically risk free. It is the reciprocal of "EV/EBITDA". It is obtained from Yahoo!Finance (under Statistics). Most use P/E and not Forward P/E (guessing the future earnings). Even if Forward P/E is used, it may not be upgraded during this fast-changing period.

[4] From Finviz.com.

From the above, I do not want to buy stocks whose Insider Trans is more than 10%. Most likely, the insiders think these stocks have approached the peaks. I would ignore the stocks that are "Cheaper by" more than -30% - another sign of over-value.

VZ is the only stock that has good value even. I may want to wait for the market crash and reevaluate them again.

4   Computer chips

As of 4/2023 (today), the U.S. chip industry is not doing well. It is primarily due to the recovery of the pandemic. During the pandemic, more people worked at home and hence the demand for laptops and related hardware was high. The increased investment on new factories gives to today's over supply of chips. The recovery would materialize hopefully by 2024, and our policy and China's is a factor.

The other reason is our sanctions on China, and China was their primary customer to many of our chip companies. We do not allow China to buy advanced products based on our technology including ASML's chip-making machines. I estimate China will have DUV (a lithography, 28 nm machine) in 2024 or 2025 that would satisfy 70% of China's chip fabrication. Based on several breakthroughs in China, I also PREDICT 14 nm chips available in 2027, and EUV that can produce 7 nm chips in 2028. Our chip companies have been suffering a lot from importing chips to China. Even more so, when China fixes these problems, the world would be flooded with cheap chips from China. Our politicians look for short-term gains.

The only positive development is the demand of high-end GPUs due to Artificial Intelligence (AI). Nvidia is the most promising stock since the introduction of Microsoft's ChatGPT during the last quarter of 2022. The new product H100 is about 4 times as fast as the current A100. Nvidia is working on reduced versions for China to overcome the sanctions. Many companies have implemented or are going to implement AI. Nvidia, many other AI chip companies, Microsoft and Google would profit.

Afterthought
My friend told me about ChatGPT and in a month Microsoft's stock appreciated by 15%; he did not buy the stock. My friend figures it wrongly that Google would be too late to dinner. Lessons follow. We need to check the impact of revolutionary products if we do not understand it (opposite to what many investors including Buffett preach). If the stock is rising, your order prices should not be too far from the current prices.

Links
China's EVU: https://www.youtube.com/watch?v=nWU6x-XHw9k
China's GPU: https://www.tomshardware.com/news/ai-and-tech-sovereignity-drive-number-of-gpu-developers-in-china
Losers: https://www.youtube.com/watch?v=3TxsVw5XWDs
Chip materials: https://www.youtube.com/watch?v=tjLEFXEbUws
AI stocks: https://www.youtube.com/watch?v=PWbEkenszec.

#Filler: Cooperation vs confrontation
Can music unite the world? I wish it could if we and the Chinese do not let our and their dumb nationalism cover our eyes. https://www.youtube.com/watch?v=gf6v59c5yuY

The song is "Hotel California", one of our best songs, being played by a Chinese girl named Moyun using a traditional Chinese instrument and is being enjoyed by the world audience.

5   Artificial Intelligence (AI)

I believe AI is at its infancy in 2023. It is a trend and it could be very profitable for the AI stocks. It is different from the internet in 2000, as many AI companies such as NVDA have profitable products. The AI companies can be divided into the following categories.

1. Hardware: NVDA (Nvidia), AMD (Advice Micro Devices, a distant second), MU (Micron for memory), TSMC (Taiwan Semiconductor Manufacturing Co. making chips), ASML (building chip fabs for TSMC), ARM, SMCI (Super Micro Computer Inc. suppling servers with liquid cooling), QCOM (phone chip) etc.
2. AI core: OpenAI (IPO soon), MSFT (Microsoft), GOOG (Google), etc.
3. Data center: GOOG, MSFT, AMZN (Amazon), etc.
4. Electricity companies: VST (Vistra Corp.), etc.
5. End-users: MSFT, GOOG, TSLA (Tesla), META, many corporations (such as drug companies), etc.

Apple should be classified in several categories when they have the phones with AI chips. So far, they are not too promising from the initial announcements.

I believe AI will benefit larger companies than the smaller ones. Many experts predict about 50% of the jobs would be replaced by AI eventually I predict AI will revolutionize drug discoveries and health care. I suggest using AI to predict the country's economy that is affected by the interest rate. My widest prediction: Replace the president with AI. Many of our leaders' decisions are based on buying votes, such as relaxing illegal immigrants for Hispanic votes, gun control, retirees, etc.

Some links on AI. Watch them with a grain of salt.
https://www.youtube.com/watch?v=ank2oncglfc
https://www.youtube.com/watch?v=OI0EjTd3PwY

Summary of AI investing performance

In 2023, you do not need to be an expert on AI to make money and I am a living example. It should include all my trading on AI stocks to my knowledge. The recent recommendations are not fundamentally sound to me. Hence, be cautious.

Stock	Buy Date	Performance	Remark
AMD	04/02/24	-14%	
AMD	05/13/24	2%	
AMZN	05/21/24	0%	
CEG	05/29/24	1%	See 3. Electric co.
DELL	04/10/24	12%	AI PC
DELL	05/01/24	14%	
GOOG	03/27/24	17%	
GOOG	05/23/24	1%	See 1
MSFT	02/14/23	64%	See 1
MSFT	02/21/23	74%	See 1
NVDA	07/21/23	194%	
NVDA	04/02/24	48%	
NVDA	12/15/22	1,206%	Sold in 2024
SMCI	12/15/22	1,133%	Sold in 2024
VST	04/12/24	22%	Electric co.
SMCI	12/15/22	900%	
SMCI	12/15/22	1067%	Sold in 2024
VST	03/26/24	17%	
MSFT	05/30/24	6%	
GOOG	2024	30%	See 2
META	06/16/24	0%	

1. Most likely it will be sold via Covered Call on 06/21/24.
2. It is harder to find the buy price from this broker. I guess it is in Feb., 2024.
3. Missed including this one initially. Performance is based on 6/21/24.

With traditional fundamental analysis, most AI stocks are over-priced. We need to consider the prospect and the recent gains such as quarter-to-quarter profit percentages. I have several trades on SMCI, but it is only one position. This time I targeted the trend of AI correctly, but not always the case.

Book 9: Insider Trading

1 Define Insider Trading

Investopedia defines it as:

"Insider trading can be illegal or legal depending on when the insider makes the trade: it is illegal when the material information is still nonpublic-- trading while having special knowledge is unfair to other investors who don't have access to such knowledge. Illegal insider trading therefore includes tipping others when you have any sort of nonpublic information. Directors are not the only ones who have the potential to be convicted of insider trading. People such as brokers and even family members can be guilty.

Insider trading is legal once the material information has been made public, at which time the insider has no direct advantage over other investors. The SEC, however, still requires all insiders to report all their transactions. So, as insiders have an insight into the workings of their company, it may be wise for an investor to look at these reports to see how insiders are legally trading their stock."

If you need more information, click this link from Wikipedia.
http://en.wikipedia.org/wiki/Insider_trading

My additions to conventional insider trading

Hopefully my additions improve the performance of this strategy that has already been proven to work most of the time.

- I add market timing to Insider Trading. You need to sell most stocks except contra ETFs before or during a market plunge and buy them back as indicated by the chart; I provide a simple marketing technique without charts.

- Diversify your portfolio. Keep 10 stocks for a portfolio less than a million. Ensure that there are not more than 3 stocks in the same sector. Keep 20 stocks for a portfolio over a million. Too many stocks would require more of your time that would be better spent in evaluating individual stocks. However, keeping too few stocks would impact your portfolio when one stock has a big loss.

It is just a recommendation. Vary your holding size and holding period according to your time, your portfolio size and your knowledge in investing.

- Stick with stocks over $2, average daily volume over 12,000 shares (8,000 for stock prices over $20) and market cap over 200 million.

  Most big winners usually are in the price range between the $2 and $15 price and market cap between 200 million to 800 million. They represent the stocks that institutional investors are ignoring due to their restrictions. This is just a general guideline and there are always exceptions. Change them according to your requirements.

  I prefer to skip stocks from most emerging countries, especially the smaller companies, as I do not trust their financial statements.

- Ignore the subscription services or books claiming they are making over 30% consistently. Some even have examples of making 5,000%. Most likely they tell you their winners but not their losers. It is easy to pick up winners that fit their strategies, but they do not tell you the real performance.

  Check whether their portfolio uses cash, as it cannot be manipulated such as using the best prices of the day to trade. I bet that most portfolios consistently making over 30% are not real. Alternatively, they have 10 portfolios, and they only show you the one that makes a good profit.

  When they back test their strategies, they cheat their performances with survivor bias (i.e., those bankrupt stocks are not in the historical database). If their returns are that great, do you think they will share their secrets with you?

  Many made great fortune, but lost it all on a bad bet. So, the turtle investors who make small profits consistently fare far better than making millions in a year and losing it all in the next year. Market timing and diversifying our portfolio are our tools and they will beat the market in the long run.

2   How to profit

My own monitor

The following is one of my performance monitors from the stocks I bought for over a period of 6 months.

All 372 stocks	77 stocks with Insiders' Purchases	Beat all stocks by
21%	28%	33%

This test was performed on 9/7/2013. They were the actual stocks I screened from the screens that had been proven. Insider Purchase is one of the fundamental metrics I monitored. The total number of stocks is 372 and 77 are identified as having heavy insider purchases. Stocks are bought in different periods. The returns are not annualized and dividends are not included. Most stocks have a holding period longer than 6 months.

If I started to collect data again, I would have used annualized returns and compared the returns to the market.

The test results are consistent with my previous tests. Beating all stocks by 33% is quite convincing. I conclude following insiders' purchases work most of the time at least in this period.

I conducted another test using the website OpenInsider on 11/2013. It listed all the insiders' purchases for more than a year. Selected insider purchases about 1 year ago by the Officer (CEO and CFO) only. I skipped the purchases that do not meet the requirements.

The annualized return is 50%. I only had about 50 stocks and it is not enough evidence to draw a conclusion. Even with 40% return, the strategy proves itself again.

My suggestion

Evaluate the purchased stocks again in 6 months. Sell the ones whose fundamental metrics have deteriorated or the price targets have been met.

Consider market timing. Sell most stocks when the chart indicates that the market is plunging.

Consider the total return. If you can wait for a month or so for less taxes on long-term capital gain, do so. If you expect that your stock does not appreciate a lot in the next few months, consider covered calls (similar to collecting rent with the renter's option to buy the housing unit at a specific price and time).

An example

Sometimes all experts are wrong on a stock except the insiders. Today (2/5/2015), GLUU is up by 23% with a good earnings report. It is 31% up since I bought it on 1/28/15, just 8 days ago. The annualized return must be astronomical.

I bought it based on the **favorable Insiders' Purchases** and confirmed by a good earnings rating (second best) from Zacks. Pow EY was 7% (passed), my short-term score 4 (failed), my long-term score 16 (just passed) and Pow Score 2 (just passed). The quarter-to-quarter profits and sales were spectacular at 200%.

The experts were wrong when I evaluated the stock: Safety Margin ridiculously negative, Blue Chip Growth C, Shorter 17%, Fidelity Equity Summary Score 4 (1 to 10 with 10 the best), ROE 3%, SMA %(10, 20 and 200 days) all negative (not good), IBD composite grade 33 (far below the average) and its SMD grade D.

Filler: How to fight terrorism?

It is interesting Poland has zero terrorist attacks so far and they refuse refugees. So is Japan.

Most of the countries that have most the terrorist attacks are those who welcome Middle East refugees. I like to help them, but we have to ensure we do not let terrorists in.

They are called terrorists by us or freedom fighters by their own citizens. We have bombed their cities so bad that most of them have no future. They cannot fight us back with their primitive weapons but using terrorism. Every action has a reaction. I hope the world would be a better one if we mind our own business.

3   Screen the Insiders' purchase.

Bring up OpenInsider.com
(http://www.openinsider.com/)

Source: OpenInsider
The following is for illustration purposes only. This screen is displayed on 11/19/2013.

If your screen is too small, bring up your PC's browser, and type:
http://ebmyth.blogspot.com/2013/12/insider-screen-for-profit-from-insider.html

Here is an illustration looking for candidates.

- Select the Officers only. Including the Director is the second choice.
- Ignore the transactions that have values less than $100,000. We only have PDII and MCBF. You should not have the same stocks on a different date. Select the stocks that have purchase values more than $100,000.
- Next bring up Finviz.com in your browser. Enter PDII and scroll all the way down to find the net purchase (= purchase amount − sold amount). For example, if the insiders bought $100,000 worth of stock and they sold $100,000 of your stock, it would not be considered as a purchase. There was no insider sell for PDII, so it is fine.
- Was the stock purchased close to the market price? From Finviz.com again, the purchase price was $5.25 and the current price is $5.29. So, it looks good.

Summary of selected criteria

The displayed screen does not have all the selection criteria as below.

- Select Officer only.
- Filing Date and Trade Date within the last 7 days.
- Transactions: Purchase only.
- Sorted by Value. Omit transactions less than $100,000 (adjust to the value you're comfortable with).

Skip the stocks if they are one of the following (change them to your own requirements).

- The purchase price is not close to the market price.
- Penny stocks (less than $2) or market cap less than 50 million. It is too risky to me, but it is your call.
- Stock daily volume less than 8,000 shares (I prefer 10,000).
- Poor fundamentals. If you do not have time to do a thorough analysis, use Fidelity's Equity Summary Score. GuruFocus.com (fee) has a nice evaluation with warning signs.
- If they are not listed in one of the three major exchanges.

My steps

Be flexible and use the tools you have.

1. Select the stocks with heavy insider trading. OpenInsider.com provides many features. Select Officers, Purchase Only, and Last 7 Trade Days and Last 7 File Days. Sorted by Trade Value.

   As an alternative, Finviz's screener using Insider Trans is easy to find these stocks.

2. Use Finviz.com. Understand the company and their fundamentals.

   If the stock cannot be found, most likely it is not traded here. Skip these companies and also the companies with small market caps and average daily volumes.

   Check the insider trade prices. If the trade prices are too low from the market prices, skip these stocks.

   Understand the company such as the country, the sector and general financial shape. I would skip most foreign countries especially from emerging countries and small companies as I do not trust their financial information.

   For safety, I would examine the fundamentals of the screened stocks.

   Skip the companies that have more than 5% appreciation in the last 5 days. We may have missed this boat, but there are many other boats.

3. Use OpenInsider.com again to list the 90 days transactions (all) for the stock. If the CEO sells 1,000 shares and buys back 1,000 shares, there is no insider purchase.

#Filler: My daughter's wedding

How to have a wedding banquet that the entire town will talk about and at the least cost? It is at the Burger King where they treat you like a king. All the fries are super-sized and the drinks are bottomless. The king's crown and the most popular party favor are included. For the reasons I do not understand, my daughter flatly refused.

4   Other Considerations

Do not bet the entire farm on any trade

We have a better chance to make money, but it is no guarantee as in everything else in life. To reduce the loss, we should evaluate the stock completely. Sometimes we still lose due to the reasons below.

- The insiders trick us to buy their company's stock.
- The stock has been manipulated.
- Even insiders make mistakes.
- The market is not rational.
- It takes the market longer to realize the potential value of the stock. In this case, hold on to the stock if it is fundamentally sound.
- The market plunges.
- Some unforeseeable event(s) happen.

Considerations

- Officers predict the stock prices better. OpenInsider.com gives us a choice on the classification of the purchasers. In addition, **ignore options exercised by the officers.**

- Consider the total value amount of the insiders' purchases. The value should be tied to the market cap. A small purchase for a small company is more significant than the same amount for a company with a market cap of several billions.

- **Compare the value to the purchase's annual salary.** If he or she bets more than his or her salary, the action is more significant.

- Any purchase by more than one officer is a good sign.

- Officers made small buys and then sold a big chunk several months later. It is called 'pump and sell'. We cannot detect it as the sell is in the future. That's why we have to evaluate the fundamentals of the company and do not bet the entire farm on a single purchase.

- Officers may make a purchase for the following reasons to jack up the price. These purchases should be ignored.

- o Most have a lot of stocks and options, so it is to their benefit to have their stock price stay high. It also explains why officers prefer stock buyback.

- o Prevent the company stock price to fall below a certain level that it would be delisted or would prevent analysts and fund managers from researching the stock.

- Watch out when the execution date (same as the trade date) and the announcement date. If it is too far apart, then it would not be a good indicator.

- Watch out for today's date. If they're too far away from the trade date, it may not be meaningful.

- Compare the number of shares purchased to the total number of shares the insider already has. If it is a very small percentage, the insider could use it to boost confidence and hence the stock price.

- Watch out for purchases after a disaster such as a bad earnings announcement. Executives are humans and they could believe wrongly that they have found the bottom value and/or they're overconfident in their own company.

- A good executive may not be a good trader and most cannot predict when the market plunges. That's why we have to watch out for market plunges.

- Most executives understand their companies and the sector their company is in. However, when they have too much confidence and love in their company, they could be biased and lose their reasoning. To illustrate that, everyone knew PCs would take over mini computers except the CEOs of the mini computer companies such as DEC and Wang. They're geniuses, but their minds had been covered by their egos, love, optimism, bias and overconfidence.

5   My trades based on insider purchase trading

Insiders' Purchases should be very positive for the appreciation of the stock. Who knows better than the insiders, the ones who run the business daily? However, I prefer sound fundamentals too. I use Finviz.com's screener on stocks that have "very positive insider transactions". The following are one test. The end date is 12/15. POZN has a wild swing.

Stock	Buy Date	Return	Annualized
POZN	05/08/15	-10%	-21%
LAKE	07/16/15	15%	55%
ABTL	07/16/15	21%	78%

Example: insider sales

On 2/22/2022, AMD dropped almost 8% to $116 ($113 by the end of the day). As in most tech stocks, AMD fell a lot from their heights recently. The Insider Sales is a good indicator to sell it earlier besides the poor fundamentals. The following are obtained from Finviz. The following is for educational purposes. I skip sales with a toal value below 1M. Also round up to 1 M for easy comprehension and round up sales price to one dollar. Gained %s are rough estimates.

Date	Share value in M	Sale price (in $)	Gained from $116
02/08/22	3.5	$122	5%
02/02/22	1.3	$130	12%
01/03/22	1.5	$151	30%
12/15/22	8.1	$133	15%
12/07/21	18.0	$144	25%
11/30/21	12.0	$162	40%
Avg.			21%

I went all the way to Feb. 24. 2021. There are no insider purchases, but all sales. The insiders are not always correct, but their trades are considerations to trades (sales in this case); ignore insiders' sales on small amounts. The insider's sales on 12/07/21 (better on 11/30/21) should trigger a sale for the owners of AMD.

Book 10: Penny stocks and micro caps

I do not recommend beginners buy penny stocks and micro-cap stocks unless you have connections or full understanding to these companies.

Most institution investors do not invest in penny stocks and micro-cap stocks as they could move them too much with their huge size of their investment on one stock. It opens the door to retail investors without their huge investment of their resources in researching these stocks. Many of these stocks have the stock prices less than $5 and the market caps less than 100M. Personally, it does not make a difference for buying $20,000 worth of a micro-cap stock or $20,000 worth of a blue chip. The only difference is the relationship between the risk and the reward (Reward/Risk). The second difference is the volatility and liquidity.

Today, many big companies used to be penny stocks, and they moved up to micro caps and even to large caps. Penny stocks are the most profitable but they are also the riskiest while micro caps are less profitable but also less risky. It is another example of "nothing risked, nothing gained". The investor could profit a lot when the big companies acquire these stocks, such a drug research company acquired by a blue-chip drug company. There are more acquisitions when the interest is low and/or the economy is improving. Microsoft has acquired many small companies with useful technologies that can be implemented with her own products.

They are not followed by institutional investors (fund managers, pension managers, and insurance companies). Once a long while the small retail investors pick up some real gems. Be warned that penny stocks are risky due to a lot of frauds (many do not have to followed SEC's rules), low volumes (easier to manipulated) and huge spreads (the price between buy and sell). The stop orders can be seen and easy to be manipulated due to low trade volume, especially during off hours. Be warned on the promotion of a microcap stock – it could be a "pump and dump".

You will be bombarded with many subscriptions making them millions with 1,000% or so returns. S/he may be trying to tell you the returns of Google, Amazon and so many of these stocks, but most likely they have not bought any of them. Even if they have bought some shares (so they can use it to advertise), they have bought a few shares, and/or they have not told you that many of the penny stocks they purchased have lost all or most of the values. If they really know some secrets to make big money, do you think s/he would share it with you?

Many brokers do not treat these stocks same as the other stocks such as higher commission rates and more restrictions. Many of them cannot be shorted and/or optioned. I do not recommend using stops as most of them fluctuated more than other stocks and they can be manipulated due to the low volumes.

These groups of stocks are different from the popular IPOs of companies such as Facebook. However, there are more companies that will fit into the most profitable category rather than the handful of big IPOs every year. I further classify this category into:

1. <u>Penny stocks</u>.
   They are stocks with prices less than $5 (with many exceptions) and are not listed in the three major stock exchanges in my own definition. They have fewer requirements from these minor or local exchanges (usually only their financial statements).

   This book usually ignores stocks less than $1 as they are far too risky. Don't buy their stocks unless you fully understand these companies.

   The majority of them described in this book are traded in <u>OTCBB</u> (OTC bulletin board) and <u>OTCQX</u> (OTC Markets Group. In addition, there are many others listed in local exchanges in both the US and foreign countries.

   Some penny stocks are also named pink sheets (with symbol names ending with '.PK'). They are very risky as the filing requirements are almost none. The inter-listed pink sheets in their own countries such as Canada and Japan could be high quality, and some provide the same information as our large caps in their own country.

2. <u>Micro caps</u>.
   These are stocks with prices ranging from $1 to $20, with a market cap between 50 and 300 million and the majority of them are listed in the three major exchanges (a good sign). This is my definition.

   Some stocks are in the gray area. I bought ALU at $1 and it had a market cap of 1 B at the time. I still consider it a micro-cap stock however for my purpose as a potential turnaround candidate.

First, practice your market timing. When the market is plunging, do not buy any stock as most stocks fall. In the early recovery, a phase of the market cycle defined by me, most stocks rise, especially the beaten down, value stocks and the potential candidates to be acquired by larger companies.

There are about 30,000 stocks including smaller and foreign exchanges. How can you find the winners?

Use one of the simple screens that are available to you free from many websites such as Finviz.com or the one from your broker to find a handful of stocks. The filter criteria could be "P/E < 5 and E> 0", "Sales Growth by 20%" or a combination. We include 'market cap > 50 and < 300' for micro caps. If the screens consistently find you winners, they are good. However, it can be more complicated than that.

A strategy consists of buying stocks and selling stocks. Screening finds a small number of stocks according to our criteria. We still have to evaluate each of them in more detail. We also have to set our criteria as to when to sell the owned stocks.

When you learn, practice and verify all these topics described in this book, the chance of success is far, far better than buying stocks without these disciplines. Avoid tips and recommendations from the media. Most likely they are not very useful by the time they reach you.

Penny stocks are harder to evaluate than micro caps. You may not be able to find any articles on them. You need to use their website to understand the company and their financial information. Most likely you buy it due to your personal contact with its management and/or employees you may know.

Links
Penny Stocks   http://en.wikipedia.org/wiki/Penny_stocks
Micro Cap   http://en.wikipedia.org/wiki/Microcap_stock
OTCBB   http://en.wikipedia.org/wiki/OTC_Bulletin_Board
OTCQX   http://en.wikipedia.org/wiki/Pink_Sheets_LLC

#Fillers Airplane mode
You should move your mobile phone far away from your bed to reduce radiation exposure. Using airplane mode would save your battery and less radiation exposure. In addition, you cut down notifications.

End of the church?
If the Church paid all the claims on the lawsuits for the lawsuits on the sex offends, there would be the end of the church.

1 My micro-cap performance

The strategies described here have been used in my book titled "Best Stocks 2014, According to Me". From 12/16/13 (the publish date) to 3/4/14, the list of all 135 selected stocks beat SPY by 103% and the list of 9 small cap stocks as you see below beat the SPY by almost 500%.

From 12/16/13 to 3/29/14 (today), the performances of the entire list of 9 small micro-cap stocks (RAS is not a micro-cap by my definition) are:

Stock	Market Cap (M)[1]	Annualized Return
ARTX	52	234%
CPSS	176	6%
RAS	602	-19%
GST	329	83%
EVC	515	65%
LEE	171	293%
SGU	313	16%
HILL	166	491%
MNTG	147	12%
Average		131%
SPY		22%[2]
Beat SPY by		496%

[1] As of 12/16/13
[2] Annualized return

Disclaimer

Past performance does not guarantee future performance. I believe both the micro-cap and the market could have reached their temporary peaks by 4/2014. Please know that these stocks have not been tested in a down market.

2   Penny stocks

They are risky as many of them do not have information as required by the SEC and the major exchanges. They are traded over the counter, OTC. They cannot be shorted (and most likely you do not want to do so even if it were allowed). Pier 1, Ford and many others were all penny stocks at one time.

Expect one winner for several losers; 1 winner for every 4 losers if I have to guess the ratio. However, the total profit could outpace the total loss if the strategy is properly implemented. The purpose of this book is to improve your odds of making a profit. Do not expect to be rich overnight.

You can buy 5000 shares at 1 cent each or one share of Apple in May 2013. When this penny stock moves up to 2 cents, you make 100%. This is not the reason to invest in penny stocks but it shows that they're very volatile. You may have a hard time trying to sell a penny stock as the average volume is very low.

Here are some good candidates.

- Established foreign companies such as Nestle and Sharp as of this writing. They want to avoid the expensive legal procedures and filing information periodically. Most are listed as pink sheets and they are not as risky as the other penny stocks.

- Fallen angels. They have been delisted due to low performance and /or the stock price falling below $1 (sometimes below $5). When they work around their problems, the stock prices may appreciate many times over. Most head to bankruptcy.

- Companies with new products such as a new technology or a new drug. They are moving up from development to the market phase of the product cycle. They may be acquired by larger companies. A recent example is the e-cigarette companies facing competition from the newly legalized drugs and/or the banning of e-cigarettes.

- New companies with quality products and/or technology. The business section of your local newspaper may have these candidates such as Aereo. Their products will most likely be challenged by the larger companies such as cable companies.

- Some could be hidden gems as no analysts have been following them. Talking about under value, I have seen one company with free cash more than its market cap!

- A money losing company could be a gem if it is developing a new technology or a new drug. Big companies such as Microsoft, Apple, and Google are consistently looking for this type of company to acquire.

Avoid the following stocks.

- Stocks that are set up as fraudulent companies. There are many small companies (foreign companies in particular) that are set up for this purpose. Even the well-established and well-funded companies fall into the trap from time to time. If they cannot spot these companies with all their resources, how can the retail investors spot them?

- Stocks with 25% or higher ownership by the owner and / or the family. Most never sell and never buy the stocks they own. There are exceptions and they are easily spotted by their fundamental metrics. For example, when a company's cash reserve is higher than its entire market cap and/or the P/Es is ridiculously low, evaluate it.

    Ensure the owners do not use it as their piggy bank for borrowing money, high compensation and/or granting options. When they do not have an independent board of directors, they can do whatever they want.

- Low volume stocks. It means you have to pay more to sell the stocks (i.e., the high spread between the ask price and the bid price).

    In addition, it is far easier to manipulate low-volume and/or low-priced stocks than large caps.

- "Pump-and-dump" strategy used by manipulators via mass email, radio/TV and news articles. The first ones may make money but the majority would lose their shirts. The 'tips' are the traps in disguise and the 'make believe' stories are bigger traps.

    As your mother would tell you, if it is too good to be true, most likely it is not.

If it is that good, why don't they act on it themselves and share this money-making idea with you, a stranger, at no charge? There is no free lunch!

- A company is running out of cash and/or heading to bankruptcy. A bargain price is no bargain.

You need to spend time to separate out the gems from garbage and fraudulent companies particularly in penny stocks. Some 'fundamentally sound' companies could be frauds as their financial statements can be manipulated.

Understand the company and its management. Call the company's investor relations department if they have one and they are willing to answer your phone call. Ask for their most updated financial statements and the prospectus of the company. Due to my limited time and a lot of stocks to evaluate, I have not done so myself.

Finding and evaluating penny stocks

Some penny stocks can only be discovered from friends or local newspapers. You should visit the company and/or talk to their investor relations person.

Besides the finance, ask how they use the capitalization and how the products/services stack up with the competition and their competitive edges. Investigate their managers' resumes and their history. Even ask how many years they have been in the current positions.

Check out whether the company files with the SEC from their website, a state regulator, or a business regulator such as a bank.

Summary on how to reduce risk in penny stocks

- Unless you have personal contact with the company which is not an established large foreign company, do not buy its stock.

- Even if they provide financial data, be careful as to whether they have been manipulated legally or illegally.

- Watch out for 'pump and dump'. These are quite common. Read the articles from the web carefully and ignore all your junk mails on promotions of any stock. If they are too good to be true, the writers will profit by buying the stock themselves. These days I see fewer junk mails of this kind than I had in the past.

- Avoid low-volume (with average daily volume less than 10,000 shares) and/or low-cap companies (with a market cap less than 50 million).

- Ensure the CEO is not using his company as an ATM.

- Some of the trading techniques are not applicable for penny stocks due to the low volume and high volatility. They are stop order (turning into market orders), market order, analyst coverage, selling short, day trading and options.

   Most of these companies do not make money initially and they do not pay dividends; they need to plow back the cash into their development / research. You need to consider whether the company has a niche in the market from its unique products and/or is following the market trend.

   The burn rate of the company and its ability to pay back loans are important. If the company burns 50% of its available cash, it can survive for two years just as an example. Most of these companies are under-capitalized.

   Many technical indicators may not work. The price and the volume of a stock can be easily manipulated to show a false uptrend.

Links
Scanning penny stocks:
https://www.youtube.com/watch?v=7iZpWmwBhel

Filler: The ideal program

I'm writing a program named IYBID (in your best interest, dummy) making all government decisions and to include twitting. It will be born and made in the USA.

3   Micro caps

I enjoy micro caps (stocks between 50M to 300M according to the SEC) more than penny stocks as they're less risky. When they're listed in one of the three major exchanges, we have a lot of info from the required filings of these companies. The tools to track other stocks can be applied to these stocks too. However, you may have a hard time finding articles on these stocks.

When these stocks move up to mid cap and even large cap, it could mean huge appreciation. Eventually and hopefully, they will be included in one of the indexes, and this would boost up the stock prices automatically, as some ETFs are required to buy them.

#Filler: Tips

When you trade 5 times or more a week, investigate whether you're eligible to trade as a business by the current tax rule. A business allows its owner to deduct business expenses.

If you create a trading plan on when and how to trade and then monitor your trades periodically, you would likely become more disciplined and a better investor.

Monitor your trades. You may need to take a breather or switch to paper trading if you have a few losses in a row. Paper trading would be useful and it serves as part of the education.

You should keep a trading log or journal to review what you may or have done wrong, and then learn from that. This may be part of the tuition for trading and there are always lessons to learn. This book can help you to reduce errors but there is no substitution for actual experiences with real money.

Technical analysis (a.k.a. charts) may not be good for penny stocks as their trade volumes are usually low. However, using charts for market timing is fine.

Be careful when using a historical database to test screens / strategies. Penny stocks have more of a chance for survivorship bias. If you have two stocks, one down to zero and one up by 100%, your total return of these 2 stocks should be zero. It could be 100% up if the database took out the losing stock. It means you never find this losing stock in your test as it is not in your database.

4 Hints

Here are some hints in searching penny and micro stocks. Some stocks may not be available from Finviz.com, which provides a screener.

Exchange. Do not exclude exchanges for penny stocks as they may be listed in local exchanges.

Stock price. It should be under $5 for penny stocks and under $15 for micro stocks.

Ensure there is enough volume and enough floating shares. I prefer not to trade small, foreign stocks as they may not have good regulations.

Most of them do not have good fundamentals: high debt/equity, high cash/share, and pay dividends and have high debt/equity. Avoid companies when the insiders are dumping their own stocks.

When they recover or finish new, profitable products, their stock prices would rocket. The signs are: insiders buying, high SMA-50 (simple moving average), better ratio comparing the current P/E to the 5-year average and positive price /free cash flow.

I expect one stock winner out of five stocks for micro stocks and worse for penny stocks. However, the winner could cover the other losses.

You should limit your losses using stop orders and protect your profits using trailing stops (renew the stops using current prices periodically).

Summary

Microcap stocks have more regulations and usually higher volume than penny stocks. I prefer microcap stocks.

Profit and risk

Penny stocks have the highest profit potential, but they are also the riskiest compared to microcap stocks. It depends on your own risk tolerance when selecting which category you want to trade.

I recommend paper trade and gradually move up to a larger percent of your portfolio. Expect your money to be tied up for a long time due to the low volatility in both volume and price. Be emotionally detached.

Do not put more than 5% of your portfolio on one stock. Unless you understand the company thoroughly and the fundamentals are very sound, making a fast 50% profit in a micro-cap stock is better than making 200% in penny stocks that have a chance of losing all value.

There are many different definitions of penny stocks. To me, usually they are stocks less than $5 and they are traded under the OTC-BB and/or named pink sheets. Exceptions abound. Refer to Wikipedia and Investopedia for their general definitions.

How to start

Open an account with your broker. Some have restrictions and/or higher commissions for penny stocks. Some provide paper trading so it is good for beginners to try this without risking their money. Paper trading for penny stocks sometimes is misleading due to the low volumes. Most provide limited or no research to penny stocks and micro caps.

When to buy
When the market is plunging, do not buy any stock (actually you should sell most of your stock holdings, especially small caps). Some small caps may not recover. Buy them back when the market is recovering as most will increase their values at a faster rate.

What to buy
Do not depend on your buy decisions on tips, emails and mail. Most are 'pump-and-dump' type of schemes. Do not listen to your brokers who have very high commissions and incentives to sell you penny stocks as illustrated in the movie Wolf of Wall Street.

Also avoid bankrupting companies (usually they have a Q at the end of their symbol). They are still listed for now. When some emerge from bankruptcy, most likely they will issue new shares and the old ones usually have 0 value.

However, if the blueprint of the company is workable for recovery and/or the company has enough assets including patented technology, customer base, and valuable inventory for example, they may have a chance to turn around in the future.

IPOs of small companies that have great products / services are promising candidates. Spend time in evaluating the products, the company's business plan, qualifications of employees and the track record of the management team. They are risky but it could bring huge profits. 2015 was not a good profit year in buying IPO stocks, but the previous two years were.

Most penny stocks have limited information from the web such as from Seeking Alpha. You may want to check out the company's website that would include financial statements, product descriptions and hopefully their business model.

Financial statements indicate how the company did in the last quarter and last year. Check out the date of the statement.

There are often few write-ups on penny stocks and most microcap stocks. Furthermore, you should not depend on the financial statements of penny stocks. You must know the company inside out. Call the company's investor relationship department or visit the local company if it is close to you.

Check out any warnings from the SEC from its website.

Here are some positive developments. The official of a small company explained that during a recession, the company did not expand their marketing effort, but expanded in the research department.

Besides the profit and its valuation (P/E), the products are the most important. Are they competitive in the current market? Even so, it cannot tell you whether they're competitive in the near future.

Check out their business models. Some do not make sense such as most internet companies were during its bubble era in 2000.

Intangible events that are not usually included in the financial statements are: potential lawsuits, expiration or the trial results of a drug, quitting of a major employee and losing a key customer.

Avoid developing countries especially with their small companies. Even if their financial statements look good, they may be frauds as I have learned the same lesson the hard way many times.

Diversifying is more important with penny and microcap stocks. Allocate no more than 5% (less in a falling market) of your portfolio on these stocks.

I prefer to hold 10 penny and microcap stocks instead of one. For taxable accounts, sell losers within a year to offset any short-term gains.

Use Stock Level 2 Quotes to show you how many buy orders and sell orders are lined up. Avoid stocks with few buy orders. In many cases, there is a market maker controlling the tempo and direction of a particular stock. Charts (Candlestick recommended) also show the price and volume. It requires you to spend more time on looking at the evolving charts.
http://www.investopedia.com/articles/trading/06/level2quotes.asp

What and when to sell
You may want to set up a target price and a price to protect from further losses. Limit Loss orders available from most brokers does not guarantee the execution of the order. Stop Loss guarantees the execution, but the market order may be at the low price of the spread. Stop loss orders may not work as the spread is too wide for low volume stocks.

Some stocks skyrocket, and some even move up to major exchanges. Patience could pay off big time. I prefer to sell at a 25% loss and adjust the loss according to the current price (not the initial price you paid for). There is no bullet-proof strategy.

Conclusion
Penny stocks are the riskiest but the most profitable stocks. Personally, I prefer micro caps that are more regulated. Monitor your strategy and adjust it accordingly. If you're doing far better in penny stocks than micro caps, stick with penny stocks, and vice versa.

Book 11: Momentum investing

Introduction

This strategy provides me with steady income by working an hour or two every week. How long will it last? I do not know. I will describe the concept here, so you can devise your own to fit your risk tolerance and requirements.

As of this writing, this strategy is having amazing returns to me. Though these returns may not be sustainable, my convictions are so strong that I am boldly increasing my investment. When the market is trending up, this strategy is very profitable particularly if the stocks are in the rising sectors. When the market is trending down, find the worst stocks and short them.

The concept of a momentum strategy

Each week, I buy about 5 stocks based on the momentum metrics and sell them within a month. I do not use the fundamental metrics a lot, as that will not be effective in such a short duration. From my current record, the average holding time is about 20 days.

The details of my strategy will not be disclosed fully but the concept is. When a strategy is used too often, it will not be effective and would end up churning the same stocks for all its followers. However, let me elaborate on the implementation of this momentum strategy and give you some ideas on how to build one for yourself.

My Theory. When a stock is on the uptrend, most likely it will continue for at least for a week or two. Do not buy stocks when the market is risky. Protect yourself by using stops and / or using technical indicators such as SMA-20 (Simple Moving Average).

Subscription services

I spent less than half an hour finding about 6 stocks to buy. My choice is helped by subscription services. Some have earnings revision information (particularly useful during earnings seasons) and most others have provided timing grades. I include the insider purchase information and short-term technical indicators. It works so far and I constantly monitor the performance.

For starters, use simple screens and procedures to find stocks without getting a subscription service. Paper trade your screens and strategies to include your average holding period and money management before you commit to use real money.

Common parameters

I subscribe to several investment services and select their recommendations. From my recent reviews, I only need a good subscription with a historical database plus the free Fidelity, Yahoo!Finance and Finviz. Most of these sites provide a timing ranking. The rank for value should take a back seat in momentum stocks.

To illustrate, the composite rank for timing in Blue Chip Growth (not free any more) is the Quantitative Score. It is also known as the buying pressure. Fidelity provides similar rankings.

http://navelliergrowth.investorplace.com/bluechip/password/index.php?plocation=%2Fbluechip%2F.

There are several common parameters on how they rank stocks. These parameters may be obtained from Finviz.com.

- Price momentum. I prefer to use SMA20% (20-day simple moving average). The higher the percentage, the better. However, they should not be too high (say greater than 15%). When it is peaking, the stock may fall.

- Change of short %. Favorable if it is over 25% (for short squeezes) and unfavorable if it is moving up (say from 5% to 15%). You need to keep track of the previous short percentages for the stocks you follow.

- Sales momentum (Sales Q/Q) and earnings momentum (EPS Q/Q or quarter earnings to quarter prior year). The higher, the better.

- Earnings revisions. Zacks (free for a single stock) has good info based on their estimates and rumors.

- Insider's Purchase. No one knows the company better than its officers. You can find the Insider Transaction from Finviz.

- Analysts' recommendation. It can be obtained from Finviz.com. However, Fidelity's Equity Summary Score provides a better one and it is based on the past performances of the analysts' predictions.

- Most momentum stocks are either in technology / pharmacy or formula sectors such as Walmart using the same formula in opening stores. Many of them no longer qualify as momentum stocks when they grow too big and/or their markets are fully exploited; most of them pay dividends.

- I usually keep them for a month. However, some big winners continue even after three months. To protect your portfolio, use stop orders (trailing stops are preferred); I prefer 20% as these stocks are usually more volatile.

- Aggressive investors can sell short on stocks having negative momentum.

Reduce Taxes

I use my Roth accounts to minimize my taxes. There are many tax advantages of a Roth account. The second choice is other retirement accounts. I converted some of my Rollover IRA to my Roth as allowed. Consult your tax lawyer or CPS for updated information about your individual situations.

Reduce losses during market downfall

My strategy works best in the up market as I seldom short stocks. However, a major market downfall could wipe out all profits for years. In 2019, I was shorting stocks more often as the market was risky.

These are two Technical Analysis tools to anticipate a market downfall. Minimize losses once a downfall of the market has been spotted.

- Do not buy any stock.

- Sell any existing positions and/or use stops to reduce further losses.

- Aggressive investors should buy contra ETFs such as DOG, SH and PSQ (against the corresponding indexes DOW, the S&P 500 and NASDAQ) when the market is too risky. It is like buying insurance (hedging your portfolio). However, do not be the entire farm.
- Be disciplined. Most likely, your strategy should be profitable despite its ups and downs of the market especially in the long run.
- Be emotionally detached. As of 4/2013, my average annualized return of 66 round-trip trades was 127%. It is so far so good, but it will not be sustainable in the longer run. I do expect some losses.
- Take a break from time to time. I have stopped this strategy for a while due to the risky market and taking a long vacation.

Monitor performance

I constantly monitor my metrics and my screens for performance. I am always looking at perfecting better systems and /or adapting to the current market conditions.

- Day of the week.
  Monday is not a good day to find stocks. Most of my subscriptions do not update their information on weekends, and the prices are the same as last Friday. I try not to trade on Fridays as I hate to leave unexecuted orders over the weekend.

- Reduce the number of stocks.
  Usually, I have an average of eight stocks for further analysis each time, and I select the five stocks or less after evaluation.

- Listen to the experts.
  If all the timing grades from different subscription services are high for a specific stock, the appreciation potential of this stock should be high

- Maximize profit.
  If this strategy proves itself and the market is not risky, I'll increase my position and vice versa.

- Improve performance and reduce risk.
  I have found that about 10% of the gains were due to good timing. If the purchased stock appreciates more than my target price, I sell it right away. My average holding period in this period is about 20 days and the gain is about 3% (the annualized return is huge due to the short average duration).

  From my limited data so far, holding stocks for 20 days gives them better performance rather than holding them longer than 60 days.

- Calculating the rate of return.
  I prefer the annualized rate of return for a better comparison. However, I would skip using those performances from trades with the holding period less than five days. I also compare my return to the return of S&P 500 on the same holding

  The better rate to calculate the rate of return is: Total Profit / Total Investment. We have cash between trades. It is too time-consuming for most.

- Money management.

In a rising market, usually too much idle cash (due to taking profits) would decrease the performance of the portfolio and vice versa in a falling market.

In a falling or risky market, limit your stock holding exposure to market risk. Instead of holding the stocks for a month, try to sell them in a week or two, and increase your cash position. You need cash to buy stocks when the market returns.

- If you do not use market orders, try to place the order price as close as the last executed price in the market. I usually submit orders after 10 am; they call the first hour (9:30 am to 10:30 am in NYC) the amateur hour for a good reason.

- My purchase prices are usually about a little less (.2%) than the market prices and sometimes even lower especially when the market is trending downward.

  When the stock is trending up, there is a good chance my purchase order is not executed. I summed up the potential profits lost and the money I saved from the discounts in my purchase prices. It turns out they even like each other. In several instances, the stocks just rocket upwards. If I cannot buy the stock after 4 or so hours, I should switch the buy order to market order.

- I prefer to beat the market by a smaller margin but more consistently.

- Using a trading plan makes it a discipline and avoids emotional influences.

Recent (4/2016) examples

Recently there were two coaster-roller stocks: Fitbits and GPro. Both stock prices surged through the roof and crashed down. Using the "Buy High and Sell Higher" strategy should have made you some money if you protected your profit via trailing stops.

The momentum is caused by the publicity and the public who follow the trend blindly. The fundamentals of both companies when they were rising, they did not justify the prices. It is like buying a hot dog cart in NYC for a million dollars. Of course, you will sell a lot of hot dogs as long as you do not have another hot dog cart next to your cart. However, your investment may never be recouped. In addition, both are single-product companies; it would be very risky when there is competition. Apple is one for Fitbits and I bet many Chinese companies are making products similar to GPro's. GPro's products could be a fad, or they may fall into a limited, specialized market.

Ignore fundamentals for momentum stocks. Ride on the bandwagon and jump off when the trend reverses.

Afterthoughts
There are several SA articles on similar topic, click here, here and here. The links are:
http://seekingalpha.com/article/1336291-does-momentum-investing-actually-work?v=1365785958&source=tracking_notify
http://seekingalpha.com/article/865091-how-price-momentum-and-bull-markets-go-together?source=kizur
http://seekingalpha.com/article/1350651-seeking-alpha-momentum-investing-with-etfs
Day trading: https://www.youtube.com/watch?v=n6pGuJxYiXQ

#Filler
Percentage wise, my momentum investing has been most profitable so far. I classify this strategy into 3 sub strategies depending on the average durations.

1   My momentum performance

The following includes all the actual transactions from September, 2013 to Dec., 2013 in my momentum portfolio. "Lot Date" is the day I evaluate what stocks to buy. Some stocks are bought on different days after the evaluation and some are not bought. I am not responsible for any errors in preparing the following tables.

Lot Date	Stock	Buy Date	Days	Ann. %
09/04/13	BOFI	09/04/13	6	(175%)
	GMCR	09/04/13	14	110%
	Z	09/04/13	6	40%
	FB	09/05/13	8	419%
	AFOP	09/04/13	6	353%
	EGAN	09/04/13	5	194%
	PB	09/06/13	10	78%
09/11/13	ARWR	09/12/13	12	136%
	CATM	09/13/13	4	136%
	GILD	09/13/13	6	157%
	YELP	09/11/13	6	242%
	TRN	09/13/13	32	24%
09/24/13	AFOP	09/26/13	22	(105%)
	DRYS	09/24/13	81	15%
	PACB	09/28/13	20	(258%)
10/02/13	ZLC	10/02/13	14	293%
	FB	10/02/13	15	20%
10/05/13	DYAX	10/08/13	16	(109%)
	FSS	10/08/13	31	160%
10/18/13	GERN	10/18/13	21	1176%
	ALGN	10/22/13	48	(22%)
	COBZ	10/22/13	62	108%
	WAL	10/18/13	21	103%
	LCI	10/22/13	10	434%
	AKRX	10/31/13	15	334%
	BREW	11/01/13	7	194%
	BCEI	10/22/13	10	434%
	RAD	10/22/13	41	142%
11/05/13	LCC merged	11/06/13	3	639%
	TRN	11/08/13	63	41%
	CIR	11/05/13	43	21%
11/12/13	LCI	11/12/13	38	138%
	TRN	11/12/13	3	785%
	UBNT	11/12/13	3	1461%
	LCC	11/12/13	61	20%
	FCN	11/12/13	38	(12%)
11/19/13	FOE	11/19/13	35	(6%)
	NUVA	12/11/13	9	93%
11/25/13	GTN	12/03/13	3	1289%
	CRY	11/26/13	49	39%

	ARC	11/26/13	24	(85%)
	BONT	12/20/13	25	(344%)
12/03/13	AIRM	12/03/13	17	44%
	FIX	12/03/13	20	(97%)
12/10/13	MDXG	12/19/13	8	1162%
	MPAA	12/16/13	7	(7%)
	LBMH	12/14/13	6	627%
	UVE	12/11/13	12	48%
	USAK	12/10/13	13	(18%)
	ARC	12/10/13	13	(144%)
	CONN	12/12/13	11	55%
	REI	12/10/13	10	192%
		Biggest loss		(344%)
		Average		200%

My best profitable month

All the stocks purchased have been sold. Some stocks were bought twice in another account and they may have been at different prices/holding durations. Stopped this strategy in 2019 due to the risky market, but will return when the market is less risky. In 2019, I switched to shorting stocks. Jan., 2014 was one of my best months then.

Lot Date	Stock	Buy Date	Days	Ann. %
01/14/14	LCI	01/14/14	30	85%
	ENDP	01/16/14	42	140%
	LCI	01/14/14	38	208%
	NSTG	01/14/14	56	36%
	BABY	01/26/14	35	156%
	NSTG	01/14/14	59	34%
	ZNGX	01/21/14	31	133%
01/22/14	ANIP	01/22/14	29	195%
	KS	01/22/14	33	115%
	CHIP	01/22/14	19	246%
	SLXP	01/22/14	33	77%
	GMCR	01/22/14	20	743%
		Biggest loss		34%
		Average		181%

Explanation

- Lot Date. I usually group the stocks I buy by weeks. When I have losses two times in a row, I would buy fewer stocks or even skip purchase altogether.
  I try to maintain a total balance for this portfolio. I would buy fewer stocks when the balance is close to this threshold. As of 3/15/14, the market is too risky (plunging or peaking), and hence I would not buy any momentum stocks. When the market falls, these momentum stocks will fall faster and steeper than the rest of the market.

- I started this momentum portfolio far earlier, but I only recorded it recently. I took a long summer break in 2013 and resumed it in September, 2013 (the start date of the first table).
  There are some positions not sold after Dec., 2013. Anyway, I have enough data for illustration purposes. Most likely, the reason for showing any 'unclosed' positions is due to housekeeping errors, not trying to present a better result than what may appear.
- I did not include the stocks that have not been bought due to my lower buy prices and/or not meeting my criteria of what to buy. When any of my subscription services tells me the stock is not a buy, I skip it. A few times, some recommended stocks just skyrocketed in prices in the open. I did not buy most if not all of these stocks.
- I've averaged the returns for the above tables. The first table has a 200% annualized return while the second one has 181%.
  However, the actual profit of this portfolio is far better in the second table – most likely due to some larger position sizes. The higher annualized return in the first table is due to shorter durations. In my actual monitor, I ignore the returns if they are less than five days, as they distort the returns.
- The actual performance should be worse due to not considering the idle cash. I also excluded the contra ETFs to hedge the portfolio. In 2013, the hedging was a losing game in a rising market. Dividends were not considered in calculating the returns.
- The better way is to compare the performances with the S&P 500 index, which is too time-consuming for me.
- My holding period is short. With many exceptions, I sell these stocks within a month or they have appreciated a lot.
- You can have a portfolio for momentum stocks and another one for value stocks.
- MTUM an ETF for momentum stocks. COWZ is an ETF for cash cows.

From my book series "Best Stocks", the performances of my recommended momentum stocks.

Book	Stocks	Return	Ann.	Beat RSP by
Best stocks to buy for 2022	5	99%	4%	4,475%
Best Stocks to buy as of July, 2021	2	12%	137%	265%
Best Stocks for 2021 2nd Edition	7	-3%	35%	-170%

The details can be found in the following link.
http://tonyp4idea.blogspot.com/2022/12/best-stocks-series.html

2 Five strategies for momentum

We have 3 strategies according to the different holding periods. The screen parameters (i.e., selection criteria) are briefly described here. Adjust them to fit your risk tolerance and requirements. Monitor them from time to time as the market always changes. Finviz does not provide most metrics for Strategy #4. Strategy #5 is a combination of the first 3 strategies and will be described separately.

Metric	Strategy #1	Strategy #2	Strategy #3	Strategy #4
Avg. holding period	< 30 days	60 days	90 days	30 to 90 days
General				
Market Cap	300 M – 2 B	300 M – 2B	2B – 10B	> 200
Avg. volume	>100K	>200K	> 300 K	> 80.000
Analyst Rec[1]	Buy or better	Buy or better	Buy or better	
Country	USA	USA	USA	USA
Price	>$5	>$10	>$10	>$1
Insider Purchases	Positive	Positive	Positive	Positive
Fundamental				
P/E	>0	>0	>0	
Forward P/E	>0	>0	>0	
Return on Equity		>10%	>10%	
EPS Growth next year		>15%	>10%	>20%
Sales Growth rate				5%
Technical				
Performance	Week up	Week up	Week up	
SMA-20%	> 5%			
SMA-50%	> 0%	>2%		>SMA-200%
SMA-200%	>0%	>0%	>0%	

[1] I usually do not care about fundamentals for momentum stocks.

In addition, they should be in one of the 3 major exchanges: NYSEX, NASDAQ and AMEX (Finviz.com allows you to select one exchange at a time).

In general, Strategy #1 does not care about fundamentals. Strategy #2 is a typical sector rotation candidate. Strategy #3 cares more about fundamentals.

I recommend paper trading your strategy using different selection criteria. When you are comfortable, commit a small amount of cash and increase your portfolio size gradually.

Vendors

Most services charge a fee. However, many free sites provide momentum (same as timing) score. Most have a score (same as rank and grade) for timing. Usually, they are based on the momentum of the price. If the price jumps very fast and high, this score is high. Use stops to protect your profits. When the price is below a set price (such as 10% from your purchase price), use a market order to sell it. When the timing score is the highest, be very cautious as it cannot go any higher, or a peak is close.

Example

Here is an example of how to find the momentum stocks for your portfolio.

Bring up Finviz.com. Select Screener. Select 20-Day Simple Moving Average above 20%. Sort the screened stocks with this parameter. Today I have about 100 stocks.

Limit your selection to fit your requirements and preferences. Here are some sample criteria: U.S. companies only, capital cap over 100 M, price over $2 and relative volume over 1. Ignore ETFs.

Check whether the screened stocks are peaking (say they have appreciated over 100%) and/or overbought (RSI(14) > 65). Check the reasons for recent surges and evaluate whether the momentum would continue or not. Check out any insider purchases at prices close to market prices.

Strategy #5

This is a variation of the described in the first three strategies. I explain it with a step-by-step approach in implementing it using Finviz.com. Bring it up by typing Finviz.com in your browser. In addition, super stocks usually are small stocks by market cap with small float and high volatility (high beta that can be found in Finviz). Strategy #5: Buy stocks whose SMA-5 is higher than SMA-20 and exit otherwise.

1. Only buy momentum stocks when the market is not risky. When the tide is up, all ships will flow up. Check out my market timing technique. In the simplest way, enter SPY (or any ETF that simulates the market) in Finviz.com. If SMA-20%, SMA-50% and SMA-200% are all positive, most likely the market is not risky. 20% is more important than the other two.
2. Screen. The following are my preferred metrics and you can change them to suit your requirements and risk tolerance.

   From the Descriptive tab, Select Small (300M to 2B) for Market Cap, Over 100K for Average Volume, Over 2 for Relative Volume, USA for Country and Over $5 for Price. Repeat it for other ranges such as 100M to 4B in the Market Cap. For 100 M market cap, use over $1 for Price; increase the price for larger market cap such as using 'over $2' for 200 M market cap.
3. From Fundamental tab, select Positive in Insider Transaction.
4. From Technical tab, select 10% above SMA-50 in SMA-20 (Simple Moving Average for the last 20 days) and 20% above 200-SMA in SMA-50. If you have too many stocks, reduce the 10% to 8% or less. Change the selection if they are not desirable for you and/or the current market conditions.

   As of 11/07/2016, I have the following 4 stocks: AAOI, BOOT, LC and NILE. They already had good price increases.
5. Click on the selected stocks one by one such as AAOI. From most other metrics, it is not a value stock. The Forward P/E is 16. Hence, it has some value despite the high P/E of 80. All SMA%s are positive which indicate it is trending up.
6. After you bought the stock, use stop loss to limit any losses especially in this risky market. Conservative investors should stay away from risky markets. I would set a 15% stop loss (i.e., sell it via a market order when it loses 15%).
7. Most likely you will not or cannot buy a stock via a discount price when the stock is trending up.
8. Save the screen with a name such as Momentum, so you do not have to reenter the metrics again.
9. Finviz does not provide a historical database. You can run the test every week (or monthly) and write down the results. Only invest with real money when you're comfortable with your tests. If your expected maximum loss is 50%, double your portfolio size as the money you can afford to lose.
10. Making 55% profitable trades could be very profitable.

11. There are many variations and parameters to this strategy such as RSI(14), Double Bottom in Pattern and New High in 52-Week High/Low.
12. If your purchased stock is moving up, review it every month (preferable every week) and set up a trailing stop. To illustrate, when it is up by 20%, set the stop at the current price (not the price you paid for the stock).
13. From a trader guru: 1. Test and select the strategy suitable for your personality and risk tolerance. 2. Learn from mistakes. 3. Select and buy from the best stocks, vice versa for shorting. 4. Protect your loss and let profits rise. 5. Diversify. 6. Reevaluate the strategy and the acquired stocks. 7. Consider the business cycle and the market cycle. 8. Stocks with prices between 1 to 10 are better for trading as most analysts do not follow them.

Link: Swing: https://www.youtube.com/watch?v=C9EQkA7uVU8
Momentum: https://www.youtube.com/watch?v=PpUlOyZrl9

#Filler: Joke on Jokes

A church-goer told me that my jokes were not funny in front of many of my friends. My readers including fund managers, business owners and professionals told me otherwise. My conclusion is that you need an education to understand my jokes, so I do not blame her. An open mind helps but it is not required.

As defined by me, the anatomy of a joke is something that is unusual unless you're 10-year-old or younger. It has one or all of the criteria below.

- Ridiculously exaggerated.

- Body (female and male) parts we do not discuss/show normally unless you have something extraordinary.

- Words with double meaning.

So, about 30% of the jokes are about sex. If you do not believe me, turn on the cable TV tonight, count and classify the jokes.

# 3	Herd theory

When the herd makes money, they think they're a genius. The last one to leave the herd will be the fool of all fools such as the last holders of Lehman Brothers, AIG, Bear Stearns, internet stocks in 2000, etc. The biggest fools are the 'value' buyers when these companies were plunging fast. When a specific stock looked great yesterday and it lost 50% today, it 'must' be super good to some. Wrong! Check out why it plunged. It could be missing some important metric, or something is really wrong with the company that did not show up in the research.

The real genius is the one who makes money all the way up, but leaves before the bubble bursts. Even a genius cannot predict the peak and the bottom, but I'll call him/her a genius if s/he is right better than 60% of the time.

Recently dividend growth stocks have the highest premium in the last 30 years. It is a mild bubble when we've many retired, or retiring folks seeking income. However, the bubble will burst when the interest rates rise. At that time, the long-term bonds with low yields will lose.

Dividend stocks will benefit when the interest rates are low. Bond holders would move to dividend stocks from their low-yield bonds. Long-term bonds lose their value when the interest rates rise, and vice versa.

It is the same for the internet bubble in 2000. I did unload most of my tech funds in early April, 2000. The more I read during that time, the more I got scared. It was partly luck and partly 'genius' to move all these sector funds to traditional industries. At that time, they did not have contra ETFs, so cash, money market funds and bonds would be the best choices.

Filler
Had you responded to the pandemic, which was confirmed on Feb., 2020? If you do, you should have shorted stocks on airline, cruise line and related sectors, or at least bought contra ETS (the market returned after the big dip due to the excessive printing of money). After the excessive printing of money, we would have bought ETFs related to gold such as GLD and RING.

4   Characteristics of momentum trading

- Usually the beta (from Finviz) is higher than 1 (the average). The higher the price fluctuation, the better for momentum stocks.

- Market caps of most momentum stocks are higher than 1B. Institutional investors move the market. However, many of my big gainers are smaller stocks; it could be due to my small bet positions.

- The 4 phases of a stock: neglect, growing, peaking and plunging. Buy at the 'growing' phase. In the 'neglect' stage, you may spot bargains, but the stock would stay in this stage for a long while. Most of the time, the stock fluctuates around 200-SMA. When the volume is high in trending up and low in pullbacks, this stock may be in stage 2, a buying opportunity.

- Do not be afraid of the daily surge of the price. Sometimes, you have to pay close to the market price for a rising stock.

- Do not sell your winners too early. Watch out for exceptions and use stops or trailing stops to protect your portfolio.

- Sell in phase 3 with the characteristics: price below 200-SMA (from Finviz), Volume higher in a losing day and lower in a profiting day and large loss after earnings announcement.

- Do not listen and follow the financial news. A lot of time, the news has been fabricated to serve the purpose of the analysts.

- From my experience, many times the insiders are wrong. Most likely they do not study the trend as described in this book.

- Do the exact opposite for shorting stocks.

5 Good News/Bad News

This is a version of the "Buy high, sell higher" strategy. It responds to the news. Hence, it is faster and it could complete the trade in a few days or even a day.

If you started on the day Trump announced the tariff and lasted today (4/2018), you should make some good money. You buy SPY (or similar ETF) when there is bad news and sell (and buy contra ETFs for more speculative traders) when there is good news such as China's announcement on negotiating trade retaliation.

You should adjust the strategy to your individual risk tolerance. In any case, use trailing stops to protect losses. To illustrate, buy SPY when it is 1% down and double the bet when it is 2% down.

This strategy will not work when there is a defined trend such as heading to a market crash. As always, practice the strategy not with real money until you're comfortable.

Recent news
When it happens, have you prepared yourself to take advantage of the situation? Aggressive investors can short stocks and/or ETFs specific to the situation.

- Pandemic. Actions: Sell casino stocks (esp. those in Macau), airlines, hotels, restaurants and stocks related to traveling. Buy related drug companies related to vaccines, cures and test kits.
- Trade war and delisting of China stocks. Actions: Sell Chinese stocks; I did not and I was guilty as charged. Buy when they hit bottoms (hard to detect). I bought BABA recently. Is it bottom or on its way further down (due to delisting)? Only time can tell.
- Ukraine war. Actions: Buy gold, silver and energy stocks. Consider Russia's supply of nickel and its impact on electric car production.
- Market fluctuation and mostly down. Buy when the market is down and sell when the market is up for a volatile market. If it is confirmed to be down (detected via market timing such as death cross), sell most stocks.

6   Business news

Business news affects the momentum of stocks and sectors. We can get daily business news from many sources. Seeking Alpha's "Wall Street Breakfast" and "Trending News" are free. The following news are also available: "Latest News" in Market Watch, Bloomberg's "Bloomberg Opinion Today" Barron's "Premarket Screener", and many others. Several websites identify stocks with recent high trade volume.

Evaluate the news. I prefer to skip the news from TV and the 'gurus' who may have their own agendas. To illustrate, the tension in the Middle East, would lead to the surge of oil price and gold price. There are many other examples such as pandemic affecting the cruise and airline sectors. Evaluate the mentioned stocks and/or related sector fundamentally and technically.

ChatGPT is an obvious innovation that will affect everything. Microsoft's stock price rose about 12% (annualized 145%) from Jan. 17, 2022 to today (Feb. 15. 2022). It is even more if it was bought a month or two earlier.

Timing is everything. Most of the time, the news is old and we may miss the opportunity. Many times we may be too ahead. In this case, I would invest about 25% of the average position and then add gradually if the news is affecting the stock or sector profitably.

Use stop orders to protect your trades. You should make good money in the long run by cutting losses early and let your winners rise. Use trailing stops for profitable stocks. Also, do not use stops for small stocks and/or stocks with low volumes to prevent manipulation.

7   Missing opportunities

We all have missed many trading opportunities. We learn and do not miss them in the future. Here are some recent examples. It seems we still profit after a few days when it happens. However, not all news can translate to profits.

- ASML. With the trade war with China, I noticed this company and it is the only company that produces high-end chips for Apple and Huawei. I did not take any action. The annualized return from 1/3/2020 to 1/3/2022 is 84% (SPY is 24%).
- FXI, an ETF for Chinese stocks. I believe in the long run Chinese stocks would do well. However, with the trade war and the possible delisting of many Chinese companies, we should stay away and the annualized return from the above period is -8% (SPY is 24%). I owned this loser.
- BABA, Alibaba. When the P/E was less than 3 on 3/15/21 and was less than $100 per share. I did buy some. Update: As of 4/1/2022, it is over $100 per share.
- MRNA, Moderna with the vaccines for this pandemic. The return from 1/3/2020 to 1/3/2022 is 1,144% (SPY is 24%) or 571% annualized. It is having wide rides with daily fluctuations of more than 5% many times. I did buy some shares. Pfizer did not perform well, as they did not own the intelligent property of the vaccine.
- Ukraine. Tesla could be affected by the supply of Russia's nickel for the battery. The price of the commodity of nickel has been skyrocketing. I did buy an aluminum company (AA) about 1 year ago due to inflation considerations. It was one of my best performers so far.

Ukraine's economy is being ruined, so is Russia and our corporations in Russia such as McDonald's and Visa. The U.S. farm companies and natural gas companies may make good profits by exporting them to Europe. The economies in EU will suffer from the expensive energy imported from places other than Russia. The status of our reserve currency is being shaken. China could gain a lot if there is no sanction for helping Russia. As of 3/2022, India is a winner with the cheap oil import from Russia.

8   Ukraine impact

We need to wear two hats: one for humanity and one for investing. My first hat does not like wars and the second one likes wars or prepares for wars as an investor. They are contractionary. If you feel guilty, donate your loot (from investing) to charities specific for your clause for humanity.

"2/12/2022" is one of my best days in investing. S&P 500 was down by 1.9% and I was up by 1.2% in my on-line statement of my main broker. It is a difference of 3.1%. I did not trade the markets according to the supply of metals such as nickel that affects electric car productions. As an investor, I hope it happens more often. Also, I closed some of my shorts with better prices in another broker account. The performance is due to several factors.

•	Contra ETFs. It is a bright day, but most are still losing. Lesson: Only buy contra ETFs when the market timing indicator (such as the Death Cross and the Golden Cross) indicates so.

•	Gold and silver. They are used to hedge inflation. Wars usually trigger the rise. Even without wars, I recommend investing about 5 to 10% in these commodities. I had almost total losses of OIL (an ETF) but good gains on USO.

•	Oil and energy stocks. I have been accumulating many oil stocks recently. My screens told me they were good buys. In this case, Forward P/E is a better metric than P/E.

•	Most of my recent stocks selected were based on value, and they have been doing better than the market. I have none (from my memory) of those high-flying tech stocks such as Facebook. Earnings of many global companies will suffer from global economies especially those who have to with draw their operations in Russia; if it happens to them in China, there will lead to huge losses.

•	With the war dragging on, hyperinflation will continue, especially in energy and food. Many poor in developing countries have been suffering most.

Everyone should have a plan. Investing is a guessing game, and do not expect that it always works to your expectation. I am not liable for your actions. Consult your investing advisor before you invest.

Winners and losers. The U.S. will gain a lot at least initially. The EU would side with us. The EU will import more expensive oil and gas from us instead of from Russia; the Nord Stream II would have financial problems. Our defense industry sector would gain a lot of sales. Inflation starting with oil prices would be another problem for us. Our USD should appreciate when some money from Europe flows to USD. However, many countries including China that are not friendly with us may dump USD and our US treasuries. Hence, our USD as a reserve currency will be shaken.

Floods of refugees would be another headache for the EU; currently most went to Poland. Russian currency has lost about 30% in the first week. Many lives have been lost and many have been suffering in Ukraine.

China is a winner if there will not be a sanction on China for helping Russia. Russia will increase trade with China for no other better options. Taiwan should be afraid, as there is no major military help to Ukraine in case of invasion from China. We have driven Russia closer to China, shaken USD's status as a reserve currency, sped up inflation and deteriorated our relationships with many countries including EU.

By March, 1, 2022, the war seemed like it would drag on. Here are what ETFs we should buy from the date and the performances one month later.

Symbol	Description	1 M	3 M	6 M	9 M
		4/1/22	6/1/22	9/1/22	12/1/22
DBA	Agriculture	1%	2%	-5%	-7%
FXE	Contra Euro	-1%	-5%	-11%	-6%
GLD	Gold	2%	-5%	-13%	-8%
PPA	Aero + Defense	-1%	-6%	-8%	3%
UNG	US Natural Gas	24%	84%	97%	29%
USO	US Oil	3%	19%	-1%	-2%
XLE	Energy	8%	24%	10%	27%
Average		5%	16%	10%	5%
SPY		5%	-5%	-8%	-5%

I cannot find an ETF dedicated to defense. You can buy a basket of defense stocks and ignore the airline stocks that can be found in PPA. We can also short an ETF on the EU rather than shorting the Euro (using FXE in this portfolio just for convenience). The first month performs the same as SPY (the market to most), and hence you can start the portfolio a month later.

From the above, besides LNG, USO and XLE, all other ETFs turn negative after 6 months. Using trailing stops could let you exit from losing money. You can also use market timing (Death Cross) for ETFs to exit. However, even if you stay in the above portfolio for 9 months, you still beat SPY by a good margin.

9   Momentum stock basic

My grandson asked me to help him in a stock competition for a duration of 3 months. In order to win, select the least number of stocks (1 is fine if allowed) and the riskiest stocks. In this way, you have a high chance of winning but lose no real money. It is not a good lesson in real life. Here is my recommendation.

First, screen stocks (using Finviz.com) for NASDAQ exchange, SMA20% (Simple Moving Average for the last 20 sessions) > 0 and Forward P/E is positive. Better candidates are:

- SMA20% > SMA50%. The current trend is better than before.
- Insider Transactions > 0.
- Insider Ownership < 30%.
- Short float% < 10.

Book 12: Dividend investing

This strategy is expected to be popular for the next 10 years or until the average CD rate beats the average dividend rate. We have a lot of retirees who depend on income from investments. The low interest rates from CDs and bonds drive these folks to dividend stocks.

Here is a simple screen to find these stocks. First find the stocks that have dividend rates more than 2% (about half of all S&P 500 stocks). Take out those sectors that give dividends as a return of equity (REITs and many partnerships). Eliminate the stocks with bad fundamentals such as high expected P/E (and earnings is negative), high debt (compared to companies in the same sector), etc. Next ensure that they have a good history of maintaining or increasing dividends (i.e., dividend growth).

As of 5-2014, it has been working well for the last five years. Be cautious on bank stocks, the drug companies, the miners and the insurers. I ignore foreign companies and ADRs (those foreign companies listed in the U.S. exchange). I prefer larger companies.

However, when a strategy is overused, it may not work any longer. There may be a mild bubble on these dividend stocks due to too many followers. We will discuss how to protect our dividend portfolios.

In addition, we should not buy (actually should sell most stocks you own) stocks during a market plunge. Since 2000, we have had two market plunges with an average loss of over 45%. We hope to have a maximum loss of 25% instead of 45%; most techniques depend on price movements and hence we cannot detect the peaks and bottoms. There are at least three variations on dividends:

1. Dividends given to stock owners (registered on and before the **ex-div date**).
2. Covered Calls. You can receive dividends while 'renting' your stocks.
3. DRIPs, Dividend Reinvest Plan.
   http://en.wikipedia.org/wiki/Dividend_reinvestment_plan

1 The basics

Basic ratios for dividend stocks

- **Ex-dividend date**

You will be eligible for dividends if you have your stock on the record. You want to buy the stock earlier, or on ex-dividend date in order to receive the dividend.

- **Payout Ratio**

It is the dividend / profit. Too high a ratio may not be good as the company does not plow back the profit into research / development. Most mature companies have higher payout ratios as they do not need to plow back into research / development compared to high-tech companies.

The other option of using the company's cash is in a stock buyback that would increase the stock values in theory.

> Earnings per share = Earnings / Outstanding Shares.

When 'Earnings' is fixed but Outstanding Shares are reduced, the ratio looks good deceptively. The management does this often as it would boost the values of their options.

- **Dividend Yield.**

It is equal to Dividend / Price.

Why companies pay dividends

Companies can use the profit by plowing back cash into research / development, buying back its stocks, acquiring companies and/or giving dividends to the stockholders. In theory, the company should consider the option most beneficial to the average stockholder. In practice, the management tries to benefit themselves by choosing the option best to appreciate their stocks and hence the stock options they own.

My additions to conventional dividend investing

Hopefully my additions would improve the performance of this strategy.

- I add market timing to dividend investing. You need to sell most stocks before a market plunge and buy them back as indicated by the market timing indicator.

- Diversify your portfolio. Keep 10 stocks for a portfolio of less than a million dollars. Ensure no more than 3 stocks are in the same sector. Keep 20 stocks for a portfolio over a million dollars. Holding too many stocks would require more of your time that would be better spent in evaluating individual stocks. Holding too few stocks would impact your portfolio when one stock has a big loss.

    It is just my recommendation. Vary your holding size, your portfolio size and your knowledge in investing.

- Stick with stocks with a stock price over $2, an average daily volume of over 10,000 shares (8,000 for stock prices over $20) and a market cap over 200 million.

    Most big winners usually are in the price range of between $2 and $15 price and a market cap of between 200 million and 800 million. They represent the stocks that institutional investors are ignoring due to their restrictions. This is just a general guideline. Change them according to your requirements.

    I prefer to skip stocks of most emerging countries, especially the smaller companies as I do not trust their financial statements.

- Ignore the subscription services or books claiming that they make over 30% consistently. Some even have examples of making 5,000%. Most likely they tell you about the winners but not their losers.

    Check whether their portfolio uses cash or not. Most likely those portfolios that consistently make over 30% are not real.

    Alternatively, they have 10 portfolios and they may only show you the one that makes a good profit. They could use the most favorable trades for the day for their virtual account. For example, the stock rose 20% late in the day and they claimed that they bought it on the open hour.

    When they back test their strategies, they can cheat on their performances with survivor bias (i.e., those bankrupted stocks are not in the historical database). If their returns are that great, do you think they really want to share their secrets with a stranger like you?

Some made a big fortune and lost it all. So, the turtle investors who make small profits consistently win. Market timing and diversifying our portfolios help us win consistently in the long run.

Besides screening dividend stocks yourself, there are many sites providing this information. You can google 'dividend stocks'. The following are some of them.

TopYields
http://www.topyields.nl/Top-dividend-yields-of-Dividend-Aristocrats.php

An ETF on Dividend Aristocrats
http://etfdb.com/index/sp-high-yield-dividend-aristocrats-index/

From Wikipedia on S&P Dividend Aristocrats
http://en.wikipedia.org/wiki/THE S&P_500_Dividend_Aristocrats
There are many sites to screen dividend stocks. I select Finviz.com as that should give us good results most of the time and it is free. In addition, we use the same site for market timing using SMA-20% and SMA-50%.

Screening is only the first step. You need to filter out the good stocks from the bad ones. When you have a handful of stocks, evaluate each one.

Links Building a portfolio: https://www.youtube.com/watch?v=ryN1aQxSefQ

Best dividend ETF: https://www.youtube.com/watch?v=TPSw7On2gUo

https://www.youtube.com/watch?v=YBCmJU8osOo
https://www.youtube.com/watch?v=8B6WqiGhfvU

Filler.
DRIP stands for dividend reinvestment plan. It uses the dividend to buy more stock of the company that pays the dividend automatically, and most likely with no commissions and some gives discounts of 2-3%.

I have participated in these plans before. After a long while, the stocks bought from dividends were worth more than the initial stock prices. You need to keep track of the cost basis of the purchased stocks when you sell these stocks.

2   More on dividend stocks

- Check out the tax rate for dividends and the tax rate for your tax bracket with a qualified professional and act accordingly.

- It makes sense to evaluate more carefully the stocks with the top 25 dividend yield stocks. If the yield is that good, they could have some problems. It also could be yesterday's darlings. Try the next 25 according to an article I read. You need to further analyze each stock especially on the fundamentals. Ensure the high-dividend yields are not due to the return of capital as in some REITs and partnerships; it could be the reason why the top 25 dividend yield stocks do not perform.

- Use CCC charts by David Fish.
  http://dripinvesting.org/tools/tools.asp

- A good article on dividend stocks.
  (http://seekingalpha.com/article/1591272-the-7-habits-of-highly-effective-dividend-growth-investors?source=kizur)

- Check their payout ratios. When the company plows back most of its profit to dividends, the company will not grow as much. Many mature companies are fine in doing this. I prefer a payout ratio between 50-70%.

- Be careful in the last quarter such as in 2012 in identifying dividend and dividend growth stocks. It is a period when companies pay extra dividends expecting higher tax rates for their stockholders next year.

  REITs must pay out 90% of their earnings to maintain their REIT status. Their dividends are taxed as ordinary income.

- Buffett on dividends.
  (http://kinderflow.blogspot.com/2013/08/dividends-warren-buffett.html)

- Buy the companies that have a lot of cash and pay little or no dividends. There is a good chance these companies will pay dividends, or increase their dividends and the stock prices would usually appreciate.

- As of 7/2013, corporations had a lot of cash with low debt comparatively. Coupled with low interest rates and a weak economy, corporations increase their dividends and buy back their own stocks.

- Here is a site to grade dividend stocks.
  http://navelliergrowth.investorplace.com/dividend-grader/

- A successful story on dividend investing.
  http://finance.yahoo.com/news/heres-janitor-amassed-8m-fortune-234459317.html

- Here is another set of criteria for dividend stocks.

    - Dividend yield over 2.5% (or at least .5% above the average of dividend yield of all the S&P 500 stocks).
    - Dividend growth for the last 5 years is zero or higher.
    - Profit growth is positive for the last 5 years.
    - Dividend payout is under 70%.
    - P/E under 25 and earnings is positive.
    - ROE is over 8%.

    If you do not find too many of these stocks, the dividend stocks may be overbought.

- There are many other sources for income besides dividends:

    - You can sell some shares. Be sure to check out the tax consequences.
    - Buy bonds. Long-term bonds are favorable when the interest rates are high. Check the S&P bond rating. Forget the bonds rated BBB and below.
    - REITs and energy royalty trusts. Many require you to file extra forms if they are in taxable accounts.

Links

Building a portfolio: https://www.youtube.com/watch?v=ryN1aQxSefQ

https://www.youtube.com/watch?v=q3IG95iWwTU

Dividend ETFs: https://www.youtube.com/watch?v=64NEiyoNBIM

3   Potential problems

When a strategy is overused, it creates a bubble. The only exception is the gold rush in 2010 due to printing too much money and gold had been down for a long time. When the shoe shine boy told a famous Wall Street investor that he was buying stocks that smart investors unloaded everything. He knew the boy did not do any research and it was the [herd](#) mentality.

When Sarah Cohen told the TV reporter that she was into dividend stocks, she seemed to be the shoe shine boy except she was prettier and she had a lot of skills but not in investing.

When the massive money flows into ETFs specialized in dividend stocks, it is a mild bubble. History tells us that the average retail investor always selects the wrong side of the market. So far, Fidelity's money fund flow has been a good contrary indicator for the market.

Past performance does not guarantee future performance unless the market conditions are the same, but it seldom happens. There are many examples such as the 2000's internet bust. Investing in dividend stocks today (2015) is still a mild bubble by many standards. Dividend stocks perform better than the market but not by a large amount. When the financial companies such as Lehman Brothers, AIG and Bear Sterns are included, dividend stocks do not perform that well.

Today there are several articles on how dividend stocks are overvalued. The premium on dividend stocks has been the highest in the last 30 years.

Consider Total Return

Total Return = Appreciation + Dividend + Covered Call (if used) - Taxes – Inflation

The institutional investors drive the market. They consider their total return. Appreciation is usually more favorable than dividend for most of their wealthy investors tax-wise in most cases.

You do not have to realize the gains (for tax purposes) on capital gains in taxable accounts. When you die, the cost basis will be stepped up. In a

word, you have more control with capital gains but not with dividends. Check the current low-tax laws.
(http://en.wikipedia.org/wiki/Dividend_tax#United_States).

Afterthoughts

- Check the dividend performances and switch when they do not perform.
  http://seekingalpha.com/data/dividends
- Myths.
  http://money.usnews.com/money/blogs/the-smarter-mutual-fund-investor/2014/02/04/7-myths-about-dividend-paying-stocks
- From YouTube, Dividend stocks, dividend ETF
  https://www.youtube.com/watch?v=4kTnAJzp94k
  https://www.youtube.com/watch?v=OwLbsIWgcBs
- SA article in 2016.
  http://seekingalpha.com/article/3901726-fate-49-dividend-aristocrats-early-1990s-may-give-nightmares

Filler

I got a call from Buffett asking me to lead their stock research.
I asked him why for a nobody such as myself. No kidding.

He told me that he should have read my book Scoring Stocks to buy Apple instead of IBM in May, 2013. It would save his company millions of dollars minus $10 for my book. Not to mention the market timing technique that had worked in the last two major market plunges.

I told him, "OK, I'll beat your mediocre returns of the last 5 years."
He said, "You can do better than that and at least beat SPY. If you do so, no one will be that stupid to leave my fund and pay the hefty capital gain taxes."

I told him, "I cannot beat the market as you are the market especially after your expensive fees. In addition, I do not know how to avoid day traders from riding my wagon in trading. Also, most of my big profits were made in small stocks that your fund cannot trade besides owning the company."

I woke up trembling. I'm glad it is only a nightmare.

4   Dividend growth

This strategy seemed to be working fine for a long time. It is partly due to the low interest rates. Retirees cannot depend on the bonds for income, so they switch to stocks that pay good dividends.

In 2015, we have to pay a premium for stocks paying high dividends. When will it end? You can examine the performance of any ETF such as DVY that specializes on high-dividend stocks for the last month and the previous three months. When they performed worse than SPY (an ETF simulating the S&P 500 stocks), most likely this mild bubble would burst soon. On 9/2015, they are not doing well as a group.

A list of dividend ETFs. http://www.dividend.com/dividend-etfs/

Filler

Quantitative Easing is supposed to stimulate the economy, create jobs and increase inflation. As of 3-2015, it has not for most countries including the U.S.

The money has not been passed to the small businesses that generate the most jobs; we should let the SBA assign the loans. Large businesses use most of the cheap money to generate products / services to increase supply and hence deflation is the norm. Stock buybacks do not generate the value as illustrated by my PE (modified from the current P/E).

My PE = (Price – Cash + Debt) / Expected Earnings
         all expressed in per share

It is better but more work to use "Net Current Asset" instead of Cash.

The big banks lend money to investors and that explains why the stock market is booming and we have record-high margin debt. It also widens the wealth gap generating inequality conflicts.

5   Are dividend stocks better?

There are continuous debates for and against dividend stocks / dividend growth stocks. I hope this article will settle the debates. If you're making money with any strategy recently, stick with it. From my test, I conclude that dividend stocks / dividend growth stocks are worse off than non-dividend stocks. Please read it with an open mind if you are a dividend lover.

Do not be biased and data fit to back up your conclusions. Ensure the test can be reproduced with identical results, and there is no cherry picking and no bias. Ensure the number of stocks and the number of tests are large enough so the results are statistically acceptable.

Here is my test procedure. It would be a sample test procedure that can be deplored for other strategies.

A test consists of selecting a number of stocks according to a specific criterion such as the 30 stocks giving top dividends. The performance of the test is defined as the average return of the specific number of stocks (30 in my test) after a period of time (a year in my test).

- I have four tests: Dividend Stocks, Dividend Growth Stocks, Non-Dividend Stocks and All Stocks. Select the top 30 stocks for each test.
- There are 10 tests for each month within each test. The first test starts at the beginning of the year and will end at the end of the year. The results of the 10 tests are averaged.
- The last ten years resemble the current market better than older dates do.
- The start date was Jan. 2 as Jan. 1 is a holiday. In some tests, it is Jan. 3 or Jan. 4 due to weekends.
- The results are annualized (= Return * 365 /No. of days tested).
- The database is S&P 500. Typically, they are the stocks of the largest companies. 'All Stocks' consists of all stocks in the S&P 500 and it is supposed to be 500.
- Using educated estimates, I add 2% dividend yield to the performance of the S&P 500 index, 5% to dividend stocks and 4% to dividend growth stocks.
  Testing other strategies, dividends may not be as important as these tests. Alternatively, I could use ^SP500TR from Yahoo!Finance. I calculated and tested estimates. It would be very time consuming and

impossible not to use estimates as the dividend yield changes every trade session.
- Dividend growth stocks have the top dividend yields and dividend growth rates equal to or greater than 10%.
- Non-dividend stocks are stocks without dividends. Just select 30 of the non-dividend stocks in the index randomly.
- You can find performance reports on dividend ETFs or funds that specialize in dividend stocks, dividend growth stocks or a combination. Compare the results to SPY. Use them to confirm or challenge my test results.

My test has a new set of 30 stocks every year, so an exceedingly good or bad year only affects one test, not all ten tests with the exception of some stocks moving up or down for many years.

I call it the window of testing as opposed to what most funds advertise by setting $10,000 or so and letting it rise and fall for a long period (say 10 years).
- Be careful on tests using small stocks that tend to bankrupt more often. We have several large companies bankrupt and most paid good dividends. Survivor bias would give them better results than the actual results.

Result

The above tests can be reproduced from a historical database. I prefer to use a database that does not take out the delisted stocks. The result is for educational purposes only. I am not responsible for any errors.

	Avg. One-Year Return	Beat All Stocks by
Dividend	10%	-1%
Dividend Growth	9%	-12%
No Dividend	16%	62%
All Stocks	10%	N/A

- From the above table, both dividend stocks and dividend growth stocks do not beat All Stocks in this database.
- Non-dividend stocks beat All Stocks in this database by a sizable margin. They represent the companies plowing back their profits into development/research and/or buyback instead of giving dividends. I was surprised by the huge return.

- You should change your tests according to what you normally do to reflect new trading. For example, you may select 3 stocks only instead of 30 and/or delete foreign countries. However, it would be cherry picking.
- If your dividend strategy has a better return than the SPY, do not change your strategy. My tests here are simple without many other filters. Most likely you can improve your returns with better ROE, low Price /Cash Flow and low Debt/Equity.
- An article (3/1/16) from MarketWatch indicated a different finding than mine; I checked it out and DVY (a dividend ETF) did not perform that well.

Improve the test if more time is available
- Use 12 months instead of one month for each test. Hence you should have 120 tests less 11 tests due to not enough data for the last year (as of 2/15/2016).
- Take out the top performer and the bottom performer in the 30 selected stocks as judging in some sports.
- More weight in the last five years than the previous five years.

Survivor bias
My historical database does not handle the delisted stocks. When I see that there are less than 500 stocks in the database for the S&P 500, I know they just deleted the stocks taken out from the &P 500 that year. However, later on it includes new stocks added to the S&P 500 index. The adverse impact of bankrupt stocks is far higher than the acquired / merged stocks. For example, the return of the test not including Lehman Brothers makes it look far better. All the tests here look better than they actually are.

The bias can be reduced or even eliminated by:
- Larger companies as in this test. Small companies tend to go bankrupt more often.
- I use "All Stocks", which consists of all the S&P 500 stocks.
- The dividend stocks should have less survivor bias than non-dividend stocks. I did not compensate for this in my test results.
- Actually, resolve the bias by including the delisted stocks if your database does not do this. You need to keep track of the delisted stocks.

A simple test
Compare DVY, a dividend ETF to SPY. Add 3% to DVY and 2% to SPY to include the estimated dividends. From the following table, 2015 was bad

for dividend stocks but the performance for the last five years is about the same as SPY.

	Avg. Ann. DVY	SPY
2015	-2%	1%
1/2011-12/31/15	13%	14%

#Fillers: I wish I have a time machine

After collecting bottles for money, an old lady ordered a bowl of plain rice and ate by herself. I wish I could have ordered a meat dish for her and I was 'ashamed' of being generous.

A well-dressed gentleman offered his just-bought hamburger to a beggar. The beggar refused and asked for money instead – most likely he needed the money to buy liquor. A tale of two citizens.

During a lunch with my fellow tourists, a beautiful girl danced for our entertainment. I did not offer her anything and it had been bothering me for years.

During college, my housemates asked me to apply for food stamps. I had used only a few stamps then as I did not cook. I feel ashamed as this is my only time to collect social welfare.

We have regrets in life and we can only bring them to our graves.

#Filler:

Teach the able welfare recipients how to fish instead of giving them fish for the rest of their lives. They will not work if you take out their welfare benefits for working.

Filler: Definitions of 'ism'

Capitalism is: You do not work, you die.
Communism is: Everyone is paid the same, so there is no incentive to work harder.
Socialism: As Margaret said, when we have nothing more to give, we all go hungry like the USA is going to.
Idealism: There is no such word in reality. It only exists in our dreams. However, many treat this as it is a reality as they're still dreaming.
Feudalism. Like the Tibetan monks in the 50s. Only the monks can learn and the rest are slaves.

6   Passive income

The major problem of dividend stocks is most of them are in mature industries, and very seldom their stock prices appreciate faster than the market. I also prefer the lower treatment of long-term capital gains.

When the dividend rates are exceptional high, find out the reason why. Besides stocks with high dividends, there are many ETFs that give you passive incomes:

REITs. REITs invest in real estate. However, you do not buy houses and manage these properties yourself. Instead, it is similar to a mutual fund. As of 2022, I do not recommend malls (due to on-line retailing) and corporate offices (many working at home). The current SEC's regulation requires REITs to distribute 90% of the profit to the investors.

Corporate bonds. You can buy ETFs or mutual funds on corporate bonds. I prefer investment-grade corporate bonds over junk corporate bonds, especially when the market is risky and/or heading to a market crash. Bonds usually depreciate when the interest rates hike – the reason the newly-issued bonds have better interest rate.

Links
REIT. https://www.investopedia.com/articles/04/030304.asp
Best dividend ETF: https://www.youtube.com/watch?v=TPSw7On2gUo

#Filler: Only in California

I was robbed of $1,000. Surprisingly the robber gave me back $50 and helped me to call the police. There is no charge for any crimes under $950, so the police can concentrate on more 'serious' crimes. The law must be passed by the lobbyists for the criminals. You need to spend money in order to make money.

Book 13: Technical Analysis (TA)

Technical analysis (TA) is the analysis of the price movements and the short-term trend and possible reversal, while fundamental analysis focuses on metrics such as price/earnings ratio and debts. TA assumes the future stock price behavior can be determined by the patterns of past price behavior – it is true more times than untrue. Traders use TA a lot and can profit by shorting stocks. Investors can use them to find the entry points and exit points and some investors only buy stocks with a positive long-term trend (using SMA-200%).

Many times stock analysis based on fundamentals fails when the evaluation is solely based on fundamentals. Technical Analysis (TA) has the following characteristics:

- Most of the time, TA is profitable in the short term (less than 3 months). The weather man is more accurate in tomorrow's weather rather than a month away. TA can also signal the reversals.
- There are too many signals if you have more than three TA parameters. To start, use SMA (Simple Moving Average) and RSI(14); both are available in Finviz.com without charting.
- You can combine TA with fundamentals such as a rising SMA50 with increasing Insider Purchases. In addition, you can use more than one TA indicator.
- For market timing, TA is a huge part, but many fundamentals should be considered too. You can use similar techniques to time the market and time stocks and/or sectors such as Golden Cross / Death Cross.

Technical analysis wins for the following reasons:
- Information such as a new product or a major lawsuit pending is not reflected timely in fundamentals, but rather in technical analysis. It gives us guidance in understanding the trend of a stock or even the entire market.
- Most TAs are based on accumulated data. For example, if RSI(14) is greater than 65, most likely this stock is overbought. If there is no reason for this condition, you may consider selling it.
- When too many investors follow TA, it would become self-prophecy.
- Do not act against the trend. The fundamentalist may buy a stock when it loses 50%, the TA investor most likely will not buy it. Many times the losing stocks will lose another 25% or so. The TA investor most likely buys it on the way up only or short it on the way down.

An example. NVRO (a stock symbol) has appreciated about 100% from mid Feb. to Oct. in 2016 despite its poor fundamentals. It has a new product that could revolutionize physical healing and eliminate pain that will not be shown in the fundamentals except by the eventual Forward P/E. Technical charts can inform us of the uptrend.

Volume is the confirmation. Institution investors drive the market. When the market (esp. the S&P 500 stocks) is down and the volume is up, there is good chance institution investors are dumping their holdings. It is obvious when most of the indicators are promising but the volume is small.

Info from free websites.
Use "Head and shoulder" as an example. Obtain the description by typing "Head and shoulder" in Investopedia. Obtain more info by entering the same in the search under YouTube.

Links:
Before you trade: https://www.youtube.com/watch?v=8hM18AHcUCs
A strategy: https://www.youtube.com/watch?v=asDBegQaupM

1   Technical analysis (TA)

The basics
Technical analysis (a.k.a. charting) is easier to learn than you might expect. It represents the trend of the market (a stock or a group of stocks) graphically. If more investors are in the market, the market would move upwards until it changes direction. We divide the trends into short-term, intermediate-term and long-term.

The chartists usually do not consider fundamentals as they believe they have already been priced into the stock price and some fundamentals are not available to the public. To illustrate, a new drug has been discovered, the stock price of the company jumps initially by insiders purchases and the informed. Its fundamental metrics do not demonstrate this right away, but many investors are buying to boost up the stock price as evidenced by the technical indicators such as SMA for 20 or 50 days.

The volume is a confirmation. When the stock moves up or down by 10% with a low volume, the trend is not yet confirmed.

The trend of the stock price is not a straight line in most cases. Hence a trend line is usually drawn to indicate the direction of the stock. Many investors believe the stocks fluctuate in certain ranges (i.e., channels) and the chart draws the upper value (the resistance line) and the lower value (the support line). In theory, the price of a stock fluctuates within the resistance line (ceiling for understanding) and support (floor). When it reaches its support, it becomes a buy and vice versa for a sell. Most charts including Finviz.com would display these lines.

When the price passes out of the channel, it is called a breakout. Darvas, one of the oldest and most successful chartists, profited from the breakouts of the resistance line and believed the stock was close to the support line of the new channel. Hence it would be a long way up in theory.

If it were so simple, there will be no poor folks
It works most of the time, but do not place all your money on it. For chartists, 51% is great (the same for playing Black Jack). Some trends reverse very fast such as the bio drug stocks in 2015. You need to hedge your bets such as placing stop orders. Most do not want to spend their lives watching the trend from a big screen.

Most novices use too many technical indicators and lose in their performances to the professionals. Recently, most chartists were not doing all that great and I did not find many books on their success than a decade ago. It could be due to too many followers in similar setups. I verified it with my recent testing using Finviz.com.

Simple Moving Average
The basic technical indicator is SMA-N. It is the average of the last N trade sessions. To illustrate, if N is 15 and the exchange is open during this period, you need 3 weeks (21 days) of data. When N is 20 (or SMA-20), we classify it as short-term. Similarly, SMA-50 is an intermediate-term and SMA-200 is long-term. Assuming 5 trade sessions per week, 20, 50 and 200 can be translated to 4, 10, and 40 weeks respectively. I prefer the default 50, 100 and 250. Day traders and swing traders can change to shorter durations such as 5, 10 and 50.

This trend duration is important. For example, do not want to place long-term purchases using the short-term SMA-50. There are many modifications to SMA such as giving more weight to recent data, but I have not found them any better. Finviz.com includes this information without charting (SMA-20, SMA-50 and SMA-100 in percentages).

Defining the trend periods is rather arbitrary. I use SMA-350 to detect the market plunges and SMA-100 for stocks. Weighted Moving Average weighs more weight on recent price data.

It can be used to determine whether we are in a bull, a bear or a sideways market using SMA-50 (or SMA-200 for longer term) for the market (using SPY), the sector (using an ETF for the sector and the specific stock. The trend is up when the price is above the SMA and the reversal of the trend. https://www.youtube.com/watch?v=jdYNaE5GJ0k

The trend is your best friend
Most traders use TA for trending in a short duration. Investors can also use TA to time the entry and exit points for better potential profits. Value investors usually are patient and they do bottom fishing and they search for 'oversold' conditions using RSI(14). Again, high volume is a confirmation.

Many sites provide charting free of charge such as Yahoo!Finance. Finviz.com provides a lot of technical indicators without charting such as SMA% and RSI(14). It also provides screen searching for stocks that meet your technical analysis criteria.

Hands on
Bring up Finviz.com and enter any stock symbol such as AAPL. You can see the daily prices of AAPL from about nine months ago to today. Three SMAs (Simple Moving Average) are displayed as SMA-20, SMA-50 and SMA-200. The first two are for short-term trends. When the price is above the SMA, it is expected to be trending up. Again, the trade volume is used as a confirmation.

You can also see the resistance line and the support line drawn. In theory, the stock will trade within these lines. When it exceeds its resistance line, it is called a breakout, and vice versa for a breakdown. Sometimes it displays some technical patterns such as Cup and Shoulder and Double Down (both are positive patterns).

Select Weekly data. The Candle chart is better described than the Daily chart. Candles give us better descriptions of the price: open, close, high and low. The green color indicates the price is up for the period (a week in this example) and the red color indicates a down period.

In addition, Finviz.com includes some technical indicators in the metric section such as RSI. Most other chart sites are similar in the basics. Use

Finviz's Help and select Technical Analysis for more description. Investopedia has enhanced descriptions on this topic.

TA patterns

There are many TA patterns such as Bollinger Bands and MACD. The patterns are based on the stock prices and many times they prove to be correct predictions especially on stocks with high volume and high market caps. Patterns have been repeating themselves many times as they are driven by investors.

Sites for TA

There are many free sites for charts with explanations of their technical indicators. Popular ones include BigCharts.com, SmallCharts.com and Yahoo!Finance. Fidelity includes some unique features in its charts such as P/E.

Why I do not use TA as a primary tool for stock picking

My investing style is different from a day trader. I prefer to 'Buy Low and Sell High' instead of 'Buy High and Sell Higher'. I try to find the real bottom price. TA will not find the bottom very easily but it tracks the trend better. As a bargain hunter, I do not expect the stock will rise fast as I'm usually swimming against the tide. However, value stocks could stay in the low price for a long time (i.e., value trap). I like to select stocks that turn around as evidenced by the SMA-20 and SMA-50.

With that said, my momentum portfolio has appreciated consistently and usually has the best performing stocks among all my portfolios. It is based on the timely grade from my subscriptions plus the metrics on TA timing.

Most chartists would also tell you to buy the stocks that have broken out (i.e., higher than the resistance line) and/or stocks at their highs. Contrary to value investing, you should exit when the trend reverses. The reversal could happen very fast and hence protect your portfolio by setting up stop loss (preferably with trailing stop) orders.

My opinion

I do not want to argue whether TA is good for you or not. You need to find that out. Most likely, the day traders and very short-term traders will profit more from TA than the investors seeking value stocks for the long-term gains.

Random remarks

Even if you do not use technical analysis, you should spend some time learning it. It is better to marry fundamentals and TA. My random remarks are:

- The Institutional investors (insurance companies, pension funds, mutual funds, etc.) use TA and they MOVE the market. A lot of times it becomes a self-fulfilling prophecy. It is better to join them as most of us cannot beat them.
- Day traders take advantage of the institutional investors by spotting their trends and jumping on the wagon.
- Most TA stocks should be good sized and have large average daily volumes. I prefer to use TA on value stocks to prevent long-term losses.
- I do know some folks making big money using TA, but I know more making good money using fundamentals. Since TA predicts the market better in the shorter term, its practitioners may have to pay higher taxes (in today's tax laws) in taxable accounts.
- Our objective should be making money with the least risk. Once you claim to belong to a certain group of either Fundamental or TA, you will be biased and forget your primary objective in investing.
- TA tracks the last two big market plunges (2000 and 2007) pretty well. The chart will not warn you right away for the upcoming plunge (as it depends on past data) to avoid the initial losses, but they will warn you to avoid bigger losses.
- You can use TA to short the stock, the sector, the country or the market.
- Risk management (with stops to reduce losses and trailing stops for rising stocks) and trade positions (more positions on stocks with better potential) could make you a fortune, even if you have only 50% correct.
- Your desire, passion, discipline, knowledge and hand-on skill (including learning from your successes and failures) are the keys to success. A well-tested strategy and TA tools to time the trend of a stock, sector and the market are the tools.

Afterthoughts
Besides searching for stocks that have potential breakouts, we should check the stocks we own for potential breakdowns.
Technical Analysis tutorial.
https://www.YouTube.com/watch?v=GENBVwV8PMs
SMA tutorial.
https://www.YouTube.com/watch?v=Na-ctpPsnks

Links
Fidelity video: Technical Analysis
https://www.fidelity.com/learning-center/technical-analysis/chart-types-video
Technical analysis: https://www.youtube.com/watch?v=LEsBoUG8_Jk

2   Examples of using TA

I have outlined how we can spot market plunges using TA and I use it to monitor the market every three months or so (I recommend doing it every month and even more frequently when the market is risky). Here is an example of how to use it to trade individual stocks.

I have to admit I do not use TA that much on individual stocks and clearly I am not an expert in TA. If this article stirs up your interest, read more books or attend seminars / classes on TA. However, this book describes the basic and most useful technical indicators. There are many good and free articles from Investopedia on this topic. Personally, I prefer to seek fundamentally sound companies at bargain prices and wait for their full appreciation. It has been proven to me many times over.

TA is very useful for momentum and day traders. With the rising volume, you can detect that the stocks are traded by managers of mutual funds, hedge funds, insurance companies and pension funds, and you profit by riding on their wagons.

Some stocks are good for TA. Usually, they are larger companies with above-average volumes and are fundamentally sound. Avoid the stocks that are trending downwards unless you're bottom fishing. Let me pick CSCO (a cyclical stock) for an illustration. I bought it several times in 2012. I sold some in 2013 and 2014 making good profits. This is quite different from what short-term traders would use during the following:

The green line is a 50-day simple moving average (SMA) for the following chart using one year data.

Buy the stock when it is above its SMA and sell when it is below. Following the chart would make good money based on this simple rule. Also, practice the strategy "Sell on May 1, Buy back on Nov. 1".

Not all stocks follow this profitable pattern. Fundamentalists may try to pick the bottom in late July while chartists enter positions on its upward trend. The chartists have an advantage to stay away from stocks in their downward trend.

Exponential Moving Average has better predictable power as it weighs more on recent prices. Some indicators / patterns work better in specific market conditions – all markets are different.

Volume is important as a confirmation. If the price of a stock is up with thin volume, the rise is questionable and it could be manipulated.

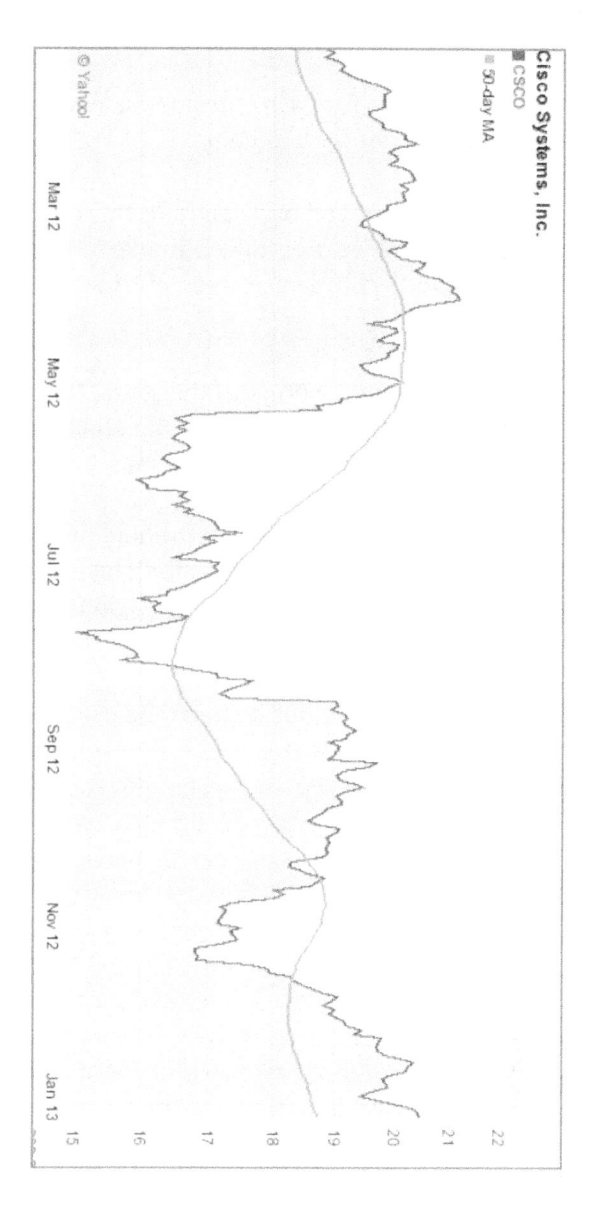

Table: CSCO 50-day SMA   Source: Yahoo!Finance (https://ebmyth.blogspot.com/2020/09/table-csco-50-day-sma.html)

We can improve the trades by:

- Use a different moving average in the number of days (50 in this example) and other indicators such as EMA (a moving average that weighs higher on more recent data). It may improve prediction accuracy and/or cut down on the number of trades. RSI(14) suggests overbought / oversold conditions.

- Instead of selling the stock for cash, consider selling the stock short. Selling short is definitely not for beginners.

- The accuracy is usually improved by a separate chart for the sector the stock belongs to and another one for the market. For CSCO, you can use an ETF for network companies and SPY (or a similar ETF) to represent the market.

  In theory and in theory only, when both the stock, the sector that the stock is in and the market all move down, the stock price has a high chance that it would move down, and vice versa.

  We use the 50 days (in SMA) for short-term holding of stocks (20 for even shorter holding periods and 200 days for longer holding periods). Personally, I use 30 days for the sector ETF. Again, 'Days' is actually 'Trade Sessions'.

TA is not for most fundamentalists but it should be used

For a bargain hunter like me, TA would not benefit me a lot for picking stocks at their bottoms. I would try to pick up CSCO with prices ranging from 15-17 and all well below the moving average line, but TA would not show me a Buy signal. However, for short-term swing traders TA is a Godsend.

To me, TA is a good indicator for growth, momentum and for short-term trading. Some fundamentalists may use TA for entry and exit points. Some recommend buying the stock when the price is above the SMA-200 (same as when SMA-200% is positive and that can be readily obtained from Finviz.com).

It should be profitable for using the 'Buy High and Sell Higher' strategy, provided you protect your profits effectively. This is also called 'Buy at a reasonable cost'. One's opinion.

In selecting a tool, you have to understand how, and why to use it and whether it fits your investing style. I use TA for market timing for the entire market more than on individual stocks. When I have more time, I probably would use TA more frequently.

Most of us cannot spot the bottom of a stock; I have had some success but most likely they were due to luck. When a stock is moving up from the bottom, there is a good chance it will move further up. TA shows it and the volume confirms it.

Conclusion
Even a fundamentalist like me can benefit a lot by using TA. This book touches on the very basics of TA.

Besides monitoring the fundamentals of the stocks you bought once every 6 months, you should analyze their technical indicators more often (1 month to 3 months depending on your available time). When the market is risky (close to the SMA average), run the SMA chart more frequently (say once a week).

Rule-based trading: https://www.youtube.com/watch?v=GAH9EyydEsM

---

3   Easy TA without charts

Bring up Finviz.com from your browser. Enter the stock you're evaluating. SMA-200% stands for Simple Moving Average of the last 200 trade sessions. RSI(14)% is the relative strength index for the last 14 trade sessions.

The following is just a suggestion with conservative parameters. Adjust the parameters according to your risk tolerance and requirements. Do not buy the stock with SMA-200% is < 0 (trending down), SMA-200% > 40 (peaking), or RSI(14)% > 65 (overbought).

Link: RSI: https://www.youtube.com/watch?v=VH84ppzmq9Q

4   Bollinger Bands

Bollinger Bands have been proven useful for traders. In theory, the stock is traded between the upper band and the lower band forming an envelope. For more info, click the following link.

http://www.investopedia.com/terms/b/bollingerbands.asp
https://www.youtube.com/watch?v=wfPf-KBuQH0
https://www.youtube.com/watch?v=2G9fHBEsauE

The following chart was drawn by Yahoo!Finance for CSCO from 8/7/2012 to 8/7/2014 selecting Bollinger Bands for the 50 days as a parameter. If you trade more often, use 20 days. If the chart is too small to display on your screen, enter the following in your PC's browser.
http://ebmyth.blogspot.com/2014/08/screen-csco-bollinger-bands-50.html

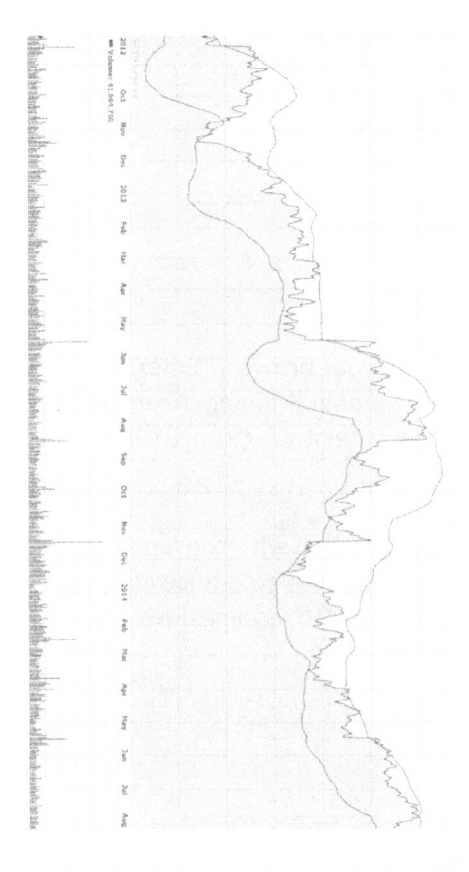

Bollinger Bands 50 Days.   Source: Yahoo!Finance

You buy the stock when the price is close to the lower band and sell the stock when it is close to the upper band.

When the stock price passes the upper band, it is called a breakout. Similar for the stock falling below the lower band. From the above, we should make some good money.

It is advisable to use at least one more technical indicator. I recommend the RSI(14), which is also accessible from Yahoo!Finance or similar sites. When it is above 70, it is overbought, so I recommend selling the stock. When it is below 30, it is oversold, so I recommend buying the stock. However, fundamentals have not been considered. Some stocks just go to zero and some just surge.

5   MACD

MACD, Moving Average Convergence Divergence, is an effective momentum (i.e., short-term) indicator used by most traders. When the stock price is crossing above the zero line, it is a buy and vice versa. It may give false signals in sideways fluctuation.

Again, try to master SMA and RSI(14) first. Using too many indicators usually harms you more than helps you. You can use Finviz.com to search stocks with technical indicators.

SMA: https://www.youtube.com/watch?v=hTDVTH8umR8
MACD: https://www.youtube.com/watch?v=SOS_YnPZSQo

A TA strategy

Buy the stock, sector or the market when: 1. The SMA-50% (from Finviz) is above SMA-200%, 2. SMA-200% is positive, and 3. The price is at least 25% above the 52-week low (i.e., do not buy at the bottom as it may stay there for a long while). Sell, vice versa. Consider other metrics such as Volume, P/E, Debt / Equity, etc. It is great in concept, but I have not been convinced so far in my recent tests.

Related YouTube: Shorter Trend
https://www.youtube.com/watch?v=GAH9EyydEsM
Finding breakout stocks using Finviz.
https://www.youtube.com/watch?v=bWpe30R2VnM
Finviz: https://www.youtube.com/watch?v=yyW8WDGjdKI
Picking bottom: https://www.youtube.com/watch?v=ygj0TPqmRK4
A TA strategy: https://www.youtube.com/watch?v=ygj0TPqmRK4
Another strategy: CCI + MA

https://school.stockcharts.com/doku.php?id=technical_indicators:commodity_channel_index_cci
https://www.youtube.com/watch?v=CuWzDo72-Rk

6   Other TA indicators/patterns

They are briefly mentioned here. Click on the links or use Investopedia for more descriptions.

Double Bottom is a bullish pattern as the support line is stronger than the resistance line.
Double Top is the opposite and is a bearish pattern. I prefer the price of the second top is less than the price of the first top. It seems there is no enough investment in this stock to break out of the second top.

Resistance and Support. The stock is supposed to fluctuate between an imaginary zone of resistance and support. Short-term traders may sell when the price is close to the resistance line and close any short positions when it is close to the support line. However, breakouts from this zone are possible and many traders trade stocks on breakouts. It is a little similar to 52-week highs and lows. The trend line indicates the trend of the stock.

Cup and handle is a bullish pattern. The stock price peaks and then forms a shape of a cup and handle.

Head & Shoulder is a bearish pattern while the reversed Head & Shoulder is a bullish pattern. It signals that the peak (the head) has been reached and the second top (the shoulder) has failed to reach the previous peak.

Stochastic Oscillator. It is similar to RSI(14). Many traders use this indicator. If it is above 65, it is overbought. If it is below 30, it is oversold. In general, I would trade on an uptrend when the stock is moving from 60 to 85; it depends on how volatile the stock is. It is better to use with other indicators and as a reference.

To illustrate when to buy, one suggestion is to buy when this indicator changes to an uptrend while the price is still going down.

Many traders follow these technical indicators and SMA. They could become "self-fulfilled" prophecies.

Link

Chart patterns. https://www.youtube.com/watch?v=o6hZma0bajE
More: https://www.youtube.com/watch?v=aRlWle9smww
Resistance: https://www.youtube.com/watch?v=C2qRW9_via4
Candle stick https://www.youtube.com/watch?v=W3PCTl5kxe0
Finviz: breakout and short
https://www.youtube.com/watch?v=YDFOFbrJRzc
Elliott Wave: https://www.youtube.com/watch?v=wAuSDVI3IJA
Support and resistance: https://www.youtube.com/watch?v=vJ-sRke6lzE

7 More on technical analysis

This chapter describes some TA indicators that can help us. Click on the following links for a better description.

- Finviz.com.
  It has SMA20%, SMA50% and SMA200% to represent the short-term, intermediate-term and the long-term indicator. SMA stands for Simple Moving Average and n for days for the duration of the average (for example, 20 days for SMA20%).

  If you are a long-term investor, use SMA-200% (or SMA-350%). Using SMA-20% would cause a lot of sells / reentries, which costs more in trading fees.

  Buy when the price is above the Moving Average line and sell when the price is below it. Finviz.com provides the percent of moving above the moving average to indicate just how much the price deviates from the average.

If you hold the stock for an average of 50 days, use SMA50%, and so on. If you hold stocks for an average of 90 days, you have to create your own SMA using one of the many websites including Yahoo!Finance and specify 90 days for the period.

Try other similar technical indicators such as EMA, which is supposed to weigh more on the more recent data. A weather man can predict tomorrow's weather better than the weather a week away.

- RSI(14) indicates whether the stock is overbought or oversold. RSI oscillates between zero and 100. Traditionally, and according to Wilder (the author of this method), RSI is considered overbought with a value above 70 and oversold with a value below 30 as described in the article.

  When it is oversold, most likely the stock will fall, and vice versa.

(http://stockcharts.com/school/doku.php?id=chart_school:technical_indicators:relative_strength_index_rsi)

Click here for another article.
(http://financial-dictionary.thefreedictionary.com/Relative+Strength+Index)

- Cup and handle is a popular indicator of when the stock price would surge.
  (http://www.investopedia.com/terms/c/cupandhandle.asp)

- Double bottom indicates that the stock will move up.
  (http://stockcharts.com/school/doku.php?id=chart_school:chart_analysis:chart_patterns:double_bottom_revers)
  It shows a double bottom for Apple in 2013.
- A trading strategy:
  https://www.youtube.com/watch?v=asDBegQaupM

#Fillers
"Hold" rating from analysts means "Sell as fast as you can". Very seldom, there is a "Sell".

8 Using Fidelity

Click "Research and News" and then "Stock". Simple charting and advanced charting are both provided.

Hints:
- Fidelity provides suggested stops.
- Click on the Support and Resistance under Technical Analysis to display the Resistance Line (upper limit). Click on the Resistance Line and you can get the Support Line (lower limit).
- Click on Advanced Chart and then click on "learn how to use the chart".
- Under Advanced Chart, select Draw and Trend Line. Select the upper line by touching the highest points and do the same for the lower line.

Links

Options trade for beginners (Part 1)
https://www.youtube.com/watch?v=4HMm6mBvGKE

#Filler: Future jobs
American blue-collar workers are facing a hard time for sure from driverless cars/trucks to robots. The future is also bleak for many professionals such as financial advisors, accountants, pharmacists...due to AI and cheap computing. The future will be owned by stock owners and the middle class will have jobs to make devices / software to remove jobs of the above workers. It may happen in our children or grandchildren's generation, and we can see it from above or below depending on what we did in life. LOL.

9   Determine the exit point

I have described 2 exit strategies: Death Cross and SMA-350 (or SMA-400 for fewer false alarms). This is a bonus technique used stand alone or together with the above two. The concept is simple, but it requires more understanding on the charting and candlestick. All the three techniques can be applied to individual stocks, sectors and the market. We demonstrate it with the market using SPY, and the reentry point is just the opposite.

All the three techniques do not identify the top and the bottom as they are based on past data. However, it tells you to exit to avoid further losses. All three have false alarms, but this one could exit earlier. We can tune all the techniques to have fewer false alarms, but it would increase more losses than the original techniques.

The institutional investors (mutual funds, pension funds, etc.) move the market. That's why the volume is important. Whenever there is high volume, most likely they are trading seriously. They may want to make the market rosier than it really is by buying, but the volume is small. When they sell a lot, most likely the market will be down for a while. The following signals that the institutional investors are selling with the exception of the option expiration dates (the Friday of the third week in March, June, September and December):

- Today's trade session is unprofitable.
- The last trade session was unprofitable or had a very tiny profit.
- The trade volume is higher than the trade volume of the last trade session; candlesticks and trade volume are available from most charts.
- The trade volume is higher than the average trade volume of the last 50 trade sessions (available from most charts).
- If the above happens more often (such as 4 times in the last month), be careful. Due to the huge number of stocks the institutional investors own, they cannot sell them fast; I estimate it takes about 2 to 4 weeks to dump the stocks.
- The market falls for no reason; the only logical reason could be the institutional investors are dumping.
- Big fall before the market open and it continues for the entire trade day. It indicates many smart moneys including the retail investors are moving out of the market.
- Most likely, Death Cross and SMA-350 (or SMA-400) would signal a down market. SMA-200 would give you a signal ahead of the described two. Using SMA-50 and SMA-200:
  https://www.youtube.com/watch?v=BaZxE12cZP4&t=218s
  https://www.youtube.com/watch?v=wMxj6iB92ZA
- The deterioration of the Buy/Sell could indicate the market is falling earlier.

Book 14: Investment advice

We need to distinguish good information from garbage.

1   Newsletters and subscriptions

Why do you not see too many reviews on investment newsletters and subscriptions from the media? If it is a bad review, most likely they will not advertise in the media. If it is a good review, they may have to face legal actions in the future if the vendor's subscription or newsletter does not perform well.

I've been using investment newsletters / subscriptions for years. Many are priced reasonably and some are even free. While a lot of them are garbage, some are very good.

When you have a lot of money to invest and you're not using a financial adviser and/or not subscribing to any investment service, it could be a big financial mistake. You do not want to be penny smart but pound foolish. Very few have the knowledge and the time to make use of the free financial data, including the guidance and articles from the web.

You need a computer, access to the Internet and a spreadsheet in order to use most subscription services effectively.

I'm not going to compare specific services / newsletters at the risk of being sued, but I will include some general pointers on how to select them. Yesterday's garbage could be a gold mine today if the subscription improves and/or the market conditions fit what they recommend.

First, you need to find out your requirements and how much time you can afford to use them. If you have $20,000 or less to invest, most likely your investment both in time and money will not pay off; just buy an ETF and practice market timing described in this book. My pointers are:

- Newsletters giving you specific stocks to buy do not require much of your time. However, if they're successful, there will be too many followers buying the recommended stocks that can drive up the prices at least temporarily. The owner of the subscription service and his insiders will buy the recommended stocks before you unless they're not allowed to do so (but who's enforcing this?). I had several of these newsletters, and so far, I have not renewed any one of them due to poor performance.

- If I found the Holy Grail of investing, do you believe I would share it with you for $100 or so? I only will after I invest my money first. My subscribers would push up the prices for me and then I could unload them before my subscribers.

  I am publishing a book (not a promise) in the June time frame every year with the title "Best Stocks for 2021" recommending a handful of stocks. Due to my relatively small positions and few buyers of the book, it will not have the adverse effects described. Most of my recommendations should be value stocks for long term hold unless the market is risky. My books will not be the Holy Grail as my objective is beating the S&P 500 Index.

- If the volume of the recommended stocks is small, they can be manipulated easily either by the newsletter owners and/or by your peer subscribers. The first ones to sell the recommended stocks win and the last ones to sell them lose.

- I prefer systems that can find a lot of stocks by providing many searches (same as screens). However, it will take a lot of time to learn and test their performances unless they provide historical databases. Most likely, you need to further research each stock screened.

  From my experience, the best performance comes from the stocks that have been screened by more than one search, especially for the short term (less than 6 months). My theory is that they've been identified by many folks and hence their prices could be jacked up. It is more profitable to buy them ahead of the herd and sell them before the herd. In any case, research the stock you are interested in.

- Most of you have received promotional mail that indicates their incredible performances such as tripling the money in a short time. Just ignore them. If it is that good, most likely they will keep it for themselves. It is the same for seminars that boost some penny stocks. Most likely the recommended stocks would rise initially to lure you and other suckers to move it. Watch out! As of 2016, I do not see these junk mail as often as before; the public is smarter. They must have switched their promotions to YouTube.

- A 'guru' told me that he made a big fortune in silver a month ago. Guess what? He also recommended selling it two months earlier and lost a lot of money in doing so. He is always right but he will not advertise the times he was wrong. We call it a double talk technique.

- There are free trial offers (or deeply discounted) for most subscription services. Take advantage of them. Some services require you to spend a lot of time, so ensure you have the time. Keep track of the performance yourself via paper trading. Do not trust their 'official' performances which can be manipulated.

- Subscribe to a newsletter that fits your style of investing. If you're a day trader, newsletters on long-term investing are not good for you. Some subscriptions handle all kinds of investing styles and you need to find the strategies and recommendations within the newsletter to fit your style. Short-term swing traders have a different set of metrics than long-term investors.

- Newsletters on penny stocks are risky to most of us. They may show you a list of big winners but they do not show you their losers.

    I define penny stocks as the stock price less than $2 (officially $5) and a market cap less than 100 M. Once in while I do trade penny stocks. Actually, I bought ALU at $1 but ALU's market cap then was about 2 billion at the time. The stocks with prices between $1 and $10 represent the most volatile stocks but a few are real gems. They are routinely ignored by most analysts.

- There are many sectors like drugs, mines, insurance and banks that retail investors cannot evaluate effectively. It is better to seek expert advice from specific newsletters. Check out their past performance and take advantage of the free trial offers.

- Remember there is no free lunch in life. The higher potential return of a stock, the riskier the stock is. To me, all trades are educated guesses. The more educated the guesses are, the higher chance they will perform in the long run. However, nothing is 100% sure.

- Some newsletters / subscriptions save us time by summarizing the financial data by providing a value rank and a growth rank. Some provide a timely rank from the price momentum. When the market favors growth, use the growth rank, and vice versa.

- Be careful with the information from radio and TV commercials. Many try to sell to peoples' fear and greed by overstating without necessarily telling the whole story. It is not possible to make 50% in covered calls consistently or make another gold rush from $400 to $2,000. One advertises the market will lose 80% in 2016. It is possible but not likely. [Update: The market was profitable in 2016.] These are tactics to get you subscribing to their services.

- TV financial shows usually exaggerate in order to sell their products. Analyze them before you act on the news.

- As retail investors, most of us cannot afford to do extensive research. Many researches and market opinions are available on the internet for free. Start to search for such information from your broker's site and financial sites such as SeekingAlpha.com, MarketWatch.com, CNNfn.com and Yahoo!Finance.com. Analyze the news and some could be obsolete, or could be manipulated with a hidden agenda.

- Most compare their performances with the S&P 500 index. Some investment newsletters inflate their performance with dividends while comparing to an index without including dividends.

    To illustrate, the S&P 500 has an average annual return of 1% on appreciation and 1.5% on dividends for a total return of 2.5%. Hence, the performance of a newsletter should compare itself to 2.5% not 1%.

- The performance of the last 10 years (I prefer the last 5 years) is more important than that of 25 years. The last 10 years is a better prediction of the newsletter than the last 25 years as the weatherman has found out.

    More than one time, I have found a popular subscription that did not beat the S&P 500 in the last 5 years but it did in the last 20 years. It could be that too many folks are using the same strategy.

- When the new major researcher takes over the subscription, s/he may not have the same expertise as the previous researcher.

- Ensure the subscriptions change their strategies according to the current market conditions. For example, 10 years ago ADRs (U.S. listed stocks of foreign countries) performed far better than today.

The trend may reverse in the future.

- Few if any use real money for their portfolios, as they cannot cheat with real money. That's why you never achieve the compatible performance by following what the portfolio trades. Some can manipulate by using the best prices of the day. Some omit their losers. Do not trust any performance claims even from reputable monitor services unless the portfolios can be verified with real money.

  Some sample portfolios trade excessively and they may not fit your investment strategy.

- When a subscription service has several strategies (say 10 for illustration purposes), they will advertise the strategies with the best returns for a specific time period.

- On 12/8/2014 TNH was down by 12% by the end of the day. If they used the open price, it would have made a difference of 12%,

- My bad experiences. I bought one book for $1. I never received the book and they charged me a small amount every month. Two subscriptions sent me spam messages and they automatically renewed the subscriptions.

Contrary to not recommending investment services, I recommend your broker for the stock research. AAII is a low-priced subscription, but Fidelity (requiring membership), Finviz and Yahoo!Finance are free today.

Filler: My favorite store

The new name of the merged companies "Family Dollar" and "Dollar Store" would be "General Family Dollar" or "Two Dollars Now".

If you want to prove the rich are more beautiful, just go to any dollar store. Must be offending a lot of folks. Sorry!

2   Advantages of a retail investor

The average retail investor does not beat the market due to switching between stocks and cash at the wrong time. Via greed, they invest at the peak of the market and via fears they divest at the bottom. They do not expect the market to return from the bottom, but it always does.

Most fund managers are smarter than I, better educated in investing than I, have ten times more research tools than I and have ten times more computer power than I. However, most of them do not beat me, the average casual retail investor. In addition, I spend less time in stock research than an average fund manager (most are working at least 60 hours a week). I hope the following help you to beat the market and the fund managers.

- They cannot beat the market all the time. When they do, more money flows in. It is very hard for them to perform with that much extra cash. When the market is depressing, everyone cashes out their funds. They need to sell stocks even though some may have better potential to appreciate.

   The saying "When there is blood in the streets, most likely it is the best time to buy" is correct. 2009 is an example. Fund managers cannot take advantage of this opportunity as many clients have cashed out.

- Most cannot play market timing freely and they have to satisfy all the rules set up for the fund. Every time they trade a stock, they need to ensure no rules have been broken such as a restricted percentage of a stock to the fund. Most funds prohibit their managers from shorting, buying contra ETFs and/or maintaining high cash positions. Basically, most are not allowed to react to the market whether it is going up or down.

- When they trade, their high volumes are easily tracked by day traders who can ride on their wagons. Hence, they have to pay more to buy and get less to sell.

- By my rough estimate, they have about 1,000 stocks (about 600 for larger funds) to deal with. I as a retail investor have about 3,000 stocks even skipping most stocks with prices below $2 or not listed in the three major exchanges.

Their stocks have been fully evaluated by analysts and newsletters / subscriptions such as Value Line and /or some firms specializing in stock research for them. Hence, they do not gain any advantage by following their peers.

The small and mid-cap stocks are risky but they are more rewarding statistically in the long run. Many fund managers cannot buy them due to the size of their funds.

- Their performance as a group is actually worse due to the closing down of non-performing funds.

- Not nimble enough.
  By the time they have done all the research and received the approval to buy a specific stock, I may have bought the same stock already. Usually, it takes at least a week for a large fund to complete trading a stock.

- The high expenses.
  The fee is about 1.5% for the average fund. Most hedge funds charge even more with the average 2% for expenses plus 20% on the profit. When the fund and the broker belong to the same company, watch out on how its brokerage arm makes profits via the trading of the fund under the same parent. Most hedge funds have no penalty for losing your money, and hence it encourages their fund managers to take big risks.

- Not spending enough time to do their own research.
  Many do not spend enough time on basic research and select the right strategies in the current market conditions. They spend a lot of time following the fund's and the company's objectives, rules and regulations.

- Wrong objective.
  The objective of most funds is beating the common index after expenses. Most fund managers do not want to take too much risk and their personal objective is job security. One will not lose the job if his performance is similar to a target index. You achieve the same objective by buying an ETF that simulates the index for less expenses.

- The reason for some of their good performance is due to taking too much unnecessary risk and/or the high leverage. Their performance improves when the market is good, but degrades when the market is down. When I see the market is coming down, I would park more cash and I only use leverage when the market is going up.

- Retail investors have a lot of advantages over fund managers. However, I advise you not to be a day trader. Statistically most amateur traders lose money as they cannot compete with experienced, disciplined traders.

    Discipline, knowledge and due diligence will make you money in the long term as a turtle investor.

Filler: Gamma rays

Gamma rays are the most effective tool for weight loss. If you die because of the gamma rays, you will lose weight gradually, naturally and surely

Filler: Victims?

We're victims of our own success: A higher living standard means higher wages, more protections for our workers and more regulations for our environment. All these will make us less competitive.
#Filler: How to end all our wars

If we send the children of our leaders to the front line, we will not have any wars.

The youths should enjoy the best time of their lives and not be sent back in body bags.

3 Future trends

As of 2021, we're at the crossroads in many areas. Let me outline some of my thoughts [Note. Updated in early 2023]. Check it out in five years (2017) or so, and see how many have materialized.

Economy
1. As of 2021, the market is fundamentally unsound but technically sound. When the technical goes down, it could be the time to exit the market. [Note. Has been materialized. If you follow my simple market timing, you should have exited the market in March, 2022].
2. As of 2021, FAANG as a group of stocks is very risky to me. [Note. Has materialized in 2022]. Oil prices will take a break before its upward trend.
3. When the oil price was at $30, I bought some oil stocks and USO. When the oil price was at $50, I sold some. I did sell some when it was over 100, but unfortunately, I bought some later when it was down but not at the bottom. No one can predict the oil price precisely and constantly.

   I expect an uptrend on oil in the next two years. It is a simple supply and demand at work. Drilling and exploration at the current $50 price range are not economically feasible. With RV replacing cars using combustion engines, the demand for oil will be reduced in 5 or so years.

   Hydro cars once considered to be the future are not promising compared to EVs. Toyota aiming at hydro cars was late to RVs, while China could be the leader in RVs in the future if not already so.

   As of early 2023, Ford planned to build a battery factory here using China's technology. It may not be passed by the Congress. If it is passed, it would put a big dent on the so-called decoupling / de-globalization. If it is not passed, our auto industry would be in great danger.
4. China's "One Belt, One Road" Initiative will have an impact on the global economy. It will benefit the participating countries and provinces in west China. Even many American companies including GE and Caterpillar will benefit by providing heavy equipment that China does not build today.
5. We have covered our eyes to that reality that China has already influenced S.E. Asia and Africa if you just look at how many roads and bridges China has already built.
6. China will eventually fix the chip fabrication bottleneck, and then our chip business would take another long-term hit. As of 2023, many chip companies have been hit financially in losing the business from China, their major customer.
7. The world should benefit from the rise of China if China does not create wars.
8. From my estimate, only one job will be gained from 10 returned jobs from Mexico and China due to automation.
9. More new drugs will be discovered in China, as it is too costly to develop them in the U.S.A.

10. The next challenge is in food and water supply. We have obvious advantages over China. Many developing countries have already starved due to the supply of food.
11. The wealth gap will be widened due to robots and the advance of artificial intelligence (AI). It could have the biggest impact since the internet. Many good-paying jobs will be replaced by AI, which many companies in these fields will benefit from, and so will their stock owners.
12. Europe will finally recover despite the rise of terrorism. With the Ukraine War, the EU has been tough in seeking energy that also affects the general economy. Without China's 5G and infrastructure projects, many second-tier cities are using 4G (or even 3G) for a long while. A famous U.S. news reporter showed that the Russia pipeline was destroyed by us, and it would decrease the trust of our EU allies.

From the above, China seems to hold many keys to the future. As of early 2023, China has many problems such as debt problems, the burst of the housing bubble, sanctions by us / our allies and corruption. Once they resolve most of these problems, they will be very formidable competitors. However, their living standard is still low compared to us.

U.S.
1. The U.S. is declining but we're still leading in many sectors. We spend too much effort on being a world policeman while China is concentrating their efforts in improving the economy.
2. As of 2020, I bet Trump will not be re-elected. Will it be the trigger to bring down the market? Only time can tell. I can tell our country has been divided by the two parties.
3. Our politicians still spend recklessly in order to buy votes. Eventually, our USD as a reserve currency would be shaken. The Ukraine War seems to be a bottomless money pit. If it ends, we may have another war to protect Taiwan. In a word, we have endless wars. The only industry that would benefit is the defense sector. We never understand the economy of wars. Shooting down a 'spy' balloon with our expensive missiles is a waste of money. Shooting down a carrier by our enemies' carrier killer is just the opposite. We cannot ignore our internal problems such as deterioration of our infrastructure (evidenced by our derailment of toxic material in 2023), constant shooting, widening wealth gap, education system, etc.
4. We used to be a nation of problem solvers, but have become people avoiding problems.
5. We need the H-1B program to attract the world's best programmers and scientists to make us more competitive. We need to monitor and enforce the program to ensure that there are more benefits than that could harm.

Link: What will the world be in 5 years (2027).
https://www.youtube.com/watch?v=LzipwDQBUyc

Book 15: Buffettology

This book has been written more than 2 years ago with recommendations to dump Buffett's funds. If you followed that advice, you would be spared by his current mediocre performance. In 2015, Buffett's funds performed very poorly. [Update. Both Buffett and Son have performed poorly in 2020 as indicated by this CNN article. It would save owners of Buffett's funds a lot of money minus $10 for my book]. Buffett usually does not invest in companies whose products he does not understand. He did not use smartphones and email. Hence, he had not invested in market-beating high-tech companies such as Apple, Microsoft, Netflix, Facebook and Google. In 2020, this article is still correct. However, the value stocks he would pick after the pandemic could perform better as the above high-flying stocks would have a hard landing.

1   Debunk the myths

Buffett Mania

Traditionally, growth stocks have higher P/Es than value stocks, but the reverse is sometimes true. As of 11/25/13, the expected P/Es (from Finviz.com) of some randomly-picked stocks were:

Growth Stocks	Expected P/E	Value Stocks	Expected P/E
Cisco	10	Coca-Cola (KO)	18
Apple	11	Colgate-Palmolive (CL)	21
San Disk	12	Verizon (VZ)	14
Average	11		18

I suspect it was caused by Buffett and his followers coupled with dividend stock seekers. During this period, dividend stocks had beaten the low interest rates from bonds and CDs. KO, CL, VZ and many others belong to the stocks that Buffett would own. They all gave dividends and had an edge such as brand name recognition and monopoly that Buffett loved. The above are only small samples of these stocks in the respective category. To me, Buffett Mania (my term) is a mild bubble and I expect the average Expected P/E of growth stocks would be over 15 in 2016 (today in 2020, they should be around 25).

This mania will not continue as we're running out of these stocks to buy. I do not believe that there will be an opportunity to buy them at 50% discount (as Buffett preaches) unless we've a market crash. When a strategy is overused, they will not be effective. **No exception.**

The Reality

Warren Buffett is one of the premier investors in our generation, if not the best. However, I believe that some of his practices are not applicable to today's market and to us, the retail investors.

Most of the money earned was for himself and not for the stockholders of Berkshire in the last three years. SPY, an ETF simulating the S&P 500 index, offers greater diversity and has seen less volatility as of this writing. If Buffett is such a hero in picking stocks, then those who constantly beat the S&P 500 Index by a sizable margin are better investor heroes, and there are many of them. We need to constantly scrutinize whom we listen to.

Performance Comparison

As of 11/1/2013, the average annualized return for the last 3 years:

BRKA	SPY
10%	11%

SPY (considered by many as the market) gives an annual dividend of about 1.5% (about 1.9% this year), while BRKA does not. Not even beating SPY from a primer investor is just mediocre. BRKA is slightly better from the beginning of 2010 to the beginning of 2021 for a period of about 11 years. However, Buffett was avoiding most of the damages in the market crashes in 2000 and 2008 using his value approach.

Why Buffett's current mediocre performance is important

I do not care how much money he made 10 years ago but what he will make in the next 10 years. Many have been utterly convinced by the many books written on his achievements many years ago. The most important to us: Are his strategies still relevant to us today?

When Peter Lynch (managing the Magellan Fund, 5/1977 to 5/1990) lost his golden touch and he quit his job, I got my money out! Most investors did not even after experiencing several years of poor returns (compared to his previous incredible performances). The result was many years of mediocre returns for the fund. Hence, Buffett's mediocre performance in the last three years matters and it could be the canary leading to his future performance.

Many of his teachings are still relevant and they are described in the next article. The following of his practices are to be debunked. I just want to seek the truth. Am I dumb to argue with the most famous investor? Read the following with an open mind and decide it for yourself.

Debunk the Myths

- **'Never sell.'**

    I believe that the "Buy and Hold" strategy has been dead since 2000. The fundamentals of most companies change after a decade or so and some even earlier.

    Market timers can detect and take advantage of the market crashes using market timing. Most books and comments that praise this strategy are based on data before 2000. This strategy should be at least replaced with "Buy and Monitor".

    Buffett made big money in KO in the first 10 years of his ownership, but not a lot in the next 10 years. If he cashed in after 10 years of ownership and then bought another stock with similar performance, he would have made far more money.

    I prefer to churn my portfolio to reflect the current market conditions. Buffett's ownership in The Washington Post (sold in recent year) was amazing then, but it could be too risky now. The paper is facing the losing battle against the free internet.

    Market fundamentals perpetually change! To illustrate this, there were ten well-known department stores ten years ago, and now only Macy's has barely survived; most others were acquired or bankrupted. The acquired ones may fare better. However, you need to analyze them again whether the combined company still fits your requirements and objectives. The internet enables Amazon.com to capture the retail sector. Most profitable companies in the last ten years such as Apple and Facebook are related to the internet and not your daddy's traditional companies.

There are so many examples to debunk the evergreen concept such as AIG, BlockBuster, HPQ and GE. The market is changing with new technology and competition. We cannot buy and sit back enjoying the present appreciation and dividends.

I read an outdated but popular book by a very famous author. A very good portion of his recommended stocks have not survived. Most of his stocks had great appreciation in the year after his recommendation, but not after a few years. It is another argument for "Buy and Monitor".

If you do not sell, you do not have cash to buy stocks when the market is cheap.

It is better to understand the new products and their profit potentials, and then make your decisions accordingly. Buffett should depend more on his extensive resources and his many analysts who should have diverse disciplines. Most highly-profitable stocks will not be matured companies but small companies with innovative products.

- **'Rule #1. Do not lose money. Rule #2. Do not forget rule #1.'**

If every stock bought is risk-free, the return could not be good; it fits into "nothing risked, nothing gained". It is similar to buying Treasury Bills that have no loss, in theory. However, holding Treasury bonds until maturity loses buying power due to inflation. Our capitalist system punishes us for not taking risk, so it is with trading stocks.

Evaluate the ratio of "return / risk" to see whether the expected return is justified for the risk. If the chance to lose 50% is the same as gaining more than 100%, then the risk is justified. It is not a science, but probability theory and common sense are decent tools. In the long term it usually works. In addition, one's personal risk tolerance determines his/her investment methods. Most retirees should be conservative.

- **'Margin of safety'.**

The margin of safety is equal to the difference between the stock price and the intrinsic value, which is quite easy to obtain from many websites. From my limited test, this metric does not beat the market most of the time.

There will be too few stocks to buy if everyone treats margin of safety as the first priority. It worked for Buffett before as few followed his 'margin of safety' practice.

Many institutional investors follow Buffett's preaching as they have learned it in colleges; they drive the market. When you follow the herd, you will not beat the market.

During a secular bull market, the market would favor momentum and growth over value and hence 'margin of safety' will not be appropriate. However, it would work better in a secular bear market.

- **'Think of Stocks as a Business'.**

    I do not have the time to run the many companies I own. I do not fire employees, do not have legal obligations, do not make day-to-day decisions, etc. I can sell the stock with a click of the button with no emotion and no legal liabilities attached. Do you really think your ideas and/or votes on how to run the company will influence the management's decisions? It may work for Buffett as he owns part and sometimes the whole company.

    Running a business is very different from investing in a company. Do not be confused! Investors' only objective is to make a profit with the least risk. The officers of a company are liable to frauds and negligence but not the stockholders.

    When a company bankrupts, most sole owners bankrupt too financially and mentally. The stockholder does not suffer the same at least not to the same degree. You may have many other assets, stocks and/or a job. You do not have to tell your loyal employees to leave. No lenders will call you unless you buy the stock on margins.

    With an optimal portfolio of 20 stocks, it is not possible to run 20 companies simultaneously. I have never attended the earnings announcement and never talked to CEOs and/or their investor relationship representative. How much would it cost for the air fares and the hotels 4 times a year for 20 companies?

- **Buffett's portfolio.**
  It was not <u>diversified</u> enough (especially in his early years). However, the portfolio under his insurance company might be.

  When he trades, he pays extra due to his huge volumes. He usually buys the entire company and most retail investors never do that.

- **Main brands** represent matured companies that will give good dividends but usually have limited growth. When they do not perform, the stock will plunge. IBM is a recent example that Buffett owns. The 'cloud' technology is risky and there are many strong competitors.

  The most profitable and riskiest companies are penny stocks. Buffett could reap the profits with their analytical skills. He chooses to stay away from most of them as they are too small for his portfolio.

- He may **miss many** of current strategies that work such as market timing, momentum strategy, technical analysis, insider trading, high tech companies, turnarounds and investing in small companies, etc. They are all described in this book.

  During the peak or during the plunge, we should accumulate cash that is needed to purchase stocks when the bottom hits. Market timing is our tool. If it works more than 50% of the time, we should make good profit. My market timing worked two times from 2000 to 2010 with one false signal that told us to exit but return shortly.

- Buffett **avoids growth companies**. He does not have Microsoft, Apple and Google in his portfolio. Google represents one of the most appreciated stocks in the last 10 years. Google is expensive by the fundamental metrics. However, it is a growth stock with technology that Buffett may not appreciate. FAANG (Facebook, Apple, Amazon, Netflix and Google) were doing well recently and they are included in the major indexes. That's one reason why Buffett cannot beat the indexes most of the time.

- Some argue that Buffett's performance is better during market plunges. It is true for most value stocks. However, you can perform better by staying in cash or even investing in contra ETFs when the market timing tells you so.

- Buffett's huge portfolio from his insurance company is the market and you cannot beat yourself after the hefty fees.
- As of 2016, dividend stocks that are favored by Buffett could be a mild bubble. When the interest rates are hiked, the dividend stocks would return to their historical values.

- There are too many followers of Buffett and it could create a bubble; all bubbles will burst sooner or later.

- Graham's (Buffett's teacher) preaching worked decades ago, but it may not work today as the market conditions are quite different.

- Many high-tech products and drugs are hard to understand. We should not ignore them just because we do not understand their products. The future belongs to these new companies. Some of the traditional businesses may not survive if they do not adapt to changes such as the Washington Post and/or the global markets such as China.

Afterthoughts
- The stockholders of his funds may have to pay a lot of capital gain taxes when they sell them. According to the current tax law, the capital gain is 0 on the day when the owner dies.
- When the day Buffett dies, will his funds plunge?
- Buffett's portfolio 1/2021.
  https://www.youtube.com/watch?v=jjXT3xTNZ4I

2 Preaching that works

Many of Buffett's preaching still works fine today. However, some need to be discussed further so we can use them effectively.

- Identify exceptional companies with durable competitive advantage.

  These are the companies with high profit margins such as Coke. Even Coke has Pepsi as its major competitor. These companies usually are matured companies and give generous dividends. They do not have to plow back all their cash into research and development. Very few (Microsoft is one) high-tech companies and drug companies belong to the group. Most use the profits to build the next better mouse traps instead of giving out dividends. Should we ignore these companies? I do not ignore them, but Buffett would.

  The Washington Post is one of these mature companies. However, the internet is changing all its advantages as most of us get our news analyses free from the internet. In addition, cutting down trees to make paper is not good for the environment. [Update: Buffett sold the Washington Post.]

  We need to monitor the companies that we have stocks on such as GE, Lehman Brothers, Enron and Boeing. When bad news is really bad, sell the stocks right away as they could go to zero.

  Microsoft is in this category monopolizing the PC operating system and Office, the most-used business software. I wonder why it is not in Buffett's portfolio and maybe Gates could give him a good friendly pointer during their bridge games. Buffett still has not bought Apple and Google as of this writing. He has missed these profit opportunities. According to Buffett, Microsoft, Apple and Google are not the companies with 'durable competitive advantage'. I do have to disagree.

  There are many innovative companies that will not fit into Buffett's 'exceptional criteria'. When they plow back most earnings to research / development, these companies usually do not have good net profits and they do not give generous dividends.

  To illustrate this, BSX was one of them finding cures to chronic pain. I read an article on the company from my Sunday paper. Even though I did not (and even today) really know how it worked, I was excited enough to buy its stock two times without doing any research (not recommended) in Oct., 2012. As of 8/2013, it was up by more than 100%.

I will buy these 'exceptional' companies if I can find them. I will sell them when their price appreciation potentials have peaked, or there are better stocks to buy.

- Get most info from financial statements.

  Today many websites such as Finviz.com and your broker's include most of the financial data and ratios. Buffett loses his edge as all these data are available to everyone. We do not have to read through the financial statements for this data. However, we do have to be careful:

  1. Ensure the ratios derived from these financial statements are up-to-date. Usually, the company's website provides the most updated data.

  2. Comparative ratios in the same sector. Many websites provide this information. To illustrate this, Price / Sale has different meanings between a supermarket and a drug company. The former makes money by selling at low profit margins.

  3. It is still important to read the footnotes and 'extraordinary' items such as those one-time charges. Settling a major lawsuit could be a one-time charge. When a virtual asset is out of ordinary, be careful.

  Success in investing today is not solely on how to get the information and understand the financial ratios. We should separate the good data from garbage, and evaluate all the immense data that are readily available from the internet. I recommend paying attention to insiders' purchases.

- Never sell.
  I have presented my opposing views on "Never Sell" philosophy in my other article. However, sometimes it has its merits. There are many companies that Buffett had or has had incredible returns after holding for over 10 years such as the Washington Post (sold recently), American Express and Coke to name a few. Personally, I usually sold

my big winners too early. I should use stops to protect my profits during their uptrends.

Very seldom do I have stocks making over 300% as I usually sell them after they make over 100%; TTWO is an exception which was gifted to my grandchildren. I keep my gainers for at least a year in taxable accounts to take advantage of the more favorable taxes on long-term capital gains. Buffett is a living example that his strategy worked at least 5 years ago. We need to identify why this strategy works and whether it is still applicable to retail investors and the current market conditions. Several thoughts:

1. These companies usually have been analyzed fully for their long-term appreciation potential. Do you have the time and the knowledge to do so? If not, depend on some reputable subscriptions and/or buy ETFs.

2. He has great vision to see the real potential of a company. Do you have that vision? However, he has missed many profitable stocks recently.

3. Institutional investors have more thorough research than us. However, most institutional investors can only trade large companies. That is why we should consider small stocks but not penny stocks.

Today commission costs are very low (even free from Fidelity and Charles Schwab) and we can postpone taxes on capital gains from non-taxable accounts (none from Roth IRAs).

- Buy the stocks at 50% discount

   Stocks are manipulated to cause temporary price erosion.

   This strategy makes him and his teacher Graham a lot of money. As opposed to Graham, Buffett still holds these stocks longer even if they have not appreciated in one or two years. He seldom sells these stocks and many times his patience has paid off.

   My suggestion is some stocks will stay low forever for good reasons. I recommend repeating the same evaluation on your purchased stocks every 6 months. Hold them if the fundamentals are not deteriorating.

The stock prices of some bad companies could go to zero. Use stops to protect your stock holdings. Buffett's stocks are usually value stocks and very seldom do they go to zero. However, we have had several big companies' stocks go to zero recently.

It is similar to buying quality companies when everyone is selling in fear. The best profit opportunity is buying quality stocks at the market bottom (easier said than done). Determining the market bottom is impossible, but there are some hints that may help us to determine whether the market is plunging.

When a company has 2 billion dollars cash and its market cap is 1 billion, most likely it is mispriced. There are exceptions such as a pending serious lawsuit.

- Buy a good business with good management at a discount.

  There were many companies on sale in 2000 and 2007. Need to separate gems from companies that would go bankrupt such as many internet companies in 2000. If the problem that causes the company to lose more than half of the value is temporary, then it could be a good buy betting on a turnaround.

  A good management is required for Buffett as he seldom wants to manage the company. Many companies go bankrupt because of frauds and / or poor management. It is a good sign that the owners have a good stake in their own companies. It is a bad sign when the CEO is overpaid compared to his peers and / or lives lavishly with huge loans from his company.
- Learn from mistakes.
  He made several mistakes as every investor did. He sold the businesses in re-insurance, airline, etc. but he seldom made the same mistake again. Learn from how he deals with his mistakes. I have repeated the same mistakes too many times, and I need to read my own books.
- He does not follow hot fads such as the internet in 2000. I prefer to follow it (a.k.a. momentum investing), but have an exit plan and protect profits via stops.
- Evaluate stocks with common sense. Mathematical models on stock evaluations are for professors to have a job and they never really resemble real life.
- Buffett has switched between bonds and stocks successfully. Most of the time, he was not the first one to exit, but he adapted to the market

- conditions better than most of us. He usually paid more, but it had turned out many times that he was right.
- Buffett as a person has a lot for us to learn from. He is frugal and generous. Making money is his career and hobby, not because he loves to make money for worldly stuff.
- Buffett has his share of bad investing decisions such as buying IBM instead of buying Google, Microsoft and Apple. https://www.youtube.com/watch?v=yRr0_gJ-3ml
- According to Buffett and Peter Lynch, they had been misled more often by getting meaningful information from calling/visiting CEOs, who have their own agenda. In addition, most of us cannot even reach anyone important in large companies on the phone.
- Most folks should follow their philosophy of owning a handful of stocks (not more than 10). Making errors is human nature. We should learn to understand
- Despite not catching the trend, Buffett ended up pretty well in 2000 and 2008 market crashes. Accumulating cash in risky markets could end up profitable when the market crashes and most stocks are in bargain bins.
- Do not buy what you do not understand such as derivatives in 2008 and Bitcoin to many. However, tech stocks will revolutionize the future, and some traditional businesses will fail such as in many retailers and printed newspapers. The best protection on buying momentum stocks (FAANG in 2015 to 2021 for example) is using trailing stops reentered every month or so.

Links
10 Rules: https://www.youtube.com/watch?v=iEgu6p_frmE
Buffett on 2021: https://www.youtube.com/watch?v=wGdbu450964
Strategy: https://www.youtube.com/watch?v=SEZwkbliJr8

#Fillers:
#A report card. According to Cruz, all politicians should have a report card to see what his/her campaign ideas/promises have been fulfilled. The words are wise but can it be enforceable? Simple concept, but big impact.

#Trending up. I missed some investing opportunities due to personal biases. I did not buy ETFs on Turkey, Europe, S. Korea, India, etc. They all have had a great year. Is it heartless to say I will buy a Turkish ETF in the next terrorist attack?

Welfare to the rich. Our government gives our corporations cash and/or reduces the interest rate. The management uses them to buy back their own stocks instead of the initial intention of reducing unemployment. Consequently, the stock prices surges, so are their bonuses and stock options.

3   Search value stocks like Buffett

Buffett stresses on value and would like to buy these companies at 25% off their intrinsic values, which are quite hard to determine. There are many screens simulated on how Buffett finds stocks. You should paper trade the stocks screened from these screens and check the performances after at least 6 months. Here are some common parameters in these screens. I also recommend not buying any stocks during market plunges.

- ROE. Check out the ROEs for the last 5 to 10 years, not just the most recent year.
- D/E. Low Debt/Equity.
- Profit Margin.
- Competitive advantage. The less competition, the better.
- Longevity. At least in business for 10 years.

From the above, Buffett cannot find too many stocks to buy during a bull market. He also ignores a lot of startups and high-tech companies. His portfolio should produce stable but not amazing performance.

In addition, he needs good managers who should be kind to his employees, paying back to the society and not using his company as his ATM besides business smart.

Using the Patriots franchise for illustration purposes, the Sullivan family did not make money even on Michael Jackson's concert in New England while everyone made good money. After Kraft took over (paying too high a price to many), the franchise turned around and became the most successful and profitable one under his helm.

Buffett's basics

From this YouTube video, Buffett's basics in selecting stocks are stable/understandable, strong long-term prospects, good management and undervalued.
https://www.youtube.com/watch?v=_uQjGz6jp2E

This strategy is good for long-term holding, valued stocks. In the last 10 years, growth stocks are better than value stocks by 7 to 3 as of 2021. That's why Buffett has performed poorly against the market. Before this period, he made a lot of money for his investors and himself. Do not follow him blindly. Here are my comments.

- Technology stocks are not classified as stable and understandable, and they have been big winners recently. As of 3/2021, they may be peaking. Buffett is not a tech guy, and he does not understand simple technology stuff such as products by Apple and Microsoft. We buy technology stocks without fully understanding their products such as heart valves, but for the potential appreciation.
  Lesson. Do not miss technology innovation, but make sure they are not a bubble such as 2000 and today too. Do not be afraid of the high P/E (most tech stocks have P/E over 25). Forward P/E is better as it estimates future profit. Use trailing stocks for rising stocks.

- Many stocks with good long-term prospects went bankrupt or lost most of their value such as Lehman Brothers, Boeing and GE.
  Lesson. Sell the stock before the company is completely bankrupt.

- Good management is good. However, even the best management cannot fight an uncontrollable situation such as the pandemic.
  Lesson. Good management is helpful, but not critical. To illustrate, all companies involved in tourism suffer during this pandemic.

- There must be a reason why a stock is undervalued, and a lot of time this stock would stay in undervalue for years. It is easy to spot value stocks, but not many of them can beat the market.
  Lesson. Prefer to buy undervalued stocks when they start moving up.

Afterthoughts
There are so many books on Buffett. Glance through them in the book stores and pick up those strategies that fit your investing philosophy and style. Many of his techniques are not applicable to retail investors, so be selective. His yearly announcement reports show his insights, discipline and knowledge. As of 2020, these books are not as popular as they used to be.

Links:
Letters: https://www.berkshirehathaway.com/letters/letters.html
Advises for 2021: https://www.youtube.com/watch?v=wGdbu450964
Value: https://www.youtube.com/watch?v=2creBZPaizl

4   Buffett

With utmost respect, Buffett's ideas may not be valid to us, the average retail investors, for the following reasons.

- We do not make big bets such as buying most or all of a company.
- He cannot usually buy small-cap stocks, which are proven to be better performers in the long run.
- He has connections and sweetheart deals that most of us do not have access to.
- We can dump losers or winners any time we want without public opinions on our trades.
- Most of his bets require him to pay extra to get in and get out.

There are exceptions. You should make money by following him to buy PetroChina and several other companies. However, he has his share of losers. As of 15/2016, he had not beaten the major index for the last five years, quite a long time for investors.

Contrary to Mr. Buffett's philosophy, I believe buy-and-hold is dead after 2000 for experienced investors. Most books / articles defending buy-and-hold are based on data before 2000. The market changes so fast that a good company could become unprofitable due to circumstances beyond its control or just due to bad management. With market timing, we can avoid some of the hefty losses in 2000 and 2007.

Insurance sector is a black swan to me. When something unexpected happens once in a blue moon, it would spoil all the fun and profit. Reinsurance companies (insuring insurers) are even riskier.

If Buffett only handled a portfolio of $10 million or so, he would beat most of us year after year by a good margin. No one including Peter Lynch can make a decent return with this huge portfolio. Lynch quit and Buffett continues, so I give Buffett more credit.

We can learn a lot from many of Buffett's sound investing philosophies / ideas and he has proven to be the greatest investor in our time. His yearly reports should benefit all investors. Many have made over 10,000% investing with Buffett but none in the last five years. He gains my respect by managing such a large portfolio. You cannot beat yourself when you are the market. I also respect him for donating most of his money to charities.

These days Buffett seems to be acting like a running dog for Obama, or he is blinded by all the glorious articles written about him, his money and his good deeds. He should concentrate on running his company whose performance has not beaten the market lately as he used to. Alternately he should retire to concentrate on his preaching about taxes and the government issues even some are controversial.

He did a great job in raising his children to be independent. However, I do not agree with his advice to the girl to be a business woman instead of a doctor who could cure thousands and save many lives.

High taxes have been proven bad for the economy and the stock market throughout our history. As opposed to the middle class, the rich have many tricks from their tax lawyers to avoid taxes. They can pass their wealth to their children and charities that allow their children to draw incomes from.

Somehow it reminds me of the Peter's Principle: When you're promoted to some job position you're not capable of, you do not perform as before.

Afterthoughts

- The announcement of the retirement of the CEO of Microsoft boosted the stock by about 7% in a day. I cannot believe it means about 20 billion dollars added to the market cap of Microsoft. What will happen to the stocks of Buffett's company when he retires or dies?
- Buffett, the person.
  https://www.youtube.com/watch?v=w-eX4sZi-Zs
- More article on Buffett.
  http://buzzonomics.wordpress.com/2013/08/30/jokes-facts-and-words-of-wisdom-from-warren-buffett/
  Warren Buffet: For beginners
  https://www.youtube.com/watch?v=yRr0_gJ-3ml

More link:
Warren's 7 rules: https://www.youtube.com/watch?v=63oF8BOMMB8
Crash ahead: https://www.youtube.com/watch?v=-53JhXlkp_o
Warren's Best ETF: https://www.youtube.com/watch?v=ycrKwTwXRa8

5   Efficient charities donation

We do not give money to an addict, because we figure that they will use it to further their addition. It is the same when we leave money to our government in various forms of taxes. They will probably spend it recklessly.

We should teach the poor how to fish instead of giving them fish for their entire lives. We should use a model specific to Africa (such as the one from China). China has been helping African countries to provide railroad to transport the ores to the port for export. Helping the poor is not a science but an art. Throwing money at the problem will not solve it long-term.
.

As Howard Buffett, Warren Buffett's son said, once Americans leave with the big machines / equipment, Africans will return to the bad old days. You do not need to automate aggressively when an abundance of cheap labor is available. From his ideas on Africa I watched on TV, I think he has some better insight and vision on how to handle his father's foundation than anyone else.

I believe that he would contribute more to the world by heading the charity instead of running his father's company. He seems to have little interest and desire to run his father's company from his conversation from the TV news magazine "60 Minutes". Making another billion is not a big deal but helping another African to survive is to him. Warren Buffett's greatest contribution to the society as well as the world is having raised great children like Howard with proper values that our society is often lacking.

The donations from Warren Buffet and Bill Gates are the noblest deed to mankind. I argue against the comments that they profit themselves. Of course, both should donate their appreciated stocks so they can maximize their donations. They should appoint their heirs to supervise their foundations and get salaries for their work to ensure the foundation is administered properly. Do you want a high school dropout or a welfare recipient to handle your foundation?

The African farming industry is being destroyed as they cannot compete with the overwhelming impact from donations. How can African farmers compete with freebies? Often donations are skimmed by the corrupt officials like many in Haiti and some African countries.

Try to identify the charities that have low overheads and are utilizing the contributions most efficiently. Some charities spend over one third of the contributions on its employees' pensions and salaries; some even use 99% of the contribution for themselves. With limited funds, you may want to limit yourself to one or two charities. The main cause of their high overhead is their various marketing campaigns to solicit donations, such as via (junk) mail, telephone solicitations, etc. Also be aware of their executive compensation schemes.

The United States and its citizens are the most generous and hope it remains so. Donate cash rather than merchandise. Donating winter clothes to Africa is very silly. Donating human milk could damage the health of the babies. The bottled water donated costs more to ship. Use common sense - not just to make yourself feel better!

As Gandhi said, the world has enough resources for all, but we're not unselfish enough to share.

At the same time, poor countries should control the population growth.

Afterthoughts
Fidelity has a charity account that is quite easy to open. Remember donating appreciated securities would make the biggest bang for the buck. Check the current tax laws. Fidelity also has a social grade for stocks.

The poor are admitted to nursing homes free of charge. The middle class like me may not afford to go to nursing homes. It defers my donation to charities as I have to ensure I have enough savings to go to a nursing home if I need to go.

Book 16: The economy

Investors should understand some basic economic concepts.

1   My economic theories

Understanding the Economic Machine
Economies are complex but can be simplified into cycles of growth and contraction. A notable resource is Ray Dalio's *How the Economic Machine Works*, available on YouTube here.

The Myth of Ending Economic Cycles
Economic cycles have persisted throughout history. Articles predicting their end, such as *The End of the Economic Cycle* (Seeking Alpha, 2019), often overlook key factors like market momentum and monetary policy.

Why Economists Often Misjudge Markets
Markets typically lead economic cycles by about six months. This explains why economists' predictions often miss the mark. For instance, in 2008, then-Fed Chairman Ben Bernanke praised the economy just months before the market crash.

Key issues impacting predictions include:
- **Unpredictable Events**: Wars, geopolitical shifts, and natural disasters (e.g., the Ukraine conflict) can disrupt markets.
- **Lagging Indicators**: Many traditional economic indicators (e.g., job reports) reflect past conditions rather than current trends.

Simple Moving Averages (SMA): A Practical Tool
Using SMA to identify market trends can help investors make timely decisions. For example:
- **SMA-350** tracks long-term trends and signals potential downturns.
- **Death Cross**: A bearish indicator where SMA-50 crosses below SMA-20.

While not perfect, these tools can prevent significant losses.

The Role of Jobs in Economic Trends
Job reports provide insights into economic health. However, excessively low unemployment often triggers interest rate hikes, reducing corporate profits. In 2022, for example, low unemployment led to aggressive rate increases, fueling fears of a recession.

Groupings of World Economies
1. **Leaders**: U.S., EU, Canada, and Australia dominate due to technological advancements and industrial history.
2. **Challengers**: Countries like China, Japan, and South Korea are emerging as significant economic powers.

China, with its vast population, is projected to surpass the U.S. as the largest economy (by GDP) within the next decade.

Factors Influencing Economic Decline
Wealthy nations often face challenges such as:
- **Aging Populations**: Shrinking workforces lead to reduced economic output.
- **Borrowing Practices**: Excessive national debt burdens future generations.
- **Productivity Decline**: Citizens demand higher wages and social benefits, reducing global competitiveness.

Population and Migration
Population dynamics play a critical role:
- **Immigration**: Countries like the U.S. benefit from skilled immigrants, boosting innovation.
- **Declining Birthrates**: Nations like Japan struggle with shrinking populations, limiting growth.

Cultural Influences on Productivity
Cultural attitudes often shape economic behavior:
- **Frugality and Education**: Influenced by Confucian values, countries like China and South Korea emphasize saving and learning.
- **Climate's Role**: Colder climates historically required more preparation and resourcefulness, fostering industriousness.

Globalization: Boon or Bane?
Globalization, championed during Reagan's era, has reshaped economies:
- **Benefits**: Lower production costs and access to global markets.
- **Drawbacks**: Widening wealth gaps, environmental damage, and trade imbalances.

For instance, China's rise as the "world's factory" created a U.S.-China trade deficit but also led to pollution and resource depletion.

Links

Growth and Crash: https://www.youtube.com/watch?v=2kJxqIO5sxQ
How the Economic Machine works.
https://www.youtube.com/watch?v=PHeObXAIuk0

I read this article predicting the "End of the economic cycle".
https://seekingalpha.com/article/4253126-weighing-week-ahead-near-end-economic-cycle?v=1554645177&comments=show

2 My Coconut Theory

Explaining Wealth and Productivity

The Coconut Theory simplifies global economic disparities using the analogy of coconuts as resources. Here's how it works:

1. **The Basics**:
   On a tropical island, a person sleeps under their coconut tree, eats a coconut when hungry, and does little else. While they may feel content, they are lazy, unproductive, and stagnant.
2. **Resource Mismanagement**:
   Borrowing coconuts without a plan for repayment or cutting down the tree for temporary gain (e.g., a canoe) without replanting leads to long-term poverty.

Application of the Theory

Country/Region Analysis Based on Coconut Theory

United States	Initially wealthy due to abundant resources ("coconuts") and industrious immigrants. Decline comes from overconsumption, reduced productivity, and reliance on welfare ("borrowing coconuts").
Norway	Wealth stems from managing natural resources (e.g., oil and fish) wisely and reinvesting globally ("planting coconut trees worldwide").
Singapore	Thrives due to strategic location and industrious citizens despite limited natural resources.
Japan	Succeeding through hard work and education despite resource scarcity but faces challenges from a declining population and restrictive immigration policies.

Country/Region Analysis Based on Coconut Theory

Haiti	Resource abundance initially (sugar plantations) was undermined by natural disasters, overpopulation, and poor governance.
Russia	Rich in resources but suffers from inefficiency and overdependence, while neighboring China uses its industrious population to leverage fewer resources effectively.

Lessons from History

Ancient civilizations like Greece, China, and India thrived but eventually exhausted their resources. Migration and innovation often follow such periods of decline, as people seek new "coconut trees" elsewhere.

Corporations and Families

- **Corporations**: Companies like Microsoft initially thrive on innovation but can stagnate by relying on past successes ("old coconut trees").
- **Families**: Wealth typically diminishes after three generations, as later generations enjoy but fail to replenish resources.

Conclusion

The Coconut Theory illustrates the importance of resource management, innovation, and hard work. Mismanagement leads to decline, while reinvestment ensures longevity.

Afterthoughts

- I did not have a coconut tree (i.e., financial aid or money from my dad), and that is why I worked two jobs in my first summer while attending college here. The first one was a busboy job from 5 pm to 10 pm. The other one was cleaning slot machines from 4 am to noon for 5 and usually 7 days a week. Lack of coconut makes you desire to work hard or you vanish. With an average IQ, I can make it by working hard in a land of coconuts.

    My children have too many coconuts and they live a more lavish lifestyle than the old man. They ask me why I work that hard during my retirement or why I still go to Burger King with a coupon, even though they do not treat me like a king.

- According to my friend Norman, the problem with a small place filled with coconuts is someone would likely to colonize you and steal your coconuts as happened to Norway during WWII. Similar to China about 250 years ago. Once a while, need to cut down one among many coconut trees to make spears to protect the rest of the coconuts.

3 American first: Challenges and risks

I totally agree, so every other country should set first priority for his/her country. However, we have done a lot that hurt us more than our enemies (China and Russia as our potential enemies for discussion). It could be due to buying votes. Here are some examples.

The Chip War
The U.S. has imposed restrictions on chip exports to China to protect intellectual property and national security. However, this has backfired in several ways:
- U.S. companies (e.g., Intel, AMD) lose significant revenue as China was a major customer.
- Encourages China to develop domestic chip production, reducing dependence on U.S. technology.
- Creates supply chain disruptions, affecting industries like automotive manufacturing.

Taiwan and Geopolitical Risks
Defending Taiwan against potential Chinese aggression risks escalating into a global conflict. The stakes include:
- Potential military confrontation with nuclear implications.
- Economic consequences, as Taiwan plays a critical role in global semiconductor manufacturing.
- Sanctions on China would add to our inflation and cause counter-actions from China.

Reserve Currency Concerns
The U.S. dollar's status as a global reserve currency is being challenged by:
1. **Russian Sanctions**: Asset freezes led other nations to question the dollar's stability.
2. **Excessive Printing**: Devalues the currency and raises inflation risks.

China and BRICS nations are pushing alternatives, including the yuan and potential new currencies, which could undermine U.S. economic dominance.

Neglected Domestic Issues
While focusing on global rivalries, the U.S. has ignored pressing internal problems:
- Aging infrastructure.
- Rising homelessness and drug crises.
- Gun violence and wealth inequality.
- Trump (first presidency) and Biden had raised our national debt to new heights. Eventually we would not be able to pay the dividends of our debts, and that would result a mild recession.
- We do not have long-term plans due to our political system.

4   Politics and the stock market

Republicans are usually pro-business, but the democratic presidency has a better track record for better market performance.

The Dow index was up 56% (from 7,949 to 12,418) in the less than 3 years since the day when Obama took office. As of 8/2012, it was 13,100, so the market had fully recovered from 2007-2008, but not the economy. If you still collect unemployment or your house has been foreclosed, you're still in deep trouble.

The S&P 500 performance under Republicans vs. Democrats since 1926:

Annualized return under Democratic presidencies: 13.74%
Annualized return under Republican presidencies: 6.25%

The President's appointees for the economy are the ones to watch as they set up the policies, if they turn out not to be the puppet of the president. As of 2012 (and also 2020), the interest rates are not a factor as it cannot go much lower. The cut in military expenses and the ending of the two wars will be good for the economy. In 2020, the trade war with our partners, especially China, will bring the global economies down after we have enjoyed globalization for the last 30 years.

The problem of the two major political parties is that they do not agree with each other, so they have to make too many compromises and waste a lot of time and effort. The efforts spent in impeaching the president in 2019 were just a waste of time as it was not feasible. These efforts should be used to improve our economy.

Afterthoughts

- Since we have more people dependent on welfare / entitlements and government jobs, they will vote accordingly and that will not cut down deficits in the foreseeable future, especially the baby boomers, who are starting to collect the entitlements.
- Do not blame the news media. They broadcast what you want to hear.
  Do not blame the politicians. They do what you want them to do.
  Do not blame me. I am speaking the truth.
  So, blame yourself.

5 The evils of printing money

Why Excessive Printing Hurts
Printing money creates immediate relief but long-term damage:
1. **Inflation**: Reduces purchasing power, especially for retirees.
2. **Debt Burden**: Passes financial obligations to future generations.
3. **Global Competitiveness**: Higher taxes and inflation make U.S. products less attractive internationally.

Examples:
- In 2020, the U.S. national debt surged to $25 trillion, partly due to pandemic-related stimulus.
- Inflation reached 7% in 2022, driven by supply chain disruptions and excessive monetary easing.

Winners and Losers
- **Winners**: Politicians and lobbyists who gain from short-term economic boosts.
- **Losers**: Average citizens, especially savers and retirees, who bear the brunt of inflation.

6 Shenzhen

The key of China's economic success is the hardworking of its citizens, from students. Professionals and workers especially.

Let's start with a video from Professor X. Click here or type the following in your browser:
https://www.YouTube.com/watch?v=SGJ5cZnoodY&t=923s

Shenzhen has transformed from a small fishing village to a modern city with 12 million citizens. Shenzhen has become the **Silicon Valley of the East**, or in the next decade we would say the US's Silicon Valley is the Shenzhen of the West.

Shenzhen could be the first major city to have all buses running in electricity and so are most taxi cabs. If you bought all the stocks in the Shenzhen Exchange, you could be very wealthy and there is no need to read my books on investing.

For example, it would take 9 months to assemble a new product but only 3 months in Shenzhen as most of the components are readily available next door or in the next street. Shenzhen's advantages are no longer tax credit and cheap labor (but highly-trained Chinese technicians, engineers and researchers). Many tech companies from over the world come to Shenzhen to set up shops in order to be successful.

There are many high-tech products from Shenzhen and they're sold all over the world. Unless you've been living in a cave for the last 10 years or you are blinded by your dumb nationalism, you should know China is catching up with technology, science and infrastructure, and the gaps are narrowing.

Under Deng's vision, Shenzhen has become one of the (if not the) wealthiest cities in China. Your homework is to study the many articles on Shenzhen starting with Wikipedia or enter the following in your browser. https://en.wikipedia.org/wiki/Shenzhen

Extra credits. There are several other YouTube videos on this amazing city. Why copying the current technology to make it better or using it for a new product is creative and profitable? Will any other countries copy Shenzhen's model and will they be successful? Do you agree from the video that open source encourages copying technology without compensation? What does our 9-year-old most likely do with no homework? Is it too early for a Chinese 9-year-old to study electronics and programming? Have a good day, class and no video game today.

My experience in Shenzhen. Shenzhen is clean and modern. Living standards could be higher than most other cities in China, but there are a lot of freebies for seniors. The streets are clean and safe. I failed to find a beggar, and it was rumored that they could take e-pay. There are many famous corporations in one street in Shenzhen. Our entire government is fighting these companies in this street.

Links

Chinese youth: https://www.youtube.com/watch?v=iyyqc9Jxdxg
From a foreigner: https://www.youtube.com/watch?v=bcVOGq4e3-8

More 1.

7 Why market rises or falls

What Drives Markets?
Institutional investors control over 70% of trades, making their strategies critical:
- Shift to bonds or cash during downturns.
- Focus on high-potential sectors during recoveries.

The Role of Cycles
Markets follow:
1. **Secular Cycles**: Long-term trends lasting 20+ years.
2. **Market Cycles**: Shorter trends within secular cycles, typically 4 years.

Foreign investment
To illustrate, when the Middle East is at war, money will flow to the US for safety and oil price would rise.

Economy
When the business climate is good such as low inflation, low interest rate and low corporate tax, corporate profits would rise and the stock prices would follow.
When the US cannot fulfill their debts, the economy would fall.

Sectors to Watch
Healthcare is in a long-term bull market due to aging populations. Tech and clean energy are also growth sectors. In 2023, it is AI (Artificial Intelligence).

8   Investors' psychology 101

Emotions control our investment decisions. We buy in greed and / or excessive optimism and sell in fears and / or excessive pessimism. They are just human nature that we have to avoid in investing. Here are some pointers:

- Emotionally detached.
  Investing is about making money at the least risk with emotions detached. Never fall in love with a stock or a group of stocks. Never be bothered by failed stocks and do not be too excited with successful trades.

- Every asset/class will return to the average value with one or two minor exceptions (gold is one but most likely it is due to the depreciation of USD). As previously stated, when a strategy has been overused, it will lose its performance.

- Do not risk the money you cannot afford to lose. One retiree lost most of his money in a market downturn and he died due to too much worry. After a year, the market recovered and he should have recovered all his losses except his life.

  Older investors should have a rainy-day fund in cash. This could be 10-30% of your total portfolio depending on its size. Younger families should have enough emergency funds for at least 6 months.
- Buy when the market is bleeding and sell when everyone is buying. Buy low and sell high is the best strategy, but it is hard to do so as our emotions do not allow us to do so.
- Diversifying your portfolio will improve your mental health besides your investment performance. Stocks could plunge with unexpected events and / or being manipulated. I had many examples in 2012. I can sleep better with one bad loss among 20, but not one among 2.
- Do not buy sin stocks like tobacco companies unless the potential profit is more important than your morals can allow. One option is to donate the 'loot' to a cause such as Lung Cancer Society for example.
- Do not follow the herd without an exit strategy. If you are against the herd (contrarian), make sure you have good reasons to do so.
- The flow to money fund proves that the average retail investor is usually wrong in market timing.

Review what we've discussed

This article reviews and summarizes the important concepts of this book. I also read my book and am reminded of the lessons I have learned from, especially from my bad experiences. I hope you can avoid the costly mistakes that are described here.

This book allows me to write down my ideas and experiences. I review them and monitor how and why some mistakes I still repeat while investing. I hope you will do the same for yourself with a trade journal. However, from my experience marketing a book like this is time-consuming, not financially rewarding and hence not highly encouraged.

1. A mistake may not be a mistake, or a win may not be a win.

Mistakes are repeated over and over again due to not staying consistent with a solid strategy and then letting our emotions influence our trading.

However, some 'mistakes' are not simple mistakes. I have evaluated my past trading records to determine whether my money losing episodes were real mistakes, just bad luck in uncontrollable circumstances or just bad financial data that I received.

If it is a real mistake, write it down to avoid repeating the same mistake. Often a trading mistake is worth more in future successes than experiencing a one-time windfall. To illustrate this, I bought a small Chinese company that had excellent financial metrics, but I discovered later that it was all a fraud and I lost most of my money in the stock. After a while, I made the same mistake again.

Cheat me once, shame on you. Cheat me twice, shame on me. I had that shame but plan not to repeat the same mistake. It was a big learning moment for me.

It is the same for a win, but in a reverse sense. We want to repeat wins by the same lesson.

Most readers do not hold a large number (about 100 to 150) of stocks as I did once. Draw your lessons by including stocks that have been evaluated even if they have not been purchased by you.

Overnight my MOS turned from a profit into a loss due to the collapse of the cartel in the potash industry. It is an event we cannot control. So, this loss is not a lesson to be learned but it teaches us not to put all eggs in the same basket (i.e., diversify your portfolio).

I read analysts' reports on lots of companies. First, I have to ensure whether or not they're written with a hidden agenda. Second, I check out whether they make sense to me. Some companies have fallen even after some good analyst reports. I reviewed them and sometimes I found their arguments were right. Several times I bought more shares and they turned out to beat the market by a good margin as a group. So, it was only wrong in the timing.

We are human and we all make mistakes. We should learn from our mistakes and reduce the chance to repeat them again. I am guilty of repeating mistakes such as buying foreign stocks that have proven to be unprofitable over a year's time.

What should we do with a losing stock? Do another evaluation. If we really make a mistake, sell it and move on. I do not recommend reversing the trade (i.e., short the loser) unless you have a better convincing argument.

2. Spotting big plunges.

Market timing does not always work. However, when it works more times than not, we can benefit in the long run. This book provides a lot of hints to detect big market plunges and avoid huge losses. Play defensively when the market is risky. Routinely monitor how risky the market is and act accordingly. Set up a schedule as to when to review the market risk. In addition, understand market cycles.

Unless the same strategy is overused, the chart should work. It may not give us ample time to react as the last two (2000 and 2008). Again, it depends on the data (the stock price), so it will not detect the bottom and the peak precisely, but it will spare you further losses and returns in time when the long-term trend of the market is up. Recently we have received more false alarms. Most of the time you do not lose much except for taxable accounts as it usually tells you to reenter the market shortly. Personally, I try to keep 50% in cash when the market is risky and 100% in stocks during the Early Recovery phase (defined by me).

When the market is plunging, do not buy stocks. When it starts to recover, this is the best time such as 2009 to buy stock as almost every stock is on sale. It is similar to flash crashes and some fierce market corrections. In the last flash crash, I participated one day too late and still made some great profits. Next time my reasoning needs to overcome my emotions.

Someone found the perfect screen producing an average return of 20% from the top 10 stocks and an average return of 5% for shorting the worst 10 stocks. However, in one abnormal year, the shorting lost 100% erasing all the gains for this strategy. It would work better using market timing.

3. Trade plan.

First, identify your objectives about investing. Next, set up a simple trade plan to start with, and then set up a schedule. Write down when to review the market risk and when to trade. For casual investors, it could be a quarterly task. Excessive (such as everyday) checking of our portfolios is a waste of time for most investors, not to mention the damage to your spirit.

Following a trading plan consistently forces you to be disciplined while investing. You should stick with the strategies that have been proven recently and avoid the bad human choices such as greed, fear and ignorance.

This book could be part of a trading plan as a source for your reference.

4. Match the ideas of this book to the current market conditions and your personal objectives and risk tolerance.

This book could bring you closer to the Holy Grail of investing: You need to adapt what works in the current market conditions including fundamental metrics and the screens you're using. There is no evergreen strategy and the predictability of metrics changes in different markets.

The market changes often and it is not always rational. Every one's investing objective is different. Even couch potatoes can benefit from this book by reading the related chapters.

5. Risk tolerance.

My objective today is to make a decent return at the least risk and conserving what I have is more important. Be a turtle investor who makes small but consistent profits. Most traders watch the screen all day long, spend a lot on commissions for the large number of trades and pay higher taxes for short-term trades.

Many of the smartest people make millions but lose it all. Avoid options, leverages and margins. The exception is for well-off investors and / or during early recovery when the profit potential is high.

I am a retiree with enough money to have a comfortable living and hopefully it will stay this way. My strategy is conservative. However, life would be no fun if I just bought CDs and treasury bills (so is losing money in reckless investing). I do not want to take any risk for the sake of selling books or boosting my ego. Here are my three major accounts.

1. Ultra conservative. I keep more cash in this account than the other two accounts. I do practice the strategy of 'all in' only in the Early Recovery stage of the market cycle. Most other times, I have cash, stocks with high values or sometimes some contra ETFs to lower my market risk.

2. Swing trading accounts. I buy deeply-valued stocks, and replace them with growth stocks during the Up and Peak stages of the market cycle (defined by me). I am conservative in the Peak stage of the market cycle with mental stops. The average holding period for me is 6 months and longer for the more advantageous treatment of long-term capital gains tax.

3. Momentum accounts (most in Roth IRAs). I switch at least some stocks to contra ETFs when the market is riskier. The average holding period for me is one month. Stress is on growth and momentum.

6. Investing advice.

Select the advice that is appropriate to your needs from good websites, magazines, newspapers, etc. The media usually emphasizes the business news and some have their own agendas. However, I have profited from some, so I do not want to ignore most of them. Take time to analyze the news and only act on it when it makes sense.

7. Evaluate your requirements and apply what makes sense.

Every one's requirements are different and my investing style may be different from yours. Actually, my current strategy is far safer than ten years ago. Write down your risk tolerance, your time available for investing and your general knowledge (and your desire to learn about investing). Only apply those ideas that make sense and fit your requirements.

If you are a beginner to investing, learn from this book and other basic books. Trade on paper. Buy ETFs but start small. Believe in due diligence. Master market timing. Luck about investing only works in the short term.

For the intermediate investors, it is better to invest in mutual funds and ETFs.

8. Be politically neutral in making investment decisions.

A political statement often offends a lot of folks. Do not let political bias distort your investment decisions. When I make political remarks on any party, I could be 100% right or 100% wrong for you according to which party you belong to.

You do not have to be politically correct in making investment decisions. In this book, I have reported my dislikes of both parties and may offend many unintentionally such as politicians on parties, union members and investment professionals.

I caution you on holding a bias that may keep you from being socially responsible for others. You can act on your beliefs and buy stocks that can enhance life in positive ways. Perhaps a promising drug that can potentially cure cancer, rather than buying a tobacco stock. You do not need to buy your company's stock either just because you work there. You should not be overconfident about the market as it is not always rational and/or the government gives out false information about the economy.

9. Trade effectively and monitor your trades.

Do not commit the same mistakes again and again. Do not buy any stock without doing a thorough analysis. Be careful of hot tips and hot stocks you learn from the media as they are usually too late and some may be manipulated, especially on small companies. Do not trade a stock days before its earnings announcement date unless you have a good reason to do so.

10. Investing is multi-disciplined.

Good investing requires knowledge in finance, accounting, the economy, psychology, probability, statistics, PC skills, politics and government... This book touches many areas in basic terms. I never stop learning about investing.

11. Best strategy.

The best strategy is not to lose big money. Please refer to the chapter on Spotting Big Plunges. Try to identify the Early Recovery phase of the market cycle and invest more aggressively in this phase. As in life, nothing is guaranteed, but following the basic market timing would give you a better chance of making money.

In other phases of the market cycle, choose one of the following strategies depending on your skill, time and risk tolerance. When everyone is making easy money, the market could be very risky. However, not participating in a rising market could be very tough. If you do participate, exit the market FAST when it is heading down; it could be the best insurance.

1. The conservative strategy. Remain more in cash all the time except during the Early Recovery phase.

2. Less conservative. Buy Low and Sell High.

3. More aggressive. Besides 'Buy Low and Sell High', add 'Buy High and Sell Higher' to a small extent. Always protect your profits and cut down your losses by using stops.

In any case, do not risk money you cannot afford to lose and check how risky the current market is. Do not bet your entire farm in one trade even if you have a good record of predictions. One bad investment could wipe out your entire savings.

This book provides you with a lot of knowledge about investing. However, you have to apply the ideas to the current market conditions and practice them.

When one strategy works consistently, stick with it. Limit your investing strategies to a few (one is fine) depending on your time and your personal objectives.

When good strategies do not work, take a break. It happens once a while including 2015 when most value stock pickers failed. In 2015, I bet it was due to 'bubble' stocks such as FANG (Facebook, Amazon, Netflix and Google). It is hard to beat the market without owning them. I encourage investing over trading. Be a turtle investor; only buy bubble stocks with clear exit strategies. However, some trading strategies explained in this book do work such as sector rotation, and understanding insider trading, etc. The difference is the holding period to me: At least 6 months for investing strategies based on value.

12. Be socially responsible and emotionally detached.

This book is my contribution to the marvelous country that allowed me to prosper and lead a comfortable life. Avoid defense companies, tobacco companies, etc. Sometimes you have to take out your humanity hat in making investment decisions. To make you feel better, donate your 'loot' to related charities such as the profit from a tobacco stock to the American Cancer Society.

Ignore daily news. My emotions could have gone wild on oil with the daily news on the oil price. Look at the long term. Short term wise, even the best experts cannot predict the direction of oil.

Epilogue

I have never taken any class in economics, accounting, business and investing except those required in my Industrial Engineering degrees. Investing is extraordinarily multi-disciplined and all we need is common sense and a desire to learn.

After my early retirement, I have been spending most of my time in investing, running thousands of simulations and reading over one hundred books on investing. Starting with the year of 2000, I have been doing very well in my investing.

It is far more financially rewarding working about my investments including finding new strategies than writing books. Writing books and articles takes time away from my investing and it actually costs me more money. However, it has been fun to write this book and to interact with my readers. Money cannot buy everything and the satisfaction of holding my printed book. I recommend keeping a trade log but not writing books, especially for unknown authors like me.

I do not believe that this book or any book can be the Holy Grail of investing. However, it has a lot of fresh ideas and good pointers that have brought me financial success (at least so far). I ask my readers to challenge my pointers and ensure they are applicable in today's market and meet their own objectives and requirements.

A good pointer can make you thousands of dollars, and a bad or misinterpreted one can do the opposite. Always do paper trading on any strategy and / or idea before you commit real money to it. Start your strategy with cash in small increments until you have more confidence.

Use the links in this book for reference and understand how we come to the conclusions. This book and similar books provide you ways on how to make decisions based on current events that can be obtained from TV, the internet and magazines.

Hopefully, this book's primary objective of enabling you to be a better investor is met. Actually, you should be a better investor than I am if you can integrate the knowledge you already have with mine – I called it adding wings to a roaring tiger. You also learn to avoid the mistakes I made.

This book should be read repeatedly to remind us (I am a reader too) of any error(s) we repeated. Some articles are not easy to read as this book is not intended to be so. You need to practice what this book suggests such as learning how to detect a market plunge.

There are many styles of investing with long-term investing as my primary tool. It is better to master one at a time than trying to master several. Personally, I selected swing trading with 3 months to renew my investment. Sector Rotation and momentum trading are my other styles I practice. Recently I have been too conservative and ignore my own market timing (i.e. Death Cross).

I have made a lot of predictions. There have been more rights than wrong compared to most other authors I have read. I never use after-the-fact predictions. Even when there are wrong predictions, I would show the logic behind.

Promoting books teaches me some human behavior, both good and bad. One oldie showed me his broker statement one day with over 8 million and asked me to show him mine with some racial remarks. Hope his racist attitude would not pass on his 'successful' children. When I told my friends about my books or reference them on a public site, I received more offensive remarks than encouragement.

The major advantage of self-publishing eBooks is the low cost to you. Without self-publishing, this book would never be done.

I will practice what I preach and what I've learned from writing this book. Jesse Livermore was probably one of our greatest traders ever. Yet he ended up losing most of his money and then killed himself. The major reason was he did not follow what he preached. We need to diversify our investments and it is better to be a turtle investor. Recently a 20-year-old Robinhood trader killed himself after losing $730,000.

A link is provided for future updates and announcements.
https://ebmyth.blogspot.com/2020/01/updates.html
My blog:
https://tonyp4idea.blogspot.com/

Final notes

Thanks for reading this book and I hope it will be beneficial to your financial health. If so, comment on it or the place you bought this book. I will be very grateful. I do not have an advertising budget for my books. You can use any name if you do not want to use your real name. They do not require your name to rate a book.

https://www.amazon.com/dp/B0DPBBRGKH

My other books:

https://tonyp4idea.blogspot.com/2020/12/book-managers.html

Afterthoughts

Thanks to Amazon for making self-publishing easy and at no cost. Promoting books is a different story, especially with no budget in advertising. Every time I mentioned my books in public, most likely it would be deleted. I received more unfavorable remarks than encouragement when I mentioned it to my friends or in mail lists of old friends and classmates. English is not my native language. Imagine how hard it is to write a book in Chinese when your native tongue is English. However, I enjoy writing books and hopefully some readers would benefit. I could be happier writing notes for myself instead of publishing it. Your positive comments are my driving force to write books.

Recommend the next books.

- "Investing Lessons and Plunders", which Includes my and gurus' experiences and many articles not included in this book. For example, the reader of "Art of Investing" would learn more about "Sector Rotation", "Shorting", "Economy", "Investing Strategies" and "Investing advices / News".

- The current book is "Best stocks for 2025" in this series.
  https://www.amazon.com/dp/B0D2459JDT

If the sales of my books in this series were based on past performances, I should have sold many books, but obviously not.

Book	Stocks	Return[3]	Ann.	Beat RSP by[1]
Best stocks to buy for 2024	8	46%	48%	132%
Best stocks to buy for 2023	8	36%	36%	290%
Best stocks to buy for 2022	10[6]	4%	4%	153%[7]
Best Stocks to buy as of July, 2021[4]	8	5%	13%	487%
Best Stocks for 2021 2nd Edition	10	42%[4]	52%	220%
Best Stocks for 2021	4	29%	44%	118%
Best Stocks to Buy from Aug, 2020	14	45%	45%	3%[5]
Avg.	9	34%	40%	208%[2]

Here is the detail:
https://tonyp4idea.blogspot.com/2024/12/best-stocks-to-buy-for-2025.html
https://www.amazon.com/dp/B09L8NVJNH

Appendix 1 - Our window to the investing world

- **General**
  Wikipedia / Investopedia /Yahoo!Finance / MarketWatch / Cnnfn / Morningstar /CNBC / Bloomberg / WSJ / Barron's / Motley Fool / TheStreet
- **Evaluate stocks**
  Finviz / SeekingAlpha / MSN Money / Zacks / Daily Finance / ADR / Fidelity / Earnings Impact / OpenInsider / NYSE / NASDAQ / SEC / SEC for 10K and 10Q (quarterly) reports required to file for listed stocks in major exchanges.
- **Charts**
  BigCharts / FreeStockCharts / StockCharts /

- **Screens**
  Yahoo!Finance / Finviz / CNBC / Morningstar /
- **Besides stocks**
  123Jump / Hoover's Online / FINRA Bond Market Data / REIT / Commodity Futures / Option Industry
- **Vendors**
  AAII / Zacks / IBD / GuruFocus / VectorVest /
  Fidelity / Interactive Brokers / Merrill Lynch /
- **Economy.**
  Econday / EcoconStats / Federal Reserve / Economist /
- **Misc.**
  Dow Jones Indices / Russell / Wilshire /
  IRS / Wikinvest / ETF Database / ETF Trends /
  Nolo (estate planning) / AARP /

Appendix 2 - ETFs / Mutual Funds

What is an ETF
ETFs have basic differences from mutual funds: 1. Lower management expenses, 2. Trade ETFs same as stocks, and 3. Usually more diversified but not more selective than the related mutual funds such as NOBL vs FRDPX.

The major classifications of ETFs are 1. Simulating an index such as SPY, QQQ and DIA, 2. Simulating a sector such as XLE and SOXX, 3. Simulating an asset class such as GLD and SLV, 4. Simulating a country or a group of countries such as EWC and FXI, 5. Managed by a manager(s) such as ARKK, 6. Betting a market or sector to go down such as SH and PSQ, and 7. Leveraged (not recommended for beginners).
Fidelity: Index ETFs (https://www.fidelity.com/etfs/overview).
Wikipedia on ETF (http://en.wikipedia.org/wiki/Exchange-traded_fund).

List of ETFs
ETF database (Recommended): http://etfdb.com/
ETF Bloomberg: http://www.bloomberg.com/markets/etfs/
ETF Trends: http://www.etftrends.com/
A list of ETFs. Seeking Alpha.
http://etf.stock-encyclopedia.com/category/)
A list of contra ETFs (or bear ETFs)
http://www.tradermike.net/inverse-short-etfs-bearish-etf-funds/
Misc.: ETFGuide, ETFReplay
Fidelity low-cost index funds: https://www.youtube.com/watch?v=zpKi4_IJvlY
Fidelity Annuity funds with performance data.
http://fundresearch.fidelity.com/annuities/category-performance-annual-total-returns-quarterly/FPRAI?refann=005
ETFs vs mutual funds; https://www.youtube.com/watch?v=Vmz0CzlQvHk
Three ETFs: https://www.youtube.com/watch?v=MVi2RhpffuU

Other resources
Most subscription services offer research on ETFs. IBD has a strategy dedicated to ETFs and so does AAII to name a couple. Seeking Alpha has extensive resources for ETF including an ETF screener and investing ideas. So is ETFdb.

Not all ETFs are created equal
Check their performances and their expenses.

When to use or not to use ETFs
I prefer sector mutual funds in some industries, as they have many bad stocks such as drug industry, banks, miners and insurers. Most mutual funds cannot time the market.

When you believe a sector is heading up (or contra ETF for heading down), but you do not have time to do research on specific stocks, buy an ETF for the sector; it is same for the market.

Half ETF

Taking out half of the stocks that score below the average in an index ETF could beat the same full ETF itself. I call it HETF (half the ETF). You heard it here first. After a decade, at least one company has a similar product.

To illustrate, sort the expected P/E (not including stocks with negative earnings) in ascending order and only include the stocks on the first half. Add more fundamental metrics. It will take a few minutes.

Disadvantages of ETFs

- When you have two stocks in a sector ETF one good one and one bad one, the ETF treats them the same. Stock pickers would buy the one that has a better appreciation potential.
- Sometimes the return could be misleading due to stock rotation. To illustrate this, on August 29, 2012, SHLD was replaced by LYB in a sector fund. SHLD was down by 4% and LYB was up by 4% primarily due to the switch. Unless you sell and buy at the right time (which is impossible), your return would not match the ETF's returns due to the replacement.
- Ensure the performance matches the corresponding index; it is hard due to excluding dividends.

Advantages of ETFs

- We have demonstrated that you can beat the market by using market timing. Between 2000 and Nov., 2013, you only exit and reenter the market 3 times and the result is astonishing.
- It is easy to rotate a sector vs. buying/selling all of the stocks in this sector. Rotating a sector is the same as trading a stock.
- The risk is spread out, and your portfolio is diversified especially for a market ETF or buying three or more ETFs in different sectors.
- Periodically the bad stocks in most funds are replaced by better stocks.
- Eliminate the time in researching stocks.

Leveraged ETFs

I do not recommend them. Some are 2x, 3x and even higher. They're too risky for beginners. However, when you are very sure or your tested strategy has very low drawdown, you may want to use them to improve performance. Most leveraged ETFs and contra ETFs have higher fees.

My basic ETF tables

I include some contra ETFs, mutual funds and Fidelity's annuity. Some of these may be interesting to you. Most Vanguard's ETFs have lower fees.

ETFs and funds come and go. Some ideas and classifications are my own interpretation. Refer to ETFdb for updated information. Not responsible for any error. Check out the ETF or fund before you take any action.

I prefer VFINX over SPY for the lower fees; both simulate the S&P 500 index. The stocks in the ETF can be either equally weighted or weighted by market caps. The latter is more like using momentum strategy, as the rising stocks usually have larger market caps. The index usually kicks out some poor-performing stocks and replaced them with better stocks. These ETFs are suited for long-term investing without constant reviews.

Table by market cap:

Category	ETF	Mutual Funds	Fidelity's Annuity	Contra ETF	Alternate
Size:					
Large Cap	DIA			DOG	
	SPY			SH	VOO VFINX RSP FXAIX
	QQQ			PSQ	FNCMX
	RYH				
Blend	IWD	BEQGX			
Growth	SPYG	FBGRX			FSPGX
Value	SPYV	DOGGX			FLCOX
Dividend	NOBL	FRDPX			
	VYM				
Mid Cap			FNBSC	MYY	
Blend	MDY	VSEQX			
Growth		STDIX			
		BPTRX			
Value		FSMVX			
Small Cap			FPRGC	SBB	FSSNX
Blend	IWM	HDPSX			
Growth		PRDSX			FECGX
Value		SKSEX			FISVX
Micro	IWC				
Multi					
Blend		VDEOX			
Growth		VHCOX			
Value		TCLCX			
Total					FSKAX VTI
Bond					
Long Term (20)	VLV	BTTTX		TBF	
Mid Term (7 – 10)	VCIT	FSTGX			
Short Term (1 – 3 yrs.)	VCSH	THOPX			
Total	BOND	PONDX			
Corp Invest Grade	VCIT	NTHEX			
High Yield	PHB	SPHIX			

(junk)						
Muni	MUB	Check state				
Special situation						
Buy back	PKW					

Table by sectors:

Sector	ETF	Mutual Funds	Fidelity's Annuity
Banking[1]		FSRBK	
Regional	IAT		
Biotech	IBB	FBIOX	
	XBI	Large	
Consumer Dis.	XLY	FSCPX	FVHAC
Consumer Staple	XLP	FDFAX	FCSAC
Defense + Aero	PPA		
Finance	KIE	FIDSX	FONNC
	IYF		
Energy	XLE	FSENX	FJLLC
Energy Service		FSESX	
Farm	DBA		
Gold	GLD	FSAGX	BAR
Gold Miner	GDX	VGPMX	
Health Care	IYH	FSPHX	FPDRC
	VHT	VGHCX	
House Builder	ITB	FSHOX	
Industrial	IYJ	FCYIX	FBALC
Material	VAW	FSDPX	GSG
	IYM		
Natural Gas	UNG		
Oil	USO		
Oil Service	OIH	FSESX	
Oil Exploration	XOP		
Real Estate	VNQ	FRIFX	FFWLC
REIT	VNQ		
Retail	RTH	FSRPX	
	XRT		
Regional bank	KRE	FSRBX	
Semi Conduct	SMH		
Software	XSW	FSCSX	
	IGV		

Technology	XLK	FSPTX	FYENC
	FDN	FBSOX	
		ROGSX	
Telecomm.	VOX	FSTCX	FVTAC
Transport	XTN		
	IYT		
Utilities	XLU	FSUTX	FKMSC
Wireless		FWRLX	

Footnote. [1] Also check Finance.

Table by countries outside the USA:

Country	ETF	Mutual Funds	Fidelity's Annuity	Alternate
Australia	EWA			
Brazil	EWZ			
Canada	EWC	FICDX		
China	FXI	FHKCX		
EAFE	EFA			
Emerging	VWO	FEMEX	FEMAC	FPADX
Europe	VGK	FIEUX		
Global	KXI	PGVFX		
Greece	GREK			
India	INDY	MINDX		
Indonesia	EIDO			
Latin America	ILF	FLATX		
Nordic		FNORX		
Mexico	EWW			
Hong Kong	EWH			
Japan	EWJ	FJPNX		
S. Africa	EZA			
S. Korea	EWY	MAKOX		
Singapore	EWS			
Taiwan	EWT			
Turkey	TUR			
United Kingdom	EWU			
Foreign: Combination				
Intern. Div.	IDV			FTIHX
Small Cap	SCZ			
Value	EFV			
Europe	VGK			

#Filler: Honey, my book can play music.
https://www.youtube.com/watch?v=HxGT5z6d-GA&list=PLMZa6mP7jZ2b1otqG4tfbgZpLEdh6YiNF

Appendix 3 - Links

The following may be repeated from the articles and it is for your convenience. To illustrate, Under YouTube (or Investopedia), search "Finviz". Some links have permanent values such as most articles from Wikipedia and Investopedia. Others reflect current events such as the current market. Learn from them and act when the current events have similar descriptions. For the printed versions and updated links, enter the following in your browser: https://tonyp4idea.blogspot.com/2023/02/links-in-my-books.html

Beginners

Common mistakes: https://www.youtube.com/watch?v=zkNueyFs8zQ

Best Vanguard ETFs https://www.youtube.com/watch?v=mSEyghlZchQ

Buy stocks/ETFs: https://www.youtube.com/watch?v=4vjkeC_4EmU

Screener

Finviz https://www.youtube.com/watch?v=cHNUMPgEYGY

Recommended YouTube: https://www.youtube.com/watch?v=CJoN7wLfWNo
PEG: http://en.wikipedia.org/wiki/PEG_ratio
Short %:
http://www.investopedia.com/university/shortselling/shortselling1.asp#axzz2LNDvpemo

Openinsider:	http://www.openinsider.com/
Finviz:	http://Finviz.com/
terms:	http://www.Finviz.com/help/screener.ashx
Insider Cow:	http://www.insidercow.com/
Current Ratio:	http://en.wikipedia.org/wiki/Current_ratio
Cash Flow:	https://www.youtube.com/watch?v=1v8hRZ36--c
Balance sheet:	https://www.youtube.com/watch?v=DZjU0CHKyV4
Earnings report:	https://www.youtube.com/watch?v=Ite4I_y08Gg

How to find quality stocks.
http://seekingalpha.com/article/2381395-how-to-identify-quality-stocks-and-is-there-really-alpha-to-be-had

Fidelity

Platform tutorial: https://www.youtube.com/watch?v=fxE5577LaxE
Fidelity index funds: https://www.youtube.com/watch?v=xdEunmLrhb4
Investing tips: https://www.youtube.com/watch?v=twMNKMhL_KY

Investing strategies

Inflation: https://www.youtube.com/watch?v=Zpthvpy3UKg\

Swing: https://www.youtube.com/watch?v=C9EQkA7uVU8
https://www.youtube.com/watch?v=a_wpfSXRSjo
https://www.youtube.com/watch?v=M8sNMhPJIN

Momentum: https://www.youtube.com/watch?v=PpUlOyZrl9
Penny stocks: https://www.youtube.com/watch?v=u7xZ3kF62u4

Scanning https://www.youtube.com/watch?v=7iZpWmwBheI

Peter lynch 2023: https://www.youtube.com/watch?v=CK1AkVVVXu8

Charlie: https://www.youtube.com/watch?v=8g2B6QJ2FEc
Dividend ETFs: https://www.youtube.com/watch?v=64NEiyoNBIM

- Innovative sectors: https://www.youtube.com/watch?v=LI1hMX8qtHg

Trading stocks
Beginners: https://www.youtube.com/watch?v=aod3cyUEu4k
Trade stocks with Fidelity: https://www.youtube.com/watch?v=wMxj6iB92ZA&t=2s

Tax Avoidance: http://en.wikipedia.org/wiki/Tax_avoidance
Tax Law: http://en.wikipedia.org/wiki/Income_tax_%28U.S.%29
Without paying (gift tax):
http://en.wikipedia.org/wiki/Gift_tax_in_the_United_States#Gift_tax_exemptions
http://www.irs.gov/Businesses/Small-Businesses-&-Self-Employed/What%27s-New---Estate-and-Gift-Tax
AMT: http://en.wikipedia.org/wiki/Alternative_minimum_tax
Estate planning fun. http://tonyp4idea.blogspot.com/2014/08/estate-planning-101-for-me.html
Taxes on stocks: https://www.youtube.com/watch?v=EKYMbsjUUtE
Tax avoidance: https://www.youtube.com/watch?v=tXou5pM7zh0
Capital gain: https://www.youtube.com/watch?v=ezPs4ibFsNU&t=2678s
Trading course: https://www.youtube.com/watch?v=8sbfrusR5Eo
How safe our brokers. https://www.youtube.com/watch?v=wz64z1YuL0A

Fidelity funds: https://www.youtube.com/watch?v=xdEunmLrhb4
Fidelity core money market fund:
https://www.youtube.com/watch?v=KU6HYRHj3jg

Government bond default? https://www.youtube.com/watch?v=wMxj6iB92ZA
Broker CDs (Recommended): https://www.youtube.com/watch?v=zhEiyW2N7KE
Money market fund: https://www.youtube.com/watch?v=N53wZ_80abU

Covered call https://www.youtube.com/watch?v=dzMOnI4Eh04
https://www.youtube.com/watch?v=7a0BRIAufBA
https://www.youtube.com/watch?v=VDzRRYADv0I
https://www.youtube.com/watch?v=hbLp63AOceo

Economy
YouTube video (highly recommended): https://www.youtube.com/watch?v=Q6NIDJZdQH4

What will the world be in 5 years (2027).
https://www.youtube.com/watch?v=LzipwDQBUyc
Inflation and interest rate: https://www.youtube.com/watch?v=q8KJSNyAHLE
Wealth gap widens with low interest rate:
https://www.youtube.com/watch?v=t6m49vNjEGs
Investing helps the economy: https://www.youtube.com/watch?v=W6ICRTqsxk8

Made in United States
Orlando, FL
06 February 2025